From Poland **with Music**

100 Years of Polish Composers Abroad
(1918–2018)

Concept:
Marlena Wieczorek

First English Edition

Published by
Fundacja MEAKULTURA
Zwycięstwa 1
44-100 Gliwice
Poland
www.fundacjameakultura.pl, 2021

Copublished and distributed by
Scala Arts & Heritage Publishers Ltd
Registered address:
27 Old Gloucester Street
London WC1N 3AX, UK
www.scalapublishers.com, 2021

ISBN (UK): 978-1-78551-407-4
ISBN (Poland): 978-83-952271-1-0

Concept: Dr. Marlena Wieczorek
Content Supervisor: Dr. hab. Beata Bolesławska-Lewandowska
Editors: Dr. hab. Małgorzata Gamrat, Dr. Marlena Wieczorek, Dr. Cindy Bylander, Dr. hab. Beata Bolesławska-Lewandowska, Dr. Magdalena Nowicka-Ciecierska (part II)
Translation: Olga Drenda
Translation Editor: Dr. Cindy Bylander
Polish Proofreading: Dr. Magdalena Nowicka-Ciecierska
Technical Proofreading: Dr. Magdalena Nowicka-Ciecierska; assistant: Marta Kaczmarczyk
Project Coordination: Dr. Marlena Wieczorek, Andrzej Kosowski, Dr. Neil Titman, Emilia Miechowicz
Cover, Illustrations, Design: Dr. hab. Max Skorwider

The first Polish edition received financial support from the Ministry of Culture and National Heritage and the Promotion of Culture Fund. The latter is part of the "Musical Trace" program subsidized by the Institute of Music and Dance. The book contains materials completed thanks to a Ministry of Culture and National Heritage scholarship granted to Marlena Wieczorek in 2017.

Partners: Ministry of Foreign Affairs; ZAiKS Association of Authors

Printing and Binding: LOTOS Poligrafia, Wał Miedzeszyński 98, 04-987, Warsaw, Poland

Table of Contents

This Is How It Usually Begins

Part I
Music in Motion: Contexts

Part II

Composers' Profiles: In Other Words, Marlena Wieczorek Asks, Experts Respond

References

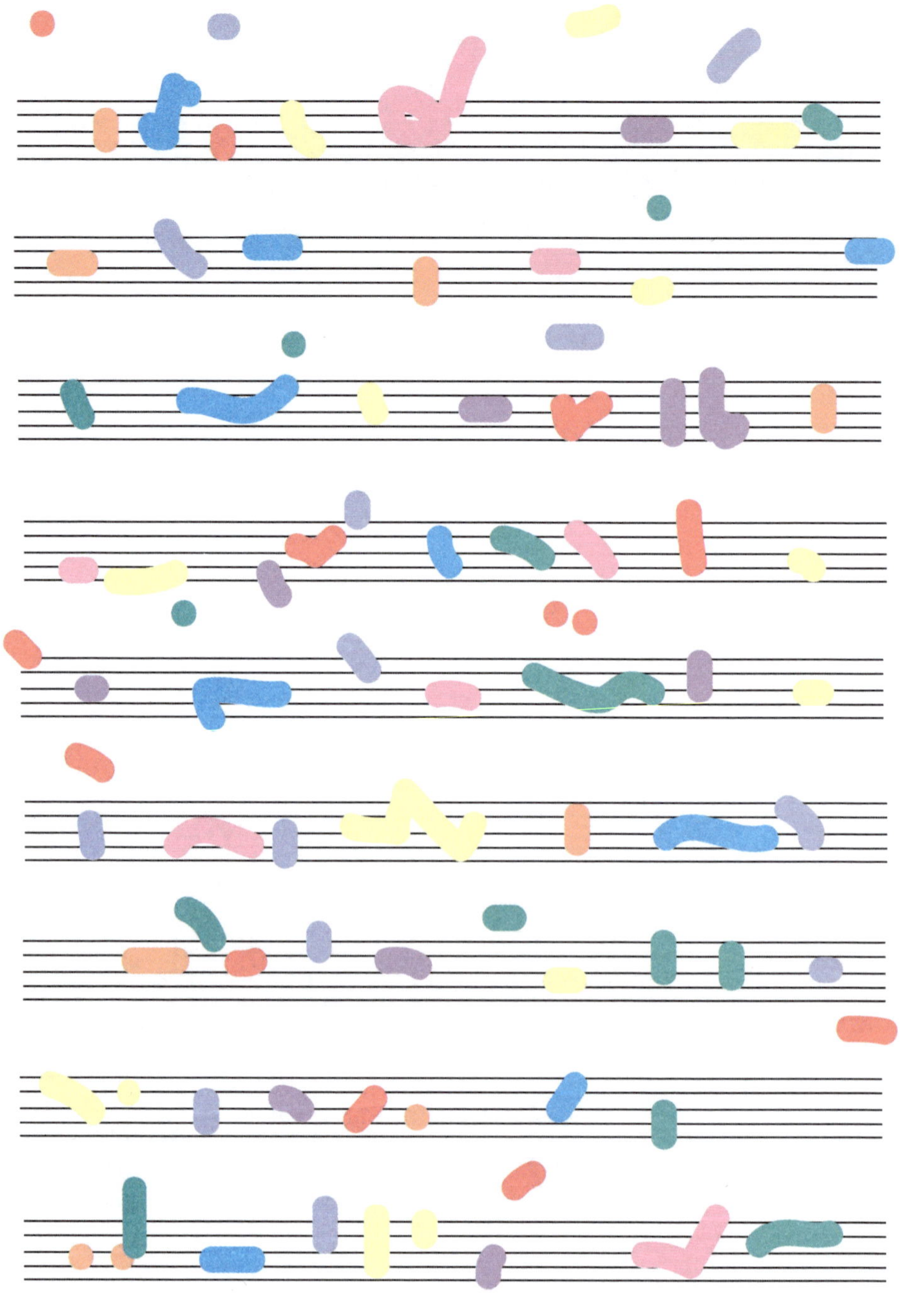

This Is How It Usually Begins[1]

100 Musical **Thanks**

We did it! This book, which was supposedly impossible to complete, is now in our hands. I've heard so many times that it was better to give up trying to do this, that it was too difficult, and that I was asking for trouble because I was trying to deal with incompatible topics. And who is an emigrant, anyway? Luckily, there were those who believed…

Here, I have to express my first thanks: to the experts who evaluated the project and made it possible to begin work on the book, as well as to the Committee of the Institute of Music and Dance for a donation from its Musical Trace program in 2018. Despite these initial achievements, we continued to seek funds for printing. Unfortunately our requests were often rejected (the list of institutions and offices is available upon request)…

I am thankful to an enormous number of people for the support they have shown. Above all: to the authors of the essays published in this book. They often had to work quickly, without any certainty that the book would be published, yet they wrote, helped, got involved, and listened. This group includes students, professors, journalists, and composers' relatives and friends. For the English version of the book, which you now hold in your hands, this group was joined by translator Olga Drenda and our outstanding editor, Dr. Cindy Bylander. Our excellent Polish editing team (Dr. hab. Małgorzata Gamrat and Dr. Magdalena Nowicka-Ciecierska) was led by content supervisor Dr. hab. Beata Bolesławska-Lewandowska. I have lost track of the total hours spent and the number of files that flew to and from our e-mail inboxes. Dr. hab. Max Skorwider, a fantastic graphic designer who, without discussing the details (even financial ones), trusted me and created incredible illustrations for the book. Thanks to his design, our publication is unique—and this was really important to me.

Dr. Miłosz Bembinow, a great composer and a terrific person who is dedicated to musical culture, aided our project and has supported our Foundation for many years. No words can express my gratitude.

I would also like to thank all the "guardians" of our Foundation who have encouraged us in body and spirit. I cannot mention all of them, but this third edition was only possible thanks to Katarzyna Sokołowska, who often indicated paths that MEAKULTURA Foundation should follow, and to the ZAiKS Association of Authors, with whom we have worked for many years. These people are truly dedicated to culture and arts.

Finally, let me salute the protagonists of our book, the composers and creators of Polish culture, who deserve many publications like this. I am thankful that I could get to know you.

Enjoy the book!
Marlena Wieczorek

Krzysztof Moraczewski
A Wor(l)d of Recommendation

The significance of emigration for the social and cultural history of Poland is a topic that has already been the subject of a considerable body of research, and yet it still seems to be far from fully explored. Poles are a nation of emigrants, or rather they became so after the era of partitions (from the late eighteenth century to the end of World War I), and this state of affairs has remained valid since then. If we compare émigré nations, the only competition for Poles in the modern age of Europe are the Irish and, to some extent, the Italians. However, the way in which the history of Poland is usually told leads to political emigration obscuring all other forms and motivations. All other emigration movements try to fit into this same context. However, it does not take much insight to understand that the mass emigration of Polish-speaking peasants from Austrian Galicia, for example, was not a political emigration, but one of an economic nature: peasants fled to the Pennsylvania mines, to Brazil, and to the American Midwest not because of any political oppression imposed by the Habsburg Empire, but because of famine. They were, after all, leaving the poorest region of Europe (next to Ireland). The descendants of the pre-partition Polish nobility did not always flee from the tsarist police to Paris; quite often they emigrated, if this word is justified here, from the Congress Kingdom of Poland to St. Petersburg to begin an impressive career in the tsarist administration or the army. Artists did not always seek to avoid tsarist, Prussian, or Communist censorship; they also sought contacts with the wider art world. They wanted to study, develop a career, and earn more money than they could in Poland.

Artistic emigration is a particularly difficult subject, as it seems to focus on all the themes of the more general history of Polish emigration. Unquestionably, it has a political aspect, which is important and sometimes crucial to consider when discussing the country's history from the partitions of Poland to the Solidarity era. But it also has an economic dimension, which was particularly important after 1989 and is probably dominant today, especially with regard to performers who join choirs and orchestras all over the world. It also has an educational dimension, including both formal education, as in the case of the Paris Committee (a movement of painters) and the Polish students of Nadia Boulanger, and a deeper need for personal participation in the cultural scene of the great artistic metropolises: Paris, Berlin, London, Munich, and St. Petersburg. It has a commercial aspect, as it is often accompanied by a justified conviction that a truly great career of an artist can be made "there," not "here." Finally, it poses a problem of artistic quality: via the careers of Adam Mickiewicz, Cyprian Kamil Norwid, Witold Gombrowicz, Czesław Miłosz, Frédéric Chopin, and Andrzej Panufnik, a large part of Poland's cultural canon was created in exile.

Therefore, there is little doubt that a study of the work of Polish musicians in exile is an extremely important undertaking, especially when the authors of this volume are fully aware of the complexity of the problem and attempt to treat it fairly. By presenting the profiles of individual artists, these writers attempt to confront the intricacies of each situation. It is more than a need to counteract the dominant, one-sided political story of artistic emigration and point out how the political motives of the times were intertwined with other justifications for leaving. It is equally important to follow the effects of emigration: from an easy entry and sometimes enthusiastic reception in a foreign artistic environment to the sheer necessity of taking up different professions in order to somehow make ends meet, from great international careers to situations when an already well-developed career in Poland was lost due to emigration, from the discovery of new creative worlds to a bitter disappointment that foreign artistic life is something completely different than it seemed to be from the outside, that one is governed by rules and values that are incomprehensible or even unacceptable. It is impossible, moreover, to reduce these successes and failures and these admirations and disappointments to artistic issues only, because sometimes success or failure abroad depended on the way of life in another country, on the possibility or impossibility of belonging to another society and a different world. These topics are not only presented in "personal questionnaires" dedicated to émigré musicians, but they are also analyzed in the various essays in this book. The selection of authors for these texts guarantees the high quality of these reflections.

The value of this book does not rely on these analyses and their attempt to shed new light on our fragmentary knowledge of Polish musical emigration. It is, in part, an effort to restore to Polish culture a collection of compositions that has been exhibited inaccurately or has been totally neglected in the country's recent musical life. Readers might be surprised by the number of names mentioned here that they did not know or had not linked to the topic of emigration. Sometimes the compositions in question are of exceptional quality, but are not known in Poland. This very lack of recognition seems to be one of the problems connected to artistic emigration. On the other hand, for a reader from outside Poland, this book not only offers knowledge, but can also serve as a type of test for the effectiveness of artistic emigration in general: To what extent did the composers discussed here—who were chosen because of their specifically Polish interests—become part of a "larger context," and to what extent did international recognition for these composers remain unachievable after emigration, and why?

Like every good book about art, this one will compel readers to revise their knowledge and opinions, to re-evaluate and seek new ways of understanding the artistic situation in which we now find ourselves. In this case, we are concerned primarily with the relationship between music and its social surroundings. We can learn much by following the changes in the output of experienced composers who, having changed the land in which they live, had to confront not only disparate traditions and musical heritages, including those as distinctive as those in Great Britain or the United States, but also audiences possessing diverse expectations.

Now, all that is left is for us to recommend reading this book and promise that it will be time well spent.

Marlena Wieczorek, Beata Bolesławska-Lewandowska

Instead of an Introduction: Let's Chat

Marlena Wieczorek: At the very beginning, we must start with a question that appears frequently in this book: What does the term "emigration" mean? What is it, actually? How should we treat a composer who is a resident/migrant/refugee? Are they all the same? Or maybe a "real" emigrant is someone who is forced to leave for political reasons and is no longer able to return to their homeland? They lose contact with their loved ones, with their native country, and their works are no longer programmed on concerts there. Does leaving in order to make a living or for educational purposes entitle one to be equated with political defectors? And finally, how does the term relate to modern times, in which one can live almost parallel lives in two countries? To develop a career abroad, but also to work professionally in Poland? How should we define the identity of such artists?

Beata Bolesławska-Lewandowska: This is a complex problem and "emigration" is definitely not an unambiguous term. In fact, the more intensively one thinks about how to define it, the more doubts arise. Emigration for Frédéric Chopin or Ignacy Jan Paderewski was different than it was for Roman Palester and Andrzej Panufnik, while arranging one's life abroad today is not the same as any of these earlier experiences, given the completely contrasting political realities of the current era.

Nevertheless, it seems to me that we can still talk about emigrants precisely in the context of the political and historical situation of Poland. We should question why a group of artists who remained in the so-called "West" after World War II were purposefully removed from the cultural consciousness of Polish society through the policies of the state. I mean here not only Roman Palester and Andrzej Panufnik, who were strictly political emigrants and thus were the most unfairly treated, but also artists such as Antoni Szałowski, Tadeusz Zygfryd Kassern, and Roman Maciejewski. These composers decided that they would link their creative lives to another homeland, but none of them deliberately wanted to break off contacts with the Polish music community. They realized, however, that the consequences of their decision would be exactly that. Their situation, however, contrasted with that of Witold Szalonek, Andrzej Dobrowolski, and Krzysztof Meyer (to mention only a few names), who left the Polish People's Republic much later. They were able to continue working in their profession without severing contacts with their native environment (except during martial law).

The situation of young artists active today is unlike that of their predecessors, as seen for example, in the case of Hanna Kulenty, who lives and works in the Netherlands and Poland, and even younger ones, including Wojtek Blecharz, Andrzej Kwieciński, and Jagoda Szmytka. In fact, it can be said that these musicians are citizens of the world, who find themselves perfectly comfortable in their original context as well as in international music circles. This is why I find it extremely important to consider the historical and political conditions for each composer. One example of this concerns Palester and Panufnik and their long absence from Polish concert stages and media. Political emigration was something different from economic emigration and its consequences were not the same—sometimes we forget about that now. The same idea applies to composers of Jewish origin who emigrated from Europe as a result of World War II; their decisions to leave were influenced by anti-Semitic policies in Hitler's Germany and the resulting imperative to save their lives, which was much more important than any desire to build a career.

Marlena: After realizing the number of possible controversies that can arise, especially when we talk about emigration from the perspective of an entire century, I decided to treat this topic broadly in this book, believing that just living in another country, where you have your home and where you work and pay taxes for many years (regardless of your identity and contacts with your homeland), is enough to prove that you have chosen a different way of life than the one available in Poland. This change by itself often influences an artist's creativity and personality. I don't mean to attach any particular value to this, but I want to indicate that some significant change occurred in an individual's way of life. Moreover, I would like to avoid claiming that any specific individuals who left the country are more "authentic," and thus more worthy of the term "emigrant."

Beata: The important question is how long such a stay lasted, because in addition to emigrants who never returned to the country (mainly for political reasons, but not only), there are also many who left only temporarily.

Marlena: I agree. It is easier to describe a situation where one's life story is quite simple: the composer left, lived most of the time outside Poland, and was buried in their new country. But we also have a number of doubtful or ambiguous cases. One example could be Krzysztof Komeda, who, at the beginning of what promised to be a successful career in the United States (he had signed professional contracts), had an accident there. He was transported back to Poland, where he died. And although it is likely that he could have been the flagship example of an émigré artist, this is only a hypothesis, because the course of his life was interrupted just as his international career was starting. We decided to include him in this book because he created a strong impression during his time abroad.

In this case, as in many others, this "abroad" category remains a stronger argument than the traditional understanding of the term "emigrant." For example, a large group of artists have been or are abroad on scholarships. Some of them have chosen to remain in their new homeland, but for others this is just one stage in the development of their compositional skills; this particular field of art favors the need for training with other masters and such travels have been occurring for centuries. And what about Eugeniusz Morawski? No one thinks of him as an emigrant, because he was professionally active after his return to Poland and he died there, yet he spent a number of years in Paris, not of his own free will. So, we decided to include him in our book. On the other hand, Zygmunt Krauze, who spent some time in France in the 1980s, was not included because the core of his creative activity is definitely connected with Poland. Finally, there is a group of artists with residences outside Poland who actually live and work in both countries. I call the latter emigrants also, although they may not even think of themselves as such, since they do not feel like they have left their homeland.

Beata: It seems that this fear of an inadequate use of the word "emigrant" also stems from the fact that, for too long, the music and activities of Polish composers who composed outside Poland in the twentieth century were treated as if they worked "parallel" to our national culture. That is why any attempt to explore the activities of composers in exile, including any potential issues concerning their work or life choices, is extremely valuable, even if in some cases we risk making mistakes. Even the composers themselves, despite sometimes living abroad for many years, do not always consider themselves emigrants and perhaps they will be surprised by our decision to include them. Others will search for their entries in this book and not find them. That is why I want to stress that we are not claiming that we have taken an entirely holistic and comprehensive approach to the subject, because that is probably impossible. However, we want to try to bring the subject to everyone's attention and outline its scope. We take this risk together.

Marlena: It's good that you used the plural we, because you're the consultant for this book. What seemed so interesting about the emigration of composers? What made you decide to devote your time and knowledge, to accept the challenge of this project?

Beata: I am simply delighted that you have come up with such a book and invited me to cooperate. The topic has been close to my heart for a long time and I also have the feeling that there has not been enough discussion about it. I think that we are combining various directions and manners of dealing with this subject in a substantive and, at the same time, an accessible way, in order to bring the subject of composers in exile to the attention of a wider circle of readers. For me, the benefit of our work lies precisely in the ability to combine scholarly research (sometimes over many years) with the popular character of our publication. The main part of this book concerns classical music, but we also include

film, jazz, and popular music, which probably no one has done so far, for usually these categories are treated separately. We also want to draw attention to composers of the younger generations, to whom the classical definition of an emigrant composer doesn't apply because the political and historical situation of our country has changed, which, in turn, has altered the possibilities of traveling and returning. In many cases, it is difficult to talk about emigration now; instead, we speak of "being abroad," which often also applies to people born before the youngest generation. Among such cases are those for whom emigration was only temporary and who eventually returned to Poland. And although we will certainly not exhaust the subject or include all possible names, I hope that, thanks to this kind of guide, we will at least be able to partially remove a barrier between composers in Poland and those in exile. I hope that the latter will become closer and more "tangible" for a wider audience, who will actually get to discover this music. At least I believe this is our aim?

Marlena: Exactly this. And to what extent are émigré artists also associated with Poland in the countries in which they actually worked? Weren't they sometimes "assigned" to the history of music of their new homelands?

Beata: In the book we try to show some indications of this, but it is still a difficult question and in order to answer it properly, more research should be done. Panufnik was knighted for his contributions to British culture and is recognized as part of the musical life of that country, although it seems to me that he is perceived there as a Polish composer, or at least one of Polish origin. He considered himself a Polish composer to the end of his life. Aleksander Tansman is often seen as a French composer of Polish (or Jewish) origin, although he also thought of himself as a Polish artist. In both cases, speaking of inscribing them into the musical culture of their adopted countries is justified. It cannot be said, however, that Kassern or Rathaus, for example, entered the American music consciousness, just as Palester, Spisak, and Szałowski are not counted among French composers. It seems that Konstanty Regamey, born half-Swiss, was part of the music scene in Switzerland, while Mieczysław Weinberg is considered a Russian composer (he spent almost his entire adult life in the Soviet Union) and it is we who are eager to recall his Polish roots. Zbigniew Bargielski, on the other hand, admitted many times that the Austrian public received his compositions with more enthusiasm than Polish audiences did, but is he perceived as an Austrian composer? I think not.

Marlena: We try to talk a lot about the biographical and sociological aspects of these composers and about the influence of their living situations on their compositions. Are there any composers who made a radical change of musical language because of the new environment in which they composed?

Beata: This is clearly the case of composers who found themselves in the United States, because of the more conservative musical life there. Karol Rathaus, previously considered to be an avant-garde artist, definitely simplified his language after his arrival in the United States and even included Polish elements in some pieces (e.g., *Symphonic Polonaise*). Kassern wrote many pedagogical and educational works in America because of the nature of his employment. Similarly, Maciejewski composed works for the choirs that he conducted. On the other hand, Weinberg, as well as Tadeusz Majerski in Lviv, had to submit to the guidelines of Soviet socialist realism. Their stylistic changes were therefore demanded by the situation in which the composers found themselves after settling abroad. It seems that those who stayed in Europe—in France or England—probably were best able to maintain their original compositional idioms; they were able to perfect their individual styles, which does not mean that they lacked Polish influences or inspirations, which, after all, still often appeared as a result of their emigration experiences.

Marlena: Nowadays, being a composer who works abroad is often an indication of international prestige. How did the Polish community treat composers in exile during the Communist era?

Beata: Differently. Palester and Panufnik were a "forbidden fruit" for many years. Their music was known primarily thanks to people who met with them during their own foreign travels and brought scores or recordings back to Poland. It was an unofficial tradition to listen to them at the headquarters of the Polish Composers' Union or in private apartments; this was mentioned many times in Zygmunt Mycielski's letters and diaries, for he regularly visited Panufnik and brought recordings and scores home with him. Certainly, Tadeusz Kaczyński was in contact at first with Palester and later also with Panufnik. He published interviews in *Ruch Muzyczny* as early as the 1960s, mostly with Polish artists who had settled in Paris; his conversation with Palester, overlooked by censors and published in 1964, almost got him fired. Spisak, Regamey, and Haubenstock-Ramati, as well as Tansman, who was older, visited Poland for both personal reasons and for performances of their compositions, although for Tansman, this occurred only at the end of his long life. Certainly, the works and activities of composers in exile were of interest to their colleagues in Poland, especially those who remembered their earlier achievements, although the younger generation often wasn't familiar with them.

Marlena: Coming back to the composers who made their debut during the interwar period, what possibilities do you see for publicizing the music of composers who were unable to do so during their lifetime and now cannot promote themselves? Isn't this a bit like archaeology?

Beata: A lot depends on us—I mean not only musicologists, whose main preoccupation is scholarly research, but the whole music community. Panufnik's music was successfully introduced into the repertoire of many orchestras, soloists, and chamber ensembles (by the way, he maintained excellent contacts with the London Symphony Orchestra and other British and American ensembles and soloists during his life), and much has been happening recently, especially concerning the work of André Tchaikowsky and Mieczysław Weinberg. The music of these composers requires the involvement of people who care about promoting their works—this actually applies to all composers. As I have already mentioned, there is certainly a lot to do in this regard. This makes such ideas as the one proposed by the MEAKULTURA Foundation all the more valuable. I was personally captivated by your enthusiasm and original, fresh approach to the subject; even now you would rather talk about our book than write a traditional introduction. From the beginning you have spoken about this publication as a guide, a lexicon, although its second part doesn't contain traditional biographical entries.

Marlena: I like this idea, although it may seem controversial. Biographies have often already been created, more or less extensively, e.g., in Marek Podhajski's dictionary,[2] and I did not want to duplicate existing publications. On the other hand, I was aware that for the reader it would be rather unattractive to publish a set of facts like: "This one wrote Requiem, here's another one, here are the statistics, and there is a bibliography." Would anyone remember such things? I decided to choose the most famous or important names and say something more about these people, approach them as...people. I asked musicologists to consider this also. The question I proposed about personality was probably the most difficult one for our contributors. Some thought that I was probably talking about the profile of the artist's work, and so they had objections about expressing subjective opinions about a composer's personality. We have fantastic contributors; I don't even know how we managed to gather them all in such a short time.

Beata: The selection of authors for the essays and the questionnaire section, as well as the choice of composers were crucial points from the start of the project. I remember our first meeting at the Institute of Art of the Polish Academy of Sciences when we discussed the criteria behind the selections. The essays for the first part didn't pose any major problems, because we know quite well who is dealing with these issues in Poland, but it was much more difficult with the questionnaires. These required a lot of knowledge from the authors, which is why we gave up on some names, such as Feliks Łabuński, because although he has been mentioned for years as belonging to an important group of Polish émigré artists, his work remains unexplored. This may be the source of other gaps as well, although we have made an effort to minimize these as much as possible.

Another issue concerned those who wrote popular music, many of whom went abroad on contracts. Although some of them spent many years away from Poland, we do not necessarily think of them as emigrants. I'm thinking here of Tomasz Stańko or Krzysztof Komeda. Moreover, many of them were also performers and so an additional question arose—whether and to what extent to include them in a publication about composers?

Also, in the case of the youngest generation of composers, any summary would seem pointless, because both their life and their music can still go in different directions. However, we have essentially assumed that we will consider composers in exile as those who not only spent some part of their lives outside Poland (for various reasons), but whose artistic activity was connected to their life abroad. Everyone has been captivated by the appendix and some of the names listed there—the composers with the greatest achievements and creative significance—are treated in more detail in the questionnaire section. Surely every reader will complete or define this list in their own way, but it is a starting point for further discussions.

Beata: We are presenting foreign readers with the first English edition of our book. What was most difficult about this project?

Marlena: Finances were the most crucial aspect. Fortunately, the ZAiKS Association of Authors in Poland quickly helped with this. They are the perfect partner for such challenges. I thought for a long time about who the translator should be. I finally selected Olga

Drenda because she is deeply familiar with cultural topics and I was interested in taking a literary approach to the text, which she was able to do. However, this book would not have been published if we had not had a good editor and proofreader. The best, actually, because Dr. Cindy Bylander accepted these responsibilities. Knowing our financial situation, I never dreamed of including such an experienced foreign scholar on our team, especially one who specializes in Polish music....But my spontaneous Facebook post brought us into contact and thankfully our biggest obstacles were overcome.

What was it like to work with the English text? Composers' names were certainly a challenge. We accepted their Polish versions in most cases (e.g., Konstanty Regamey, not Constantin Regamey), but we made an exception for two composers. One is Andrzej Czajkowski (in Polish), who is commonly known elsewhere as André Tchaikowsky (similar to his Russian predecessor); the composer himself adopted this form after years of living in Great Britain. For Mieczysław Weinberg, it is more complicated. In Poland, his name is often spelled Wajnberg, since that is how it appears, among other places, on his birth certificate and many of his manuscript scores. For the rest of the world, however, it is usually Weinberg. This topic is rather delicate, especially since the composer definitely preferred the Polish spelling of his last name.[3] There are also many names of cities in the book, all of which appear in their Polish spelling, except for Warsaw (which in Polish is Warszawa).

Beata: What are your expectations for the English edition? Why did you undertake such an ambitious task, when even mass book publishers in Poland see no point in publishing books in other languages?

Marlena: Of course, I thought about a publisher from outside of Poland and even submitted a fantastic proposal guaranteeing global distribution. Unfortunately, the Book Institute in Poland declined to finance it. So, the Foundation decided to deal with the project on its own. Why? Because, in effect, this book functions as an advocate for Polish culture, for the talents of our composers and the knowledge of our musicologists. It also demonstrates the importance of our non-governmental organization (MEAKULTURA Foundation) for our country's culture.

This book illuminates Polish history. It tells the stories of hundreds of exceptional "individual lives." It is my dream that these (often forgotten) names will be "restored" to Poland and the world. Perhaps thanks to this book, foreign communities will remember that—for their benefit or for a given university or orchestra—an outstanding artist from Poland once worked in their midst. Perhaps they will also include the works of young émigré composers in their own repertoire simply because we "spoke" about them in such an interesting way. This publication provides wonderful material for promoters of culture, artists, scholars, foreign libraries...The potential is enormous.

Of course, I also have deeply hidden personal dreams. One is the hope that, for example, some representatives of the Polish diaspora who appreciate culture will learn of our achievements and become patrons of the MEAKULTURA Foundation, so that we can further our missionary activities. Oh, I said it aloud, do you think it will become true? (laugh)

On the other hand, we should answer the question about why we even "battled" to produce this English edition. We didn't calculate this in economic terms or by considering any "trend" that is fashionable today. We did it because it's worth it. That's it.

Beata: Yes, it's "worth it and that's it"! Now, let me change the topic a bit, I would like to point out that I was positively surprised by the graphic design you proposed. I remember that even before it was clear whether the book would be published, you said that you didn't want photos of the composers.

Marlena: Yes, I have been working with Max Skorwider at the MEAKULTURA Foundation for years. We trust each other, so I did not hesitate to put this challenge before him. I asked for colorful portraits of composers and authors' illustrations. It often irritates me that for books about cooking soup you get to have colors and nice paper, while for humanities publications, you usually must stick to low-budget standards. Therefore, from the beginning I insisted on an original, quality graphic design, although sometimes I felt that it was perceived as a folly.

Beata: And thanks to your vision and decisiveness, we have received an original (not only in terms of design) publication in which anyone interested in Polish émigré composers can find crucial information provided by experts and explained in an accessible way. Even though we haven't exhausted the entire complex of phenomena and problems, we have significantly widened the perspective and opened the way for further research and discussion. It's a great joy and satisfaction!

Marlena and Beata: Finally, we would like to thank all our authors for participating in this slightly mad enterprise. Thanks to their knowledge and involvement and also to the hard work of the entire editorial team (of which we are part), we managed to come to a happy ending. We hope that the outcome meets your expectations. We would like to wish everyone pleasant reading and fascinating music discoveries!

Part I

Music in Motion: Contexts

Danuta Gwizdalanka
The History of Music Often Means **the History of Emigrants**

At the Père Lachaise cemetery in Paris, three graves are always decorated with fresh flowers: those of Frédéric Chopin, Edith Piaf, and Jim Morrison. Several centuries earlier, these musical stars would not even have been allowed to be buried there, because those who, while wandering from place to place, sang and played for others, were considered unworthy of resting in consecrated soil. As you can see, much has changed since then. However, mobility has remained an attribute of a musician's profession (although Chopin is perhaps not the best example here). If, therefore, we consider any person who leaves his or her country of origin and settles permanently or temporarily in another country as an emigrant (because of the constant changes of borders, this is a nightmare for any historian investigating the problem), we will find that music history has been shaped to a great extent by emigrants. The Fleming Orlando di Lasso worked in Italy and Bavaria, the Florentine Giovanni Battista Lulli ruled in French musical life as Jean Baptiste Lully, the Saxon Georg Friedrich Händel made his career in England, and the Pole Chopin in Paris. The Russian Igor Stravinsky lived in Switzerland, France and the United States, being a Russian, French, and finally an American citizen, and, in the meantime, he also applied for Polish citizenship.[4]

These musicians emigrated in search of (better) work, for artistic reasons, and sometimes for personal ones. In other cases, the motivation was political in nature. In recent decades these politically inspired instances have aroused lively interest among scholars and musicians, causing Central Europe's refugee composers to become the subjects of special seminars and publications. These events were inspired by those who left during the Stalinist era to avoid enslavement and unwanted artistic compromise. Nothing stimulates curiosity (and emotions) more than attempts to limit the freedom of art and artists.

Dreaming of a career, a singer, instrumentalist, or conductor becomes, then, a professional wanderer. Composers seem to be relatively less threatened by such a fate, because since the invention of print, their music "wanders" anyway and they can write from the peace

of their homes—but until the middle of the twentieth century, composers were first and foremost performers. Conversely, it was customary for performers to learn composition, because audiences expected them to improvise. Therefore, the names of famous artists such as Paweł Kochański or Wanda Landowska, rarely thought of as composers today, continue to appear in the annals of composition history, for it was once unthinkable for a composer not to also perform publicly.

At the Courts

We owe the beginning of Polish musical traditions to pious immigrants from western and southern regions of Europe. Arriving in Polish lands, which had been incorporated into the community of Christian countries, these monks were musicians "on the side," because their song was primarily prayer. This "side product," however, launched a musical culture of previously unknown richness and complexity. For several centuries, this immigration of religious musicians, and gradually also laymen, occurred in greater numbers than did any emigration from Polish areas. For various periods of time, musicians from Italy, Flanders, Germany, and sometimes France served at Polish courts.

The first accounts of movement in the opposite direction could be observed in the fifteenth century, when the presence of several Poles was noted in the courts in Straubing (Bavaria), Leipzig, Innsbruck, and Hamburg.[5] The most common evidence of this were accounts of a "polnische Geige" played by Polish musicians in Germany, Denmark, and Sweden, where they enjoyed great popularity at the local courts. In the sixteenth century, a few organists and lute players from Poland also made their careers abroad. Today, the most remembered of these is Jakob Polak-Reys, who in 1574, at the age of twenty-five, followed Henry III of France to Paris. There, he spent the remaining four decades of his life as a royal court lute player—a virtuoso and composer who wrote under the name of Jacques Polonais or Jacques Reys. It is unlikely that Reys considered himself a Polish emigrant, although we could grant him such a status today, just as we could call Adam Jarzębski a "re-emigrant." Born in Polish territory, Jarzębski was a member of an ensemble of the Elector of Brandenburg in Berlin between 1612 and 1615. A few years later he arrived in Warsaw, where he stayed for the rest of his life, playing for successive Polish kings. Is it possible that he did so because of nostalgia for his homeland? After all, he had been born in Warka, less than sixty kilometers from Warsaw. Musicians as outstanding as Jarzębski chose the most attractive employer possible, and in the early seventeenth century the Warsaw court definitely towered over the Berlin one, as was reflected by the number of foreign musicians coming to Poland. One of these was Vincenzo Gigli from Italy, who in the early seventeenth century was employed in the royal band in Warsaw. Eventually, he Polonized his name to Wincenty Lilius, and his son Franciszek, kapellmeister of the Wawel Cathedral, is today considered one of the most important composers of the Polish Baroque. The Republic of Poland maintained its magnetism even in the eighteenth century. Many newcomers adapted themselves to the new country and, like Gigli, changed their names to Polish-sounding ones. In this way, the son of Frenchman Durant, kapellmeister of the Ogiński family in Słonim, was known by the name of August Fryderyk Duranowski and was later successful in Europe as a violin virtuoso.

Foreigners also built the foundations of Polish opera. At the court of the Radziwiłłs in Nesvizh, Italian Alessandro Danesi composed *Agatha, or The Arrival of the Lord* [*Agatka, czyli Przyjazd Pana*], staged in 1784 to celebrate the visit of King Stanislaw August, and Johann David Holland from Germany wrote *Another Man's Property Is Good for No One* [*Cudzy majątek nikomu nie służy*].[6] At the time, Warsaw was still one of the most important hubs of Central European culture. There, *Poverty Made Happy* [*Nędza uszczęśliwiona*] was composed by Slovak Maciej Kamieński and *Krakovians and Highlanders* [*Krakowiacy i górale*] by the Czech composer Jan Stefani.

Even though in nineteenth-century Europe, court patronage was already a marginal phenomenon, beginning in 1839 Karol Lipiński became the concertmaster of the Saxon King Frederick August's orchestra in Dresden (after his retirement two decades later, he returned to his estate of Urlov near Lviv). Even in the second half of the century, several virtuosos (and also composers) were considered to be court artists. Antoni Kątski, and later also Natalia Janotha, could introduce themselves as court pianists of the Prussian king.

Before that, the title of "First Pianist of Their Majesties Tsarinas Elisabeth Alexandrovna and Maria Fiedorovna" belonged to Maria Szymanowska. Her example shows perfectly that the dictionary definition of an emigrant does not fit everyone. The future pianist was born in 1789 in Warsaw, then still the capital of Poland. Seven years later, Warsaw was briefly incorporated into Prussia. Szymanowska thus started her career as a subject of Tsar Alexander. When she settled in St. Petersburg with her family in 1827, she was not formally an emigrant. Henryk Wieniawski found himself in a similar situation. As a native of Lublin, he came from a Russian provincial town. When he took up a post at the tsarist court in 1860, he worked for the head of his homeland. He could have been called an emigrant fourteen years later when he moved to Brussels to be a professor at the local Conservatory, but having studied in Paris, he probably felt at home there as well.

Towards Metropolises

As the importance of royal courts diminished, the attractiveness of cities grew. Increasing numbers of noblemen and burghers were eager to pay for the pleasure of listening to music. Seventeenth-century Venice saw the creation of the first public operas and London began to organize concerts open to anyone who paid a fee. The largest metropolitan areas were located in countries that were politically and administratively consolidated; these included the capitals of France and England, later those of Russia and Austria, and eventually united Germany. In the middle of the nineteenth century, when London had more than two million residents and Paris more than one million, only eleven cities in Poland exceeded twenty thousand inhabitants. It is therefore hardly surprising that many musicians, especially the most outstanding, looked for their fortunes—or to be more precise, audiences for their art—abroad.

Poland, with its disappearance from the map of Europe at the end of the eighteenth century, lost its attractiveness to foreign artists. Aside from cases of spectacular Polonization, as in the case of Józef Elsner, in the nineteenth century emigrants clearly outnumbered immigrants. After all, musical life in Poland was not supported either by a rich state that cared for an imperial image—as was the case in the French or Austrian capital—or by a sizable, musically educated bourgeoisie, which allowed this art to flourish in Germanic countries. On the contrary, one of the consequences of the loss of political independence was a poor educational system (which affected music as well) and the handicapping of cultural development through intense Russification in the tsarist partition and Germanization in Prussia. Those in the Austrian partition enjoyed the greatest freedom, but the region's poor economic situation was not conducive to the flourishing of art. For the most talented composers, emigration to large foreign cities proved to be the most advantageous solution.

In eighteenth-century London, musical life was dominated by Italians and Germans. Jakob Kremberg, a lute player, composer, and music entrepreneur gained experience in the ensemble of the Polish king, and later in Halle, Stockholm, and Dresden. In London he boasted of successes he allegedly had in Italy. Around 1710, as a member of the "24 Violins," he became the only foreigner in the court ensemble of Anna Stuart, the first queen of Great Britain (which was not just the territory of England anymore). Almost a hundred years later, Feliks Janiewicz, with equally rich international professional experiences, remained in Britain after debuting successfully in London in 1792. Kremberg was primarily a court musician, giving public concerts only from time to time. For Janiewicz, this new form of professional concertizing became the basis of his existence. In 1813, already as Felix Yaniewicz, he became one of the founders of the Philharmonic Society, a professional orchestra that gave regular performances for the public. Two years later, he co-organized the first Edinburgh Festival, which remains the biggest cultural attraction in Scotland today. Janiewicz died as a distinguished citizen of Edinburgh, having reached the impressive age of eighty-six, which was unusual at that time. Born in Vilnius, he spent his first eighteen years in Poland. Could he have felt like a Polish emigrant?

Antoni Kątski chose London as his residence for sixteen years. At the end of nineteenth century, Natalia Janotha also settled there. Soon afterwards, Emil Młynarski enjoyed success as a conductor; it was thanks to his initiative that Edward Elgar composed *Polonia*. Several decades later, Andrzej Panufnik asked for asylum in London. Then André Tchaikowsky (known in Poland as Andrzej Czajkowski) joined him. Gradually the community of Polish musicians grew, many of them also changing the spelling of their surnames for reasons similar to Janiewicz's (while the biggest challenge for Poles would have been to get used to the new spelling of Jacek Kasprzyk's name as Kaspszyk).

Paris seemed to attract Polish musicians more successfully. Its location in the center of continental Europe, the attractiveness of its local conservatory, its abundance of music salons and potential students, as well as the fairly common knowledge of the French language in Poland (as opposed to English, which became fashionable much later) were all compelling factors for composers looking for a second home. In 1828, Albert Sowiński settled in Paris. He made his living by teaching and composing; he is also recognized as the author of the first dictionary of Polish musicians, published in France in 1874. The situation of Józef Michał Ksawery Poniatowski was completely different; several of his operas were staged between 1858 and 1868, among them the spectacular *Pierre de Medicis* at the Paris Opera. He may deserve to be called a Polish emigrant, but above all, he was a cosmopolitan who, as an Austrian and Italian prince, settled down in Paris after a few years of diplomatic service to Tuscany, and thus found himself in the immediate vicinity of Napoleon III.

"I can barely remember how they sing in the country," wrote Chopin in the fall of 1848. These words became a symbol of the fate of the Polish immigrant in Paris, often quoted alongside the poetry of the homesick Adam Mickiewicz. However, in less frequently quoted words written in the autumn of 1831, Chopin stated: "I am content with what I found here; I have the world's leading musicians and its finest opera." It was for this very reason that musicians from all over Europe were attracted to the "music capital," among them Poles, including Stanisław and Apolinary Kątski and later the Wieniawski brothers, whose success during their years at the Paris Conservatory launched their international careers, or later Wanda Landowska, who became a Parisian by choice in the early twentieth century. There were also others, who did not find their place in the elite circles of stars, but still found a place for themselves in Parisian musical life—for example, two Varsovians: Józef

Z. Szulc, a successful musician in Paris after 1910, and Józef Eugeniusz Szyfer, a conductor of the Grand Opera between 1927 and 1940.

Paris remained the primary destination for Polish musicians after the emergence of independent Poland. In 1919, Aleksander Tansman arrived there. In subsequent years, the community of Polish composers, violinists, and pianists grew, as state scholarships enabled foreign study for those who previously could not afford it. Since French remained the most popular foreign language in Poland, Paris was the most attractive option for musicians. A previously loose group of artists became more of a regular community: L'Association des Jeunes Musiciens Polonais à Paris (Association of Young Polish Musicians in Paris) was founded in 1926, and by the time World War II broke out, the group had one hundred and forty members. Contact with the bustling musical life of Paris weakened their attachment to Romanticism, which was still very much alive among musicians in Poland. "The atmosphere of Paris...is very desirable for young musicians," they explained in a brochure published in 1930, "because it does not allow one to become pigeonholed. By coming into contact with foreign musical culture and the achievements of other composers, this has prompted a constant race of ingenuity, often at a dizzying pace."[7] The majority of young composers returned to Poland after their studies, but Szymon Laks, Antoni Szałowski, and Michał Spisak decided to stay in Paris.

Among previously mentioned composers, only Tansman achieved sustained success. Szałowski enjoyed a spectacular but brief moment of fame when his *Overture* for orchestra received a gold medal at the 1937 Universal Exhibition; this piece soon became the most frequently performed Polish work. Spisak was noticed, but only after World War II. In 1954, his *Serenade* received an award at a composers' competition in Brussels; one year later, he won the competition for an opening anthem for the Melbourne Olympics, and in 1957, thanks to another prize, international stages welcomed his *Concerto Giocoso*. Spisak's music generated interest in the early 1960s in France but, unfortunately, these performances and recordings arrived only at the very end of his life, for he died in 1965.

Vienna competed with Paris, but despite its geographical proximity to Poland, it was a much less popular destination for Polish composers. Bazyli Bohdanowicz, a native of the country's Lesser Poland region, went down in Viennese history as a clown rather than a musician, entertaining the public from 1785 on with pieces played by his wife and eight children in the most bizarre ways: for example, three children played one violin or four children played the same piano at the same time. Tomasz Nidecki was active for a decade (1828–1838) exhibiting his operettas. But overall, for the Viennese, Slavic musicians, as a "national minority" living on the borders of the monarchy, were not an attraction.[8] Hence, in 1911 Grzegorz Fitelberg made his debut as a Russian conductor, Kochański was announced by the local press as a musician from Leipzig, and Landowska performed as a Frenchwoman, which she was entitled to do given her French citizenship. Karol Szymanowski's hopes for career in Vienna also remained unfulfilled. In the spring of 1912, together with Fitelberg, he rented an apartment in the most creative district, right next to the Karlskirche, but a year later he left the capital of the Habsburg Empire with debts and dubious consolation: a score for *Hagith*, rejected by the Hofoper.

Berlin was a more popular destination, especially for composition students. The city joined the ranks of European metropolises after 1871, when it became the capital of the united Germany. Among composers who studied there and remained for several years were Wanda Landowska, Mieczysław Karlowicz, Leopold Godowski, Zygmunt Noskowski, Feliks Nowowiejski, Ludomir Różycki, Karol Tausig, and Tadeusz Tyszkiewicz.[9] In 1905, Berlin saw the birth of "Young Poland." According to Adolf Chybiński, Young Poland was "a publishing association whose goal was to print compositions by young Polish authors in the center of the European music movement, namely in Berlin."[10] In the 1920s, Berlin surpassed Vienna as a music capital; Karol Rathaus moved there, following his professor Franz Schreker, and Jerzy Fitelberg and Bronisław Kaper arrived from Warsaw. After 1933, they all went into exile again, forced to do so as the result of an official anti-Semitic campaign.

Of the three partitioned areas of Poland, the most noticeable role played by Polish musicians occurred in the capital of Russia. Józef Kozłowski, between 1803 and 1819 the musical director of the tsarist theaters in St. Petersburg, popularized the polonaise in Russia. An exceptionally picturesque, now forgotten figure was Ludwig-Wilhelm Tepper de Ferguson, son of a Warsaw banker and a diplomat by profession, who is still remembered in Russia as Alexander Pushkin's music teacher (by the way, Tepper was the grandson of a Scottish immigrant named Ferguson and the son of a French immigrant). Maria Szymanowska settled on the Neva in 1828, but only three years later she fell victim to cholera. In 1842, disappointed with the provinciality of Vilnius, Wiktor Każyński moved to St. Petersburg; nowadays he is remembered mostly as the author of *Notes from Travels Around Europe* [*Notatki z podróży po Europie*]. Apolinary Kątski's position as a soloist at the tsar's court allowed him to obtain permission to open the Music Institute in Warsaw. His brother Antoni, a pianist, lived in St. Petersburg between 1854 and 1867 and performed together with Wieniawski.

London, Paris and St. Petersburg offered incomparably higher earnings than other centers, but at the end of the nineteenth century, America entered the game. Virtuosos like Wieniawski, and later Ignacy Jan Paderewski, made fortunes thanks to their journeys across the ocean. Gradually, a growing number of musicians decided to emigrate from Europe to the New World. Among them was the Adamowski family, which contributed much to the musical life in Boston, the second city (after New York) to have a permanent symphony orchestra. Chicago soon became attractive, as the rapidly growing Polish community there offered possibilities for finding employment in an ethnically close-knit environment; Aleksander Karczyński, who went there in 1907, was one who took advantage of this opportunity. An important role was also played by Polish musicians in Philadelphia.[11] Józef Hofman co-founded the Curtis Institute of Music, where Artur Rodziński and Emil Młynarski taught. Młynarski also composed "on the side." In the post-World War II years, the Institute's staff often taught descendants of emigrants, such as Aaron Rosand, whose father came from the Warsaw region and his mother from Minsk. In 1957 Rosand caused a sensation when he bought his Guarneri del Gesu from Paweł Kochański's widow. Half a century later, he sold it for ten million dollars—allegedly the highest amount ever paid for a violin—and donated some of the money to the Institute. The aforementioned Kochański also received an offer to teach at the Juilliard School of Music in New York. He decided to go to America permanently, tempted by this very job.

Polish musicians in the United States, both temporary and lifelong emigrants, worked in Polish communities, in orchestras, and for film studios in Hollywood. Only film composers could count on fame and fortune, as Kaper experienced while creating music for one hundred and fifty films. In 1953 he was awarded an Oscar for the music to the film *Lili* with the then popular song *Hi-Lili, Hi-Lo*, known in Poland as *Laleczki, moje laleczki* [*Dolls, My Dolls*].

Some musicians were globetrotters rather than emigrants per se. For example, Tadeusz Jarecki, born in 1889 in Lviv, studied in his hometown, in Moscow, and in Hellerau near Dresden, where he accepted his first job at Émile Jaques-Dalcroze's Institute of Rhythmics. In 1917 he left for the United States, but a year later returned to Poland and voluntarily joined the army. In 1920 he left Europe again to live in New York. He spent the years 1932–1936 in Lviv and Stanisławów (today Ivano-Frankivsk, Ukraine), then he went to the States again, to Paris, and eventually to London, where he worked for the government in exile during World War II. After three decades of peregrinations among continents, he settled permanently in the United States. He died in New York in 1955.

Hundreds of Polish musicians have found—and continue to do so today—employment in orchestras worldwide, from Mexico to Iceland. Wojciech Frankowski, in his book *Columbus Discovered America and Łódź Musicians Discovered Finland* [*Kolumb odkrył Amerykę, a łódzcy muzycy Finlandię*], described the era of international contracts arranged by the Pagart agency during the Communist era in Poland. Among conductors, three long-time emigrants stand out: Artur Rodziński, Paweł Klecki, and Stanisław Skrowaczewski. Today, composers are offered permanent jobs, primarily at universities. In the nineteenth century, however, Henryk Wieniawski taught violin in Brussels and Juliusz Zarębski gave piano lessons in the same city. Szymanowski rejected a proposal to teach composition at the Cairo conservatory. The first foreigners to teach composition were probably Klecki in Milan in the 1930s and, during the next decade, Feliks Roderyk Łabuński at an American college. Only in the 1970s were Poles employed abroad as composition professors: Witold Szalonek in West Berlin, Andrzej Dobrowolski in Graz, Bogusław Schaeffer in Salzburg, and Krzysztof Meyer in Cologne. Marta Ptaszyńska, who has taught composition at Berkeley, Santa Barbara, Bloomington, and the University of Chicago, is sort of a record holder in this group.

Exiles and Fugitives

The first musicians forced to emigrate—or to say it more dramatically, the first fugitives and exiles—were court lute players. The Hungarian Balint Bakfark served at the court of Sigismund II Augustus in 1549–1566, until it transpired that he was spying for the Prussian prince. He was lucky that he managed to escape before his sentence was carried out. A dozen or so years later, Wojciech Długoraj, a musician at Stefan Batory's court, found himself in similar trouble. For reasons that are still unclear today, he was spying on his former patron, Samuel Zborowski, for the Polish king. From letters retrieved by Długoraj, it was learned that a plot to assassinate the king was in the works; Zborowski was beheaded, and Długoraj, presumably fearing the family's revenge, left Poland and spent the rest of his life in Germany.

Natalia Janotha's exile had a completely different background. In 1915 she was—literally—expelled from London, where she had lived for several years. The reason was due to her title, "Court Pianist of the King of Prussia," which she had been granted in 1885. In the British newspaper *The Times* on 10 August 1915, we read: "Maria Cecilia Natalie Janotha, the Emperor's favorite pianist, was arrested in London on Sunday by two Scotland Yard officers and expelled from the country. She was not allowed to take any things and was taken away in a carriage within two minutes of the detectives' appearance." She spent the rest of her life in neutral Holland. Three years after Janotha's eviction, the dethroned Emperor Wilhelm II Hohenzollern also asked for asylum in the same country. He then lived eighty kilometers away from his "favorite pianist."

The collapse of the Republic of Poland at the end of the eighteenth century and the country's subsequent unsuccessful attempts to regain independence were followed by a new wave of emigration. Michał Kleofas Ogiński, author of *Farewell to the Fatherland* [*Pożegnanie ojczyzny*] polonaise, was the leading figure among these patriot-refugees. His piece, like Teofil Kwiatkowski's painting *The Ball at the Lambert Hotel in Paris* [*Bal w Hotelu Lambert w Paryżu*], with its specters of dancing to music played by Chopin, is still recognized as a symbol of emigration for that era.

Among those who left Poland after the defeat of the November Uprising in 1830–1831, the most famous musician possessing compositional aspirations was Chopin's friend, Julian Fontana. He went to America, but returned to Paris after some time. More musically well-educated amateurs from noble families also travelled across the ocean via Germany and France. Under new conditions, they earned money by performing, teaching, and composing.[12] Ignacy Feliks Dobrzyński found himself among those composers who left Poland, which at that point was non-existent. During his artistic journey around Germany in 1845, he was forced to stay in Berlin for a longer period of time; having written several patriotic songs, such as music to Adam Mickiewicz's poem *To the Polish Mother* [*Do matki Polki*], he was not welcome back home (he was forbidden from returning to Warsaw until September 1847). Half a century later, Eugeniusz Morawski spent many more years abroad out of necessity. In 1907 he was imprisoned on charges of plotting an attack on the police. He was sentenced to four years of exile to Siberia by the tsarist military court, but thanks to his father's efforts, the penalty was changed to banishment. He left Poland for Paris, where he continued his studies. He remained there until 1930, when returned to Poland.

Due to the open borders of the Second Polish Republic, a large group of composers were surprised to find themselves outside the country at the outbreak of World War II. Michał Kondracki headed first for Brazil and then for the United States. Roman Ryterband was in Switzerland, from where he emigrated to Canada and then to the United States. Spisak, Szałowski, Tansman, and Jerzy Fitelberg travelled from Paris to southern France. They all applied for American visas, but only Tansman and Fitelberg were able to get one. Rathaus also managed to take refuge in America, where he found taught and wrote film music. He had to give up his ambitions to compose more serious music due to the relative disinterest in modernism in American music circles. Laks was deported to Auschwitz, where he survived by working in the camp orchestra, and later was taken to Dachau; after liberation, he returned to Paris.

About 300,000–350,000 Poles with Jewish roots escaped from the German-occupied territories to lands occupied by the Soviet Union; several thousand managed to leave for Sweden, Palestine, the United States, Canada, and Australia, among them musicians who joined or followed Anders' Army.[13] The Holocaust and emigration decimated the community of entertainment musicians, which had been dominated before the war by Jewish composers and conductors. Thus, after 1945 Poland did not lack symphony and oratorio creators, but there was a clear shortage of composers able to write popular songs. Some authors of interwar hits, including Henryk Wars and Henryk Gold, settled in America. So did Jerzy Petersburski, who, unlike his colleagues, returned to Warsaw in 1968.

The fact that Poland found itself in the Soviet sphere after the war prompted dilemmas among artists. Roman Palester, having lived through the years of war in Poland, officially left for Paris in 1947. Many times he asked himself, "Where can I serve Poland better? Here or in exile?" After the notorious Łagów composers conference in 1949 and in the face of growing political pressure, he decided not to return to Poland, choosing to avoid life under Communist dictatorship.

"Until now, it seemed that it was our duty to stay in the country. This is still the view shared by the vast majority of Poles," Palester responded in 1951:

> From a basic human point of view, it is, of course, quite understandable that a person decides to escape and endure even the worst conditions of living in exile in order to ensure his elementary legal freedom and a peaceful night's sleep....At the same time, however, you should be aware that having chosen the path of exile, you will, as an artist, find yourself almost in the situation you were in twenty years ago, at the start of your career....You will remain in a tragic situation...without any contact with audiences who understood you.[14]

Tadeusz Zygfryd Kassern made a similar decision. He worked as a diplomat in the United States but in 1948, seeing that the imposition of Communist rule in Poland was inevitable, he decided to stay abroad. He suffered the consequences, exactly as Palester had described. Unlike Czesław Miłosz, who in 1951 asked for asylum in Paris and was ostracized later by the émigré community, who blamed him for cooperating earlier with the Polish authorities, Kassern encountered problems with the American authorities because his asylum application was denied. After being refused again in 1955, Kassern, in desperation, tried to commit suicide. His application was not approved until the fall of 1956.

The image of a "free West" combined with emigrants' expectations about life there usually proved to be incompatible with reality. In 1988 Palester described his experiences: "My first postwar trip abroad was to London. In July 1946 my *Violin Concerto*, written during the war, was played there at the Festival of Contemporary Music." Palester then described a situation that at the time was impossible to imagine in Poland:

> This journey, regardless of its artistic success, was not pleasant....Why? Because there, for the first time, we encountered, *ad oculos*, an incredibly painful symptom: an aversion to Polish emigrants and an exaggerated enthusiasm for newcomers 'from there'. We experienced this personally later, when we were already emigrants, in France, and especially in Germany....These English people at all the parties, cocktails, and other meetings almost threw themselves around our necks, declaring with delight how happy they were to finally see 'real' Poles, as opposed to the terrible 'Arciszewski-Poles', who wanted them to subvert their system of alliances and who do nothing but protest everywhere. Of course there is no need to generalize—we have met English people who understood everything and were sorry, but overall it was quite unpleasant.[15]

He was even more surprised by reactions in Paris:

> My French friends—and I had many at the time—strongly urged me not to go back to Poland, eloquently explaining to me everything that I knew much better. But when one day I told the music director of French Radio that I already had refugee status, he, terrified, made a real scene: What will I do now, what will happen to me, and how could I be so foolish. He started to explain that every artist must have the support of some kind of government—any kind—but a government of some sort. I would find that out all too well over the next decades, when most of the great manifestations of international artistic life were pushed into a tight framework of various 'cultural arrangements' between governments.[16]

Unlike those who moved abroad in the 1920s or 1930s—for example, Tansman, Ludomir Rogowski, and Roman Maciejewski—who maintained their profession, sometimes even previously successful postwar emigrants lost the possibility of creative work. Kondracki, Kassern, and the Łabuński brothers did not succeed in becoming part of their local music communities. Palester's works were performed for some time thanks to the opportunities offered by his role as a "representative in exile" at the International Society for Contemporary Music. However, after 1957, when as a result of changes in Poland's political situation, musicians living in that country renewed contact with the Society, Palester lost this support (making the Paris radio director's words seem prophetic) but remained censored in Poland. Andrzej Panufnik was luckier. Initially, he turned out to be as naive as Palester and was sadly surprised to find that there was no escape from politics even in the West. Later, in his memoirs, he described his situation briefly as "from number one to no one." Over time, however, he managed to obtain a good position, first as a conductor and, after several years, also as a composer, while finding such influential promoters as Leopold Stokowski and Yehudi Menuhin. Other composers, either as renowned as Stanisław Skrowaczewski or lesser known, also took advantage of invitations to foreign concerts, or remained abroad after a contract ended, settling mainly in the United States, Canada, Germany, and France (or, more precisely, in Paris).[17]

Polish Jews

As mentioned before, changes of Poland's borders, let alone the loss of sovereignty, make the use of the term "emigrant" complicated; for example, after 1945 the Lviv-based composers Tadeusz Majerski, Adam Sołtys, and Andrzej Nikodemowicz could feel like emigrants in their own city, which now was part of the Soviet Union. The adjective "Polish" poses a similar problem. The former Republic of Poland was a multinational country, in which many musicians—including the most outstanding ones—came from Jewish families. About one third of European Jews lived in the Russian partition. During the late nineteenth and early twentieth centuries, many left in successive waves of emigration.[18] During the Second Polish Republic era, the anti-Semitic attitude of a large part of society, who demanded a nation-state (i.e., one that was Polish-Catholic), combined with an economic crisis that limited the income of many liberal arts professionals, prompted the departure of tens of thousands of people. This included musicians, although their motivation was more often a desire to try their artistic luck internationally rather than a need to escape oppression.

Karol Rathaus left his hometown of Tarnopol at the age of eighteen and went to Vienna to study. From there, he moved to Berlin, where in the 1920s he had developed into one of the most interesting composers of the younger generation. The events of 1933 prompted him to leave Germany, along with many other artists of Jewish origin (Kaper also did). He lived in Paris, London, and, in 1938, settled in the United States, where he gained a reputation as an experienced teacher and film music composer. In America, Rathaus adopted the identity of an emigrant and rediscovered his ties with Poland (he spoke Polish at home). Placed by Goebbels on a list of "degenerate composers," he gradually lost his previous sense of belonging to Austrian and German musical culture.

The reason for Tansman's departure was hardly anti-Semitism, although we occasionally come across such suggestions. Awarded three prizes at a 1919 composition competition in Warsaw, but soon discouraged by the first reviews of his works, the young and promising artist made the bold but sensible decision to leave for the city then regarded as the artistic capital of Europe. His talent and hard work, along with a great deal of luck, enabled him to obtain an excellent position there in a relatively short time, as one of the few Polish composers who tried to conquer that city. It is a fact, however, that aversion to Jews was demonstrated many times in interwar Poland, including in music circles.

After the outbreak of World War II, many musicians from Warsaw fled to the east. Among them was twenty-year-old pianist Mieczysław Weinberg. He was granted Soviet citizenship and sent to the conservatory in Minsk for composition. The fates of Edi Tyrmand, Henryk Wagner, and Ryszard Sielicki were similar. Three of these fugitives remained in the Soviet Union for the rest of their lives, while Sielicki repatriated to Poland years later. In autumn 1949, when about 30,000 Polish citizens of Jewish nationality were granted one-way passports, Roman Haubenstock-Ramati took advantage of the opportunity. He emigrated first to Israel and from there went to Vienna. From 1956–1960 a certain liberalization of Poland's passport policy also led many Jews to leave the country, for reasons similar to those of ethnic Poles—exhaustion with the atmosphere in the country as well as its economic crisis (a similar decision was made by the parents of then eleven-year-old Gabriel Chmura). After the six-day war, the anti-Semitic campaign launched in Poland in March 1968, and waves of persecution and dismissals from jobs, about thirteen thousand people—of Jewish origin and defining themselves as Poles—left the country. Many of them were members of the intelligentsia, including artists such as pianist Ryszard Bakst and composer Jan Radzyński.

Remembering the Absent

In the case of Polish emigrants, the saying "out of sight, out of mind" was true. In the Polish People's Republic, the process of "forgetting" was facilitated by governmental censorship and the "deletion" of political emigrants: Kassern, Palester, and Panufnik (when *Ruch Muzyczny* published an interview with Palester in 1964, the editorial staff suffered the consequences of doing so). In the late 1950s and early 1960s a certain liberalization occurred in the country, but at the same time, the music community's interests changed. Thus Tansman, who remained faithful to neoclassicism, had no chance to re-emerge in Polish life. Maciejewski's *Requiem*, performed in 1960 at the Warsaw Autumn Festival, went unnoticed. In the mid-1960s, Weinberg was met with total indifference; he was treated as a representative of Soviet music, and as such, was unwelcome. When he came to Poland in 1966, nobody remembered him as a composer from the interwar period. Only Konstanty Regamey, who left for Switzerland after the war, and Roman Haubenstock-Ramati aroused interest as avant-gardists. Moreover, performances of works by composers living abroad were sometimes hindered by bureaucratic and foreign exchange issues, as was the case at a Chopin Competition, when Spisak's *Serenade*, awarded at a competition under the Belgian queen's patronage, was to be played to celebrate her visit.

Palester and Panufnik remained unknown in their homeland during the decades when their best works were composed. In this respect, the position of music was worse than that of émigré literature, which at least could be smuggled across the border. While abroad, composers lost contact with their influential native communities and, most importantly, with performers. Even if no political objections were raised, émigré composers struggled to find musicians willing to perform their music. Panufnik was relatively successful in this respect; his works with political overtones quickly aroused understandable interest and were performed in the 1980s.

Relations between these emigrants and Poland were ambivalent. Szałowski did not visit a single time. Spisak did, however, and maintained regular contacts with his colleagues and even with the Polish embassy. He was a member of the Polish Composers' Union, which spared him financial difficulties for many years. His normal professional development was hindered by his physical disability, so commissions or awards from Poland provided invaluable assistance for the artist, who was otherwise dependent on the income of his French wife. In 1954, after receiving an award in Brussels, he confided in Stefan Jarociński: "The financial gain from this allowed me to pay off my terrible debts; for some time, I will be free of wondering: What will tomorrow bring?"[19] The fate of Palester, who was subject to censorship in Poland, was completely different. Working for the Munich-based radio station Radio Free Europe as manager of its cultural department gave him financial security as well as a chance to travel and follow European artistic life. His living conditions also allowed him to compose. In Poland, however, his music did not appear on stage until 1977 (at a concert celebrating the 50th anniversary of the Association of Young Polish Musicians in Paris).

The "repatriation" of émigré art began late. Gradually, music of the neoclassicists was "re-discovered." In 1996 Tansman lived to see a festival dedicated to his music. In subsequent years Weinberg aroused interest; in his case, the impulse came from abroad, thanks to an emerging interest in a Soviet composer born in Warsaw.

"Cosmopoles"

Because many virtuosos and composers of the past changed their places of residence many times, they do not fit the strict definition of an emigrant. A record holder in this respect was Kraków-born Antoni Kątski, who lived in Berlin, Lisbon, London, and even in Buffalo, New York. For a dozen or so years, it was impossible to determine the permanent place of residence of the Warsaw-born Natalia Janotha, whose last address, The Hague, could be considered a place of forced emigration, as mentioned previously. In the case of the biggest stars, it is difficult to talk about emigration because they felt at home everywhere; however, they were usually performers, not composers.

Interest in émigré composers increased due to the closed borders of the Polish People's Republic. Until 1989, the word "emigrant" was associated with escape or exile, and as such it carried negative emotions of parting, separation, compulsion, or desperation (recently recorded in Paweł Pawlikowski's 2018 film *Cold War*, whose protagonist is a musician). Once the borders were opened, the problem lost its relevance. Today, according to estimates, about one third of people born in Poland or with Polish roots live abroad, among them, of course, composers. In contrast to their predecessors, they can easily remain in touch with their homeland. Sometimes, they simply use two addresses, such as Hanna Kulenty, a Polish-Dutch composer since 1992, or Krzysztof Meyer, who divides his time between Poland and Germany. There are also those who come back years later, like Zbigniew Bargielski from Austria. On the polmic.pl website we meet a lot of "Cosmopoles": Piotr Radko, Mikołaj Piotr Górecki, Jarosław Kapuściński, Piotr Grella-Możejko, Marzena Komsta, Tomasz Praszczałek (for the convenience of foreigners, he uses Prasqual), Jacek Sobieraj, and Paweł B. Sydor. One symbol of normalization is the Festival of Premieres, organized for years by the National Polish Radio Symphony Orchestra in Katowice and open to Polish composers regardless of their place of residence.

In Polish society, the attitude to emigration remains ambivalent. According to the latest research, even though 56 percent of those surveyed share the opinion that "emigration means hope for success in a new country," negative feelings prevail, because still "most contemporary Poles (66 percent) associate emigration with sadness, regret or longing."[20] This shows that a community perspective prevails over an individual one. However, among artists, the "I" is usually more important than the "we," so their attitude to the phenomenon of emigration is likely to be different.

Perhaps the approach to this issue will also change as the result of a process that has been ongoing since the emergence of the Third Republic of Poland and the country's entry into the European Union. International instrumentalists and singers are now hardly a rarity in Polish orchestras and operas; the same is true of conductors who lead these ensembles. Foreign composition students have become a part of the landscape of Polish music universities. Compositions are also commissioned from foreign composers. Slowly, the emigration movement has ceased to be one-way and the profile of its participants has begun to diversify.

Marlena Wieczorek

Life Choices: Causes and Effects of Migration

The twentieth century, taken in its entirety, was an unusually dynamic time for the world and for Poland, a country that did not exist at the beginning of that century and that, after it returned to the map, soon faced the struggles of World War II and Communism. Poland's difficult history consists of millions of individual biographies. These biographies tell the story of struggles for personal liberties, creative freedom, money, career, education, and often for life itself.

This historical complexity, as well as the reality of technological progress, makes it difficult to compare the situation of composers who had been creating, for example, in the interwar period with those working in the current European Union, in the era of the Internet, cell phones, freedom of creative expression, and the ability to move easily to any country (or even between continents). Composers generously use the possibilities offered by the present day. Mobility no longer means resigning from a career in their homeland, because leaving is not the last resort and emigration is not exile anymore. And yet not so long ago Tomas Venclova wrote in a letter to Czesław Miłosz: "We must get used to a second life in the West. In a sense, it will be a posthumous life. We meet people we had no hope of meeting in this world and we are separated from our old friends forever. Contacts with them are of a slightly spiritual nature."[21] In this context, the private and professional lives of all those musicians who today, living in different parts of the world, use Skype for concert rehearsals, seem so different.

Motivations for Leaving

Why did composers decide to emigrate? For varied reasons, of course. Often it is difficult to distinguish the most important incentive for leaving one's homeland, but it is almost never an easy decision and sometimes it is one that has to be made quickly. Sometimes composers can explain why they planned to emigrate, but often only coincidence or other circumstances prompt such a radical step (e.g., the outbreak of war while a composer is out of the country).

The most frequent reasons for emigration from Poland include:
- escaping war to save one's life
- rampant anti-Semitism in the country
- lack of opportunities for development along with the disapproval of a conservative artistic environment
- refusal to live in a totalitarian state
- educational motivations (scholarships, education in a chosen school, internships, etc.)
- work-based migrations (specific professional contracts or expanding career opportunities)

– personal reasons (e.g., family tragedy)
– coincidence (including a change in a country's borders)

Another important factor is the new reality connected with Poland's accession to the European Union, but also crucial is the specificity of today's nomadic times, in which an artist's life can become almost a never-ending journey.

Life Above All

Fear for one's own life often provides the strongest impulse to escape, even from one's home, with its cost of parting from loved ones. Such a threat may happen in times of war, but also in times of relative peace, if this apparent serenity is disturbed by widespread hatred directed towards a particular group of people. With anti-Semitism, such hatred was experienced by Polish composers shortly after Hitler gained power in 1933, before the outbreak of World War II. Karol Rathaus and Bronisław Kaper gave up promising careers in Germany in order to avoid persecution. It is highly likely that emigration saved them from death.

For many, leaving Poland provided an escape from a dangerous area. In August 1939, Tadeusz Zygfryd Kassern evacuated first to Lviv (together with the entire General Prosecutor's Office) and then, because of his Jewish origin, he hid in various Polish cities (he was wanted by the Gestapo). In 1939, an escape from Warsaw (attacked by Nazis on 1 September) to the east of Poland (which was invaded by the Soviet Union on 17 September) saved the life of Mieczysław Weinberg; unfortunately, his younger sister Estera, also a pianist, and their parents remained in occupied Poland and died a tragic death in the Trawniki concentration camp in 1943. His departure from Poland closed, as the composer stated, "the best and happiest period in his life."[22] On the other hand, it extended life itself for many: Ryszard Sielicki also found himself in the Soviet Union during the war, along with Stanisław Landau, who joined Anders' Army; later, Landau took part in the battle of Monte Cassino and finally emigrated to England.

Serving in Anders' Army was not an unfamiliar experience for other artists as well. Roman Haubenstock-Ramati studied composition under Józef Koffler at the M. Lysenko State Conservatory in Lviv from 1939. His studies were interrupted by the war, arrest, and finally deportation to Odessa and Tomsk. He joined Anders' Army thanks to an amnesty in 1942 and became a member of its orchestra.[23] Joining Anders' Army was associated with the risk of death, but in some cases, it influenced a decision to emigrate. One interesting example of this type concerns Alfred Schütz, who joined Anders' soldiers in 1941 together with Henryk Wars, Kazimierz Krukowski, and Konrad Tom:

> After the evacuation [of the army] to Iran, he performed in Tehran with the Polish Soldiers Theatre [*Teatr Polskiego Żołnierza*]....He also prepared and hosted radio broadcasts for Poles in Cairo, Baghdad, and Jerusalem, and later in Rome and Florence....In 1947 he left for Brazil, where he spent 14 years.

> Together with Jerzy Petersburski he created a piano duo and gave concerts in Rio de Janeiro, São Paulo and the clubs of Copacabana.[24]

A number of composers did not survive the war; we may assume that if they had emigrated from Poland, their lives would not have ended so tragically. Zygmunt Moczyński was murdered by the Gestapo on September 17, 1940 in Palmiry, Jakub Mund was sent to the Janów camp in Lviv around 1942, and in the same year Feliks Halperin died in the Łódź Ghetto, while the place of Leon Zelman's death is unknown. Wiktor Hausman died in a prison in Płock in 1943, after being arrested for participating in the resistance movement. Józef Koffler, one of the most interesting Polish composers of the interwar period, probably survived the liquidation of the Wieliczka Ghetto in 1942, but he did not succeed in fleeing from the Nazis and was murdered together with his family in 1943 or 1944. Roman Padlewski, whose *String Quartet* remains a testimony to his talent, was killed in the Warsaw Uprising. Joachim Mendelssohn was shot in the Warsaw Ghetto, the same place where Marian Neuteich, in whom Aleksander Tansman saw great talent before the war, was also murdered.

Kazimierz Jerzy Oberfeld also suffered a tragic fate. Although he emigrated from Poland to France as early as 1931, when the Italians handed Nice over to the Germans in 1943, he was arrested and sent to Auschwitz. He died on the train during the camp's evacuation in January 1945. Jan Sztwiertnia, who, in 1939, while preparing for a year-long scholarship to study composition in Paris, was arrested (probably by mistake) and transported to the Gusen concentration camp, where he died on August 29, 1940. Cieszyn, the composer's hometown, still commemorates him. Bronislaw Wolfstahl died on September 15, 1944 during the evacuation of Warsaw's Wola district. Korneliusz Brzozowski was wounded in the Warsaw Uprising and died on September 19, 1944. Alfred Stadler was arrested, held hostage, and shot in Lviv in 1944. Polish composers did not die only at the hands of Nazis. Henryk Skirmuntt was arrested in Moladava, Belarus just after the Soviet Union invaded Poland; he was brutally tortured and shot, together with his sister, by Soviet activists on September 20, 1939.

Among émigré biographies, especially those spanning the Second World War, the stories of two brothers, Michał and Stanisław Freszko, are especially compelling. Both of them were involved in entertainment before the war and both composed and were pianists (Michał was appreciated for his interpretations of Chopin). Stanisław left for Vienna in 1937 and then went to Palestine, eventually settling in the United States in 1952. As a musician he was quite successful, earning the name of the "Israeli Gershwin." Michał, on the other hand, stayed in Poland, took part in the September campaign in 1939 and, beginning in 1940, was a member of Artur Gold's orchestra in the Warsaw Ghetto. He did not survive the war. Gold's story was similar; he was murdered in Treblinka towards the end of the camp's existence (even though he had led an orchestra there, which presumably might have saved him from death). His younger brother Henryk established a dance and jazz orchestra band with Jerzy Petersburski in the Soviet Union in 1939, then from 1942–1945 served in Anders' Army and the Second Polish Corps.[25] He spent part of his long postwar life in Paris, later moving to the United States.

It goes without saying that the nightmare of war prevented the talents of many people from seeing the light of day. Many promising artists had died before 1939 and an enormous amount of their work did not survive the turmoil of military operations. For many artists, the war meant the collapse of their developing careers, often permanently. For some, psychological issues became a concern (e.g., following his horrifying concentration camp experiences, Szymon Laks was unable to compose for many years).

Lack of Acceptance

Roman Palester decided to leave Poland in the late 1940s because of his unwillingness to work within a totalitarian system. The composer did not agree with the restrictions imposed on individual liberties, including creative freedom; he was also disgusted with the growing push to create music for "the masses." In his own words:

> Before the war we composers and musicians—artists in general—created a homogeneous and close-knit community. Nothing in Polish musical life happened without our knowledge. In Łagów, I noticed a strange kind of distance among my colleagues. They avoided conversation, they didn't look into each other's eyes, they didn't talk about things honestly. It was the beginning of an era of lies, but these lies always had some 'lining', some 'second layer', which meant that both parties didn't take what they said to each other seriously. Everything was done tongue-in-cheek. And this is what I couldn't figure out....I left Łagów feeling that one could only partly distinguish between the truth and a lie. Growing tired of having to recognize what is not yet a lie, but might be in a moment, removes the ground from under your feet. You begin to fear that tomorrow we may not be able to distinguish between good and evil, truth and lie, loyalty and betrayal—and that, therefore, you have to escape.[26]

Palester finally decided to accept the status of a political emigrant, which resulted in his removal from the Polish Composers' Union and the banning of his work from publishing and distribution inside Poland. Although he managed to rebuild his life outside the country, he always regretted how his former colleagues treated him. As he wrote to Andrzej Panufnik in March 1961:

> I'll admit to you that I wouldn't defend our friends there....They are now acting like 'free' people in the eyes of the West, but quietly complain that their [cultural] programs are controlled, and that you and I are not allowed to be performed. (Meanwhile, I am convinced that this is their fear, because a brave enough kapellmeister could smuggle us in.) So as free as they pretend to be, they are not, but they ask not to say it aloud, because it 'may harm them'. By the way, I have some doubts about whether this is true at all. And I will admit to you honestly that I have no intention of going at loggerheads with them, because they don't really care about us, and their careers are easier now that we're gone. Besides, the West is already bored with this reminder of the political side of the issue, so I have come to the conclusion that it is not worth defending our colleagues—as a whole, of course, because one or another of them may be a decent person and a friend, but deep down they are resentful about the fact that we are right. Therefore they don't like us.[27]

Panufnik shared a similar revulsion towards the new cultural policies of the Polish People's Republic. Once the government's favorite composer, who had good opportunities to build a career in his homeland, Panufnik decided instead to ask for asylum in Great Britain. This decision was an extremely courageous step, considering his professional life in Poland appeared to be excellent and he was recognized internationally; in 1950 he became vice-president of the Conseil international de la musique at UNESCO in Paris. Panufnik strived for creative freedom and acceptance of his own choices. He refused to write music for the masses and to yield to the pressure of Poland's cultural policies. A curtain of silence fell on him, also.

Disagreement with the current state of things, artistic frustration, and opposition to authorities' interference in creative freedom also compelled Roman Haubenstock-Ramati to leave Poland; initially he and his family settled in Israel. For him, professional issues and a need to remain faithful to one's own talent were strongly connected with honesty, understood in a broad sense. Tadeusz Kassern's decision to give up his position as the Polish consul in the United States was made in harmony with his conscience and personal freedom. As he wrote, "I resigned from the Consuls' post in 1948 as a protest against the growth of Communism and the Soviet occupation of Poland."[28]

Not all composers in exile manifested their views openly, but even this did not protect them from alienation. As Roman Palester wrote:

> Szałowski was the only composer from this group to have suffered from collateral damage. He had more or less the same views as Panufnik and I, but he did not speak of them very often. Administrative bans hit him simply because in the 1950s the three of us were considered official composers in exile. We took part in various events, we made statements together...and because Panufnik and I supported the Congress for Cultural Freedom, it backfired on Antek as well.[29]

Perspectives for Development

Among the main reasons that young composers go abroad are to learn new skills, expand their network of personal connections, and enrich their knowledge of music and other aspects of life. Residencies abroad provide relative financial security, in part due to scholarships (e.g., from the government). Moreover, they know that they can return to Poland at any time. Often, artists decide to extend their stays in new countries; either they receive attractive commissions or they are otherwise inundated with new opportunities. In the twentieth century, the most popular destinations included France, Germany, Austria, and the United States, which is a special site of inspiration for jazz and film musicians. Of course, this is a generalization, but we are talking about a phenomenon that has lasted for almost a century. The table below shows selected universities where Poles studied in 1918–2018 (the names indicated obviously do not exhaust the whole phenomenon).

Name	France	Germany	United States	Russia	Others
Władysław Eiger	École Normale de Musique in Paris				
Adam Falkiewicz					Royal Conservatory in The Hague, the Netherlands
Jerzy Fitelberg		Hochschule für Musik in Berlin			
Aleksander Gabryś					Musik-Akademie der Stadt Basel, Switzerland
Isabelle (Wiesława Alicja) Garr	Conservatoire National Supérieur de Musique et de Danse de Paris				
Katarzyna Głowicka					Royal Conservatory in The Hague; Sonic Arts Research Centre, Queen's University Belfast (doctorate)
Mikołaj Górecki			Indiana University, Bloomington (Ph.D. in composition)		
Piotr Grella-Możejko					University of Alberta, Edmonton, Canada
Barbara Jaźwińska (Jazwinski)			City University of New York (doctorate)		
Jarosław Kapuściński			University of California at San Diego (doctorate)		
Paweł Klecki		Hochschule für Music in Berlin			
Marzena Komsta	Conservatoire National Supérieur de Musique, Lyon				
Hanna Kulenty					Royal Conservatory in The Hague
Dobrochna Daria Kwiatkowska			Cornell University, Ithaca, NY (doctorate)		
Maciej Małecki			Eastman School of Music, Rochester, NY		
Marta Ptaszyńska			Cleveland Institute of Music, Ohio		
Jan Radzyński			Yale University, New Haven, CT		Buchmann-Mehta School of Music, Tel-Aviv, Israel
Mirosław Rogala					University of Wales, (first doctorate in interdisciplinary arts by a Pole)
Jerzy Sapiejewski			Catholic University of America, Washington, DC		

Name	France	Germany	United States	Russia	Others
Ryszard Sielicki				Moscow State Tchaikovsky Conservatory	
Bettina Skrzypczak					Musik-Akademie der Stadt Basel, Switzerland
Paweł Bartłomiej Sydor			Oberlin Conservatory of Music, Ohio		
Michał Talma-Sutt		Hochschule für Musik, Stuttgart			
Ewa Trębacz			University of Washington, Seattle		
Olga Widawska-Kotulecki					Hochschule für Musik und darstellende Kunst, Vienna
Wojciech Widłak					Royal Academy of Music, Copenhagen
Krzysztof Wołek			University of Chicago, Illinois		Royal Conservatory in The Hague
Maciej Zieliński					Royal Academy of Music, London

In addition to studies, there were also many opportunities related to courses, trainings, workshops, internships, and private lessons (which, of course, did not necessarily mean emigration, but rather a temporary stay).

The most popular destinations for these purposes included:

- **Paris:** These were mainly courses with Nadia Boulanger. A large number of composers from Poland studied with her and some later decided to emigrate permanently: Michał Kondracki, Felix Roderyk Łabuński, Antoni Szałowski, Michał Spisak, Bernadetta Matuszczak, Roman Maciejewski (although he did not stay long), Piotr Paweł Koprowski, Zbigniew Bargielski, Krzysztof Meyer, Joanna Bruzdowicz, Marta Ptaszyńska, and Marek Żebrowski. In addition to lessons with Boulanger, Polish artists also studied with Paul Dukas (Zygmunt Mycielski) and conductor Philippe Gaubert (Panufnik) prior to World War II. In later years Elżbieta Sikora studied with Pierre Schaeffer in his Parisian electronic music studio. Younger generations of composers crowd IRCAM, the "mecca" of electroacoustic and computer music.
- **Darmstadt** and DAAD (Deutscher Akademischer Austauschdienst): Internationale Ferienkurse für Neue Musik (Eugeniusz Knapik, Krzysztof Knittel, Włodzimierz Kotoński, Aleksander Lasoń, Wiesław Rentowski, Zbigniew Bargielski, and Hanna Kulenty).
- **Graz:** Hochschule für Musik (Zbigniew Bargielski).
- **Burgas:** International Course for Composers (Aleksander Lasoń).
- **Avignon:** contemporary music performance courses (Robert Jędrzejewski, Marzena Komsta).
- **Marseille:** training at the experimental music studio (Grażyna Pstrokońska-Nawratil).
- **The Netherlands:** Conservatorium Hogeschool Enschede (Katarzyna Głowicka, Olga Hawryluk).

- **United States:** Fulbright scholarships for composition (Andrzej Dutkiewicz, Tomasz Sikorski).
- **Canada:** Banff Centre for Arts and Creativity, scholarship (Mikołaj Piotr Górecki).

For some composers the completion of an educational scholarship did not lead to a return home, but rather to a decision to stay. Szałowski, for example, remained in France hoping to develop his international career.[30] Before World War II, Spisak left Poland after receiving a scholarship (granted for his outstanding academic achievements) and never returned.

Classes and internships, aside from providing an opportunity to study at a foreign university, also offer a chance to stay near leading musicians and remain in direct contact with them. For Michał Urbaniak, the United States were a kind of creative mecca. This composer and jazz instrumentalist was well aware that musical inspirations are best drawn directly from the source, which meant not living in Communist Poland. In the world of contemporary music, a similar impulse appeared for Ptaszyńska, who saw in her trip to the United States a chance to learn about the latest trends in percussion techniques. While still in Poland, she joined the American Percussion Society and then receive a coveted scholarship to the Cleveland Institute of Music. Sikora emphasized that her departure was driven by her long-time love for French culture,[31] hence her decision to begin electroacoustic studies in Paris in 1968. She returned to Poland for private reasons and did not decide to settle permanently in Paris until 1981, with the start of martial law.

Career and Money Also Matter

Some artists left Poland for other professional reasons. Before World War II, Jerzy Bojanowski moved to Chicago at the Polish government's invitation; he took the position of cultural attaché and also did some guest conducting.[32] Jerzy Fitelberg, an experienced traveler, moved to Paris in 1933.

In later years, a so-called "stuffy political atmosphere" prompted many composers to leave Poland. Apart from a need to distance themselves from the oppressive climate they perceived in their home country, some of them hoped for better commissions and a chance for better life, perhaps even fame. Dorota Szwarcman recalls:

> My professor of composition, Dobrowolski, emigrated because he was offered a professorship in Graz. In his case it was obvious, because the Warsaw school at that time brought down everyone who excelled above a certain level. Dobrowolski, a professional and a decent man, never joined the Party, which was probably another reason why his career was blocked. When about to leave, he told me, 'at this academy, I wouldn't ever be anyone more important than an associate professor [docent]'. In Graz, he was fully appreciated, which is why he stayed there.[33]

Other decisive reasons for emigrating included personal ambition and a desire for professional development. This was the situation with Krzysztof Meyer, known and respected in

Poland, who accepted an offer of a professorship at the Hochschule für Musik in Cologne and began to divide his life between the two countries. Zygmunt Krauze accepted Pierre Boulez's offer and in 1982 became a music advisor at IRCAM. This allowed him to function in two worlds (although his seminars and courses took place in various countries).

During the Communist era in Poland, many artists traveled abroad to earn money for reasons that had nothing to do with professional ambitions. Usually these involved contracts (which were sometimes long-term) with Poland's state Pagart agency to perform in venues, circus orchestras, on ships, or in spa towns (this was often a specialty of composers who were also instrumentalists, such as Jan Drzewiecki in Scandinavia or Wojciech Karolak and his many bands). Of course, some emigrants benefited from contracts that enabled them to work with some of the finest foreign artists, which would not have been possible without leaving Poland. Zbigniew Seifert, for example, took advantage of such an offer in 1973, thanks to which he became internationally acclaimed. A similar opportunity was also taken by Adam Makowicz, who left for the United States after receiving an invitation from John Hammond in 1978.

Offers from the American film market, which attracted composers comfortable with writing for cinema, also deserve special attention. Bronisław Kaper left for the United States in 1935 at the invitation of Louis Mayer, the head of Metro-Goldwyn-Mayer. More recently, Abel Korzeniowski has found his place in Hollywood, which has made more use of his creative potential than would have been possible in his native country.

The desire to improve one's financial situation and professional position often is a strong motivating factor to change one's country of residence. Often, however, economic and career possibilities are not the only reasons for departing. Sometimes emigration can be a kind of escape from a personal situation, or a way to "rescue" oneself. Ludomir Michał Rogowski used this possibility before World War II. A cosmopolitan composer who had lived and studied in Leipzig, Munich, Rome, and Paris, he returned to his native Poland after completing his education, only to emigrate again because he was unable to situate himself artistically among the pragmatic musicians of Warsaw.

The reasons for the departure of André Tchaikowsky are not entirely known. Probably the most important rationale was the scope of his ambitions—he hoped to have an international career as a piano virtuoso. After receiving eighth prize at the 1955 International Chopin Piano Competition in Warsaw, he took part in the Queen Elisabeth of Belgium International Music Competition in Brussels, where he was awarded third prize. This professional success facilitated his decision to emigrate. The West gave him other opportunities to develop his musical talent, but was it only about opportunities? Tchaikowsky had studied earlier in Paris, so he knew what life was like in both countries. He was aware of the freedom of creative expression abroad, and he also...discovered personal freedom. Being Jewish and gay, it seems that he hoped for a life where he could be himself without being ostracized. This is what he cared most about.[34] Maybe private life coincided with professional hopes and frustrations, but perhaps a combination of these reasons prompted his eventual decision to leave?

Others wanted to join their loved ones: Szymon Laks, immediately after leaving the Dachau concentration camp, joined his two brothers in Paris, a city he was acquainted with from his university days. Dobromiła Jaskot moved to Australia because of her relationship with Dominik Karski, yet the reasons for their decisions were also more complex. These included the lack of opportunities for permanent work in Poland and the chance for further development abroad.

Hanna Kulenty's decision seems to have been prompted by professional reasons, but when we asked her friend Maja Trochimczyk, we learn:

> She went to study with Andriessen. She had more performances there and a better opportunity to have an international career, thanks to promotion efforts made by Donemus. Speaking of personal issues, after her daughter Misia (Maria) died in a fatal car accident in 1993, she had had enough of Poland and driving on Polish roads. Doctors and friends in the Netherlands helped her recover from the shock.[35]

Not everybody wanted to speak openly about personal tragedies behind emigration, yet Rachel Knobler, who was Jewish, did. She moved to Germany when her mother was killed in Słomniki by Polish nationalists soon after the Second World War. The composer could not forget this, especially given that her family was severely affected by war tragedies—they had also experienced the ghetto, a concentration camp, her father's death, and the shooting of her young sister. As a result of this trauma, she did not want to return to Poland; she became a German citizen, although her integration with the Polish community allows us to say that in spirit, she remained connected to her native country.[36]

For Jerzy Abratowski, emigration was a way to escape his memories. His wife Ludmiła Jakubczak had died in a car accident at the age of 22 while Abratowski was driving. When Sława Przybylska asked him about the possibility of returning to Poland, he revealed the scale of his tragedy: "What for, to die on Lusia's grave?"[37]

Accidents Happen

Emigration does not always have to be deliberate—sometimes it happens by accident. Maciejewski (who already lived in Paris, having received a state scholarship) did not intend to stay in Sweden initially. When he went in Scandinavia with his newly married wife in order to meet his in-laws, World War II began. After about 12 years, he moved again, this time to Los Angeles. He wrote about his experiences in Göteborg:

> I have experienced a lot here, maybe more than in my entire life prior to coming to Sweden. I also owe much to this country. I have learned many things and confirmed many truths, grown more mature. I see life more brightly. I walk through the world more consciously. Yet I don't feel any attachment to this country and I could leave even tomorrow!!! It's too cold!!! It's the North, alien to us Poles.[38]

It may be surprising to learn that Maciejewski returned later to the place he seemed to dislike. Once more, fate intervened. As Maciejewski wrote from Göteborg:

> On the second day after my arrival [a second time], by chance I walked into a piano shop where I discovered an incredible instrument, a pre-war Swedish piano in near mint condition for a ridiculously low price, probably because it was out of style. I had dreamed about one like this. The tone….Mr Wacek! I could cry when I am about to play. I immediately paid a deposit.[39]

Maciejewski, not knowing what to do with the instrument, decided to buy an apartment to go with it. However, the pragmatic aspect of this decision should be mentioned here as well—by staying in Sweden, he was granted a pension, which allowed him not only to live out his old age with dignity, but also to spend the winter months in the Canary Islands.

Similar scenarios can be observed in the case of other composers as well. Kondracki was on a boat in the Mediterranean Sea when the Second World War broke out. From there, he went to Brazil. During the same invasion of Poland, Aleksander Brachocki was in New York to give concerts in connection with the World's Fair. The war prompted other cases of accidental emigration, which sometimes sent composers around the world. For example, in 1938 Władysław Eiger left Poland for Paris and found himself in the so-called free zone in the southern part of France during the German occupation of that country. After obtaining a Dutch visa, he left for Curaçao and finally settled in the United States in 1942. Roman Ryterband moved to France on July 30, 1939 for educational purposes, but ended up in a refugee camp in Switzerland. He finally obtained Swiss citizenship, but in 1955 he left for Canada and five years later for the United States. Although Jan A. P. Kaczmarek did not leave Poland intending to stay in the United States, he spontaneously responded to a chance that determined his whole career, as he eventually extended his stay on a State Department scholarship in order to stay in Los Angeles permanently. It should be remembered, however, that he established the Rozbitek Foundation in Poland and often visits the country, usually related to the organization of the Transatlantic [Transatlantyk] Festival.[40]

The example of Jacek Kaczmarski shows how diverse the motivations connected with emigration might be. His departure in 1981 was not his choice, but was forced upon him by politics (the start of martial law). When he left a second time, in 1995, he left willingly, hoping to find peace and a joyous life in Australia.

Other interesting examples of "accidental" emigration are those caused by a change of borders as the result of historical events. Tadeusz Majerski was born and died in Lviv, but after the Second World War, the city was no longer Polish.

What If…

When one thinks about an individual's biography, the question arises: What would his or her life have been like if other choices had been made? The same is true of composers' lives: How different would their musical language have been if it had not been for some trip, what would they have achieved in Poland, and what new opportunities would arise in a different cultural circle? Let's ponder a few responses to "what if…":

1. Creative freedom

This phrase keeps recurring. Opportunities for creative freedom certainly allowed some emigrants to relocate away from Poland and its canons of socialist realist aesthetics, to actually spread their wings (Palester), and also to write against the fashions prevailing in their home country (Maciejewski and Szałowski). In today's world, this freedom is often identified with financial opportunities (e.g., film production, as in the case of Jan A. P. Kaczmarek). As we know, insufficient budgets can often kill artistic momentum.

2. A turn towards folklore and national elements

A sentiment towards Polishness is almost certainly one reason for such a turn. Distance can deepen a connection to one's own culture, while nostalgia can influence the choice of musical inspirations, which perhaps would be different if a composer stayed in his or her native country. One example of such a state of affairs is Panufnik, for the composer "documented" his emotional connection with his lost homeland through music. As his wife, Lady Camilla Panufnik, said:

> He felt the need to create music with a strong Polish accent, inspired by political protests in Poland. This was the case, for example, with his *Sinfonia Sacra*, composed to celebrate the millennium of Polish Christianity and statehood, but also written with the idea that celebrating such a great anniversary through music would be a kind of anathema for governmental authorities in the 1960s, who hoped for the complete abolition of the Polish state. His *Katyn Epitaph* [*Epitafium katyńskie*] carried a powerful message that impacted the Stalinists, while his *Bassoon Concerto*, dedicated to the memory of Father Popiełuszko, and *Sinfonia Votiva* were expressions of aversion to the country's regime and support for the ideals of Solidarity. In many of his works, regardless of earlier or later musical language, one could discern strong Polish roots.[41]

Similarly, the mazurkas of Tansman and Maciejewski (the latter composed them throughout nearly his entire life) mirrored their longing for their homeland in a kind of emigrant's "diary." Rogowski also reached for Polish folklore in his music.

3. Moving away from Polishness

It is impossible to say to what extent a lack of references to Polish music tradition is driven by a change of residence and a life in a new place, and to what extent it is a deliberate decision about compositional style. Palester, for instance, did not incorporate Polish inspirations in his musical language, but he did use lyrics of Polish poets. An interesting approach to Palester and Panufnik's creative choices can be found in an article by Beata Bolesławska-Lewandowska:

> Palester remained objective in his music. The only trace of his Polish interests was his reaching for poetry.…This attitude can be attributed to the fact

that Roman Palester, for the twenty years of his work for Radio Free Europe, remained the closest to issues in Poland and it was on his radio broadcasts that he shared his feelings and dilemmas regarding his homeland; Panufnik, however, clearly transferred his emotional involvement in Polish affairs into his music.[42]

4. Chances for international recognition

Leaving the country often presented opportunities to present oneself to a wider audience. Two such composers were Panufnik and Tansman, whose music became popular in their new countries. Recently André Tchaikowsky has been rediscovered, not only by Polish promoters, but also, to a greater extent, by British music lovers (for example, David Pountney).

5. No influence on style

It seems that in the case of some composers, emigration did not make a significant impact on their musical language. Maciejewski remained a neoclassicist all his life; he wrote mazurkas as a student in Warsaw as well as while a pensioner in Sweden. Krzysztof Meyer, upon his departure from Poland, was already a mature artist, so he did not feel the need to pursue further experiments. Panufnik, almost by default, distanced himself from the avant-garde trends that dominated in Polish music after 1956 (he left Poland in 1954). Instead, he sought his own language, his own individual style of artistic expression.

6. Inspirations found in new culture

Weinberg, a composer of many musical incarnations, has been adopted by the Russians as their own composer. For many years Poles forgot that he was their compatriot. During one conference, Zofia Helman mentioned that during Weinberg's stay in Poland at a Warsaw Autumn Festival, everyone treated him as a Soviet artist. Both his studies and his environment shaped his musical language, which was close to that of Shostakovich, and the nature of his commissions (e.g., he wrote for Soviet cinema). Despite this, he did not resign from inspirations drawn from his first homeland. He reached for the texts of Polish poets as well as for musical quotations from Poland (Tuwim's poems and *The Passenger*, an opera based on Zofia Posmysz's short story). Karol Rathaus, on the other hand, although he used Polish and Hebrew folklore in his work, was not interested in Polish lyrics for his vocal works (e.g., *Five Moods after American Poets*, op. 57 and *Three Choral Songs*, op. 70 for mixed choir).

Inspirations for composers in a new culture can come from many directions. Sometimes a composer follows a specific professional task. Sikora went to Paris to broaden her knowledge of electroacoustic music, which involved not only acquiring new skills but also gaining access to technology and modern equipment. Panufnik wrote his cantata *Universal Prayer* to a poem by Alexander Pope, an English poet who once lived in the same town as Panufnik—Twickenham, near London. He also wrote a short piece celebrating the eightieth anniversary of the Queen Mother and a cantata for children, *Thames Pageant*, depicting various events in the history of England (including the famous rowing competition on the Thames between teams of Oxford and Cambridge students). Kassern, during his stay in the United States, composed operas to English librettos and pedagogical works for his students. Maciejewski composed Swedish dances for the piano and, when he lived in the United States, masses in English. He also composed music for Ingmar Bergman's plays. There are certainly more examples of Polish inspirations as well as references to the culture of the country where the composers lived in exile; these existed side by side or became intertwined with one another.

In Their Own Words

In conclusion, it is worth noting how artists themselves (or their relatives) perceived their emigration and the emotions connected with it. Let's start with those who, because of war and Communism, were excluded from musical culture in Poland for a long time. The most painful experiences were shared by "blacklisted" composers such as Panufnik or Palester. The latter wrote about the "costs" of his emigration:

> It was a blow from which you never really completely recover. My name was crossed out of all publications, encyclopedias, etc. My music was no longer allowed to be played or discussed in writing. All of my printed works were sent to be destroyed and library copies were confiscated. Ochlewski was only able to save two or three copies of individual scores and all publishing contracts in progress were canceled.[43]

Panufnik said:

> During my emigration, I have always composed music inspired by events in Poland. My absence was only physical; for 36 years, I have lived in England, but my music has always been closely attached to Poland and recognized as Polish. I was inspired by events from our nation's history, both old and new.…Despite my British passport and gratitude to Great Britain, which has accepted me and facilitated my creative work, I consider myself a Polish composer.[44]

Both composers, despite the pain of rejection, which they suffered due to a lack of interest in their work in Poland, and their longing for their homeland, decided to visit only late in their lives (although the ban on their names and music was lifted in 1977). Palester appeared in 1983, while Panufnik waited until Communism in Poland had officially collapsed, a delay that strengthened the tone of his protest. For him, only the first free elections were a guarantee of real change, so only in 1990 did he accept an invitation to appear as a special guest of the Warsaw Autumn Festival.

It would seem that artists such as Maciejewski suffered fewer professional losses as a result of emigration because they did not officially oppose the government. But can we be sure? Although his works were not withdrawn from libraries, they were not published, played, or promoted (except for a few from the interwar period). Maciejewski himself concluded bitterly,

I had a strange experience: on a recent evening, when I was listening to a concert organized by the Polish Music Publishers in Kraków on which my *Triptych* for piano was played, Mr Ochlewski introduced each composer. I felt a bit like a defector when Ochlewski announced that I had disappeared and despite their best efforts, nobody could find me. I will probably write to these genius hunters and reveal my hiding place to them.[45]

It was not until the end of the twentieth century that the activities of the composer's brother, Wojciech Maciejewski, made it possible to get to know Roman's works, including those previously unknown that exist only in manuscripts and also the monumental *Requiem*, which had been presented at the Warsaw Autumn in the 1960s.

Many composers (possibly even most of them), despite living or having lived abroad, did not break their ties with their homeland. Even Palester, who perhaps was subjected to the most repression, wrote:

> What they have failed at was separating me from the core of Polish music and culture and, above all, from everyday affairs in Poland. During the first twenty years of my life in exile, I was closely connected to the life of our country. I reacted heatedly to what was happening and discussed all musical and general artistic events. That's why all this talk about emigration is quite ridiculous, since I was literally connected with national issues from morning to evening! No – it certainly wasn't emigration![46]

Lady Panufnik adds about her husband:

> Of course he missed Poland. Every day he looked through newspapers in search of political news from the country. We talked endlessly about politics and music. You can imagine the excitement in our home when the Solidarity strikes broke out, as well as during subsequent political changes....No, he did not regret leaving Poland. He could no longer stand interference in his life and beliefs. Mainly this was because music was the basis of his existence.[47]

Another level of relationship refers to Trochimczyk's discussion of having two homelands at the same time. She wrote this about Kulenty, a contemporary composer whose political, technical, and financial opportunities facilitated operating in two cultural worlds almost simultaneously:

> She is not an émigré, but a citizen of both countries. Her children, Kaja and Piotr, have completed two secondary schools, have two matriculation exams (Polish and Dutch), and speak both languages fluently. They are studying in The Hague, thanks to its higher level of musical education and better financial conditions (e.g., free train transportation). They have a house in Arnhem and an apartment in Warsaw, so it is difficult to consider it a complete emigration. Instead she has developed a career in two countries at the same time as well as a double artistic personality.[48]

What should we say about recent times, in which passports and frequent plane flights are not unusual? Dobromiła Jaskot and Dominik Karski are probably in the most difficult situation, because they live far away in Australia. In their interview for the magazine meakultura.pl we can read:

Ewa Chorościan: We are discussing the subject of Polish composers' emigration. Do you feel like émigré composers, Polish-Australian composers, or perhaps 'citizens of the world'?

Jaskot: In my case, I left Poland so recently that I am still very far from feeling Polish-Australian. I definitely feel like a Polish composer. I still need many more years of experience in my new country. But the biggest problem is that in Australia, the music we make sounds strange. We don't fit into the local new music scene, especially in Western Australia, where we live, so it is difficult to talk about finding ourselves in a new environment yet. It is also difficult to find performers who would devote long months to preparing our compositions. Here, it is primarily graphic writing that is practiced, so the arduous reading of complex scores is a kind of extinct element in Western Australia.

Karski: I have never felt a need to define myself, but given this question, it seems to me that I am an émigré Polish-Australian composer who feels like a citizen of the world. Many years have passed since I emigrated from Poland. Australia is my second homeland and my music is now performed in various countries. I would also like to mention that after fifteen years in Australia, I tried to live in Poland permanently (2007–2014), but for several reasons unrelated to the new music scene, I found that in Australia I feel more like I am "at home."[49]

Various Thoughts at the End

Karski's statement shows how complex threads about emigration may be and how complicated emotions accompany the notion of belonging to any particular country. This was strongly emphasized during World War II, when many Poles of Jewish descent suddenly became strangers at home. Adam Michnik wrote interestingly about this phenomenon:

> I always have a sense of a certain lack of clarity about my own status—the status of a Pole of Jewish origin, not a Polish Jew. Also, a Pole who really wants to be a Jew for anti-Semites and who always says 'I am a Jew' directly in the faces of anti-Semites. This is a special kind of Pole. I don't hesitate to call anti-Semitism in Poland what it is. This is because I am Polish. This is my national pride and my cultural identity. If I did anything good, I did it within Polish culture and for everything bad, I did that within Polish culture also. At the same time, I feel, excuse my egocentrism, that my grandparents all died in the Holocaust and nobody asked them who they were, whether they were Poles, Jews, or maybe Ukrainians. It was decided for them that they were Jewish and because of this, they had to die. Therefore it is my duty to repeat: 'I am Jewish'. Because otherwise I would spit on the ashes of my murdered family. I am also a strange Pole who identifies himself with Poland and has

> no other identity, neither cultural, moral, or ideological, but I am also someone who, when an anti-Semitic phrase is uttered, says: "I am Jewish."[50]

Weinberg, who was born in Warsaw but became a Soviet composer, was in a particularly difficult position. Such a long-term emigration may also cause a sense of homelessness (or perhaps quite the contrary, does owning many homes, as today's patchwork families do, cause the same emotion?). This issue remains very sensitive; it is different for everyone. An extended emigration forces questions about one's own identity, belonging, and roots.

In this context, we can name two types of identity:
- hybrid (coexistence of various cultural influences), as in the case of Karol Rathaus, a Polish-Jewish composer who also succeeded in finding a place in America.
- transnational (often referring to people who were not deported from their own countries but feel a sense of solidarity with other nations, for example due to a history of colonization). An example here would be Ludomir Rogowski, in reference to his works related to Slavic folklore.[51]

The story of some émigré composers has been, and often still is, a story of a lost generation. This term, as used by Tadeusz Kaczyński, describes a group of intellectuals and artists who successfully debuted during the interwar period but later had to emigrate due to political and personal reasons. This caused their lives and compositions to gradually disappear from common knowledge in Poland. This situation was made worse by a reluctance to promote artists living abroad; such a position was common in postwar Poland. In the case of music, the issue of style also played a role, because the musical language of composers who debuted before the war was conservative in comparison with the mid-twentieth-century avant-garde. Kaczyński wrote in the 1970s:

> Isn't it time to get rid of the common aversion shared by the postwar generation towards prewar composers? Are musicologists really right in their claims that this music is entirely unoriginal? Were attacks on it justified? Did we miss terrific works among the supposed neoclassical trash that we got rid of so happily?....Some musicians of that generation have already died, but others, even worse, were prematurely buried. It is our duty to bring them back into our musical life, not only for the generation that is now passing, but also for the current and future ones.[52]

Nowadays, the concept of emigration has become very blurred in relation to that of the Cold War, for example. The experiences of living in two places, of frequent migrations, and of learning abroad are not alien to many people. With such a complex subject, it may be interesting to answer the question of how artists define themselves, whether a composer considers himself to be an emigrant, or to what extent he simply resides in another geographical area, but is emotionally, mentally, and often professionally connected with his homeland, as if he had never left. Hence questions about emigration and the discussion of its various manifestations are a fascinating and far from exhausted topic.

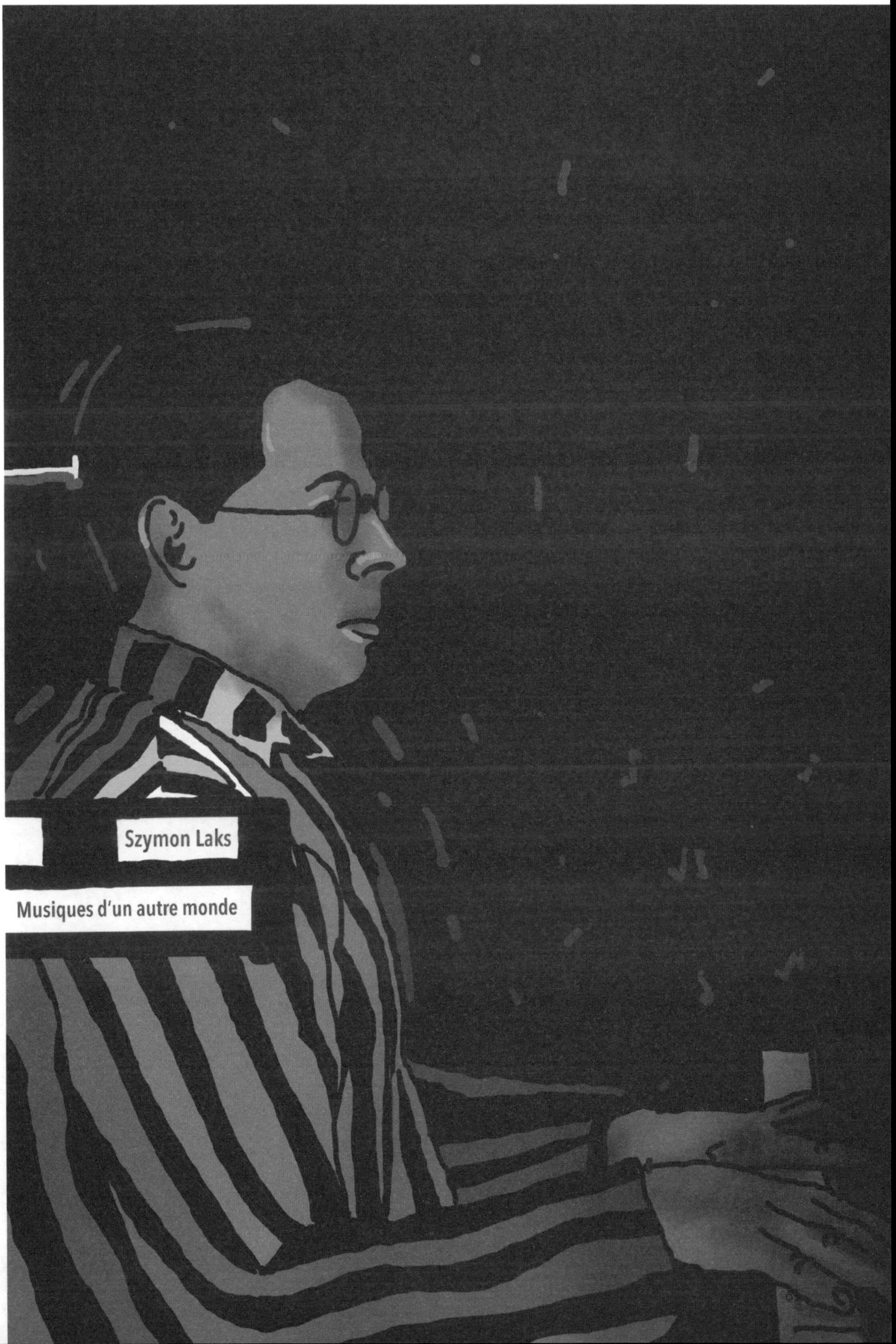
Szymon Laks
Musiques d'un autre monde

Jolanta Guzy-Pasiak

Towards the Four Corners of the World: Directions of Emigration

The issue of migration is a topic of interest today in various scientific disciplines in which the directions, motivations, and effects of population movement are being analyzed. Migrations can be divided into voluntary and forced, legal and illegal, permanent and circular, and intrastate and interstate (or international). In terms of their causes, we can distinguish between political, ideological, racial, and economic migrations. The effects of population movements are felt by both sending and receiving countries.[53]

To summarize briefly, the first emigrants left Poland for political reasons in the eighteenth century: Bar Confederates and Kościuszko's insurgents. During the next century, revolutionaries of the November (1830–1831) and January (1863–1864) uprisings followed.[54] Polish communities emerged primarily in France, Great Britain, Belgium, Switzerland, Germany, and the United States. In Russia, people sent into political exile constituted quite a large Polish community. The nucleus of the post-uprising emigrations was formed by the nobility, artists, and intelligentsia. These groups created a kind of "emigration ethos," rooted in the fact that they departed Poland during the partition period. Patriotic norms of conduct also shaped emigrants' attitudes after World War II. The Great Emigration gained its name because of its size and the important role it played for Polish culture in the nineteenth century. Artist-refugees from the Polish People's Republic are sometimes described as forming the Second Emigration, as analogies can be created between the two exoduses with regard to the scope of the phenomenon and the contributions made for their homeland by Poles living abroad.

The economic migration in the late nineteenth and early twentieth centuries, which consisted mostly of peasants searching for work and fleeing (primarily to North America) from poverty in the Polish countryside, is of little importance for this essay, but it was significant in terms of numbers. By World War I, a huge number of Poles, estimated at about three million, found themselves in the United States; this emigration continued until the economic crisis of the 1930s.[55] Regaining independence, in fact, facilitated studying and working abroad for many Poles.

Even though migrations had been a phenomenon since ancient times, it was the twentieth century that earned the name of the "emigration century,"[56] due to the waves of migration prompted by two world wars, decolonization, globalization, and technological developments that facilitated communication and transport. As a result of both world wars, many Poles found themselves outside their country. Living under Nazi and Communist totalitarian systems also proved to be extremely difficult experiences for artists, since these regimes rendered professional activity practically impossible to conduct (not to mention factoring in the basic difficulties of living and the limitations of freedoms that affected all citizens).

During the interwar period, the rise of Nazism in Germany and the resulting persecutions of the Jewish community, which began in 1933 and limited Jews' participation in public life, led to a mass exodus from Germany and Austria to the United States, with "stopovers" of a few years in Czechoslovakia, France, and Great Britain. Poles were among these emigrating groups as well. Only the most famous artists were able to continue their careers in important cultural centers such as Paris or London, due to the large number of newcomers looking for work at the same time. For many, the war interrupted any attempts to pursue their professions. Still, those who managed to escape Europe most often saved their own lives—while their loved ones were killed in concentration camps. After World War II, people opposed to the implementation of Communist power and the accompanying socialist realist cultural policy left Poland, usually illegally. After 1956, conditions for leaving became more favorable. More serious waves of emigration took place after 1968 due to an anti-Semitic campaign launched by the authorities of the Polish People's Republic, which led to about fifteen thousand people of Jewish origin leaving the country for Israel and the United States. After martial law was declared in 1981, people departed for political and, in part, economic reasons. For the years 1951–1980 and again for the 1980s there are similar estimates of the number of Poles deciding to leave—each time, approximately 800,000 to one million moved to other countries.[57] The year 1989, when Poland regained its independence, marked the end of politically motivated emigration and travels "without return." Most recent migrations have been driven by economic reasons or by a search for better professional conditions; they are not generally associated with remaining abroad permanently. For this reason, these migrations will not be taken into account here.

The largest Polish diaspora, or Polonia, remains in the United States, while of the European countries, Germany, France, and Great Britain stand out. Poles have created a number of cultural institutions abroad of local and supranational influence, such as the Literary Institute in Maisons-Laffitte near Paris (founded in 1946), the J. Pilsudski Institute in New

York (1943) and London (1947), and the Polish Institute of Arts and Sciences in America (1942). Some of the notable Polonia magazines have existed for a few dozen years, including the Parisian *Kultura* (1948–2000), *Zeszyty Literackie* (published in Warsaw since 1990), and the London-based *Wiadomości* (1946–1981). Polish musicians have collaborated with all these cultural institutions, contributing in the fields of music and journalism.

Reasons and Places

The twentieth century was a period in which musical culture, art in general, and science were intertwined with political and social events on an unprecedented scale. Robert Morgan, the author of one of the most popular music history textbooks, has set the caesurae in the periodization of twentieth-century music by taking into account not stylistic tendencies but historical events, especially the two world wars that interrupted normal cultural development. Morgan's perspective is also visible in most studies of Polish music in the twentieth century; in fact, it is their common denominator.[58] The biographies of composers who survived the nightmare of armed conflicts, the rise of Fascism and Communism, and the forced emigrations that saved their lives all have a common denominator as well. The question of the relationship between artistic creation and the external conditions in which these creations emerge is frequently raised by contemporary music researchers.

To date, the extent of the emigration of musicians of Polish origin has not been determined. One of the reasons for this is that some of them were born during the partitions, so that they are often treated in German or English-speaking sources as citizens of one of the three states that occupied Polish lands from the late eighteenth century until 1918. In foreign-language studies on emigration, there is only scant mention of Polish musicians, but the situation is no better in Polish lexicons either. These omit a number of names, other than those composers who, in addition to working as musicians, also performed state duties, such as Paderewski.[59]

The primary destination for artists fleeing Nazi repression or the nightmare of World War II was the United States, which welcomed Karol Rathaus, Jerzy Fitelberg, Wanda Landowska, and Michał Kondracki. Opponents of Communism, including Tadeusz Zygfryd Kassern and Mateusz Gliński, also received asylum there.

Composers' lives obviously depended on the political and, in part, the economic situation of the country in which they resided. However, one difference that does not affect other professional groups is that an artist's job inherently includes movement—an instrumentalist travels for education and concert tours and composers do the same out of a desire to find inspiration and gain experience in the finest music centers, even at the cost of parting with their native land. For these reasons, the United States has always been the most popular choice of musicians, both before World War II (Zygmunt Stojowski, Tadeusz Jarecki, Wiktor Łabuński, Feliks Roderyk Łabuński, and Ignacy Jan Paderewski, who spent many years there) and afterwards (Stanisław Skrowaczewski and Marta Ptaszyńska), as well as today. Speaking of the United States, one should also mention composers known primarily for their activity in the thriving film industry, including Bronisław Kaper, Henryk Wars, and Roman Ryterband. These classically educated musicians, who became popular music stars, also composed for concert halls. In some of these cases, attempts to bring their work out of oblivion have been observed in recent years.

Another nation that attracted Polish artists was France (particularly Paris), partly thanks to Karol Szymanowski, who influenced the choices and lives of an entire generation of composers educated there—the members of the Association of Young Polish Musicians in Paris (Antoni Szałowski, Szymon Laks, and Michał Spisak). A separate story is needed for the outstanding international career of Aleksander Tansman, a member of the older generation. France also became a place of refuge from Communist authorities, for example, for Roman Palester and later Elżbieta Sikora, who was there when martial law was introduced in 1981. During the first half of the twentieth century, Switzerland also played a major role as a new homeland for Polish composers, including Ignacy Jan Paderewski, Czesław Marek, Henryk Opieński, Paweł Klecki, and Konstanty Regamey.

A review of the biographies of the most well-known Polish composers working in exile shows that some of them departed during wider waves of migration, but others left the country independently. A few were driven both by the desire to find suitable conditions for creative work (Ludomir Michał Rogowski, Roman Maciejewski, Zbigniew Bargielski, and Krzysztof Meyer) and by an eagerness to escape Communist authorities (Andrzej Panufnik, Roman Berger, and Roman Haubenstock-Ramati). They settled in countries such as Sweden (Roman Maciejewski), Great Britain (Andrzej Panufnik), Czechoslovakia (Roman Berger), Austria (Roman Haubenstock-Ramati and Zbigniew Bargielski), Germany (Krzysztof Meyer), and Croatia (Ludomir Michał Rogowski, whose decision to emigrate was probably the only case not influenced by political factors).

Although the stories of our composers fit into a wider panorama of Polish emigration, the path each of them took after leaving Poland was distinctive, as was the way in which they rebuilt their careers. It must be admitted, however, that all of them gradually reached a high professional position, even if in their new reality they devoted themselves more to teaching than to composition itself. A short description of their development in exile is given at the end of this text. From this point of view, eminent émigré musicians employed in American universities enjoyed a remarkable stature and made an important contribution to the process of transferring European musical culture to America. These observations do not, of course, apply to composers who also made a career as virtuosos or conductors, such as Ignacy Jan Paderewski, Aleksander Tansman, and Stanisław Skrowaczewski.

When considering the situation of Polish artists abroad, one should not forget those artists who, while not counted as emigrants, found themselves outside Poland due to a change of borders. It is difficult to provide an exact number of Polish citizens who after 1945 remained in the territories incorporated into the Soviet Union, but it has been estimated that there were no fewer than 2 million of them. We should mention some of the fine musical inhabitants of Lviv, one of the main centers of Polish science and culture in the period of Polish independence: Adam Soltys, Tadeusz Majerski, and Andrzej Nikodemowicz.

To summarize our information about the destinations of Polish composers (very briefly out of necessity), a list of countries of residence has been included at the end of this essay. It includes composers whose stature in Poland and their successes in their new homelands were substantial; memory of them has survived until today. They formed (and still comprise) a minority in comparison to the total number of émigré artists, whose names are sometimes still unknown even to their fellow countrymen (this gap can be filled thanks to the appendix attached to this book). Therefore, apart from some of the most outstanding composers, we will also mention those who—having played a lesser role (or started their careers relatively recently)—have also made a Polish presence in art known abroad.

The list includes basic information about the centers where they studied (often chosen later as their place of residence), the date of their permanent settlement in a given country, and brief information about their professional careers. The names of countries (arranged by continents) appear in order depending on the number of Polish artists who played an important role in these new locations; the order of names depends on their time of settlement in a new country.

Emigration Directions for the Most Important Polish Composers[60]

NORTH AMERICA

UNITED STATES OF AMERICA

- **Zygmunt Stojowski** (1870–1946), pianist and composer, educated in Paris, student of Ignacy Jan Paderewski, moved to New York City in 1905, in 1918 founded his own music school. He published writings on piano pedagogy.
- **Tadeusz Jarecki** (1889–1955), composer, conductor, and teacher, studied in Lviv, Moscow, and Hellerau near Dresden with Émile Jaques-Dalcroze (1912–1913), where he also worked as a lecturer for some time. As of 1917, he spent most of his professional life in the United States, working as a conductor and as a lecturer at Columbia University. He was also involved in composition and journalism. During World War II, he held various positions in the Polish government in exile in London; in 1940 he became the head of its Ministry of Information department, while from 1940–1943 he organized and led the Polish Musicians of London association.
- **Wiktor Łabuński** (1895–1974), pianist, composer, and conductor, studied piano at St. Petersburg Conservatory. Beginning in 1928 he performed and taught piano in the United States, eventually becoming the director of the Conservatory of Music in Kansas City (now part of the University of Missouri-Kansas City). He also wrote pieces for piano.
- **Bronisław Kaper** (1902–1983), composer, pianist, and lawyer, graduated from the Music Conservatory in Warsaw, worked in Berlin and Paris, lived in the United States by 1935, employed by Metro-Goldwyn-Mayer Studios Inc. He became a leading film composer.

- **Feliks Roderyk Łabuński** (1892–1979), pianist, composer, student of Nadia Boulanger and Paul Dukas in Paris, affiliated with the Association of Young Polish Musicians in Paris, in the United States since 1936. Teacher in American and Canadian schools, concert pianist, columnist (*Modern Music* and *Musical America*), radio journalist, and promoter of Polish contemporary music.
- **Karol Rathaus** (1895–1954), studied with Franz Schreker in Vienna and Berlin. The rise of Nazism forced him to travel to Paris (1932–1933) and then London (1934–1938). He sought refuge in the United States, where, following a short stay in Los Angeles (1938–1940), he finally settled in New York (1940–1954). Employed at the City University of New York, he laid the foundations for the Queens College Department of Music; his work there in the areas of composition and theory has been highly acclaimed. The newly erected building for the Queens College art department was posthumously named after him and the Karol Rathaus Memorial Association was founded.
- **Jerzy Fitelberg** (1903–1951), son of the conductor Grzegorz Fitelberg. Like Karol Rathaus, he was one of Franz Schreker's students at Berlin's Hochschule für Musik. Forced to leave Berlin, like Rathaus, he left for Paris, from where, in 1939, he went to the United States. He won many composing awards.
- **Wanda Landowsk**a (1879–1959), harpsichordist and composer, educated in Berlin and Paris. She started the first harpsichord class in Berlin in 1913 and a school dedicated to early music in France in 1927. Forced to flee France in 1941, she settled in the United States, continuing her solo career.
- **Michał Kondracki** (1902–1984), composer and pianist, studied in Warsaw and Paris, affiliated with the Association of Young Polish Musicians in Paris. After the outbreak of war, he reached Brazil in 1940 and moved to the United States in 1943. Active as a piano teacher and TV journalist, he also wrote for the Polish music biweekly *Ruch Muzyczny*.
- **Henryk Wars** (1902–1977), a composer, studied at Warsaw Conservatory, wrote film music beginning in the 1930s, and created many famous hits. Starting in 1947 he worked as a composer of film music for the largest studios in the United States and also composed symphonic works.
- **Tadeusz Zygfryd Kassern** (1904–1957), composer and pianist, studied in Lviv and Poznań, member of the Association of Young Polish Musicians in Paris. In 1945 he became a cultural attaché in New York City and a cultural consul at the United Nations. In 1948 he cut contacts with the government of the Polish People's Republic and remained in the United States as an émigré, where he dedicated himself to composing and teaching, among other places, at the Dalcroze School of Music in New York.
- **Roman Ryterband** (1914–1979), pianist, composer, musicologist, and lawyer, studied piano at the Helena Kijeńska Conservatory in Łódź and musicology at the University of Bern. In 1955 he moved to Canada and in 1960 he settled in the United States. He worked as a pianist, conductor, composer, and director of the Chicago Conservatory of Music.
- **Stanisław Skrowaczewski** (1923–2017), pianist, conductor, and composer, studied in Kraków and Paris (with Nadia Boulanger), went to the United States in 1960, where he conducted the best American orchestras.
- **Marta Ptaszyńska** (b. 1943), composer and percussionist, studied in Warsaw and Paris (with Nadia Boulanger, Olivier Messiaen, and Pierre Schaeffer), has lived in the United States since 1972, where she has taught composition at several prestigious American universities.

CANADA

- **Mateusz Gliński** (1892–1976), musicologist, composer, conductor, teacher, and music critic, in Rome by 1949, where he directed the F. Chopin International Institute; in 1956 he moved to the United States and founded the International Chopin Foundation in Detroit. In 1959 he moved to Canada, where he worked at the University of Windsor until 1965. From 1956–1976 he conducted the Niagara Symphony Orchestra in Welland.
- **Mieczysław Koliński** (1901–1981), composer and ethnomusicologist. He studied in Berlin at the Hochschule für Musik and at the University and was an assistant for Erich von Hornbostel, with whom he made many recordings of folk music from 1926–1933. From 1938–1951 he lived in Belgium (Brussels) and from 1951–1966 in the United States (New York), where he founded the Society for Ethnomusicology. In 1966 he moved to Canada, where from 1966–1976 he worked at the University of Toronto.
- **Piotr Paweł Koprowski** (b. 1947), composer and theorist. He studied in Kraków, Paris, and Toronto. In 1971 he left for Canada, where he taught at the University of Western Ontario. Active as an educator and composer.
- **Piotr Grella-Możejko** (b. 1961), composer and literary scholar. He studied journalism in Katowice, took composition lessons privately with Bogusław Schaeffer, and then studied music at the University of Alberta in Edmonton. Since 1989, he has been a successful composer in Canada. Also, he holds a doctorate in Comparative Literature from the University of Alberta (2008).

EUROPE

FRANCE

- **Aleksander Tansman** (1897–1986), pianist and composer, lived permanently in Paris from 1919 until his death, except during World War II, when he lived in the United States (where, among other things, he wrote film music). He was known internationally as a performer and composer.
- **Antoni Szałowski** (1907–1973), violinist and composer, after studying in Warsaw, he studied in Paris with Nadia Boulanger, member of the Association of Young Polish Musicians in Paris. In France since 1931, he remained abroad for the rest of his life. Associated with French Radio, he composed many works commissioned by this organization.
- **Szymon Laks** (1901–1983), composer and writer, studied mathematics in Vilnius and composition in Warsaw and Paris (1927), member of the Association of Young Polish Musicians in Paris. During World War II, he was deported from France to concentration camps (Auschwitz, then Dachau). After liberation he returned to Paris, where he lived for the rest of his life. In addition to composing, he wrote books on his experiences in the camps, which he survived thanks to his experience as an orchestra conductor.
- **Michał Spisak** (1914–1965), violinist and composer, studied in Katowice and Paris, associated with the Association of Young Polish Musicians in Paris. Having left for France in 1937, like Szałowski, he remained there until his death, composing and popularizing Polish music in his new homeland.
- **Roman Palester** (1907–1989), composer, member of the Association of Young Polish Musicians in Paris from 1936–1938, left Poland in 1947 without planning to emigrate

(he made that decision in 1950). He spent most of his life in France, except for an extended residence in Munich (1952–1972), where he worked as head of the cultural department of the Polish section of Radio Free Europe. He was the first outstanding Polish composer to "choose freedom."

- **Elżbieta Sikora** (b. 1943), composer of electronic music, studied in Warsaw and Paris, in France since 1981; she stayed there after martial law was declared. She taught composition at the Angoulême Conservatory.

SWITZERLAND

- **Ignacy Jan Paderewski** (1860–1941), pianist, composer, and politician, "citizen of the world," spent most of his life abroad (he lived, among other places, in the United States), and performed on several continents. The artist's museum is located in Morges.
- **Czesław Marek** (1891–1985), composer, pianist, and teacher, studied in Lviv, Vienna, and Strasbourg. During World War I he went via Prague to Zurich (1915), where he settled permanently.
- **Henryk Opieński** (1870–1942), musicologist, composer, violinist, and conductor. Initiator of many important musical ventures (among others, he organized the first music academy in Poland, in Poznań, and founded the first musicological magazine in the country, *Kwartalnik Muzyczny*), moved in 1926 to Morges, where he led the early music vocal ensemble Motet et Madrigal.
- **Paweł Klecki** (1900–1973), conductor and composer, studied in Warsaw and Berlin, forced to leave Germany in 1933, stayed in Italy and the Soviet Union, settled in Switzerland in 1939. After the war he was mainly active as a conductor.
- **Konstanty Regamey** (1907–1982), pianist, composer, linguist specializing in oriental languages, and academic lecturer. He actively participated in the resistance movement during the Second World War. Due to his Swiss citizenship, he avoided being sent to a concentration camp. Beginning in 1944, he lived in Lausanne.
- **Bettina Skrzypczak** (b. 1963), composer and musicologist, left for Switzerland after graduating from Poznań's Academy of Music in 1988. There she continued her studies in composition and musicology at the Academy of Music in Basel and the University of Fribourg. Since 1995, she has taught at the Lucerne School of Music.

UKRAINE

- **Adam Sołtys** (1890–1968). Conductor, composer, and teacher. He studied in Lviv, Charlottenburg, and Berlin (where he received his doctorate). Lecturer at the conservatory in Lviv, where he lived until the end of his life. As of 1945 he resided in the Soviet Union due to a change of borders.
- **Tadeusz Majerski** (1888–1963). Composer, pianist, and teacher. He studied in Lviv and Leipzig. Lecturer at the conservatory in Lviv, where he lived until the end of his life. As of 1945 he lived in the Soviet Union due to a change of borders.
- **Andrzej Nikodemowicz** (1925–2017). Composer, pianist, and teacher. He studied in Lviv. As of 1945 he lived in the Soviet Union due to a change of borders. He worked at

the Lviv State Conservatory and as an organist at St. Mary Magdalene's Church (until its closure in 1961 and transformation by Soviet authorities into a concert hall). In 1980 he moved to Lublin, Poland, where he lectured at the Maria Curie-Skłodowska University and the Catholic University of Lublin.

THE NETHERLANDS

- **Natalia Janotha** (1856–1932), pianist and composer. She studied in Warsaw and Berlin (with Clara Schumann and Johannes Brahms, among others). She lived in London and, as of 1916, in The Hague. She also performed across Europe.
- **Hanna Kulenty** (b. 1961), after graduating from the Academy of Music in Warsaw, she studied with Louis Andriessen in Amsterdam (1986–1988) and stayed in the Netherlands, where she has worked as an independent composer since 1989. Since 1992 she has lived both in Arnhem and Warsaw. Her compositions are published by the Dutch publishing house Donemus.

GREAT BRITAIN

- **Andrzej Panufnik** (1914–1991), composer and conductor, studied in Warsaw and Vienna (and privately in Paris and London). In 1954 he asked for political asylum in the United Kingdom, thus condemning himself to banishment from the Polish People's Republic. He conducted and composed abroad.
- **André Tchaikowsky** (1935–1982), pianist and composer, studied in Paris, Warsaw, and Brussels. He left for Brussels in 1956 and moved to London in 1960. He gave concerts in many European countries and outside Europe; he also composed.

AUSTRIA

- **Roman Haubenstock-Ramati** (1919–1994), composer, left for Israel in 1950, where he taught at the Music Academy in Tel Aviv; in 1957 he moved to Vienna and was professor of composition at the Hochschule für Musik und darstellende Kunst.
- **Zbigniew Bargielski** (b. 1937), composer, studied in Warsaw, Paris (with Nadia Boulanger), and Graz. In Austria since 1976, he has also been teaching composition in Bydgoszcz (since 2002) and Kraków (since 2003).

ITALY

- **Magdalena Komiażyk** (b. 1945), pianist and composer. She studied in Warsaw. In Italy since 1974, where since 1980 she has taught at the Conservatorio Statale di Musica in Verona.
- **Piotr Lachert** (1938–2018), pianist, conductor, and composer. He studied in Warsaw, Hannover, Brussels, and Paris. From 1974–1978 he was a professor at the Royal Conser-

vatory in Brussels; from 1971–1991 he ran his own piano school. He moved to Italy in 1992, where from 1992 to 2001 he was the professor of piano at the Academy of Music in Pescara.

BELGIUM

- **Joanna Bruzdowicz** (b. 1943), composer, graduated from the State Higher School of Music in Warsaw in 1966, studied composition in Paris with Nadia Boulanger beginning in 1968. In 1975 she moved to Belgium, where she gained wide recognition. She is acclaimed primarily for her stage work (the operas *Penal Colony* [*Kolonia Karna*], *Women of Troy* [*Trojanki*], and *Gates of Paradise* [*Bramy raju*]). She founded the F. Chopin Society and K. Szymanowski Society in Belgium. Since 2011 she has been living in the French part of the Pyrenees.
- **Zbigniew Kruczek** (b. 1952), composer and organist. He studied in Poznań and Brussels. Since 1977 he has lived in Belgium, where he is a lecturer and an organist. His compositional output includes organ, choral, chamber, and symphonic works.

NORWAY

- **Anna Jastrzębska** (b. 1950). Composer, pianist, and conductor. She studied in Wrocław, Warsaw, and Oslo. In Norway since 1976.
- **Zbigniew Zuchowicz** (b. 1965), pianist, organist, and composer. As of 1992 in Iceland, then moved to Norway in 1995, where he studied and has served as an organist in various churches. He composes music for organ.

CROATIA

- **Ludomir Michał Rogowski** (1883–1954), composer and conductor, studied in Warsaw, Leipzig, and Paris. In 1926 he moved to the Kingdom of Serbs, Croats and Slovenes, which became Yugoslavia. He composed and conducted choral ensembles.

SWEDEN

- **Roman Maciejewski** (1910–1998), composer, pianist, and conductor, studied piano and composition in Berlin, Poznań, Warsaw, and Paris (with Nadia Boulanger), member of the Association of Young Polish Musicians in Paris. For most of his life he lived in Sweden (1939–1950, 1977–1998), but also has resided in Great Britain and the United States. Associated with ballet (Great Britain), theater (Sweden), and film (United States). He worked for fifteen years on his *Requiem*.

RUSSIA

- **Mieczysław Weinberg** (1919–1996), composer and pianist. Educated in Warsaw and Belarussian Minsk. After 1939 he was in the Soviet Union. He composed classical works and also music for film and circus.

SLOVAKIA

- **Roman Berger** (1930–2020), composer, pianist, and music theorist, studied in Katowice and Bratislava. As of 1952 he lived in Slovakia (then part of Czechoslovakia), where he taught piano and theory at the Higher School of Music in Bratislava and worked at the Slovak Academy of Sciences and Slovak TV.

ICELAND

- **Szymon Kuran** (1955–2005), violinist (also jazz), and composer, studied in Gdańsk and London. Moved to Iceland in 1984, where until 2000 he was employed as concertmaster of the Icelandic Symphony Orchestra in Reykjavik.

GERMANY

- **Krzysztof Meyer** (b. 1943), composer, pianist, publicist, studied in Kraków and Paris (with Nadia Boulanger), since 1987 in Germany. He taught composition at the music academies in Cologne and Kraków.

SOUTH AMERICA

BRAZIL

- **Borys Lomani** (1893–1975), pianist and composer. He studied in St. Petersburg. Between 1927 and 1951 he lived in Brazil, where as of 1939 he worked as conductor of the São Paulo Radio Orchestra. After returning to Poland he was employed by Polish Radio.

ASIA

ISRAEL

- **Józef Kamiński** (1903–1972), composer and violinist. He studied in Berlin and Vienna. Later, in Warsaw, he became first violinist in the Warsaw Radio Orchestra. As of 1937 he lived in Palestine (now Israel), where until 1969 he worked as the concertmaster of the Israel Philharmonic Orchestra in Tel Aviv (after being invited there by Huberman). He enjoyed success as a violinist and composer.

- **Ignacy Friedman** (1882–1948), pianist, composer, and musicologist. He studied in Leipzig and Vienna, became famous as an outstanding pianist, and was also active as a composer. In Sydney since 1941.

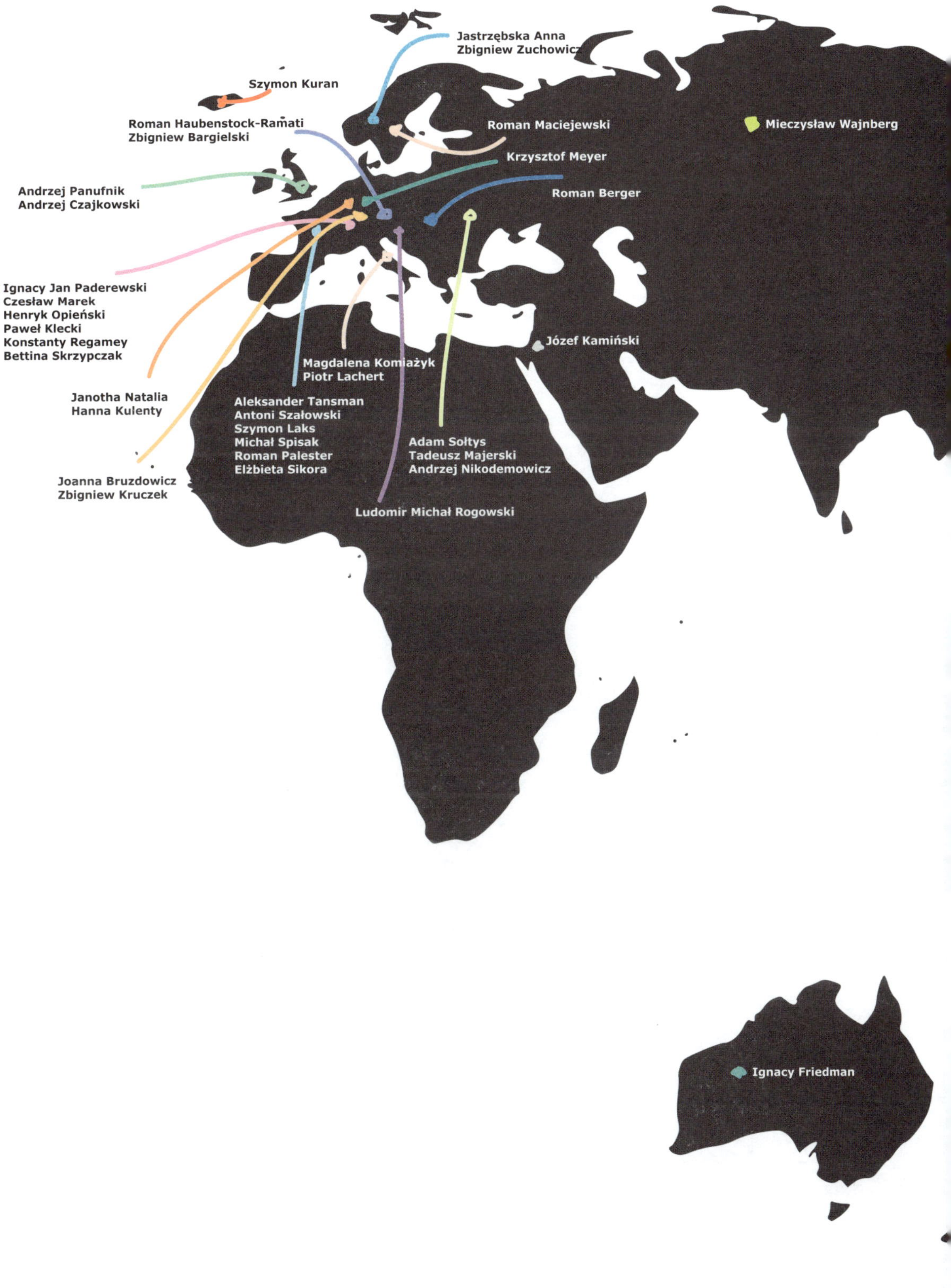
Jastrzębska Anna
Zbigniew Zuchowicz
Szymon Kuran
Roman Haubenstock-Ramati
Zbigniew Bargielski
Roman Maciejewski
Mieczysław Wajnberg
Krzysztof Meyer
Andrzej Panufnik
Andrzej Czajkowski
Roman Berger
Ignacy Jan Paderewski
Czesław Marek
Henryk Opieński
Paweł Klecki
Konstanty Regamey
Bettina Skrzypczak
Józef Kamiński
Magdalena Komiażyk
Piotr Lachert
Janotha Natalia
Hanna Kulenty
Aleksander Tansman
Antoni Szałowski
Szymon Laks
Michał Spisak
Roman Palester
Elżbieta Sikora
Adam Sołtys
Tadeusz Majerski
Andrzej Nikodemowicz
Joanna Bruzdowicz
Zbigniew Kruczek
Ludomir Michał Rogowski
Ignacy Friedman

Iwona Lindstedt

Music in Transit: Currents and Styles

> When considering the entire body of postwar music created in exile, it is relatively easy to integrate it into the mainstream of Polish art, since they are closely related. External conditions (life circumstances, political systems, economic systems) were not decisive factors determining the character of composition or the stylistic differences between domestic and émigré music. What turned out to be more important was a way of thinking about composition that was common to this generation and that was formed on the basis of a common national tradition, as well as a connection with the universal values of European culture. Music in exile, on the other hand, owes its specific features to outstanding individuals.[61]

These words, written by Zofia Helman in the last decade of the twentieth century, refer to the generation of composers born between 1892 and 1920 who remained abroad after the end of World War II or who left Poland in the late 1940s and early 1950s. It can be assumed, however, that they describe something of a more general nature, which I will try to verify here. In my reflections, I will consider both the context intended by the author quoted above as well as a broader one that includes the artists who found themselves in the countries of the so-called Eastern Bloc (e.g., Roman Berger, Andrzej Nikodemowicz, and Mieczysław Weinberg) and those members of the younger generation who decided to leave Poland after 1956 (which, as we know, marked a significant caesura in the history of Polish musical culture), but before 1989. This year, in turn, symbolizes not only the collapse of the Communist system in Poland, but also a qualitative breakthrough in research on Polish composers in exile, which began with a musicology conference sponsored by the Polish Composers' Union in December 1988 (the proceedings from this meeting were published as *Music Wrongly Present*) [*Muzyka źle obecna*].[62]

There is no doubt that the fact of living and working abroad did not keep émigré composers from feeling as if they belonged to the Polish community, even when they were isolated from domestic musical life and officially banned. Quite the contrary, they were aware that, regardless of the place where they lived, they contributed to Polish musical culture and somehow served it. This is demonstrated by the words of Roman Palester, who said in an interview during his visit to Poland in 1983:

> I return with a sense of certainty that all of us, regardless of the place where we were thrown by fate—I am thinking of Polish artists—are doing the same work. We work for Polish culture. There are fluids in Polish culture that hold us together and form an unusually strong national bond, thanks to which artists in exile experience the affairs of their Homeland no less than those living in the country.[63]

In correspondence between Andrzej Panufnik and Zygmunt Mycielski,[64] we can find not only many signs of Panufnik's interest in the music created in Poland, but also his concern for the condition of contemporary music in Great Britain and worldwide—its dominating trends, key concepts, successes, and failures. After all, Polish composers in exile were also part of the current musical scene in their new countries. And although the perception of their work was diverse, many were quite successful. For example, Feliks Roderyk Łabuński was one of the heads of the American branch of the International Society for Contemporary Music from 1941–1944, Jerzy Fitelberg received a prestigious American Academy of Arts and Letters award in 1945, and Michał Spisak was twice a Grand Prix winner at the Queen Elisabeth International Composition Competition in Brussels.

Undoubtedly, the activities of Polish composers in exile strengthened their sense of belonging to the European musical community, which in turn influenced their specific artistic experiences and offered free access to cutting-edge musical trends. However, in the case of composers who found themselves on the eastern side of the Iron Curtain, we must recall that barriers to information existed, as did dangers related to working in conditions where creative freedom was impeded by political constraints. For example, Roman Berger, a supporter of the Prague Spring, was expelled from the Slovak Composers' Union and for many years was deprived of permanent employment. Weinberg was accused of "Jewish nationalism" and imprisoned in the Lubyanka prison in Moscow soon after a 1953 concert that featured his *Rhapsody on Moldavian Themes* [*Rapsodia na tematy mołdawskie*]. However, the complexity of conditions outside of the field of music, and even the aforementioned examples of actual repression, did not rule out the possibility of implementing one's own artistic visions and individual compositional strategies. Thanks to this, the work of composers in exile not only reflects but also—and most importantly—enriches and provides nuances to the panorama of twentieth-century Polish music.

Ubiquitous Neoclassicism

The first and most resonating stylistic phenomenon in the works of twentieth-century Polish composers, regardless of their place of residence, was neoclassicism, whose principle was to take patterns from the musical past that are considered classic (i.e., exemplary, perfect) and incorporate them into a modern musical language.[65] For some composers mentioned here, neoclassicism, in fact, can be likened to an essential and inalienable musical identity. Antoni Szałowski, utilizing a wide range of classical and Baroque forms, created works featuring an expressive *sérénité*, i.e., full of moderation, joy, and lightness; it was emotional, but at the same time far from theatricality. In his legacy, we can find stage works (e.g., the ballet *L'Auberge ensorcelée*, or *Enchanted Inn* from 1945), as well as symphonies and concertos (e.g., the *Violin Concerto* completed in 1954), vocal and instrumental works (e.g., the 1960 *Cantata* for female voices and string orchestra), and chamber works (e.g., four string quartets).

Spisak is also considered to be one of the leading representatives of neoclassicism in Polish music, impressing with his outstanding craftsmanship, vitality, logic, and humor derived from French-Parisian origins. Spisak developed his own formal and expressive concepts;

his music remains the epitome of transparent textures and clarity of form (e.g., *Symphonie Concertante No. 2* from 1956 and *Concerto Giocoso* from 1957), all based on solid compositional skill.

Model examples of neoclassical style can be also found in the oeuvre of Aleksander Tansman, who lived abroad as early as 1919 and who is associated with the so-called École Paris, an informal group of Central and Eastern European composers who brought many of their own original elements into the French musical tradition. Reaching for genres and forms of classical music (*Concerto pour Orchestra*, *Symphonie Concertante*), his affinity for instrumental music was accompanied by inspirations from many sources, which affected the quality and general sound of his works. Expanded, complex harmonics (including his typical "Tansman chords") or his so-called "bridge form" are key elements that describe Tansman's individual style. Additionally, some of his works express a "Polish character," already noticeable during the interwar period (*Mazurkas*, *Polish Album* [*Album polski*]), but also present in his later compositions due to their dance rhythms as well as their melodic and harmonic features (*Alla Polacca* for viola and piano, 1985, or *Hommage à Lech Wałęsa*, a mazurka for guitar, 1982).

National Tradition and Folklore

References to Polish national and folk traditions, or the evocation of Polishness in a variety of ways, are also present in many works of other émigré composers. Even Karol Rathaus, a student of Franz Schreker, who in the first stage of his modernist-oriented work avoided folk references, composed several works referring to Polish traditions during the Second World War (e.g., *Three Polish Dances* [*Trzy polskie tańce*] from 1942 or *Polonaise symphonique*, commissioned by Artur Rodziński and performed in 1943 at Carnegie Hall). The works of another Polish composer who settled in the United States, Jerzy Fitelberg, also come from the war period or shortly thereafter. These include *Three Polish Songs* [*Trzy polskie pieśni*] for a cappella choir (1941), *Golden Harp: Variations on a Polish Folk Song* for string orchestra (1943), and *Polish Pictures* (1946), a suite for string orchestra.[66]

Tributes to the traditions of a composer's native culture can also be noticed in the titles and dedications of Panufnik's compositions. Works such as *Sinfonia Sacra* (1963), dedicated to the millennium of the Polish state and Christianity in Poland; *Katyn Epitaph* [*Epitafium Katyńskie*] (1967); and *Bassoon Concerto* (1985), dedicated to Father Jerzy Popiełuszko, are the most important examples, alongside the *Polonia* suite (a study of Polish dances, 1959), the stylized *Jagiellonian Triptych* (1966); or the *Third String Quartet "Papercuts"* [*III Kwartet smyczkowy "Wycinanki"*] (1990), which were inspired by the symmetry of the folk art masterpieces from the Kurpian region of Poland, although without reaching directly for folk quotations. Reminiscences or even the atmosphere of Polish folk melodies (e.g., *Landscape*, 1962; *Violin Concerto*, 1971)[67] have been blended into his individual musical language.

In the output of Szymon Laks, next to the *Third String Quartet "On Polish Folk Themes"* [*III Kwartet smyczkowy "Na polskie tematy ludowe"*] (1945), we find a number of works referring to Jewish themes, such as *Huit chants populaires juifs* set to Yiddish texts (1947), whose compositions coincided with the publication of his memoirs about Auschwitz,[68] and *Elegy of Jewish Towns* (1961), set to a poem by Antoni Słonimski. Laks's works, which combine traditions of romantic vocal lyricism, French neoclassicism, and the songs of Weill, lead to another important thread reflective of the stylistic diversity of the music of Polish composers in exile—references to the folklore of the European Jewish diaspora.

Such attributions were an important element in the works of Mieczysław Weinberg, who lived and composed in the Soviet Union. His oeuvre was dominated by neoclassical features maintained in a Russian style reminiscent of Sergei Prokofiev or Dmitri Shostakovich. He also wrote works based on lyrics by Polish poets (e.g., Mickiewicz, Staff, Broniewski, and, most of all, the composer's beloved Tuwim, exemplified by his 1964 *Symphony No. 8 "Polish Flowers"* [*VIII Symfonia "Kwiaty polskie"*]. His music also reflects various classical and ethnic colorings synonymous with the composer's identity, which is divided between three worlds. Danuta Gwizdalanka explains the inspirations present in his work with the following words:

> He grew up in the world of Jewish music of prewar Warsaw—that was his first world. As a pianist he explored European music: Bach, Beethoven, and Chopin. Despite having played works by Turski and Panufnik, he didn't want to be involved in new music. That was his second world. Then came the Russian tradition, which Zolotariov gave him. These three worlds overlapped.[69]

Weinberg's extremely communicative music is situated between tradition and modernity, incorporating harmonic and rhythmic complexities, sometimes linking sharp dissonances with lyricism and Jewish motifs. The latter were used by the composer both to commemorate the victims of the Holocaust, including his own family, and to recall his Jewish heritage (e.g., in *Jewish Songs* [*Pieśni żydowskie*], op. 17, which recounts the harrowing story of the mass executions of Jews in Babi Yar: *Tife griber, royte leym – Deep Graves, Red Clay* [*Tife griber, royte leym – Głębokie groby, czerwona glina*]).

Tansman's music also referred to Jewish traditions through his styling of the melodies in his 1959 opera *Sabbataï Zévi, le faux Messie* and through his recollection of Old Testament traditions in his oratorios *Isaïe le prophète* (1950), *Rhapsody hébraïque* (1938) and *Apostrophe à Zion* (1978). The theme of the false Messiah was also taken up by Tadeusz Zygfryd Kassern, who settled in the United States and whose opera *The Anointed* (1949–1951) became his emotional and ideological credo; its libretto, written by the composer, is based on the story of a seventeenth-century Jewish mystic. In the opera, Kassern applied an original harmonic system, which more or less continued the principles of dodecaphony while rejecting its strict regimen. The composer also sought to modify pre-existing compositional techniques and means; the styles and idioms he used stretched from neoclassicism in its pure form to a neoclassic style that was either "archaic and romantic" or "radical" or a style that could be described as "post-neoclassical expressionism."[70]

Religious Traditions

In the first post-World War II decade, sacred genres were almost completely omitted in compositions by composers living in Poland, mainly due to the political situation in the country. The same was not true of émigré composers. In the years 1949–1959, for example, Roman Maciejewski's monumental *Requiem* was created. The composer described it as follows:

> In *Requiem*, I tried to apply a musical language that would form a bridge between past and present and that, through its direct clarity, would contribute to the fulfilment of the social role of music, born of the spirit of Peace, which unites both art and people of different eras and beliefs.[71]

In 1951 Palester composed *Missa Brevis*, a very personal composition referring to pre-Baroque traditions, which is ascetic in expression, focused in mood, and clear in texture. In 1979 the same artist dedicated his *Te Deum* for three choirs (including one children's) and three instrumental groups to the newly elected Pope John Paul II, thus expressing not only his own religiosity, but also emphasizing his connections to his homeland and to the importance of the event, which brought such great hopes for change in Poland. We should remember that the announcement of the Polish Pope, John Paul II, and his subsequent visits to Poland also provided a creative impulse for many other composers, both those remaining in the country (Krzysztof Penderecki, Henryk Mikołaj Górecki, Wojciech Kilar, and Augustyn Bloch) and those abroad.

Among the latter, let us mention Joanna Bruzdowicz and her *Sonate d'Octobre* (1978, the association of the title with the October Revolution is correct) and Piotr Moss, who dedicated his composition *Salve Regina* (1981) to John Paul II.

The universalist and humanist approach to religious music signaled by Maciejewski's *Requiem* was also reflected in the works Panufnik created in exile. Although we do not find among them the typical genres and forms of religious music, they still bear many references to faith. Alongside the *Sinfonia Votiva* dedicated to the Black Madonna (1981), we should mention *Universal Prayer* (1968–1969) to lyrics by Alexander Pope, which conveys the idea of an ecumenical prayer by people of all religions and races to the "Father of All," as well as a short composition *Prayer to Our Lady of Skepe* [*Modlitwa do Matki Boskiej Skępskiej*] (1990) and the much earlier *Song to the Virgin Mary* [*Pieśń do Marii Panny*] (1964).

It is also worth remembering that in Eastern Europe, an outstanding creator of religious music was Andrzej Nikodemowicz, who in 1973 was dismissed from work at the Lviv Conservatory "for his religious beliefs." Even before his return to Poland, where he finally settled in 1980, he used religious texts or religious-themed folk poetry in his music, creating the cantatas *Virginis cum Cruce I* (1969), *Ad Christum* (1965–1966), *Loreto Litany I* [*Litania loretańska*] for an a cappella choir of 20 tenors (1968), and *Lamentation I* [*Lamentacja I*] for solo soprano, two clarinets, bassoon, and cello (1971).

Émigré Avant-Garde

It would seem that in the face of the international recognition of the 1960s phenomenon called the "Polish school of composition,"[72] music created in exile could contribute little to the image of Polish modernist or avant-garde composition as it was depicted by critics. Nothing could be further from the truth, since it was compositions written abroad that introduced the first references to atonality, expressionist poetics, and dodecaphony soon after World War II. Such early solutions as these can be found in the oeuvre of Konstanty Regamey, Palester, and Roman Haubenstock-Ramati. All of them, although focused on their own creative ideas, made twelve-tone technique an important point of reference. Regamey had already amazed the Warsaw music community during the Nazi occupation with his dodecaphonic pieces—the fifth movement of *Persian Songs* [*Pieśni perskie*] (1942) and the *Quintet* for clarinet, bassoon, violin, cello, and piano (1942–1944)—that were performed during underground concerts. Regamey, however, was far from strict about the principles of twelve-tone technique; he used his own version, claiming that any kind of music could be written in this way, "even in Mozart's style"![73] In his works we find a desire to synthesize various stylistic elements, which he drew from both past and present as well as from traditions of the Far East, and to enrich the sonic material, for example with microtones (i.e., smaller than half-tone distances between sounds) in the solo violin part of the *Autographe* for orchestra.

One of the first manifestations of Palester's new sound language was his *Fourth Symphony* (1948–1952), which is an example of the free use of dodecaphony in combination with classical principles of shaping form. He also used twelve-tone technique in his later works, including his finest works, *La mort de Don Juan*, the *Viola Concerto,* and the *Fifth Symphony*. In *Varianti* for two pianos (1963–1964) and *Metamorphoses* [*Metamorfozy*] for orchestra (1966–1968), this technique was met with "controlled" aleatorism. Thus, Regamey brought an important voice to Poland's artistic "discussion" on the use of chance in music (for example, in compositions by Witold Lutosławski and Kazimierz Serocki).

Haubenstock-Ramati, convinced of the need to reconstruct and modify traditional ways of thinking about musical form, solved a similar problem in his own work. The composer worked on his own concept of "cyclic thinking," from which came the later idea of a mobile, i.e., by analogy to Alexander Calder's moving sculptures, a form whose frame is set by the composer but whose final shape depends on the performers. Simultaneously providing repetition and variability of the musical material, this can be seen in such pieces as *Recitativo ed Aria* (1954), *Liaisons* (1958), *Credentials* (1960), *Tableau I* (1967), and his string quartets (1973 and 1977). Starting with *Ricercari* for string trio, composed in 1948 before the composer left Poland but published in Israel, Regamey paid a lot of attention to "serial thinking" (*Serielle Denken*) as a way to dialog with dodecaphony, sometimes in an original way. For example, he attempted to combine these ideas with a desire to reproduce old Jewish traditions in new music. Suffice it to say that in order to create an original sound concept in *Blessings* for voice and nine instruments (1951), the composer used both Jewish cantor singing as well as Arabic maqam and elements of Byzantine music. The works of Haubenstock-Ramati also include many examples of graphic notation, in which symbols invented by the composer are used instead of traditional notes. Thus, an unusual synthesis of music and painting was created (e.g., in *Konstellationen*, 1971) that paralleled the experiments carried out in Poland by Bogusław Schaeffer.

We must also mention Tadeusz Majerski, who was developing twelve-tone technique in Lviv before World War II, which places him alongside Józef Koffler as one of the pioneer Polish dodecaphonists. In his postwar work (he stayed in Lviv), there are few traces left of his experiments from the 1930s. Instead, the composer turned to the diversification and refinement of melody, rhythm, and harmony as well as to the enrichment of musical texture and expression. However, Majerski, regarded as a formalist by Soviet authorities and as such criticized and marginalized, returned to dodecaphony in his unfinished *Violin Concerto* from 1962, written with his young niece, Kaja Danczowska, in mind.

However, it should be remembered that the avant-garde tendencies exploding in music after the Second World War were also the subject of debate. For example, Stanisław Skrowaczewski, who lived in Paris in 1947–1949, was a member of Le Zodiaque group, whose aim was to defend the idea of artistic freedom through, among other things, the exploration of one's own cultural roots. One expression of these tendencies in Skrowaczewski's work can be seen in his orchestral *Night Music* (1949), which offers a balance between neoclassical tonal language and twelve-tone technique.

Sound Above All Else

The works of Polish émigré composers also complement the image of the 1960s Polish school of composition in terms of their search for sound, sometimes described as "sonoristics" [sonorystyka][74] but, more broadly speaking, referring to the musical trend called sonorism. An integral part of the achievements of the Polish school of composition is the work of Roman Berger, also an outstanding theorist of this phenomenon.[75] Technically excellent and also full of emotional commitment, Berger's compositions explored almost all available means, including serialism (expanding dodecaphony to elements other than pitch, for example, rhythm or dynamics) and aleatorism (e.g., *Transformations* [*Transformacje*], 1954–1965; *Memento,* 1973–1974) as well as electronic sound processing. His works also contain references to Polish musical traditions and poetry (e.g., *Violin Sonata from a Motive of Karol Szymanowski*, 1982–1983, and *De Profundis Monodrama* for bass, piano, cello, and electronic devices, set to poems by Tadeusz Różewicz, 1980).

A direct response to innovative musical techniques, inspired by the composer's visit to the first Warsaw Autumn Festival in 1956, can be found in the work of Nikodemowicz, who wrote a series of works reflecting his interest in sonic phenomena. His cycle *Composizione sonoristica* (1966–1971) forms a compendium of his sonoristic technique. There, the composer used not only a series of unconventional articulations for each instrument, but also an inventive way of indicating them in the score. The sonic layer was integrated with dodecaphony and neoclassical properties. It is worth noting that Nikodemowicz reached for avant-garde means only once; apparently, after exploring their possibilities, he felt no need to return to them.

Between Avant-Garde and Tradition: On Diversity

The deeper we reach into the twentieth century, the more diverse the image of Polish composition (including works by artists living permanently outside the country) becomes. This is probably due to the variety of means of artistic expression that existed in the sonic arts in the second half of the twentieth century. The multitude of modernist and postmodern "-isms," which in creative terms were transformed into individual artistic propositions, often made it impossible to categorize compositions unequivocally as representative of particular trends. What is important is that after 1956 in Poland, the circumstances driving composers' decisions to emigrate were generally different than they had been during World War II and the first postwar decade. As time progressed, the manifestation of ideological control in Poland on the music of émigré composers also disappeared. Similarly, it became impossible to speak of preventing artists living outside Poland from participating in Polish musical life.

Three composers can serve as an example: Andrzej Dobrowolski (1921–1990), who had been associated with the Hochschule für Musik und Darstellende Kunst in Graz since 1976; Witold Szalonek (1927–2001), professor of the Hochschule der Künste in West Berlin since 1973; and Krzysztof Meyer (b. 1943), professor of composition at the Hochschule für Musik in Cologne since 1987. All of them were (or still are) active in Polish musical life, participating in the Polish Composers' Union, in Warsaw Autumn Festival circles, or in the local music community. Szalonek created music of unparalleled sound quality, which he codified in his *On the Unused Sonoristic Values of Woodwind Instruments* [*O niewykorzystanych walorach sonorystycznych instrumentów dętych drewnianych*], written in 1968 and published in 1972. In the last years of his life, he combined sonorism with folk elements from the Podhale region in *Inside? – Outside?* for bass clarinet and string quartet (1987) and *Symphony of Rituals* [*Symfonia rytuałów*] for string quartet (1991–1996), in the process creating works of outstanding quality. Dobrowolski, a pioneer of Polish electroacoustic and electronic-instrumental music, proved that even in the field of symphonic music there is a place for electronics, in his case obtained by manipulations of orchestral sounds. He remained faithful to electronic music until the end of his career; in 1988 he completed *Passacaglia für TX*, in which he used digital computer equipment (including a sixteen-voice, eight-color Yamaha synthesizer, which provided the title of the piece). Meyer, on the other hand, starting from dodecaphony and sonic explorations (as in the 1963 *String Quartet No. 1* or, a year later, *Symphony No. 1*), has been more inclined towards technical diversity and has shown that connecting to tradition at the level of aesthetic categories such as formal order, convincing dramaturgy, sonic beauty, and balance of compositional elements does not conflict with the use of a fully modern compositional skillset. As Meyer has said:

> When I was a very young boy, I had the opportunity to listen to chamber concerts, which were regularly held in our house. Hence my first impressions of music were provided by the music of Beethoven, Schubert and Brahms.... It is likely that these first impressions had a significant impact on my future interests and my hierarchy of values. Beethoven's extremely intricate forms, with their repertoire of ways to affect a listener's mind, later became a refer-

ence point for many of my thoughts. The wealth of nuances in the music of Schubert and Brahms also influenced my way of thinking.[76]

Within the context of the diversity of artistic achievements of Polish émigré composers, the work of Elżbieta Sikora, who settled in France, is quite interesting. It significantly enriches the panorama of Polish electroacoustic music, because the composer refers first to the recorded material recorded and then to its processed version. She explains it as follows:

> I have composed many electronic or instrumental-electronic pieces based on real sounds that I have recorded in the city. For example, *Lisbon, Tram 28* [*Lizbona, tramwaj 28*] uses specific sounds recorded in Lisbon. *Chicago al fresco* is based on sounds recorded in Chicago. I always stick to the specific sound; the nucleus of my works is always the original sound. I have written very little music that has come from synthesizing the sound, in other words from electronic trends.[77]

An important, yet infrequently used genre in Sikora's work is opera (e.g., *Derrière son double*, 1983, a radio opera commissioned by Radio France, and *L'Arrache-cœur*, 1986). We can also mention other examples of opera written by composers residing outside Poland. In addition to Kassern, Tansman, and Palester, who have already been mentioned, these include Joanna Bruzdowicz, who settled in Belgium and was the author of *Penal Colony* [*Kolonia Karna*], commissioned by the opera in Prague (1968) but not premiered for political reasons, *Trojans* [*Trojanki*] (1973), and *Gates of Paradise* [*Bramy Raju*] (1987). Weinberg composed *The Passenger* [*Pasażerka*], completed in 1968, which was not pre-

miered until 2010 at the theater festival in Bregenz. André Tchaikowsky was the creator of *The Merchant of Venice* [*Kupiec wenecki*], an opera composed on his deathbed (1982), which, like Weinberg's work, was brought to the stage by the head of the Bremen festival, David Pountey. Marta Ptaszyńska, who lives in the United States, also composed operas (mainly for children, such as *Mr. Marimba* [*Pan Marimba*] (1996) or *Magic Doremik* (2007). She has demonstrated a great sensitivity to the visual arts and has also shown the possibilities of various sound colors (e.g., *Linear Constructions in Space*, 1997–1998, and *Mobile*, 1976), which portray a kind of continuation of sonorism in Polish composition. Moreover, Ptaszyńska's music maintains an unwavering link with Polish cultural traditions, which is manifested—as with many other composers already mentioned in this text—via inspirations from patriotic ideas (e.g., the cantata *Polish Letters* [*Listy polskie*], 1988, and *Conductus - a Ceremonial for Winds*, 1982).

Music for Practical Use

Twentieth-century Polish composers working in exile, as well as those who never permanently left, were often also involved in making music for practical uses. Sometimes these activities were driven by material reasons, but sometimes the motivation came from their deeper reflection or even their desire to specialize in this area. Until 1933, Karol Rathaus was an outstanding composer of music made for the first European sound films. He went down in history thanks to his collaboration with Moscow-born Fyodor Ozep on *Der Mörder Dimitri Karamasoff*, a free adaptation of excerpts from Fyodor Dostoyevsky's novel. Although the music was given a primary role in this film, it was not synchronized with the picture. Instead, the film was made to match Rathaus's music. One of the composer's texts about film music states:

> A musician creates music for film just as he creates an opera; both arise from the common ground of art and are subject to the same laws. If optical and acoustic impressions are so integrated into an inseparable whole that an illusion of two-sided, mutual illustration is created in the film, where the image cannot be separated from the music or the music from the image, then the music must be appreciated. It seems to me that I managed to achieve such a degree of optical-acoustic unity in my film *Der Mörder Dimitri Karamasoff*, in the scene with the 'troika'. Perhaps a layman will notice here only a skillful illustration, but this is by no means the case, because the music was not something secondary and subordinate at this point, but formed a completely independent idea.[78]

The example mentioned above concerns a fragment of the film in which a ride with a three-horse carriage (the so-called "troika") is accompanied by a precisely shaped piece for percussion ensemble. In other words, this music drove the film's narrative, which turned it, as the composer wanted, into a true "musical experience."

Rathaus also wrote film music in the United States, but at that time the motivation for his work was purely financial; he composed music for short educational or documentary productions such as *Building a Nation* (1945), *Gateway to Freedom* (1946), *Before Your Telephone Rings* (1948), and *Preface to a Life* (1950). Similar reasons prompted Tansman's venture into film; in fact, during his stay in Hollywood film composing was his primary occupation. Among other ventures, he wrote soundtracks for *Flesh and Fantasy* (1943) and *Destiny* (1944), directed by Julien Duvivier. It is worth remembering that Tansman had worked with this master of early sound cinema in the 1930s in France. At that time, he wrote interesting and dramatic music to *The Redhead* [*Poil de Carotte*] (1932), especially in the scene where the title character attempted suicide. Other important film scores that came from Tansman's pen are *Sister Kenny* (1946), directed by Dudley Nichols, and *Paris Underground* (1945), directed by Gregory Ratoff. For the latter film, Tansman received an Oscar nomination, the first Polish composer so honored. (Of the 21 nominees, Miklós Rózsa won for his soundtrack to Alfred Hitchcock's legendary *Spellbound*.) Jerzy Fitelberg also worked for film in the United States, composing music for *Poland Fights On* and *Polish Pictures*.

Film scores were an important source of income for Weinberg, who had been familiar with entertainment music since his early days. In prewar Warsaw he played in boulevard theaters, at Jewish weddings, and in cinemas. In the Soviet Union, he wrote music to more than sixty films, including the famous melodrama directed by Mikhail Kalatozov, *Flying Cranes* (1957), which received the Palme d'Or award in Cannes. Weinberg also wrote music for classics of Russian animation (this was where he actually began his adventure with film in 1948), such as Fyodor Khitruk's *Toptushka the Bear* and *Winni-Puch*.

Palester left Poland as a respected film music composer, having made significant contributions to this genre both in the interwar period and in the first postwar years. Two of these films were *The People of Vistula* [*Ludzie Wisły*], directed by Aleksander Ford and Jerzy Zarzycki, and *Forbidden Songs* [*Zakazane piosenki,*], directed by Leopold Buczkowski. After emigrating, however, he returned to this field only once. In 1971 he wrote the soundtrack to Alexander Ford's last film, *First Circle* [*Den Foerste Kreds / Pierwszy krąg*], based on the prose of Alexander Solzhenitsyn.

Mentioning every example of Polish émigré composers' excursions into "useful music" would be impossible. However, it is worth mentioning that Fitelberg composed his "light" works such as *Lost Fantasies*, *Silverblue*, and *A Timely Tale* under the pseudonym Steve Terry, while Weinberg also wrote many pieces for radio and even composed music for circus performances, which were highly appreciated in the Soviet Union. Echoes of this genre can be heard in some of Weinberg's "serious" works, such as the orchestral *Suite* from 1950 (especially the final *Gallop*). While in Göteborg, Roman Maciejewski collaborated with Ingmar Bergman and wrote music for theater productions staged at the local Municipal Theatre. He contributed to *Caligula* by Albert Camus (1946), William Shakespeare's *Macbeth* (1948), and *Divinas Palabras* by Ramón del Valle-Inclán (1950). A remarkable example from outside so-called serious music was Spisak's first prize at the 1955 competition for an official Olympic anthem. His piece was chosen from among 392 scores and was heard at the opening of the Olympic Winter Games in Cortina d'Ampezzo and at the Olympic Games in Melbourne, both in 1956.

***

I must end my short story here. I do not pretend to have examined the topic thoroughly. However, from the multitude of techniques, forms, and genres, as well as the subtlety of individual styles described here, we can observe a diverse picture of the work of Polish composers operating outside Poland during the last century. Their works testify to the relative independence between political, social, and religious conditions or place of residence and the development of musical styles. Therefore, they confirm the view expressed at the beginning. The output of Polish composers in exile is undoubtedly a contribution to the global identity of twentieth-century music. However, in their case, the use of universal artistic means was often tinged with a sense of strong connections to the traditions of their homeland, as expressed in titles, dedications, purposes, or in the musical matter itself. Explaining why this is the case and, to a greater extent, describing exactly how experiences of emigration, either voluntary or forced, affected the music itself would require another essay. This would have to be based on the conviction that a musical work is capable of reflecting the deepest layers of a creator's emotional life, as a kind of emotional autobiography. Such a perspective seems fascinating and hopefully will be taken up in the future.

Beata Bolesławska-Lewandowska, Krzysztof Stefański

Do We Know Them? **Does the World Know Them?** The Presence of Musical 'Nomads' in Poland and Abroad

During a 1995 conference about Polish music of the past half-century, Krzysztof Droba asked selected participants to present a list of the most important compositions of those decades. The jurors included Krzysztof Bilica, Andrzej Chłopecki, Krzysztof Droba, Małgorzata Gąsiorowska, Irina Nikolska, Olgierd Pisarenko, Bohdan Pociej, Marta Szoka, Krzysztof Szwajgier, Paweł Szymański, Mieczysław Tomaszewski, and Joanna Wnuk-Nazarowa. Among the sixty-two compositions by twenty-two composers mentioned, there were nine works by five émigré composers, who had been cut off from Polish music life for various reasons. Among these composers were Andrzej Panufnik, with five compositions (*Autumn Music* [*Muzyka jesieni*], *Arbor Cosmica*, *Sinfonia di Sfere*, *Sinfonia di Speranza*, and *Symphony No. 10*), Roman Maciejewski (*Requiem: Missa pro Defunctis*), Roman Palester (*Symphony No. 5*), Zbigniew Bargielski (*Im Niemandsland*), and Roman Haubenstock-Ramati (*Equilibre*). Later, this selection was expanded by additional titles, again by Panufnik (*Twelve Miniature Studies* [*Krąg kwintowy*], *Sinfonia Sacra*, *Tragic Overture* [*Uwertura tragiczna*], and *Violin Concerto*), Konstanty Regamey (*Alfa*), and Roman Berger (*Memento*).[79] Does this number, as well as the mere presence of works by émigré composers, prove that the Polish music community is aware of and appreciates this music? After all, esteemed members of the same community at the end of the twentieth century had named quite a few pieces by these composers as examples of valuable compositions. Going further, however, have the works of Polish composers created abroad been included in the history of Polish music, as broadly understood? And finally, do they exist in the consciousness of listeners and music lovers on an equal footing with the music of composers active in Poland?

The answer to this question is not obvious. It would seem that it should be natural to include the works of Polish "emigrants" in musicological reflections about Polish music in the twentieth century. The aforementioned session was, in fact, a significant step in this direction, since papers presented in the main part of the conference were related equally to composers working in Poland and to those working abroad (Zygmunt Mycielski, Roman Palester, Roman Maciejewski, Witold Lutosławski, Panufnik, Krystyna Moszumańska-Nazar, Tadeusz Baird, Zbigniew Bujarski, Krzysztof Penderecki, Henryk Mikołaj Górecki, Marek Stachowski, Zygmunt Krauze, Tomasz Sikorski, Eugeniusz Knapik, and Paweł Szymański). Moreover, Tomaszewski, in his essay on Polish symphonies of the postwar years, placed equal weight on the works of Lutosławski and Penderecki and those of Panufnik and Palester, including them in the repertoire that every musicologist or theorist dealing with Polish music of the past century should know. A similar approach was adopted by authors of other essays. However, is it true that mentioning these émigré artists in a discussion of Polish music of the last fifty years is analogous to indicating that they have become permanently embedded in the history of twentieth-century Polish musical culture? Before we answer this question, let us take a closer look at the reasons why their names and music disappeared, or were deliberately removed for a number of years from the panorama of twentieth-century Polish music.

Censor's Cut: Political Constraints

A few years before the aforementioned session on Polish music in the second half of the twentieth century, the works of composers who after 1945 decided—or were forced—to remain outside the borders of Communist Poland were described only in terms of being "wrongly present" (or neglected) compositions. This phrase was used as the title of a conference organized by the Musicology Section of the Polish Composers' Union in 1988 (still in Communist Poland), which also featured concerts of works by these "wrongly present" composers. The performances, as well as the subsequent publication of the conference proceedings,[80] comprised the names of nine composers: Roman Berger, Haubenstock-Ramati, Tadeusz Zygfryd Kassern, Michał Kondracki, Szymon Laks, Maciejewski, Palester, Panufnik, and Michał Spisak. Why were these particular composers chosen? For sure, this is not an exhaustive list, and not all of those named were cited as "wrongly present" composers for the same reasons. Both of these issues were pointed out by Palester, whom organizers had asked for a statement because he could not come to Poland personally. First, he brought up the name of Antoni Szałowski, whose absence on this list created a kind of scandal. Second, he pointed out the entangled reasons why these particular composers were selected for a discussion of "wrongly present music." Varied explanations were offered and it was important for Palester to discuss them in order to avoid applying the same considerations to all Polish composers living in exile. His main goal was to distinguish composers who chose to emigrate due to political oppression from those who found themselves abroad for other reasons. The former had been repressed by the Communist authorities of Poland through censorship and a ban on performances of their music in the country, while the latter often maintained contact with their homeland without clearly defining their views and without encountering political restrictions from the Polish government.

Perhaps it is worthwhile to stop here in order to discuss the policy of Polish Communist authorities towards artists who remained outside the country. In trying to determine the presence or absence of a given composer's works in Poland, it is impossible to ignore such a fundamental issue as state policy and especially the related restrictions that affected composers whom the Communist authorities considered "hostile" to their system. These constraints were primarily related to the imposition of censorship, i.e., a deliberate and obligatory erasure of composers' names from official records and from the consciousness of Polish audiences. Such a ban was officially imposed in the late 1940s and early 1950s on four composers: Kassern, Palester, Szałowski, and Panufnik. They were treated as political enemies in the country. And while Kassern, Palester, and Panufnik openly emigrated for political reasons, having consciously broken off relations with their Communist homeland in order to stay in exile, Szałowski's case was not so obvious. The composer remained in Paris, where he had lived since before World War II, just as Spisak and Aleksander Tansman had. But while the latter two composers did not sever contact with Poland after 1945, with Spisak even visiting regularly and maintaining relations with other composers,

Szałowski fell victim to censorship. It's difficult to explain why—he did not personally express political opinions detrimental to Poland and his neoclassical works were free of so-called "formalist influences." Probably Palester was correct when he stated that:

> Szałowski...had views more or less like Panufnik or myself, but he didn't express them frequently. The ban affected him simply because we were considered three official émigré composers in the 1950s....And because Panufnik and I supported the Congress for Cultural Freedom, it backfired on Antek as well.[81]

Indeed, the works of Szałowski, like Kassern, Palester, and Panufnik, disappeared from Polish concert halls at the beginning of the 1950s (in the case of Panufnik, after 1954, when he left the country permanently). It is worth adding that the situation concerning the presentation of compositions by composers who remained abroad after the war became problematic only when policies tightened in the late 1940s and the doctrine of socialist realism was implemented in 1949.

In the first years after World War II, the music of Polish composers living outside of Poland was performed both in their native country and—perhaps more often—in other areas of Europe, often with the assistance of Polish conductors, for example, Panufnik, Paweł Klecki, and Zbigniew Górzyński. Information on this subject can be found in the first postwar issues of *Ruch Muzyczny*, in the sections entitled "Polish Music and Musicians Abroad" or in their regularly printed chronicles of musical events. European stages hosted works by Tansman, Palester, Panufnik, Szałowski, Spisak, Kassern, and Regamey. The latter, a Swiss citizen (thanks to his father) and a resident of Lausanne since 1944, even answered questions about the presence of Polish music abroad during his stay in Poland in 1947. He recalled the foreign performances of his Polish colleagues at the time, complaining only about difficulties in obtaining orchestral materials, which made it difficult to promote new compositions and meant that many Western conductors were still familiar only with prewar compositions by Polish composers (for example, Palester's *Dance From Osmołoda* [*Taniec z Osmołody*] and Szałowski's *Overture*).[82] Nevertheless, until the end of the 1940s all of these composers remained in international (mainly European) circulation, promoted by performers and conductors traveling from Poland to perform abroad.

This was not the case with the composers who remained in the United States: Karol Rathaus, the Łabuński brothers, Jerzy Fitelberg, Kondracki, Maciejewski, and, after his decision to break off contacts with Poland, also Kassern. These composers devoted themselves primarily to educational work in an effort to make a living. Maciejewski, who came to America in 1951 from Sweden (where he lived before the war, having married a Swedish dancer), worked there as an organist and conductor of church choirs, while creating his *magnum opus*, the *Requiem*: *Missa pro Defunctis* (1944–1959). Kondracki gave up composing almost entirely and became active as a music critic and an American correspondent for *Ruch Muzyczny*.

Of all of them, only Kassern's works were officially banned from Polish stages—because only he, while a cultural attaché of the government of the Polish People's Republic, had decided—as late as 1948—to break off contact with the country and stay abroad. The other artists had left earlier, so there was no reason to harass them with censorship, although in the period up to 1956 it was certainly impossible to even discuss them, write about them, or perform their works in Poland. The situation changed after 1956, when, as a result of the political thaw, the music of emigrants could return to their native stages. Even the most politically "incorrect" composers, Palester and Panufnik, had performances of their works in Poland in the late 1950s. In fact, Palester's *Symphony No. 4* was presented during the Warsaw Autumn Festival in 1958 (conducted by his pupil, Stanisław Skrowaczewski, who was soon to join the group of emigrants himself, leaving for the United States in 1960). At the beginning of the 1960s, however, censorship again took hold, affecting primarily Palester and Panufnik. In the case of other émigré composers, their lack of presence in Poland's musical life after the thaw was influenced more by stylistic considerations than by political ones.

In the Embrace of the Avant-Garde

With the so-called political thaw in 1956 and the establishment of the Warsaw Autumn International Festival of Contemporary Music the same year, avant-garde music resonated on Polish stages. Artificially paused during the years when a socialist realist aesthetic was imposed by authorities, now it flourished. In the late 1950s and early 1960s, this resulted in a number of pieces not only stylistically close to the most radical Western proposals, but often surpassing them. At that time, the world heard about the "Polish school of composition," marked by sonoristic experiments in works by the youngest composers, Krzysztof Penderecki, Henryk Mikołaj Górecki, Wojciech Kilar and Witold Szalonek, and bravely accompanied by the achievements of Tadeusz Baird, Kazimierz Serocki, and Witold Lutosławski. A new era had dawned in Polish music. What was the relation of our émigré composers to this phenomenon? Unfortunately, most of them still did not find a place in Polish musical reality, this time primarily for artistic reasons.

The music of Kassern (who died in 1957), as was the case with the works of his American colleagues, was considered neoclassical and conservative in relation to new expectations. The same was true of Szałowski and Spisak, although the latter almost until his death (in 1965) kept coming to the Warsaw Autumn Festival, where his compositions were performed from time to time. Maciejewski appeared in Poland for the premiere of his *Requiem* in 1960, also at the Warsaw Autumn Festival.[83] Contrary to his expectations, however, the reception of this work was far from enthusiastic. Both the theme of the work, dedicated to the victims of wars and composed over almost fifteen years, as well as its eclectic language that referred to musical traditions, did not appeal to the festival audience, which was hungry for the most avant-garde innovations. The work's importance was probably first appreciated by Kondracki, who in 1961 wrote:

> The composer writes a tonal, highly emotional, almost programmatic and visionary piece, shocking in its breadth, power, momentum, broadness of phrasing, suggestive force, sincerity, and fervor. Maciejewski's *Requiem* can be considered an enduring, timeless work of art.[84]

Nevertheless, the proper reception of this composition, aided by numerous performances, recordings, and sheet music editions, did not occur until the 1990s, when, having left avant-garde prejudices behind, one could look again at music representing a very different—which does not mean worse—style and sonic language.

In the years of Warsaw Autumn Festival experiments, the music of Szałowski was completely ignored. In 1956 his prewar *Overture* was performed and two years later his *Trio* for oboe, clarinet, and bassoon [*Trio stroikowe*]; these remain the only performances of his music at this festival. Also mostly absent were compositions by Aleksander Tansman (only his *Concerto for Orchestra* was performed in 1960 and two of the string quartets as late as 1997) and the works of the most talented of the émigré artists, Panufnik and Palester, whose works began to appear only after 1977, when the censorship ban on their names and music was finally lifted. It seems that Palester's work, in particular, suffered greatly from this forced absence, because his musical language, which engages in a dialogue with the achievements of the so-called second avant-garde, would have fitted very well into the world of Polish music presented at the Warsaw Autumn Festival. Still welcome in Poland were Haubenstock-Ramati (eleven performances at the Warsaw Autumn Festival as of 2016), Regamey (six), and Berger (ten); Berger, who, after the geopolitical divisions enacted following World War II had found himself in Czechoslovakia, remained a member of the Polish Composers' Union. In the mid-1960s, the Warsaw Autumn Festival featured two performances of compositions by Mieczysław Weinberg, who was not regarded by the Polish community as an émigré composer, but as an artist representing the Soviet Union. Since the music of composers from this region, due to their separation from Western compositional trends, did not generally arouse much interest in Warsaw, no one was particularly interested in Weinberg either.

Difficult Returns: The Restored Presence

Of course, it can be said that the Warsaw Autumn Festival was not (and still is not) the only platform in Poland for performing music by Polish composers, including those in exile; however, especially in the years of the Polish People's Republic, it was the most important stage that would testify to the presence of a given Polish artist in the consciousness of the local music community. This situation changed after 1989; indeed, 1990 brought the triumphant return of Panufnik to Poland and, as expected, his music was heard at the Warsaw Autumn Festival. A few years later the Tansman Festival, which still exists today, was established in Łódź, effectively restoring the work of this composer to public awareness. In addition, the International Spisak Music Competition has been organized in Dąbrowa Górnicza for years, in 2010 Maciejewski's *Requiem* (previously heard in Poland) was included in the program of the Polish season in Great Britain and was successfully performed in London's Westminster Cathedral, and the works of Kassern were successfully presented in Gdańsk.

The music of Palester, despite a monograph about him published in the late nineties,[85] is only beginning to appear live and on recordings, thanks to the activities of the Archive of Polish Composers at Warsaw University: a website dedicated to Palester was launched in late 2016[86] and an album with compositions for piano, two violins, and pianoforte was published,[87] followed in 2017 by additional recordings and publication of the composer's memoirs, previously extant only in manuscript.[88] However, there is still a long way to go to bring this artist back to the consciousness of music audiences, both because of the difficulty of performing his works and because of a backlog of publications that for now has resulted in a lack of easily accessible musical materials. Palester, considered immediately after the war to be Karol Szymanowski's successor, suffered probably the most by his stay in exile, which was exacerbated by his work for Radio Free Europe. He was completely absent in Poland due to censorship, while performances of his compositions in Europe, at first fairly frequent, diminished over time; his last big success was probably the concert premiere of the opera *La Mort de Don Juan* in 1965 in Brussels. After 1977, he was performed in Poland again, but as Zofia Helman noted:

> The long years of silence have done their job. To the younger generation of listeners, the name Palester no longer says anything. They willingly put him into the category of prewar neoclassicists together with Szałowski and Spisak, without taking the trouble to learn about his new work.[89]

A similar gap of consciousness also applied to Panufnik, who, however, managed to gain a stable place in the international music world and actually returned to the Polish stage after years of silence as the only composer among Poland's émigré artists to achieve success in foreign lands. His success can be measured by commissions from eminent artists and orchestras in the United Kingdom and America, as well as by a collaboration with the London Symphony Orchestra and the appearance of a number of recordings.[90] The composer's discography today includes nearly all of his pieces, many of them having been recorded by various performers. While still alive, Panufnik enjoyed a well-deserved reputation in his second homeland, which, less than a year before his death, also honored him with a title of nobility in recognition of his contributions to British culture (since 1961 he had been a British citizen). In his case, an extraordinary leap in the number of performances and recordings came in 2014, the centenary of his birthday. The composer's music was heard almost worldwide at that time. At the same time, many recordings and other projects related to him and his music were produced.[91] Probably none of Poland's émigré composers can compete with Panufnik in terms of international success.

It is worth mentioning here, however, that Regamey, for example, enjoyed recognition in the musical life of Switzerland, where some of his works were released on recordings. In his case, however, it should not be forgotten that at the same time he worked as a valued linguist, a specialist in Oriental languages, and his compositional work was, in a way, overshadowed by his full-time scholarly activities. It is also impossible not to mention Tansman, who even before the outbreak of the Second World War was one of the most frequently performed Polish composers abroad and who during his long life could not complain about a lack of performances or interest, either at home or abroad. Although during the years of the Polish People's Republic, his work was considered conservatively neoclassical, he was not completely unknown here. He was also the only artist living in exile whose biography was published in Communist Poland; an extensive, two-volume monograph appeared in the late 1980s.[92] Today, as has already been mentioned, Tansman is not only the protagonist of a large, international festival held every two years in Łódź, but, like Panufnik, his discography is rich and extensive and publications devoted to him have appeared both in Poland and France (where there is also a company named after him).

Almost all of the artists mentioned here have already had monographs published about them, and those who haven't are still discussed in musicology circles; hopefully, in the near future, our knowledge about them will be expanded through broader scholarly studies. Nevertheless, the most important way to indicate the presence of a composer in popular consciousness is through performances and recordings. This situation is still far from perfect, although certainly in recent years much has been achieved in the area of recordings. The most important of these is the *Poland Abroad* series produced by the German publisher EDA, in which six CDs with music by Laks, Kassern, Rathaus, Fitelberg, Regamey, Tansman, and Spisak, among others, have already been released.[93] Recently, we have also seen a renewal of interest in the work of André Tchaikowsky, a musician who died prematurely and who during his lifetime was known mostly as a charismatic pianist. His opera *The Merchant of Venice* [*Kupiec wenecki*] had its first performance in 2013 in Bregenz. A year later it was presented at the Grand Theater – National Opera in Warsaw and in 2017 it was staged in Great Britain. Pianist Maciej Grzybowski is dedicated to performing and promoting Tchaikowsky's solo works and piano concerto, which he has recorded for British Toccata Classics;[94] renowned singer Agata Zubel recorded his *Seven Sonnets by Shakespeare* [*Siedem Sonetów Szekspira*] with Finnish pianist Joonas Ahonen in 2015 for CD Accord.[95]

Recent years have also seen a great interest in the work of Weinberg, whose homeland is trying to restore him to the chronicles of twentieth-century Polish musical culture, despite the fact that as a Jewish defector from Warsaw, he spent the war years and his postwar life in the Soviet Union. A friend of Dmitri Shostakovich, he found a place in the music community there. The fact that he had not forgotten his Polish roots (he studied in Warsaw in the 1930s) is evidenced by his music, which frequently reaches for Polish texts and themes. His compositions are becoming more and more popular in Poland; the late Gabriel Chmura often included them in his concerts, and Jacek Kaspszyk also likes to conduct them, while his string quartets have been recorded by the Silesian Quartet, among others.

It seems that recent decades have brought a significant improvement in the reception of the music of Polish composers in exile, as the names of the artists mentioned above are slowly becoming an increasingly conspicuous part of the panorama of twentieth-century Polish music. New books and articles and, above all, recordings and performances of their works, have significantly enriched the current perception of Polish music. Recent tendencies among performers and researchers to search for previously unknown or less current works give hope that this perception will continue to expand, gradually revealing the richness of musical styles presented by Polish composers, who for various reasons were writing music far from their homeland.

In Reborn Poland

Interest in the activity of émigré composers—and, in turn, their interest in Poland—seemed particularly strong during the first years of the political and economic transformation in Poland, as if attempts were being made to make up for the time lost due to the difficult political situation of the country before 1989. New interviews with Barbara Jaźwińska, Krzysztof Meyer, Marta Ptaszyńska, and Piotr Moss, among others, have been published in *Ruch Muzyczny*. Compared to the first half of the 1990s, however, less attention was devoted to Polish artists living abroad in the latter part of the same decade. Composers had to make a considerable effort to make themselves known in the broader consciousness of the Polish music community. Piotr Moss is an admirable example of such self-promotion. As early as 1989, he enjoyed a reputation as a "talented author of useful music" in Poland,[96] thanks to a persistent publicity campaign in which, on the pages of *Ruch Muzyczny,* occasional news items began with the words "the composer Piotr Moss visited our editorial office" or "Piotr Moss gave us some information about his activity." This campaign must have been successful because the composer's works have been included in programs such as the Warsaw Music Meetings, the Laboratory of Contemporary Music in Białystok, the Poznań Musical Spring Festival, Musica Polonica Nova, and the 1994 Warsaw Autumn Festival.

A suitable reception of Krzysztof Meyer's work was ensured by musicologist Maciej Jabłoński, who from 1989–1990 conducted four (!) interviews with the composer, published in *Ruch Muzyczny*. These were later included in the book *Krzysztof Meyer: To and From the Composer* [*Krzysztof Meyer. Do i od kompozytora*], published under Jabłoński's editorship in 1994; the publication also contains the composer's own lyrics and analytical sketches of individual works.[97] Meyer's music is widely available in Polish concert life, especially in Poznań, where he is considered "local" enough to be heard not only during the Poznań Musical Spring, but also at the opera, philharmonic, and even during Poznań Composers Days. However, Meyer's music has also been performed in other Polish cities: in 1992 he was a composer-in-residence at the Musica Polonica Nova festival and his compositions have been heard many times at the Warsaw Autumn Festival. It is difficult to believe the words of Władysław Malinowski, written on the tenth anniversary of the composer's residency abroad: "Krzysztof Meyer's presence in Germany is more noticeable to the Germans than, unfortunately, for Poles—where he is absent."[98] However, this only proves how successful the composer has been outside his home country.

Marta Ptaszyńska has also enjoyed positive press coverage; her activities and international successes (including the premiere of *Holocaust Memorial Cantata*) have been regularly reported by *Ruch Muzyczny*. Certainly, the composer's recognition in Poland has been influenced by the Bydgoszcz Percussion Workshop, in which Ptaszyńska has been involved in the double role of composer and percussionist. One sign of the composer's popularity is the fact that during the difficult years of transformation, which were especially tough for culture, she was featured in two monographic concerts at the National Philharmonic in Warsaw, held in 1989 and in 1994. Stage works by two other composers should also be considered a significant success: *The Penal Colony* [*Kolonia Karna*] by Joanna Bruzdowicz at the Grand Theater in 1995 and the premiere of Elżbieta Sikora's *L'Arrache-cœur* at the Warsaw Autumn Festival the same year.

Rebels and Outsiders

Despite financial difficulties, the Warsaw Autumn Festival has continued to be the leading contemporary music festival in Poland and a performance of a composition at that event is still considered to represent the highest recognition of the Polish music community. Out of the nearly forty composers I know in exile who left before 1989, only eight have appeared in the festival program in the Third Republic [since 1989] (apart from the aforementioned Palester and Panufnik). These include Bargielski, Meyer, Moss, Ptaszyńska, Jan Radzyński, Sikora, Skrowaczewski, and Bettina Skrzypczak. Apart from Moss, Radzyński and Skrzypczak, all these composers made their Festival debut earlier. Three of them (Moss, Ptaszyńska and Radzyński) have seen only a single composition performed at the Festival since 1989. These numbers look a little better for the group of composers who emigrated after 1989. Out of almost thirty names, as many as nine composers have had pieces presented at the Festival: Katarzyna Arnhold, Aleksander Gabryś, Jarosław Kapuściński, Marzena Komsta, Hanna Kulenty, Michał Talma-Sutt, Ewa Trębacz, Krzysztof Wołek, and Joanna Woźny. Of this group, only the first two composers have had only a single performance, while only Talma-Sutt debuted at the festival before he moved abroad. Does this mean that after the fall of the Iron Curtain, emigration did not mean ties with the homeland were severed anymore, and international success could even facilitate a debut on the most important Polish contemporary music stage? Certainly yes, yet it is worth remembering that some of these composers, such as Kulenty, were well known and performed locally before their emigration.

The gatekeeping of the Warsaw Autumn Festival prompted criticism during the Festival's biggest crisis, in 1995, which came from Piotr Lachert, an Italy-based pianist, composer, and organizer of piano competitions in Pescara. Lachert accused the Festival of hermeticism: "When I read *Ruch Muzyczny* and see the names of Warsaw Autumn organizers being repeated year after year, it is difficult for me to think of it as anything other than a society of mutual adoration."[99] Lachert wrote these words from the perspective of a composer "printed by eight publishers," but he could not hide his grudge from the times when he had unsuccessfully presented his works to the Festival commission.

Relations between Poland and Miłosz Magin, a pianist and composer living in Paris, looked similar. *Ruch Muzyczny* was kept informed about the Magin piano competition held in Paris, and Józef Kański wrote about one of Magin's piano recitals:

> Magin remains one of the few contemporary composers who can really write for the piano, utilizing all possibilities of the instrument, not only the 'percussive' ones.[100]

The composer's popularity still remains limited to piano circles; he is ignored by the contemporary music world. Another "outsider," at least in his own eyes, was Witold Szalonek, who complained in an interview with *Ruch Muzyczny* that his works had never been recorded by Polish Radio and he had received no performances with the Great Polish Radio and TV Symphony Orchestra in Katowice. Moreover, his submissions to the Warsaw Autumn Festival were consistently ignored and "the Polish Music Publishing company has been quite unkind."[101] At the same time, when asked about the reception of his music in Berlin, where he had been living since 1972, he replied: "Nothing…nothing…all of Berlin has refused me," although he emphasized his success as a teacher: "I've become known as a good teacher."

Szalonek's reports on his own marginalization should be taken here with a grain of salt. He actively promoted his music in Poland, which can be proven by the article "Festiwal Witolda Szalonka?" [Witold Szalonek's Festival?] in *Ruch Muzyczny*, which was dedicated to the third Upper Silesian Festival of Chamber Music, for which the composer was a member of the Artistic and Program Council. According to one reviewer, "his works clearly prevailed in the festival program (performances of nine pieces, some of them repeated in various cities), as well as 'Evenings of Mystique and Music', which he hosted."[102] Szalonek's works were also regularly presented at the Warsaw Autumn Festival and other such events in Poland, even after his death in 2001. Only one year after that, a catalogue of works and a selection of composer's writings, edited by Lilianna M. Moll, was published.[103]

It would also be difficult to count on the appreciation of Polish academic circles for Zbigniew Karkowski and Kasper T. Toeplitz, world-renowned composers of electronic music and *noise* who met in Japan in the 1990s and, in addition to their solo activities, created the duo Le Depéupleur. Although they both had a classical compositional education received from the legends of the European avant-garde (Karkowski studied composition in Göteborg and attended courses with Iannis Xenakis, Olivier Messiaen, Pierre Boulez, and Georghes Aperghis; Toeplitz worked with the Parisian GRM and IRCAM electronic music centers), their music was better known abroad than in Poland, where, with some difficulties, it eventually reached alternative clubs. While Toeplitz's works were performed at the Warsaw Autumn Festival in 2003 and 2015, Karkowski's works did not appear at any contemporary music festivals until 2016, when they were performed at the Poznań Musical Spring and Sacrum Profanum. The vision that Jacek Skolimowski spread a few weeks after Karkowski's death in 2013—"Imagine that in ten years' time the Minister of Culture announces 2023 as his year and the most important festivals of contemporary music organize huge monographic concerts [of his music]"—still seems unrealistic, although perhaps a little less now than in the past.[104]

Interestingly, spectacular successes achieved abroad may significantly affect the popularity of contemporary artists in their home country. The best example is Jan A. P. Kaczmarek, a film music composer who has worked in Hollywood since 1989. Only after he won an Oscar for the music to *Finding Neverland* (2005) did he gain attention in Poland, which resulted in a number of prestigious commissions, including works for the twenty-fifth anniversary of the Solidarity labor union and the fiftieth anniversary of the June 1956 workers' protests in Poznań. Of note also is the fact that the greatest media success of Polish popular music in the 1990s, Edyta Górniak's second place at the 1994 Eurovision Song Contest, involved the participation of a musical emigrant: Stanisław Syrewicz, living in Paris and author of the song *Once in a Lifetime* [in Polish this is known as *To nie ja!*].

Making Émigré Music Better Known

On the eve of the 1989 political changes in Poland, musicologists coined the term "wrongly present music" to describe the work of émigré composers who for various reasons were not widely known in Poland. One of the main challenges of musical life in the Third Republic of Poland involved making this music better known. Certainly, the works of musicologists who published monographs of these composers were helpful in achieving this goal. Aside from Panufnik and Palester, these monographs covered the life and works of Haubenstock-Ramati,[105] Kassern,[106] Maciejewski,[107] Spisak,[108] Szałowski,[109] and Rogowski.[110] A collection of writings by Roman Berger was published as well.[111] Yet despite these efforts, a number of "wrongly present composers" still await similar publications: Kondracki, Regamey, and Laks. Unfortunately, these efforts have not been translated into concert presentations of works by these composers.

Such a breakthrough, thanks to the efforts of Łukasz Borowicz, who consistently revisits forgotten Polish music, would occur only in the twenty-first century. Michał Bristiger also made significant contributions to the growing interest in the music of Weinberg and André Tchaikowsky. In the field of recordings, the outlook was hardly more optimistic. Jan A. Jarnicki's label Acte Préalable, established in 1997 with a goal of promoting Polish music, including "forgotten" works, produced many first recordings not only of individual

pieces, but also of composers who were represented by a recording for the first time, although the quality of these recordings often leaves much to be desired.

Without Borders

At the 2003 Eurovision Song Contest, Michał Wiśniewski, from the band Ich Troje, who grew up in Germany, sang *Keine Grenzen* (*Without Borders*). Indeed, although borders have not disappeared altogether, they have become somewhat blurred. Poland entered the European Union in 2004 and the Schengen Area in 2007, which enabled an unprecedented flow of people and goods to and from Poland (in more precise terms, people moved "from" while goods came "to"). Polish students were able to study all over Europe and the pool of funds allocated for such mobility as part of the Erasmus and, later, the Erasmus+ programs has increased. More labor markets opened up to Poles and the "Polish plumber" became a cultural phenomenon. These new opportunities were also taken advantage of by composers of the younger generation, who were willing to go to foreign universities, especially in German-speaking countries, Benelux (Belgium, the Netherlands, and Luxembourg), and Scandinavia as part of such mobility programs. Sometimes, a trip to a foreign country funded via scholarship and the resulting establishment of new artistic contacts formed a prelude to a permanent move, which might involve studies at another university, as was the case with Rafał Zalech undertaking studies in Vienna. Much more often, however, composers returned to Poland enriched by new experiences. For others, a scholarship trip preceded studies at another university, which then opened additional prospects for further education or work elsewhere. "When I decided to go to Germany, I did not intend to look for a master. I wanted to find myself between several strong magnets. It is better to find one's own ground if you avoid close contact with only one personality. It is better to remain in between, because then you can make up your own mind"—with these words, Jagoda Szmytka described her experiences from study trips to Graz, Frankfurt am Main, and Karlsruhe.[112]

The twenty-first century brought a significant development of musical culture in Poland. The Warsaw Autumn Festival regained stability during Tadeusz Wielecki's long term as chair of the program committee (1999–2016), new festivals were established (among them, Sacrum Profanum, Musica Electronica Nova, and the Festival of Premieres), and others slowly recovered from the financial and organizational problems that had hindered their development (Poznań Musical Spring and Musica Polonica Nova). One breakthrough in the effort to aid professional composers was the launch of a Composers' Commissions program at the Ministry of Culture and National Heritage, an undertaking managed by the Institute of Music and Dance. These changes have turned Poland into an attractive market for composers. Mikołaj Laskowski expressed his hopes for these changes: "It seems that Poland will do splendidly. Among other things, a system of composers' commissions has been created and it seems that Polish musical culture will begin to flourish. But we will see how it goes."[113]

Wojciech Blecharz is an ideal example of someone for whom a permanent stay abroad does not exclude intensive activities in Poland. While living in San Diego and later in Berlin, he became a co-curator (together with Paweł Mykietyn) of the Install-Actions

[Instalakcje] festival organized by Warsaw's New Theater [Teatr Nowy]. The year 2012 brought the composer's debut at the Warsaw Autumn Festival and a nomination for the Polityka's Passport award. The following year saw the premiere of his opera *Transcryptum* at the Grand Theater – National Opera as part of that institution's "P" Project. Wrote Jan Topolski at that time:

> The time has come for Wojtek Blecharz: a nomination for Polityka's Passport, a commission from the National Opera, a doctorate from the University of California [at San Diego] and, finally, he is no longer confused with Rafał Blechacz [a pianist]. However, these are only external manifestations of a much more important internal development.[114]

Since then, Blecharz has created a number of opera-installations that actively engage the audience: *Soundwork* at the Variety [Rozmaitości] Theater in Warsaw, *House of Sound* [*Dom Dźwięku*] in the Lesser Poland [Małopolska] Art Garden, *Park-Opera* at the Universal [Powszechny] Theater in Warsaw (even though, according to the title, the action was set at the Skaryszewski park) and *Body-Opera* at the New Theater, also in Warsaw. An overview of institutions which Blecharz has been working with recently shows that he works in the "second circuit," outside of major festivals. His ideas have been received with mixed feelings in the world of contemporary music. Sebastian Smoliński asked after *Soundwork*, "which stank of didacticism": "Who removed Blecharz's claws? Maybe he did himself?"[115] Ewa Szczecińska opined that *Body-Opera* turned out to be "too bland to be deeply remembered."[116] Aside from these skeptical opinions, Blecharz has not lost the trust of critics—the same authors have called him "one of the most popular composers of the young generation,"[117] who "has become a master at penetrating the boundaries between arts and linking them together."[118]

Blecharz was not the only one creating spectacular projects while living abroad. On the same evening as *Transcryptum* was presented, Szmytka, now living in Karlsruhe, premiered *For Hands and Voices* [*Dla rąk i głosów*]. Two years later, at the Warsaw Autumn Festival, she presented her multimedia opera *LOST*. This piece by "one of the most talented and original Polish composers of the young generation"[119] prompted Tomasz Biernacki to note that while "the artist at one time began from very interesting positions," she has since been shifting into an "increasingly noisy populism."[120]

Prasqual, who resides in Cologne, has created his two musical and theatrical "architectures" at the Wrocław Opera in Poland: *Architecture of the World* [*Architektura światła*] and *Five Chants from the Cage* [*Pięć śpiewów z klatki*]. He also composed two spatial works for performance at the new headquarters of the National Polish Radio Symphony Orchestra: *MUQUARNYAS* and *MASHARABIYYA*. Andrzej Kwiecinski, who lives in the Netherlands, became a composer-in-residence of the Łódź Philharmonic for the 2011–2012 season; in 2016 he staged his opera *Personaggi: Euridice* at Warsaw's New Theater. In the case of Mikołaj Laskowski, studies in the Netherlands and a subsequent move to Berlin did not prevent him from co-founding the Sultan Hagavik ensemble with Jacek Sotomski, who lives in Wrocław. Laskowski's piece *The Tiger Left Me Unsatisfied* represented Poland at the UNESCO International Rostrum of Composers in 2015, where he received a so-called "recommendation" in the category of composers under thirty.

Spectacular successes in Poland have not been only the domain of young composers. As evidence, we need only note the performances of the following operas: *Penal Colony* [*Kolonia Karna*] by Bruzdowicz in 2008, *Mother of Black-Winged Dreams* [*Matka czarnoskrzydłych snów*] by Kulenty in 2010 at the Wrocław Opera, *Madame Curie* by Sikora in 2011 at the Baltic Opera in Gdańsk, *The Cyberiad* by Krzysztof Meyer in 2014 at the Grand Theatre in Poznań, and *The Players*, an opera by Shostakovich completed by Meyer, in 2013 at the Baltic Opera in Gdańsk. It is also worth noting the monographic albums published in the Portraits of Contemporary Polish Composers series, in which two of the ten albums were dedicated to artists in exile: Ewa Trębacz and Michał Talma-Sutt.

The Festival of Premieres in Katowice is often the site of performances of works by composers of the middle and older generations. The works of emigrants are also regularly performed there; during the second festival in 2005, they comprised as much as one third of the program (twelve of thirty-six pieces). In the past, this festival has presented many works by Bargielski, Mikołaj Górecki, Meyer, Moss, and Kulenty. Works by Jacek Domagała have been heard three times, although he is much less known in Poland and now lives in Berlin. The festival has also featured music by the younger generation: Kwieciński, Blecharz, Prasqual, and Wołek. Another interesting case is the Musica Electronica Nova festival, which during its short history—it has occurred biennially since 2005—has managed to employ as many as two directors living abroad: Talma-Sutt, who prepared the program in 2007, and Sikora, who directed the festival from 2011 to 2017.

Just as an emigrant's mature age does not exclude successes in Poland, neither does one's young age assure them. Despite two presentations of her own work at the Warsaw Autumn Festival, Martyna Kosecka has not enjoyed much interest from Polish critics. After she left for Iran, the composer and her husband, Idin Samimi Mofakham, founded Spectro: Centre for New Music and co-founded the International Festival of Contemporary Music in Tehran. Her recognition in Poland was not even enhanced by her success at the 2015 Zagreb Music Biennale, where she won the five-minute opera competition. Only two years later, her full-scale opera, the festival-commissioned *Klótho* finally turned critics' attention to her style, described as "post-expressionism or post-sonorism approached in an original manner."[121]

A separate case can be made for emigrant composer-instrumentalists, whose frequent performances in Poland do not necessarily translate into recognition of their work. Double bass player Aleksander Gabryś, a member of the Basel-based Phoenix Ensemble, has performed many times with his band and as a soloist in Poland, but his own music is much less known here. One of the few performances of Gabriel's works occurred during the New Music Days in Gdańsk in 2017, where the Phoenix Ensemble also performed. Similarly, viola player and composer Rafał Zalech performed with the Ensemble PHACE, SCENATET and Nimikry groups three times at the Warsaw Autumn Festival as of 2017, but his own compositions were heard only at the 2017 Musica Electronica Nova festival. As a co-founder of the Vienna Platypus Ensemble, cellist Tomasz Skweres presents his works in Poland when he performs with his band; among other events, his music was heard in 2016 during the Słuchalnia festival in Toruń and at the Musica Polonica Nova festival in 2018.

***

Recently, Aarhus in Denmark, where Simon Steen-Andersen (recognized in Darmstadt circles) is employed as a composition teacher, has become a fashionable destination for Polish students. Piotr Peszat was the first to study with Steen-Andersen, graduating in 2016. In the same year Marta Śniady started her education in Denmark. A year later, three Polish composers followed in their footsteps: Aleksandra Kaca, Paweł Malinowski, and Rafał Ryterski. After returning from Aarhus, Peszat undertook doctoral studies at the Academy of Music in Kraków. While studying herself, Śniady taught at the Academy of Music in Łódź. What will be the fate of the other three? How many more young Polish composers will link their musical futures to Aarhus? In unifying Europe, similar questions seem to be of less and less importance.

Marta Wryk

Independent and True to Themselves: The Migration of Young Polish Composers[122]

The fact that the words "composer" and "abroad" appear so close to each other in the title of this book brings to mind an unhappy Chopin "thundering away on the piano" in Vienna during the November Uprising,[123] as well as the experiences of two other Polish composers: Andrzej Panufnik, who was unable to return to Poland for 36 years, and André Tchaikowsky, who moved away permanently, seeing no chances for developing his career behind the Iron Curtain.[124] The protagonists of this chapter, born in the 1980s, are citizens of a free Europe and the world. In comparison to their predecessors, they are fortunate. They can choose whether they want to live and work in Poland or go abroad for such activities. They can also travel frequently. The world is open to them. I will try to find an answer to the question: What is the decisive factor for composers when they decide where to live? I also will question how living abroad influences how and what composers create. Finally, I will ask what conditions these new countries of residence offer to artists.

To illustrate these issues, I have sketched three portraits of selected composers. The first is Prasqual, a well-known composer in Poland. Later, I will prioritize two composers who have experienced success abroad but whose music is not well known in Poland: Szymon Brzóska and Jakub Ciupiński. I have purposely omitted composers who are already recognized and appreciated in Poland, for example, Wojtek Blecharz, who lives in Berlin, or Jagoda Szmytka from Frankfurt, because much has already been written about them. Their names, however, will appear throughout this chapter.

Following Passion or Escaping the Familiar: Motives for Going Abroad

It is probably no surprise that, in most cases, composers born in the 1980s started their adventures abroad via university exchanges (for example, the Socrates-Erasmus program, today's Erasmus+), foreign scholarships (e.g., DAAD), or doctoral studies. But what influences the choice of a given university? Today, after all, it would be difficult to identify teachers and institutions similar to Nadia Boulanger, to whom students from all over the world flocked in the twentieth century. Indeed, composers do not always decide to go somewhere because of a particular teacher. As the aforementioned composer, multimedia author, and performer Szmytka said in an interview for *Przekrój*:

> When I decided to go to Germany, I did not intend to look for a master. I wanted to find myself between several strong magnets. It is better to find one's own ground if you avoid close contact with only one personality. It is better to remain in between, because then you can make up your own mind. I sent compositions to several composers and established contact with them.[125]

Asked about important people or moments of inspiration on her artistic path, the composer answered, "Every person I meet is important. You need to keep the curiosity of a child, remain open to people and things happening around you. Everything can be an inspiration."[126]

Contemporary composers usually leave Poland with several years of studies behind them, aware of the direction they want to go. The motive for their departure is, therefore, often a desire to develop any early interests that still inspire them. In the case of Brzóska, this was an interest in dance, which soon turned into cooperation with some of the greatest contemporary choreographers. For Ciupiński, it was his passion for electronic music, which the young artist is still developing today, not only through composing, but also as the artistic director of the Purchase Orchestra Electric at the State University of New York at Purchase.

There are also composers such as Blecharz, who know in which direction they do not want to go, and they leave in order to rest, to distance themselves from what they know, and to find their artistic identity:

> A breakthrough in Blecharz's artistic development was his graduation from the Music Academy [in Warsaw]. Having lost faith in the solutions offered to him by the conventional attitude of the Academy, he began to search for his own path. He was able to do this at the University of California at San Diego, where Blecharz began his doctoral studies in 2008.[127]

In an interview with *Glissando*, the composer said:

> When I moved to San Diego, I began to realize that the knowledge I had gained during my composition studies in Warsaw didn't belong to me, in the sense of [acquiring some sort of] artistic expression. My experience during those days confirmed to me that this was not my language....Halfway through my research in San Diego, I realized that my Ph.D. should be dedicated to identity.[128]

Currently, Blecharz lives in Berlin. In an interview for meakultura.pl magazine, he explained how living in this electronic music capital prompted him to move away from classic concert halls towards long club raves.[129] This, in turn, made him question the entire classical concert situation. He began to search for a new form in which a listener experiences music not only by sitting passively in a philharmonic hall, but also through an experience involving their entire body and all their senses. *Body-Opera* and *Park-Opera* resulted from these investigations.

To sum up, the most common reason for going abroad among young artists was to further their education and, while choosing a particular university, they either wanted to expand their pre-existing passions and interests or distance themselves from the familiar and find a new formula for themselves and their art.

Scholarships and What Next?

Poles who live abroad today often go home for holidays and vacations. Still, I am interested here in composers' motives for living outside of Poland. Most of my interviews[130] have shown that education provides a valuable network of professional and private contacts. Composers therefore consider staying abroad to be a natural progression of their career development. Few say that they have stayed abroad because the contemporary music scene in Poland has less to offer. On the contrary, they speak very positively about it. Some, however, have expressed concern about an increasingly visible tendency in Poland to favor national and patriotic-themed works on concerts and other spectacles.

Most of the artists I have talked to are not only working in the country where they live, but are still traveling around the world. Szmytka says that there was a time when she did not have a permanent home at all because she was constantly travelling in connection with her projects, living in hotels for weeks at a time. It is worth noting that this is a situation typical for contemporary artists—their work concerns more than making music. Often they stay for weeks wherever a given project takes place. Szmytka considers her so-called community projects to be an important part of her work because of their social impact. These are activities in which an artist invites representatives of a given social group to co-create a work, such as DIY or DIE, for which Szmytka worked for several weeks with paintball players and activists from the Green Party.[131] Blecharz recalls the time when he worked on his *Soundwork*:

> Meeting a group of wonderful people (actors, not musicians) for two months, five days a week, in order to make music together and to work on sound was a special, even dreamy experience. Usually a composer works with musicians during two or three rehearsals before the concert; here it was quite the opposite. My practice with sounds was passed through a process, not by delivering a polished score.[132]

Composers living in Germany and Belgium also praise the social system of these countries, which supports artists in various ways, either by exempting them from some insurance premiums or by providing benefits when they have no projects. Not all countries provide a similar system of support. In the United States, for example, where the situation of artists is not easy, rarely does a composer make ends meet without a job at a university or without working on commercial projects (for example, arranging or music for advertising).[133]

Any decision to stay abroad is usually a natural consequence of professional and private contacts established during a composer's educational days. However, for the protagonists of this chapter, the place of residence is often only an address where they check in from time to time. They work all over the world, and the open borders of Europe along with careful living and access to the Internet allow them to be constantly inspired by the cultural products of the entire planet.

Looking for a More Capacious Form

Prasqual, born in 1981, has recently been associated with his works for Polish Radio Symphony Orchestra and its excellent concert hall in Katowice. These pieces utilize the hall's space and sonic possibilities to the max: *Muqarnyas* for accordion, double orchestra in six groups, and electronics (2015) and *Masharabiyya: Poem of a Wandering Light* [*Masharabiyya. Poemat wędrującego światła*] for English horn/oboe, French horn, 93 orchestra musicians in six groups, and electronics (2017), a piece that was critically praised.[134] These works, however, like most Prasqual's works, were created not in Poland, but in Cologne, where the composer has lived for over ten years.

When in 2003 the Poznań Academy of Music started working with the Hochschule für Musik und Tanz in Cologne, Prasqual, then studying composition with Grażyna Pstrokońska-Nawratil, was one of the first to decide to go to the Rhineland as a part of the Socrates-Erasmus program (today Erasmus+). He was attracted by the opportunity to get to know the country and the environment of one of his composing idols, Karlheinz Stockhausen. Over the following years, Prasqual returned to Cologne for postgraduate studies in composition with York Höller and Manfred Trojahn, in electronic composition with Hans Ulrich Humpert, and in piano with Klaus Oldemeyer. Since 2001 he has also taken part in master classes with Brian Ferneyhough, Ivan Fedele, Peter Eötvös, Christian Wolff, and Stockhausen; after the composer's death, Prasqual supervised the production of Stockhausen's opera *Sonntag* at the Cologne Opera. Cologne turned out to be so inspiring and comfortable for the composer that he decided to settle down there.

When asked about the influences of the teachers and masters with whom he worked in Germany, Prasqual answered that Stockhausen had been influential, but he also claimed that he was largely self-taught. He stressed the importance of the lush musical life that Cologne offers, including the important new music festival Acht Brücken. He named two events that became important inspirations for him: seeing the entire Wagner *Ring* cycle at the Cologne Opera (directed by Robert Carsen in 2006), and getting to know the music of Romanian composer Horatiu Radulescu. He attended four monographic concerts of Radulescu's music in Cologne, including one at the Columbus Museum in 2013. As a result, Prasqual changed his thinking about spectralism. Those who know Prasqual's music will probably immediately understand the relevance of these inspirations.

The composer's fascination with the *Ring* cycle should not come as a surprise, either, since he has always been fascinated by "total" forms, which combine different arts and means of expression and affect many senses of the listener. Among his early works, we find the opera *Ester* for five soloists, choir, and chamber orchestra (2005), *Ophelia* for three soloists, instrumental ensemble, and electronic music (2011), and electronic music for the ballet *Six Wings of an Angel for Eight Loudspeakers Set in a Cubic Space* [*Sześć skrzydeł anioła na osiem głośników rozstawionych w kubicznej przestrzeni*] (2012). The composer considers his breakthrough work to be *Architecture of Light* [*Architektura światła*] (2013) for soprano, trumpet, 23 orchestra musicians moving around the performing space, an electronic layer, and eight dancers. The piece consists of eight "Rituals" and is part of a larger project entitled *Orlando. Architecture of Light* was first performed at the Poznań International Fair, then in Cologne's St. Peter's Church (a DVD was made of this performance). Each time, the performing venue underwent a metamorphosis. It was no longer a concert space, traditionally divided into a place where the audience sits and a section where the musical and stage action takes place. The space became simultaneously a site of ritual, where the spectators are witnesses and co-participants, and a large resonating box, in which the "ritual sound theater," as the composer calls it, takes place. The space itself becomes an instrument that co-creates acoustic and light phenomena. The movement of sound becomes the protagonist of the production as well as the demiurgic beginning and end of the artistic and ritual events. One of the compositional techniques that Prasqual uses in *Architecture of Light* is spectralism. The journey takes place here on two levels: travel into the depths of sound symbolizes the spectral microcosm, while the movement of light, sound, and action in the architectural space, with the participation of artists and audiences, represents the human macrocosm. It also symbolizes the cosmic order, the creation of everything from the very first sound.

Further explorations of sound and movement in space came in the form of such pieces as the *Nevermore* ballet (2014) for two drummers and electronic music and *Five Songs from the Cage* [*Pięć śpiewów z klatki*] for mezzo-soprano, baritone, reciter, orchestra in seven groups, and electronics (2014), commissioned by the Wrocław Opera on the occasion of the 85th birthday of Tadeusz Różewicz. The previously mentioned works for the National Polish Radio Symphonic Orchestra also are examples of these explorations.

Prasqual highly values his cooperation with the National Polish Radio Symphonic Orchestra, believing it to be one of the best and most accessible orchestras, even in comparison with German ensembles. Although most of the composer's large musical commissions come from Poland, he is also satisfied with the artistic support system that Germany provides. There, artists who do not work on a full-time basis can register with the artists' social security fund (Künstlersozialkasse), after which half of their contributions are paid by the state. Germany's cultural offerings are also richer than those of Poland, in part because there are many more theaters and concert halls. But there is also more competition there, as Prasqual pointed out in an interview with *Deutsche Welle*.[135]

Prasqual's art, erudite and spiritual, draws from European tradition, but he is also fascinated by Islamic architecture and literature. He is searching, in the words of Miłosz, for "a more capacious form." His art should not be omitted from discussions on contemporary Polish music. His most recent projects include *Conversations with Death* [*Rozmowy ze śmiercią*] for contralto, basso profondo, reciter, and double orchestra with basso continuo, set to the poetry of Jan Kochanowski and the ancient *Egyptian Book of the Dead*. In an initial description of the piece, Prasqual mentioned two separate worlds, embodied by two differently tuned orchestras: baroque (415 Hz), representing the journey of the dead person, and classical (430 Hz), symbolizing the journey of the one who remained.[136] The work was premiered by the {oh!} Historical Orchestra in Katowice, on 17 September 2019.

Faithful to his Path

When Szymon Brzóska (b. 1981), who studied composition in Poznań with Mirosław Bukowski (b. 1936), left Poland in 2004 for a three-month scholarship to Leuven, he already knew what he wanted to do and how he wanted to write. His interests focused on writing music for ballet, theater, and film; for his thesis, he created music for the ballet *Ice Palace* (based on Tarjei Vesaas's novel of the same title). Thanks to his studies with Bukowski, he felt that he had mastered the craft of composition. He went to Belgium in order to broaden his horizons, since he was curious about the country that is currently the mecca of contemporary dance. His three-month stay in Leuven and his work with Lucio van Hove resulted in an invitation to study at the Royal Conservatory in Antwerp. During the last week of his stay in that city, Brzóska saw the ballet *Myth* by the famous choreographer Siri Larbi Cherkaoui (b. 1976). Delighted with the production, he decided to see it again, this time taking a recording of his own music, which he intended to give to the choreographer. Three days later he received an email from him. Cherkaoui had listened to the recording and was enchanted by the calm, meditative character, gentle harmonies, and melodies in Brzóska's music. He proposed that Brzóska write music for his *Sutra* project, a ballet involving Buddhist monks and Kung Fu masters from Shaolin Monastery in China that was premiered in 2008. The spectacle has gained great fame; since its premiere it has been watched by over 160,000 spectators in twenty-eight countries and has been staged in the most famous theaters in the world. The tour continues to this day and is now being performed by a fifth "generation" of monks. For Brzóska, this project became an entrance pass to the international dance theater scene. Together with Cherkaoui, he has produced six more ballets, including *Icarus*, a ballet written for the legendary Russian dancer Vladimir Malakov that premiered at the Staatsoper Berlin in 2014; *Orbo Nuovo*, for the Cedar Lake Contemporary Ballet in New York; and *Dunas*, for the Maria Pages Company in Madrid, with choreography by Cherkaoui and the famous flamenco dancer Maria Pages, 2009.

In 2013, he started working with another great choreographer, David Dawson. For the Dutch National Ballet they created *Overture* (2013) and *Citizen Nowhere* (2017). In 2015, their ballet based on *Tristan and Isolde* for Semperoper Dresden was highly successful. Today, the composer lives in Belgium, although he still travels to work on his projects and commissions. When he is not working on commissioned works, he writes chamber music and small pieces. His compositions have been performed at various festivals: Sounds New Contemporary Music Festival in Canterbury, Operadagen in Rotterdam, Tehran International Contemporary Music Festival, En Avant Mars Festival in Ghent, and the Music@ venture in Antwerp.

Brzóska's career and artistic development are extremely interesting in the context of reflections on the composers of the young generation, because he is someone whose first important work, *Sutra*, was based on a clash of cultures. The performance was co-created by the Flemish-Moroccan choreographer Siri Larbi Cherkaoui, British set designer and sculptor Antony Gormley, 19 monks from Shaolim Monastery in China, and Brzóska. While working on the project, he made several trips to China and spent several weeks in a Buddhist monastery. Interestingly, however, in an interview for the New York-based *Przegląd Polski*, the composer answered a question about whether he was inspired by Far Eastern music by saying:

> Not really. Each of us was supposed to bring to this spectacle what is natural for his own cultural circle. So I wrote in my own compositional language. I wanted to avoid a banal imitation of Chinese music. The only connecting element is the use of the muju—a percussion instrument shaped like Buddha's belly—and glissandos in the string instruments.[137]

In my conversation with the composer, Brzóska confirmed that neither living abroad nor travelling has influenced his compositional style. Brzóska emphasized that Bukowski, his teacher in Poznań, taught him how to think musically and to understand the development of music across the centuries. He said, "I have good foundations that I can turn upside down when necessary,"[138] and added that it was important to have received commissions and work with an orchestra early on: "It takes making some mistakes early. Something has to sound wrong in order to learn the secrets of orchestration, proportions, and how music functions in time. Composing cannot be learned any other way except through practicing."[139] In this regard, Brzóska seems to be a composer standing firmly on the ground, focused on simply writing good music. He is not the type of composer who has chosen to live abroad because of a need to be inspired by something exotic or to seek new ways. Brzóska knew how he wanted to write when he left Poland and he remains faithful to his own compositional path.

When it comes to his compositional style, Brzóska places himself somewhere between the modern avant-garde, the tradition of extended tonality, and minimalism. His music is captivating with its gentle, but deeply moving expression (e.g., *Rumi Partita* for harpsichord and strings, 2017, and *The King's Speech* from the *Tristan and Isolde* ballet, 2015), and its moments of theatrical grotesqueness, for example, the distorted melodies and rhythms reminiscent of Shostakovich and Prokofiev in *Tres somni: Horror* for piano and cello (2010).

Brzóska has no plans to return to Poland. He seems happy to live in a country that is the center of contemporary dance. In Poland, compared to Belgium, much less is happening in the sphere of ballet. He has also gained the so-called status of an artist, needed for tax purposes. Belgium's tax system is similar to France's, where artists have to prove that they have at least three large contracts a year or work for a certain number of days per year. For days when they do not work, the state pays artists a fixed benefit rate. Each contract is signed by Intermin, the state art agency. However, Brzóska is also glad to have his music performed in Poland, especially in his hometown of Poznań. Among his Polish projects, the most important ones are the *Desert* ballet choreographed by Paulina Wycichowska for the Polish Dance Theatre (2011) and *Oh Noh*, a project with Kaja Kołodziejczyk shown at the Centre for Contemporary Art at the Ujazdowski Castle in Warsaw (2012). His music has been presented at the Malta Festival in Poznań, the Ars Polonia Biennial in Opole, and the Polish Piano Festival in Słupsk, where his *Hommage à Schnittke* for piano, strings, and percussion, with Barbara Drążkowska as soloist, was performed. Drążkowska is popularizing Szymon Brzóska's music in Poland: in 2017 she did a concert tour of Poland, traveling by bicycle (the Green Pianist/Green Velo Tour). During her concerts she played music that will be available on the *Murmur* album. So far, Brzóska has released two original albums, *Migrations* and *The Wanderer*. A CD with his music for the *Sutra* ballet is also available.

Dancing with a Theremin

Jakub Ciupiński (b. 1981) was 18 years old when he recorded *Abomey*, his first album with electronic music, for Sony, using the pseudonym Jakub Żak. His education took place in Kraków, where he studied with Zbigniew Bujarski and Krzysztof Penderecki. Thirsty for new perspectives and inspiration, he decided to continue his studies with Christopher Rouse at New York's Juilliard School of Music and then with Edwin Roxburgh and Joe Cutler at the Birmingham Conservatory. Today, Ciupiński's works are performed on both continents. He has been appointed Dean of the Faculty of Studio Composition at the State University of New York at Purchase and the Art Director of Purchase Electronic Orchestra, a multimedia project combining orchestra with electronics, light installations, and video projections.

In the United States, Ciupiński has continued to experiment with sound and computers. He has developed software that allows for live composing and reacting to a live performance. This method has been used by the composer during concerts of the Blind Ear Music collective, which he co-established. During concerts, Ciupiński and musicians playing various percussion instruments have laptops instead of music stands holding pages of notes. The composer sends music to the performers and gives them the tempo, which they hear in headphones. The musicians repeat the given loop; the composer can remotely ask each of them to change the tempo or dynamics, introduce a new loop, suggest that they improvise, etc. Due to the repeated loops and the sound of marimba, dulcimer, and other percussion instruments, the music of the Blind Ear Music collective can resemble a gamelan, whose sound, however, is fully controlled and created live by a leader standing in front of a laptop.

Another of Ciupiński's ideas involves a new application for the theremin (an electronic instrument emitting sounds that react to vibrations generated by hand movements in the air), which the composer uses in conjunction with his laptop. The software he created reacts to information received from the theremin and decides which sounds and elements will be emitted through the speakers. Ciupiński, with his hands, or rather his entire body (more complex sonic structures require fast and smooth movements that engage the whole body), thus composes live electronic music. Thanks to this, he develops a more direct contact with his audience, which can experience the creative process not only through their ears but also their eyes. Works made via this technique have been enthusiastically received by audiences and critics alike.

In his compositions, both traditional ones (such as *Guitar Concerto*, 2014), as well as those combining live instruments and electronics (such as *Glitsch* for violin and theremin, 2014), Ciupiński uses expanded tonality. In an interview with *Przegląd Polski*, he said, "My harmonic language is characterized by changes in tonality, from minor to major. It becomes almost a principle, like moving from dominant to tonic. There is still a lot of unused space in tonal music."[140] This deep exploration of the minor-major system as well as his contrasting of beautiful, simple melodies with disturbing glissandos and amplified background can be heard in *The Wrecks of Umbria* for violin and orchestra, which premiered during Kraków's Last Night of the Proms in 2016. Soloist Anne Akiko Meyers, on her Avi Records release *Mirror in Mirror* (2018), has included various compositions by Ciupiński.

Ciupiński has found his place in the United States, even though it is not easy to be a musician there. The state does not support artists within its tax and insurance systems. Most musicians decide to work at universities; this situation has positive aspects, not only in terms of insurance provisions, but also creative ones. Ciupiński has emphasized the significance for his own development of working with students and establishing contacts with the community, saying "one learns the most by teaching others."[141]

"Actually, I'm on the Internet": Final Thoughts

For the sake of this essay, I spoke with Marcin Banasik (b. 1982), a composer who, following his studies with Mirosław Bukowski at the Academy of Music in Poznań, went to the University of York for his Ph.D. Later, for private reasons, he went to Shanghai. Several months ago, Banasik decided to return to Poznań with his family. When discussing his migration during a phone call, he admitted "Actually, I'm on the Internet."[142] Indeed, Banasik has an extensive website where you can buy and listen to his works, as well as read his poems and prose and view his paintings (Banasik is an extremely versatile artist). His statement about "being on the Internet" summarizes this chapter perfectly. Thanks to the Internet, composers are present in the consciousness of contemporary music fans around the world. Their recordings sometimes have thousands of views on YouTube. I may add, provokingly, that among the many works by young Polish composers that I have watched on YouTube, the highest number of views has probably been given to a piece by Szmytka: *F* for music* (2012). Those who click on her piece, intrigued or excited with the title, will not be disappointed; it is a perfectly written, brilliant composition that probably refers to a documentary about a group of German activists, *Fuck for Forest.*

The Internet is an important tool for young artists that allows them to create an image consistent with their music. Their websites and other social media sites are often small works of art with excellent designs and photographs (especially Szmytka's website, Blecharz's Instagram site, and the Twitter profile of the Netherlands-based composer Katarzyna Głowicka). This online presence is, of course, a trademark of the generation of composers born in the 1980s. Some well-known Polish composers of earlier generations, including Paweł Mykietyn, Paweł Szymański, Zbigniew Bargielski, and Rafał Augustyn, do not have their own websites at all.

The Internet can be a perfect metaphor for how composers function in today's post-Iron Curtain world. They have unlimited possibilities for travel, establishing contacts, and working in different countries. They are unhindered by censorship; the only exception in this regard known to me is the *Sutra* ballet with music by Brzóska, which had to be approved by the Chinese government. "The borders have been open for a long time," says Szmytka. "Now it's all about having open borders in our heads."[143]

Agnieszka Cieślak, Mariusz Gradowski

The Paths of Film Music[144]

Did émigré composers write film music? Of course, and quite a lot. What's interesting is that we hardly know about this work. Film composers who have worked abroad remain only marginally interesting to people in Poland who deal with music for cinema. While it is possible, perhaps, to understand this state of affairs in the case of contemporary composers, whose work still continues, it is surprising to discover a lack of studies on the oeuvre of such important composers as Bronisław Kaper or Henryk Wars, who were true masters of Polish film music. Without aspiring to exhaust the topic at all, we propose a small reconnaissance in this area.

It is worth emphasizing at this point that we applied a broad understanding of the term "film music" in deciding what to examine for this essay. Thus, we include not only original scores for feature films, but also music for documentaries, short films, student efforts, television series and films, and songs written for films. After all, everything mentioned here can be heard in films! We define a particular composer as a Polish émigré artist either through the presence of at least one aspect of his or her life (e.g., Polish origin, surname, citizenship, use of the Polish language, publishing in Polish, or a direct connection with Poland) or through previously published recognition as such (articles in Polish and international encyclopedias, monographs, being defined as Polish in biographies, press articles, and other media texts). All types of migration are considered, from social and economic (early twentieth century) to politically conditioned (mid-twentieth century), and to departures prompted by opportunities for professional development (late twentieth and early twenty-first centuries).

Categorizing a composer as an émigré artist can, of course, be debated. The professional lives of artists of the middle and younger generation are still evolving and their career prospects are seemingly unlimited. Nevertheless, we have decided to discuss a group of composers who have remained outside Poland for a relatively long period of time, which places them in a different position than composers who work exclusively in Poland. Krzysztof Komeda is a problematic case. He worked with Jerzy Skolimowski, Henning Carlsen, Tom Segerberg and, for the longest time, Roman Polański. He would often leave Poland to compose and record abroad. His last trip turned out to be particularly important artistically, for his successful scores for the films *Fearless Vampire Killers* (1967) and *Rosemary's Baby* (1968) made it advantageous for Paramount Pictures to offer the Los Angeles-based composer a lucrative contract. In her memoirs, Zofia Komeda claimed that her husband Krzysztof was supposed to have the opportunity to write music in Poland and send finished material to the United States. This proposal also included working visits to Hollywood. How would this have worked? Would Krzysztof Komeda have returned to his family in Poland and worked with Hollywood remotely? Would he have chosen to emigrate, inviting Zofia Komeda and her son to come to the United States, or would he have decided to break up the family? These questions must remain unanswered, given the composer's unexpected death in 1968 due to an unfortunate accident.

Many Polish composers, especially those of Jewish origin, were forced to emigrate by the economic crisis after World War I and, later, by the rise of Nazism and the outbreak of World War II. They were educated in renowned European conservatories (e.g., in Berlin, Vienna, Paris, Moscow, St. Petersburg, and Warsaw) under the tutelage of such esteemed teachers as Arnold Schoenberg, Nadia Boulanger, and Karol Szymanowski. The diversity of the approaches to composition presented by the representatives of these schools—from traditional European concert music to the avant-garde—shows the rich potential that these emigrants took abroad. Before their departure, some of them had held prestigious positions in institutions such as operas, orchestras, and theaters. Others had chosen the popular music industry from the beginning, working as cabaret musicians or leading their own jazz ensembles. Even before emigration, some of them had been writing for film, although some abandoned this activity over the course of their professional careers. Going abroad, usually overseas to the United States, was associated with hopes for better social, political, economic, and cultural conditions. Emigrants learned a new language, often changed their names, and adapted to a new musical environment. Most of them never returned to their homeland.

Direction: America

One of the first Polish composers to make an impression in the field of American cinematography was Bronisław Mirski (1887–1927), known as Nek Mirskey. He went to the United States at the end of 1914 as the orchestral conductor on a White Star Line ship. His ambition was, he claimed, "to study the appropriate musical accompaniment for moving images in the country that has contributed most to their popularity." For many years he was associated with the Famous Players-Lasky firm (later Paramount Pictures). He also worked as the music director of cinemas in Washington, Boston, Kansas City, and Dallas and was responsible for the final shape of the musical arrangements that were prepared for silent films. Since the accompaniments to these early films were primarily compilations of various pieces (classical music excerpts, popular melodies, and short compositions created specifically for cinema), Mirski cannot, strictly speaking, be called a composer of film music. Nevertheless, his creative contribution to the music arrangements for over two hundred silent movies makes it necessary to recognize his accomplishments.

Film music formed the core of Bronisław Kaper's career (1902–1983). He was probably the biggest émigré star of Polish film music. A graduate in piano and composition from Warsaw Conservatory, he took his first professional steps in Berlin, Vienna, London, and Paris, writing music for over thirty films. His talent, exemplified by the hit song *Ninon*, which was sung across all of Europe in the 1930s, was recognized by Louis B. Mayer, head of the Metro-Goldwyn-Mayer label. With Mayer's help, Kaper moved permanently to Hollywood in 1940. Over 28 years of collaboration with MGM, he composed music for over a hundred films. The high point of his career was being awarded an Oscar for the musical *Lili* (1954), directed by Charles Walters. Many of the themes from the films illustrated by Kaper became popular, including *Green Dolphin Street* (1947, with the title song recorded by Miles Davis in 1958), *Invitation* (1952) and the atmospheric and exotic *Follow Me* from the film *Mutiny on the Bounty* (1962). In the mid-1960s, Kaper began working for television. Among other things, he composed the main theme of *The F.B.I.* series (1965). Kaper's style was rooted in late Romanticism, but it combined elements of symphonic and popular music, especially jazz. His work can be viewed as a benchmark of Hollywood's golden age of music alongside the achievements of such giants as Max Steiner, Erich Korngold, and Miklós Rózsa. Kaper belongs to this same league of composers.

Henryk Wars (1902–1977) also contributed to American cinema. His songs, such as *Love Forgives Everything* [*Miłość ci wszystko wybaczy*], *I'm Going to Meet Her at 9* [*Umówiłem się z nią na dziewiątą*], and *I'm Such a Cold Scoundrel* [*Już taki jestem zimny drań*], are well known in Poland. A slightly less well known fact is that Wars was also a pioneer of jazz in Poland. But he was a prolific composer of film music. Beginning with one of Poland's first sound films, *Exile to Siberia* [*Na Sybir*] (1930), Wars created musical settings for more than fifty interwar films, including *The Singer of Warsaw* [*Pieśniarz Warszawy*] (1934), *Love Maneuvers* [*Manewry miłosne*] (1935), *The Quack* [*Znachor*] (1937), *Paweł and Gaweł* [*Paweł i Gaweł*] (1938). After the turbulent war years, he settled in Los Angeles, where he continued his successful career in the film industry. Between 1953 and 1971, he

composed music for more than sixty films produced by leading Hollywood film companies such as Columbia, Universal, 20th Century Fox, and MGM. He gained the most popularity for his music for the film and children's TV series *Flipper* (1963–1966). Making use of his talent for writing memorable melodies, Wars continued to write songs, including *Sleep My Child* and *Never Say You'll Never Fall in Love.* An impressive list of artists sang them, including Bing Crosby, Doris Day, and Brenda Lee.

Let's stop for a moment on the subject of Polish interwar cinema. Three composers abandoned working for film after they emigrated, which is perhaps why they are somewhat forgotten. The first one, Iwo Wesby (Ignacy Singer, 1902–1961), worked from 1934 to 1939 as a conductor, composer, and music manager for about fifteen Polish productions, including the last films made in Yiddish before the Nazis attacked Poland. Wesby was the musical director of one of the two melodramatic films directed by the famous actor Eugeniusz Bodo, *Queen of the Suburbs* [*Królowa przedmieścia*] (1937), to which music was composed by the aforementioned Henryk Wars. When working on the film *Wacuś* (1935), he came into contact with Władysław Daniłowski and his ensemble Dan's Choir [Chór Dana]. This choral group performed in several Polish films, singing lyrics written by the great poet Julian Tuwim! Daniłowski, the second of the three forgotten composers, who created music for ten Polish films, including *The Story of Sin* [*Dzieje grzechu*] (1933). He also appeared as a vocalist in the film *Palace on Wheels* [*Pałac na kółkach*] (1932), for which Michał Kondracki prepared the score. Kondracki, the third of the three composers, is remembered today mainly as a composer of "non-film" music, but it is worth remembering, for example, that he worked on the film *A Girl Is Looking for Love* [*Dziewczyna szuka miłości*] (1937) with Marian Neuteich. After the outbreak of World War II, all three composers settled in the United States, devoting themselves mainly to pedagogical and journalistic activities.

A separate paragraph should be dedicated to Karol Rathaus (1895–1954). Before the outbreak of World War II, he wrote scores for important films, first in Germany (*Der Mörder Dimitri Karamasoff* and *Die Koffer des Herrn O. F.*, 1931), then in France (*Amok*, 1934) and Great Britain (*The Dictator*, 1935). It seemed that working in Hollywood would have been a natural continuation of his European experience. It turned out, however, that he wrote music for only one film there, *Let Us Live* (1939). The pace of work and commercial pressure of the studio system discouraged him from working on additional films. After moving to New York, however, he did not completely abandon this activity. In the 1940s and 1950s he composed music for several short films (*Headquarters United Nations*, 1947), documentaries (*Jaguas*, 1942, *Histadruth I*, 1945, and *Histadruth II*, 1946) and feature films (*Out of Evil*, in Hebrew *Mi Klalah Le Brachah*, 1950). He also wrote so-called stock music for B-class movies, doing so anonymously.

Emigrants by Choice

The non-film work of Karol Rathaus is often compared to the output of composers whom Zofia Helman has described as "emigrants by choice." Film music comprised part of the output of these composers. Aleksander Tansman can be used as an example. Tansman left for Paris at the age of 22 and became a French citizen—a bit ostentatiously, after suffering years of hostility from Polish music critics. In France he began working with Jean Epstein (*Mor Vran*, 1931 and *La Châtelaine du Liban*, 1934) and Julien Duvivier (*Poil de carotte*, 1932). He spent World War II in the United States, as did Duvivier, for whom he later wrote music to *Flesh and Fantasy* (1943) and *Destiny* (1944). Tansman's talent was confirmed by an Oscar nomination for his music to Gregory Ratoff's film *Paris Underground* (1945). This seems to be a bit paradoxical, because it proved to occupy the penultimate position in the composer's film music oeuvre, followed only by the music to *Sister Kenny* (1946), directed by Dudley Nichols. He focused on other compositional endeavors for the rest of his career. After his return to France, Tansman worked almost exclusively in the classical music arena, with only sporadic contributions to theater, radio, and documentaries.

Roman Palester (1907–1989) is also referred to as an "emigrant by choice." He spent World War II in Poland, leaving for Paris only in 1947; a few years later, he decided to emigrate permanently. Unlike Tansman, Palester wrote film music exclusively for Polish films. He collaborated with many well-known directors, including Józef Lejtes (*Girls from Nowolipki Street* [*Dziewczęta z Nowolipek*], 1937), Leonard Buczkowski (*Forbidden Songs* [*Zakazane piosenki*], 1947), and Aleksander Ford (*Border Street* [*Ulica graniczna*], 1948).

Andrzej Panufnik (1914–1991) left Poland and made his way to Great Britain in 1954. As early as 1938, he had composed music for the movie *Fears* [*Strachy*], starring Eugeniusz Bodo in the lead role. He also worked on Jerzy Zarzycki's film *Treacherous Heart* [*Zdradzieckie serce*] (1947), but the film was never released. Panufnik also composed music for documentaries made in the Military Film Studio, most of which presented propaganda content. Panufnik's compositions have great potential for imagery, which was taken advantage of by Andrzej Wajda in 2016 for his film *Afterimages* [*Powidoki*], which tells the story of the painter and art theorist Władysław Strzemiński.

Like Panufnik, Allan Gray (birth name Józef Żmigród, 1902–1973) also emigrated to Great Britain. A student of Arnold Schoenberg, he began by writing music for German cinema, including *Emil und die Detektive* (1931). In 1933 he settled permanently in England, where he worked for London Films and other British labels. Together with Michael Powell and Emerik Pressburger, a duo of directors known as The Archers, he worked on such films as *I Know Where I'm Going!* (1945) and *A Matter of Life and Death* (1946).

Mieczysław Weinberg (1919–1996) went in a different direction. In 1939 he escaped from Warsaw to the Soviet Union, settling permanently in Moscow four years later. While still in Warsaw, Weinberg wrote music for Zbigniew Ziembiński's film *Fredek Makes the World Happy* [*Fredek uszczęśliwia świat*] (1936). In the Soviet Union, he composed music for many films, leaving behind scores for about sixty short and long feature films. Of these, Mikhail Kalatozov's drama *The Cranes Are Flying* (1957), honored with a Palme d'Or at the Cannes Film Festival, won the greatest recognition.

Joseph Kumok (1901–1979) settled in Prague after World War I, where he worked as a conductor and composer in the Barrandov film studio and cooperated with the UFA studio in Berlin. His music for Julien Duvivier's film *Golem* (1936) brought him international fame. Many of his songs for film gained great popularity, including *Rosita* from the film *Lelíček ve službách Sherlocka Holmese* (1932). In 1938 Kumok emigrated to Argentina, where—as George Andreani—he worked mainly for Lumiton Studios. He became famous as a composer of music for more than 75 films during the golden age of Argentinian cinema (c. 1937–1959). His story, or what we know of it, is a classic example of a blank spot in our knowledge of composers in exile. Andreani's oeuvre is impressive...and maybe somebody will be tempted to investigate it more closely.

With Polish Blood in Their Veins

A separate group we should discuss are American film music composers who were born in Poland but left the country at an early age. Their relationship with Poland was very loose, but since we are using a broad understanding of emigration, they are worth mentioning. For example, Paul Lamkoff (Peter Lampcovici, 1888–1953), who started his career as a violinist in the Moscow Symphony Orchestra, emigrated to the United States in the 1920s and settled with his wife and daughter in Los Angeles. He worked as a vocal teacher (and taught Al Jolson) and as an orchestrator and composer for MGM. Another emigrant, Fred Rich (Frederic Ephram Rich, 1898–1956), wrote music for eight Hollywood productions in the 1940s, such as Frank Borzage's *Stage Door Cantine* (1943) and Lewis Milestone's *A Walk in the Sun* (1945).

Jay Gorney (Abraham Jacob Gornetzsky, 1894–1990) began his career on Tin Pan Alley in New York City, working on many Broadway productions. One of his most popular songs was *Brother Can You Spare a Dime* to Yip Harburg's lyrics, based on a lullaby melody that Gorney remembered from his childhood on Polish soil. There was also Paul Sawtell (Sawatzki, 1906–1991), who wrote music for over 330 films and TV productions, including Irwin Allen's Oscar-winning documentary *The Sea Around Us* (1953). Finally, two Polish-born American songwriters were honored by the Songwriters Hall of Fame for their contributions to the popularity of songs from Hollywood productions of the 1930s and 1940s. They are Jack Yellen (Jacek Jeleń, 1892–1991), author of *Happy Days Are Here Again* and *Ain't She Sweet*, and Mack Gordon (Morris Gittler, 1904–1959), an Oscar winner for his song *You'll Never Know* from the film *Hello, Frisco, Hello* (1943).

Among those in the Polish diaspora who maintained a close relationship with Poland was Victor Young (Abe Young, 1901–1956), an important figure in the world of film music. Born in Chicago to a family of Jewish immigrants from Poland, he was sent to Warsaw to learn composition with Roman Statkowski and violin with Stanislaw Barcewicz. His relationship with Poland was strengthened by the fact that after completing his education, he stayed in Warsaw for a few years, earning money as a cinema pianist, among other things. After returning to the United States, he developed a career as a theater and film composer, earning 22 Oscar nominations and a 1956 statuette for the film *Around the World in 80 Days*.

Other representatives of the Polish film community are Leopold Stokowski (1882–1977), the winner of an honorary Oscar for creating a new form of visualized music in the animated Walt Disney film *Fantasia* (1940), and Robert Muczyński (1929–2010), author of the music for nine award-winning documentaries produced by the film department at the University of Arizona in Tucson; these included *The Great Unfenced* (1963), *Terra Sancta* (1967), and *Journey Through Eden* (1975). This group also includes the French composer Marcel Landowski (1915–1999), son of the sculptor Paul Landowski (author of the statue of Christ in Rio de Janeiro), and grandson of Edward Landowski (an insurgent in the January Uprising of 1863–1864). Everyone interested in composers from the Polish diaspora should consider Landowski's impressive output, which includes music for several dozen films.

While political reasons for emigration prevailed until the 1950s, economic and professional considerations were the most important factors for artists born after World War II. Only a few Polish composers writing contemporary film music found themselves abroad for political reasons. Perhaps such motivations can be considered in the case of Stanisław Syrewicz, whose return from Paris, scheduled for 13 December 1981, was stopped by the imposition of martial law. Cezary Skubiszewski also recalls the "political stuffiness" that reinforced his decision to emigrate to Australia. But in these cases, one can also see what most composers themselves emphasize: their stay abroad opened up new possibilities for composing film music. This is particularly clear with regard to the American market. Even today, the film music world accepts Hollywood as its main point of reference, perhaps not for purely artistic reasons, but certainly on the basis of its prestige (productions viewed worldwide and high-profile film awards, including the Oscars), commercial possibilities (high budgets), and publishing opportunities (recordings).

New Horizons

In recent years, the history of Polish film music created in the United States has been determined by two composers: Jan A. P. Kaczmarek and Abel Korzeniowski.[145] Kaczmarek went to Los Angeles in 1989 as a musician and composer with experience in theater (mainly as a member of the Orchestra of the Eighth Day [Orkiestra Ósmego Dnia]) and a film composer (*Shadow* [*Cień*], 1981; the *1944* series, 1984; and *Blind Man's Game* [*Gra w ślepcal*], 1985). His first period in Hollywood, during which he composed several music scores to lesser known films, ended with Agnieszka Holland's *Total Eclipse* (1995). The success of this film contributed to the popularity of Kaczmarek's music and had a key impact on his future collaborations with Holland (*Washington Square,* 1997 and *The Third Miracle,* 1999). It also paved the way for other famous films such as *Aimee and Jaguar* (1998), *Unfaithful* (2002), and *Finding Neverland* (2004), for which the composer received an Oscar. Kaczmarek has not lost touch with Polish film. In 1992 he wrote the music for Magdalena Łazarkiewicz's *White Marriage* [*Białe Małżeństwo*], in 2002 he illustrated Jerzy Kawalerowicz's *Quo Vadis,* and in later years he composed music for the films *Who Never Lived* [*Kto nigdy nie żył* by Andrzej Seweryn (2006), Janusz Kamiński's *Hania* (2007), and Aneta Kopacz's *Joanna* (2013). Kaczmarek writes distinctive music that combines the full sound of a symphonic orchestra with a minimalist style. He has used the sounds of Fischer's fiddles, folk instruments, and also electronic instruments.

Abel Korzeniowski's creative path is similar to that of Kaczmarek. Korzeniowski went to Los Angeles as a composer who had created music for the well-received feature films *Big Animal* [*Duże zwierzę*] (2000), *An Angel in Kraków* [*Anioł w Krakowie*] (2002) and *Weather for Tomorrow* [*Pogoda na jutro*] (2003), as well as for television films and spectacles. His stay in the United States turned out to be fruitful; he is known for his artistic collaborations with Tom Ford, which include *A Single Man* (2009) and *Nocturnal Animals* (2016), and his music for the series *Penny Dreadful* (2014–2016), which received a BAFTA award. As with Kaczmarek, Korzeniowski did not lose touch with Polish cinematography, as evidenced by the films *The Star of Copernicus* [*Gwiazda Kopernika*] (2009) and *Grains of Truth* [*Ziarno prawdy*] (2015). Korzeniowski's music takes advantage of minimalism; he also employs small ensembles in which a string orchestra dominates, which situates him within a film trend characterized by the use of chamber music.

Since 2014, Bartłomiej Gliniak (b. 1973) has also been working in Los Angeles. Korzeniowski's peer, he has written music for over forty films, including *To My* (2000], *My Nikifor* [*Mój Nikifor*] (2004), *The Bailiff* [*Komornik*] (2006), *Palimpsest* (2006), *Officers* [*Oficerowie*] (2006), and *Deceived* [*Oszukane*] (2013). His stay abroad has not yet resulted in soundtracks for American films, but in the meantime, Gliniak has continued his cooperation with Polish directors such as Wojciech Kasperski (*On the Border* [*Na granicy*], 2016), Kuba Czekaj (*The Erlprince* [*Królewicz olch*], 2016) and Maciej Sobieszczański (*The Reconciliation* [*Zgoda*], 2017).

Thanks to new technologies, Cezary Skubiszewski discovered Polish cinematography. No matter where the composer lives, the Internet enables contact, cooperation, and file sharing, even from the other side of the world. Skubiszewski left Poland in 1974 as an instrumentalist. After arriving in Australia, he began veterinary studies, but eventually returned to music as a composer. Associated with Australian cinema since 1994, his most important compositions include scores for *Lilian's Story* (1996), *The Sound of One Hand Clapping* (1998), *Red Dog* (2011), and *The Sapphires* (2012). In 2012 he started working with Polish directors, which resulted in music for *Felix, Net, and Nika and the Theoretically Possible Catastrophe* [*Felix, Net i Nika oraz teoretycznie możliwa katastrofa*] (2012), *Jeziorak* (2014), and *Karbala* (2015), the latter with the wonderful participation of Lisa Gerrard, a member of Dead Can Dance.

Among other composers working in exile, there is the composer and violinist Zbigniew Paleta (b. 1942). Today he is virtually unknown, but in the 1960s and 1970s he was associated with the famous Cellar under the Rams [Piwnica pod Baranami] cabaret and also performed with Ewa Demarczyk and the band Anawa. Paleta's emigration was prompted by the possibility of an unusual kind of employment: in 1980 he won a competition to be a violinist in one of Mexico's orchestras. He emigrated with his wife and daughters, Dominika and Ludwik, who began their acting careers in the 1990s and are now Mexican cinema stars. Perhaps this is why Paleta, formerly a cabaret violinist, rock musician, and songwriter, eventually became interested in film. He has written soundtracks for several feature films, two of which were nominated for an Ariel Mexican Academy Award (two nominations for music and song to *Libre de culpas*, 1997, and one for music to *Su alteza serenísima*, 2001). In his music, Paleta exploits the possibilities of the solo violin. His playing style influences the nature of his own film music; the echoes of his collaborations with Cellar under the Rams and especially with Zbigniew Preisner can be heard.

Other composers decided to stay closer to their native country. Of the film music émigrés who remained in Europe, Stanisław Syrewicz was the most successful. Even before his emigration to France, he had made himself known as a film composer. From that early period, he is remembered above all his debut film *Charming Eyes* [*Oczy uroczne*] (1977) and his music for the series *Sherlock Holmes and Doctor Watson* (1980). During his first years in exile, Syrewicz worked as a musician and, as in Poland, composed songs. After four years he successfully returned to film with his score for *The Holcroft Covenant* (1985), whose success brought further commissions from the United States, Great Britain, and France. After 1989, Syrewicz's professional contacts with Poland became more frequent. His music for television became particularly recognizable (*The House at the Lake* [*Dom nad Rozlewiskiem*], *The Secret of the Code Fortress* [*Tajemnica Twierdzy Szyfrów*], and *Law of the City* [*Prawo miasta*]). Songs are one of the trademarks of Syrewicz's work, along with his expressive and catchy melodies.

Joanna Bruzdowicz is also associated with France. In 1968, while still a student, she went to Paris on a scholarship; after two years, she decided to stay abroad. In 1975 she became a French citizen. Bruzdowicz's work is perceived in Poland primarily through the prism of her non film-related compositions, but this picture is not complete without her more functional pieces, including her film scores. Joanna Bruzdowicz's cooperation with Agnes Varda has been particularly important. She started with the film *Vagabond* (1985), working with fragments of a string quartet reworked especially for the film. She writes for feature films, documentaries, and television productions. Bruzdowicz has also worked on English productions, including the film *The White King* (2016). Her overall musical style is characterized in part by an ease of handling the various elements of contemporary music, which can also be heard in her film music.

Composers active in France who also occasionally create film music include Elżbieta Sikora and Piotr Moss. Even before her departure from Poland in 1981, Sikora composed music for Krzysztof Rogulski's television films (e.g., *On the Run* [*W biegu*], 1978, and *Papa Stamm*, 1978) and for cinema (e.g., *Before the Departure* [*Przed odlotem*], 1980, and *Great May Day* [*Wielka majówka*], 1981). In 1991 she also wrote the music to Rogulski's 1991 film *Children of the Wind*, aka *Children of War* [*Dzieci wiatru* or *Dzieci wojny*]. Although film music remains on the margins of her compositional interests, we should point out that she has maintained a consistent musical language in all genres, including film.

The same is true of Piotr Moss. His film music is almost exclusively dedicated to documentaries. He has collaborated with Andrzej Titkow many times and has also written music for films by Jerzy Tuszyński and Stanisław Różewicz. Różewicz's *Passion* (1977) is the only feature film scored by Moss.

Within the circle of composers operating in France, or more broadly, in the Francophone countries, are artists who were born into families of Polish emigrants. The one most closely connected with Poland is Henri Seroka (b. 1949), who in the 1960s performed as a singer in "the old country." Involved in film music since the 1970s, he has worked closely with director Jacek Bromski. Indeed, he has composed the music for most of Bromski's films, beginning with the student work *The Cyclist* [*Kolarz*] (1976), through *Alice* (1980), *Kill Me, Cop* [*Zabij mnie, glino*] (1987), and *The Art of Love* [*Sztuka kochania*] (1988), to *In God's Garden* [*U Pana Boga w ogródku*] (2007). Apart from the music for Bromski's films, Seroka's soundtracks for TV films, documentaries, and children's series (including the popular *Smurfs*) stand out.

Karol Beffa (b. 1973), professor at the Collège de France, pianist, musicologist, and composer, is another name associated with Poland. He is an important figure, as evidenced by the fact that in 2013 he received the "Bene Merito" Honorary Award granted by Poland's Minister of Foreign Affairs to Polish citizens and citizens of foreign countries for activities contributing to Poland's international stature. Apart from composing for various film genres (short films, feature films, and documentaries), Beffa's work also includes newly composed music for old silent movies, including *Romeo e Giulietta*, directed by Ugo Falena (1912, 2003), *Broken Blossoms,* directed by D. W Griffith (1919, 2009), and *Le Double Amour*, directed by Jean Epstein (1925, 2014). His music for Stéphane Breton's experimental documentary films is also compelling.

Optic Fibers and Staves

The youngest generation of film music composers operates within the reality of Poland's membership of the European Union. These artists are highly mobile and maintain close contacts with Polish cinema (or, more broadly understood, Polish musical culture). This is the case of Antoni Komasa Łazarkiewicz (b. 1980) and Karol Obara (b. 1978), both active in Germany since 2007. Łazarkiewicz stems from a family with rich film traditions, to which he owes his early debut. In 1995, at the age of fifteen, he composed the music for the TV show *Atmosphere* [*Klimaty*] directed by Magdalena Łazarkiewicz, who is also the composer's mother. Currently, he is one of the most recognizable artists of the young generation. He has been acclaimed for the music to the film *In Darkness* (2011), which was awarded the "Eagle" Polish Film Award in 2012, and his soundtrack to the series *Burning Bush* [*Hořící keř*] (2013), which received awards from the Czech Academy of Film and Television Arts and Czech Film Critics. Łazarkiewicz has recently composed music for feature films such as *City of 44* [*Miasto 44*] (2014), *Convoy* [*Konwój*] (2016), and *Spoor* [*Pokot*] (2017). Among his foreign films, next to *The Burning Bush*, we should mention his attempt to confront Krzysztof Komeda's legacy in the series *Rosemary's Baby* (2014).

Karol Obara, who lives in Stuttgart, has written music for several short films, including the futuristic *Kryo* (2015). In 2016 his music debuted on the big screen in the German film *Immigration Game*. Tomasz Opałka (b. 1983) chose a path similar to that taken by Kaczmarek, Korzeniowski, and Gliniak. Since 2012 he has been dividing his time between Warsaw and Los Angeles. Opałka's film music is currently only complementary to his concert career, however. Nonetheless, a considerable number of compositions for short films, including animations and documentaries, and feature films, offer a good prognosis for his future development. Good examples of Opałka's recent film work include such films as *The Lumberjack* [*Drwal*] (2011), directed by Paweł Dębski, *Bridging Urban America* (2016), directed by Basia and Leonard Myszyński, *Hugo* (2017), and *Signs* [*Znaki*] (2018), both directed by Wojciech Klimala.

Despite the fact that film music usually constitutes only a portion of the works of Polish composers in exile, the aforementioned names, of which there are nearly forty, create a significant group of artists. Much more can be written about all of them. Such factors as their backgrounds, education, initial professional experiences, and reasons for emigration should all be taken into account when trying to interpret their film music. For most of these composers, the emigration experience proved to be successful professionally, as evidenced by the recognition of their local communities and the awards they have received.

Of course, one should not forget about the changing social and economic conditions faced by artists active in the twentieth century. Until the 1960s, composers migrating to Hollywood found employment within the structures of the studio system, working for film studios with huge budgets. Their work for film seems impressive today, but it should be remembered that they (with the exception of Bronislaw Kaper, Henryk Wars, and Victor Young, perhaps) had relatively little influence on the final shape of a film's music, which was the result of a collaborative effort. Composers operating after the collapse of the studio system gained more individual creative opportunities, but these always had to fit within the framework of a specific director's vision. Those for whom working in such a system did not fulfill their vision of the "American dream" migrated to other geographical regions. Polish filmmakers have been quite successful in German, British, French, Russian, Czech, Argentinian, and Israeli cinematography, often finding satisfaction in independent film production.

One might risk stating that for contemporary filmmakers, the traditional meaning of the notion of emigration is blurred. Open borders and the freedom of working in Europe, the rapid development of digital media, and better equipment and software for making music have opened up new possibilities for composers. In the global world, the virtual cooperation of a Polish composer with a foreign director is not a problem; quite the contrary, it even has a chance to become the norm.

Grzegorz Piotrowski

Particular Existences: Jazz and Popular Music Composers

With regard to jazz and popular musicians,[146] the phenomenon of emigration seems particularly blurred. If music is considered a "wandering" profession, then representatives of the musical entertainment community appear to be its most mobile members. There are several reasons for this. The market for jazz and pop music, which is largely dependent on financial considerations, distribution channels (concert agencies, record companies, etc.), and music technology, has always been much more global, flexible, and open than the market for so-called serious (classical) music, which is entangled in dependencies on the patronage of governments, institutions (often public), and agencies of musical authority, such as orchestras, opera houses, music critics, musicologists, and music educators. One of the manifestations of the flexibility of popular music is its hybridization,[147] or the opening of sonic art to various "influences and flows," including the migrating, creative human element. Moreover, neoliberal ideology,[148] the expansion of digital technologies, and communication developments (more traditionally understood in the reality of a "united" world) make artists and everyone related to the music business independent of the need to exist in the "here and now," especially in the sense of "for good." This possibility and, at the same time, the awareness of the facile shaping of one's own career and private life significantly impact musicians' identities. As a result, emigration becomes, at least mentally, easier to familiarize and internalize, and, as a phenomenon and condition, perhaps even fades from thought.

Red Poppies at Green Dolphin Street

The first significant waves of Polish emigration related to jazz[149] and popular music in the twentieth century are connected to the political reality of the 1930s and also that of the following decades, including World War II and its Nazi and Soviet occupations as well as the ramifications of these after 1945. As Krystian Brodacki aptly notes,[150] Bronisław Kaper (1902–1983) opened the wave. After studying at Warsaw Conservatory, he left for Germany, from where, like many other Jewish artists, he emigrated in 1933 after Hitler came to power, severing his successful cooperation with German cinematography. He lived for a short time in France and later settled in the United States, where he achieved great success as a film composer associated with the Metro-Goldwyn-Mayer company. Moreover, many of Kaper's songs crossed the boundaries of cinema to become jazz standards, such as *On Green Dolphin Street* (1947, with lyrics by Ned Washington) or *Invitation* (1944, 1952, lyrics by Paul Francis Webster). The fate of Henryk Wars (1902–1977) was to some extent similar, but different in certain ways as well. He did not return to Poland from his wartime exile, probably due to fear of sharing the same fate as other members of Anders' Army.[151] Wars had a decidedly different start in Hollywood than Kaper; eventually he joined the ranks of B-grade film music composers,[152] even though he was also an author of songs performed, among others, by Doris Day, Brenda Lee, and Margaret Whiting (the latter recorded Wars's greatest international hit, *Over and Over and Over*).[153] Other members of Anders' Army included Jerzy Petersburski (1897–1979) and Alfred Schütz (1910–1999), who collaborated with Wars. They both settled in South America. Petersburski, one of the greatest songwriters in the interwar period, spent more than twenty years in Argentina; he worked as a conductor at the Teatro El Nacional in Buenos Aires and cooperated with Radio El Mundo. He also composed songs and eventually returned to Poland in 1967. Schütz, famous for his song *Red Poppies on Monte Cassino* [*Czerwone maki na Monte Cassino*], worked in the revues of São Paulo and Rio de Janeiro; in 1961 he settled in Munich, where he became a regular contributor to Polish Radio Free Europe.

The emigration biographies of Kaper, Wars, Schütz, and Petersburski can be interpreted as attempts to assimilate and redevelop working life in new conditions. It must, of course, be assumed that Petersburski's return to Poland was connected to his private life: the death of his wife and his new marriage, which, after the birth of his son in 1969, sealed his decision to remain in his homeland. But that is only one side of the story. The emigration careers of Petersburski as well as Schütz and Wars—even though they didn't lack in significant achievements—were not the same as Kaper's. In the case of Kaper and Wars, this was related not only to the place of emigration—a music market other than in Hollywood—but also to the artists' creative temperament and probably to the relative scale of their success. Kaper, like Kurt Weill or Erich Wolfgang Korngold, managed to assimilate both a new musical language and a new way of working in the music business. He created a synthesis of American elements with his own individual style, which allowed him to become an American composer in the full sense of the word. According to Iwona Sowińska, as far as Wars is concerned, "the ingenuity of his pre-war hits...disappeared [in Hollywood] without a trace."[154] In the case of Petersburski, on the other hand, although several of his songs gained worldwide popularity (for example, *Tango Milonga*), he made no changes in compositional style that were significant enough to allow him to fully assimilate or function in the world. In this situation, the status of the "converted classic songwriter" in Poland would be attractive for the composer. However, Schütz's decision to work for Radio Free Europe—a declaration of a political and ethical nature—meant losing official contact with his homeland.

Other Ways

Of course, there were also other paths to emigration, among them one in which artistic activity abroad was restricted mainly to the Polish diaspora; this was related to a myth of the "real" Poland (the one existing in exile) being a "besieged fortress abandoned by the Allies." This type of emigration occurred with Władysław Daniłowski (1902–2000; known in the United States as Walter Dan), who was the founder of Dan's Choir [Chór Dana],[155] and many artists associated with the Polish Hearth Club in London. Whether these men made internal, autonomous decisions, dictated, for example, by patriotism and a sense of mission, or they were instead forced by their external circumstances and the realities of life in foreign countries is difficult to determine. Later, in the 1960s, a wave of emigration occurred that was connected to the lifting of the Iron Curtain and the opening of certain professional prospects in the West. These were initiated by contracts established by Polish musicians in Scandinavia,[156] as well as by radio concerts and occasional performances at festivals or at the Olympia in Paris (which drew the world's attention to Ewa Demarczyk, Violetta Villas, and Czesław Niemen).

However, these emigrations sometimes forced one's identity (including the artistic one) to operate flexibly, as in the case of Michaj Burano (b. 1944, in the West he performed as John Mike Arlow),[157] which ultimately ended in professional failure. Maciej Kossowski (b. 1937) and, a little later, Bernard Kawka (b. 1943, he used the name Kafka in the United States), among others, left Poland at the same time. After the infamous events of 1968 (when an anti-Semitic campaign was launched by the authorities of the Polish People's Republic), the "classic" Zygmunt Karasiński (1898–1973) also left.[158]

An Artist Cannot Create Without Freedom

Now we face the problems of motivation and the consequences associated with decisions to emigrate, which prompt all kinds of "why?" and "what for?" questions. This is a difficult area. In the modernist formation of Western culture, the condition of an emigrant is created (in the case of Poles and the "Polish spirit") by an overly sensitive sheen of existential choices and ethical burdens. During the period of the mature Polish People's Republic, these values were associated with, for example, the extremes of freedom and material affluence or dissent and conformity, which from internal (Polish) and external (emigration) perspectives appear to be strongly polarized. In the case of classical music composers (such as Andrzej Panufnik), the motivation of freedom ("an artist cannot create without freedom") emerged automatically, discreetly obscuring all other needs and conditions. In the case of musicians representing light (and carefree?) music, the opposite is true—here it was and is easier to raise suspicions or even accusations concerning a (reprehensible?) desire for career and money, or an "easy life."

As we shuffle cultural stereotypes, the image shifts and depends on one's point of view. During the Communist era, it might have seemed conformist both to remain in the country as well as to choose the fate of an emigrant (the *Diaries* of renowned Polish poet and writer Jarosław Iwaszkiewicz are a clear testimony to such hesitations and evaluations). Probably for these reasons, émigré artists sometimes decided to stay silent or, in contrast, emphasized the necessity of choosing freedom. This issue is related to the construction of identity—a category always strongly entangled in stereotypes and rhetorical strategies. Thus, Aneta Norek-Skrycka notes about Zbigniew Seifert (1946–1979): "Zbyszek was never an expatriate. He signed contracts, on the basis of which he received legal papers entitling him to stay abroad, come to Poland, and return to Germany."[159] In turn, Tomasz Stańko (1942–2018) declared: "I am a free man. All my life I have been alone and free. Therefore, why should I not exercise my freedom?"[160]

I Love Poland

Two factors determining the mobility of jazz and pop musicians in the People's Republic of Poland are worth noting. The first one concerns limitations in travel and opportunities for international activity, the latter of which was related, among other things, to rules established by Pagart, the Polish Artistic Agency. Since 1957 this agency had not only made decisions concerning the foreign careers of Polish artists, but also played a negative role through the implementation of top-down censorship of specific names, as well as through all kinds of personal antipathies and backstage plots, which resulted in offers of tours for some artists being set aside.[161] Another important factor was a natural desire to stay in touch with European and world music. One can risk claiming that pop and jazz music, to a much greater extent than classical music, requires a live, direct contact among musicians—they simply need to exchange, play together, and surround themselves with sounds. As Adam Makowicz (b. 1940) said about his American experiences, "I am closer to real jazz than when I lived in Poland."[162]

Michał Urbaniak (b. 1943) concurred:

> I did not miss Europe, not Stockholm or Paris...but I dreamed of New York all the time....I am not ashamed to admit it. A soldier, politician, or some other son of a bitch, who supposedly did everything for Poland and then emigrated for money, may be ashamed. I was a jazz musician and wanted to emigrate for jazz. Since America is the cradle of jazz, I, a jazzman, have the right to treat it as a homeland. And this is how I still treat it today. I wasn't born a January insurgent or any other hero, so I had to shake off my Polishness. And I love Poland as well, but that is another matter. I have American and Polish citizenship.[163]

What also matters is that "it takes five or ten years of playing any new kind of music in the United States before it can finally be accepted in Europe, which is conceited, airtight, and waterproof, and still thinks that it knows better."[164] This resonates with Seifert's words, who dreamed of going to the United States and, as he wrote from Dortmund to his family in Poland in 1976, "We are fed up with this 'beautiful' country, we need changes, new impulses. Here, we are increasingly annoyed by people's mentality, language, and by this whole thing about ordering reality down to the last pebble!"[165]

The great émigré stars of the 1970s (Urbaniak, Urszula Dudziak, Seifert, and Makowicz) were in some way prepared for a different type of impactful entry into the prestigious European jazz scene. "We were like kings," as Stańko described the situation of Polish jazz musicians in the 1970s.[166] Indeed, this period can be considered a *tour de force* of Polish jazz, which had been preceded by a phase of *Sturm und Drang* (1969–1973) that had been apparent at many prestigious events, especially those in the Federal Republic of Germany and Scandinavia, and also in projects such as the album *We'll Remember Komeda*, prepared in 1973 on the initiative of Joachim-Ernst Berendt, who promoted many Polish jazzmen. This situation is illustrated best by Seifert's path, who, before he moved to Darmstadt in 1973, achieved recognition as a member of Tomasz Stańko's quintet (starting with his first foreign performance at the Berliner Jazztage in 1970).[167] He continued to develop, eventually recording his own album *Solo Violin* and performing at the Monterey Jazz Festival (both in 1976). He also was asked to take over the violin class at Berklee College of Music and signed a recording contract with the Capitol label in the United States. Thus, his career was built step by step. At the same time, he remained in close contact with inspiring musicians (such as Stańko did with Edward Vesala and later Cecil Taylor), with new musical styles, and even with technology (this was also important for Dudziak's development and crystallization of her style and vocal techniques).[168]

Thus—let's repeat—perhaps the paradoxical ability to assimilate external influences, to catch the wave, and at the same time to expose one's own original and fascinating individuality, to be "alien" but also "familiar," paved the way for artists to grow in a transnational social, aesthetic, and cultural context. A good example is Anna Prucnal (b. 1940), an artist gifted with phenomenal vocal, technical, and interpretative capabilities (she often inspired and co-created songs written for her by such renowned artists as Oswald d'Andréa and Francis Lai), who was the only Polish woman besides Basia Trzetrzelewska (b. 1954) to achieve worldwide success as a singer. In the 1960s she played leading roles in East German films and studied with Walter Felsenstein at Berlin's Komische Oper. After marrying French director and poet Jean Mailland and leaving Poland in 1970, she became successful in avant-garde operas and drama productions staged at the Avignon Festival, among other places; she also appeared in films by Federico Fellini, Dušan Makavejev, and Michel Deville.[169] All of these experiences allowed her to create a unique singing style[170] associated with the French chanson tradition, but at the same time exceeding it. She enjoyed great success not only in France, but also in Canada, Switzerland, and Japan, marked by the recording of several albums for the RCA label.

From Poland, Back to Poland (and the World)

In a sense, the emigration of later generations of artists seems similar: this group includes Basia Trzetrzelewska, who left Poland in the late Gierek era (1979), Władysław (Vladislav) Sendecki, who left the country during the "Carnival of Solidarity," (1980–1981) and—emigrating at the end of the Polish People's Republic—Grażyna Auguścik and Witold Szczurek (in the West, known as Vitold Rek). All of them were successful in Poland or at least active on its professional music scene. However, we can assume they all experienced some disappointment with Poland as well as a lack of wider developmental opportunities. As Sendecki wrote (he was expelled from the Academy of Music in Katowice for his involvement with Solidarity):

> I went to a Solidarity meeting at the PSJ [Polish Jazz Association]. I look, and here, behind the green table I saw the same people who did anything to have an easy life in the Polish People's Republic....I was lost. I was overwhelmed by hopelessness and apathy.[171]

In the modern jazz environment, this discouragement was also linked to Poland's difficult economic situation[172] as well as to the growing gap between the mainstream and the young generation. Basia, Sendecki, Auguścik, and Rek, like the aforementioned Prucnal, have developed significantly in exile; they have assimilated their new cultures and communities, but at the same time they have discovered the depths of their own selves. They have found that their possibilities could develop properly only in the transnational melting pot of the West. In the case of Auguścik, for example, jazz studies at the Berklee College of Music certainly became a catalyst, while in the case of Basia, a journey through different musical experiences as a background vocalist provided an opportunity to become an expert in vocal harmony and in the borderline area between pop and smooth jazz.

The meandering of careers of such artists as Stańko and Zbigniew Namysłowski (b. 1939), who lived for two years in the United States in the late 1970s, or others who made various "returns to Poland after many years"[173] show how difficult it is to indicate a dividing line between true emigration and international professional activity. Sometimes, the dynamics of such careers are dependent more on the fluctuations of professional life, which are entangled in various areas and contacts between people and cultures. At times, the dynamics of such careers rely more on a fluctuation of work-related activities, entangled in various areas and contacts between people and cultures, and sometimes it depends on individual qualities, perhaps on a type of personality that is afraid to settle down. It may, therefore, be the case of the market, of personal temperament, or various other factors. Contemporary biographies of such artists as Pati Yang (b. 1980), Julia Marcell (b. 1982), and Greg Szlapczyński (b. 1971) prove that a musician in the reality of an "open" world can work anywhere there is demand for their art. Being an artist can be seen as a curse, a condemnation to eternal wandering, in which one becomes their own homeland. As Stańko said, "No association, no group, no patriotism, only PE. I am Polish, I was born here, this is my language, and I feel a deep connection to this land, but in general, I feel that I am Tomasz Stańko. A Particular Existence."[174]

KRZYSZTOF KOMEDA
1931-1969

Piotr Matla

Enclaves of Young Polish Jazz

When we discuss the subject of young Polish jazz musicians working outside of Poland, it is difficult to talk about emigration per se, because artists often change places of residence. They live and work where they have opportunities to create and earn, then go to another place that will provide better conditions and ensure inspiration for creative work, searching for new sounds, new colors, and cooperation with other artists. Still, they do not break off ties with their colleagues in Poland. This sort of migration is prompted by a need for creative development, rather than the desire to escape something. It has a completely different meaning than in the twentieth century, during the era of the Communist regime and its closed borders.

Poland's accession to the European Union on May 1, 2004 opened frontiers for Polish artists. Restrictions on movement and earning money internationally disappeared. This resulted in the increased mobility of Polish artists, including jazz musicians. Escape from political and cultural limitations ceased to be motivating factors for changing residences. However, the economic aspect of migration still remains an important factor, often connected to the possibility of collaboration with foreign colleagues. In the current century, yet another reason could be added to this list—the opportunity for artistic development and education at foreign universities. Polish musicians had studied at American and European academies in the twentieth century, but it was only after Poland joined the European Union that opportunities at international schools became widely available, thanks to numerous scholarship programs.

Many of today's 30-year-olds embarked on journeys to Denmark, the Netherlands, and Germany in order to study according to a different model than that offered by Polish universities. Denmark has become a favorite among young jazz musicians. At one point, the Rhythmic Music Conservatory in Copenhagen had so many Polish students that the music community started to call the Danish capital "the most dynamic Polish jazz center."[175] The list of students and graduates of this school over just one decade includes Franciszek Pośpieszalski, Marek and Maciej Kądziela, Jędrzej Łagodziński, Kuba Więcek, Artur Tuźnik, Szymon "Pimpon" Gąsiorek, Anna Rybacka, Tomasz Licak, Radek Wośko, Kamil Piotrowicz, Grzegorz Tarwid, and many others. Some of these young artists returned to Poland after their studies, others moved on to different parts of the world. A large group of Polish jazz musicians continues to develop their careers in Denmark.

Denmark and Germany

Artur Tuźnik is a Polish pianist and composer who, after graduating from the Rhythmic Music Conservatory and completing the prestigious "soloist class" postgraduate program at the same university, decided to settle down in Denmark. He is still active on the Polish jazz scene and has performed with such renowned names as Tomasz Stańko and Piotr Wojtasik. He debuted on the international jazz circuit with the *Quintet* album, which featured Tomasz Licak and Anders Mogensen in addition to Tuźnik. The album, released by the Danish label BlackOut in 2011, was critically acclaimed as an "excellent contemporary record and a real must listen," while Tuźnik was described as an unusually talented improviser. He is often invited to cooperate as a sideman with his Polish colleagues and others, although he has concentrated on his own work for quite a while. In 2016, together with his Danish colleagues Nils Davidsen and Jakob Høier, he released the album *Artur Tuźnik Trio*, which served to confirm his importance on the international jazz and improvised music scene. Tuźnik doesn't distance himself from his Polish roots; his music is clearly inspired by folk music, which he creatively combines with Scandinavian jazz traditions. As he has said, he received the highest possible Danish education in jazz and now he is dedicating himself to studying classical music.[176] He tries to avoid defining his music. In fact, he would willingly call his current pieces "contemporary music by Artur Tuźnik." Working in Denmark has allowed him to compose without sticking to any specific genre. Although he has not released an album for several years, he is involved in numerous projects. In 2018, commissioned by Copenhagen Jazz Festival, he created music for a nonet. During the same festival, he performed his compositions together with Irek Wojtczak, the Atom String Quartet, and Danish musicians (double bass player Joel Illerhag and percussionist Simon Olderskog Albertsen).

Copenhagen has also become the new home of Polish percussionist and composer Radosław Wośko. After completing his medical studies in Szczecin, he decided to reorganize his life. He moved to Denmark and began studying at The Academy of Music & Dramatic Arts in Odense to learn the principles of jazz and improvised music. As it turned out, this was a great decision. Wośko has taken part in numerous projects, both as a sideman and leader. He has performed and recorded in Poland, Denmark, Germany, the United States, Canada, Great Britain, Norway, Ghana, Benin, Kenya, and Tanzania. He has also worked with Stańko and guitarists Gilad Hekselman and Lionel Loueke. Wośko is active in the Danish and Polish jazz scenes, although he has not abandoned his academic plans, either. For his Ph.D., he chose to examine how contemporary music can be combined with modern jazz percussion. Wośko is also a member of The Beat Freaks band founded by Michał Starkiewicz; other members are graduates of the same Danish university: saxophonist Tomasz Licak and bassist Paweł Grzesiuk. In 2015, Wośko recorded the album *Atlantic* with his band, the Radek Wośko Atlantic Quartet. Guitarist Gilad Hekselman, pianist Søren Gemmer, and Polish bassist Mariusz Praśniewski also performed on this recording. It is actually a kind of monographic album because, with the exception of the song *Man of The Light* by Zbigniew Seifert, it contains only Wośko's pieces, which combine the melancholy of Scandinavian jazz and the emotionality of Slavic roots with the energy of downtown New York.

When writing about Copenhagen, one must not forget Jędrzej Łagodziński, a Polish saxophonist and composer. He started playing late, at the age of 22, when he was a sociology student. He then studied at the Kraków School of Jazz and Contemporary Music. However, inspired by guitarist Marek Kądziela, he stopped those courses and left for Denmark. After graduation, he stayed there but did not sever contacts with Poland; in fact, he often performs and records with his Polish colleagues. His own project, the LOVE sextet, is extremely important to him. What is characteristic of his music is not complicated phrases and formal intricacies, but the expressions and emotions that he evokes in the audience. In Copenhagen, Łagodziński, together with drummer Szymon Gąsiorek and double bass player Franciszek Pośpieszalski, created a democratic jazz trio (which means that each

musician participated equally in decision-making) entitled The Love And Beauty Seekers, which released the album *Żar* in 2016.

Szymon "Pimpon" Gąsiorek is another Polish emigrant living in Copenhagen. He has extraordinary creativity and energy, finding time to compose, record, perform, and even organize a festival in his hometown of Wschowa. Gąsiorek is also the leader of the Polish-Danish-Norwegian nonet called the Pimpono Ensemble, which is known for its unusual instrumentation: a trumpet, three double basses, bass tuba, guitar, baritone and alto saxophones, and percussion. The musicians describe their music as a combination of punk energy, free improvisation, and experimentation with beautiful nostalgic melodies and the noise-ish sound of a jazz orchestra. Friends say that Gąsiorek does not accept any compromises and acts deliberately. He knows perfectly well what effect he wants to achieve, although he also grants great freedom to the artists performing with him. This freedom is manifested, among other things, in the fact that Gąsiorek avoids classic musical notation, preferring to use a graphic style that has icons and colors, which allows other musicians more freedom of interpretation. He looks for non-obvious sounds and prepares his own instrument with this in mind. With his expressive musical language, his album *Hope Love Peace Faith* immediately stood out on the Scandinavian avant-garde scene. Certainly, Gąsiorek is the most colorful character on the Polish-Danish avant-garde jazz scene. Unfortunately, he is not appreciated yet in Poland.

An extraordinary figure of the Polish jazz scene in Denmark is Ania Rybacka, a singer, composer, and songwriter, who does not limit herself exclusively to jazz music. She left for Scandinavia after graduating with a degree in psychology (which included studies related to jazz) from Warsaw's University of Social Sciences and Humanities. After studying at the Rhythmic Music Conservatory, she decided to stay in Copenhagen. She has performed with world-class artists such as Adam Rudolph, Kresten Osgood, Anders Filipsen, Stefan Pasborg, and Frederik Lundin, as well as the Odense Symphony Orchestra and the Danish Radio Orchestra. Due to her extraordinary musical expression and creativity, she has received awards at competitions in Poland, Finland, Germany, and Turkey. She can enchant with her music and with her main instrument, her voice. In her case it is difficult to talk about one style or one voice. She has a talent for storytelling and impersonating different characters in her singing. This caused problems during her studies, because her teachers wanted her to develop a characteristic and recognizable style instead of exhibiting such versatility. Today, however, we can be certain that stylistic openness and variety is actually her trademark and her greatest asset.

Avant-garde composer and pianist Sebastian Zawadzki also lives in Copenhagen. He started his musical career in Toruń, then moved to Denmark, where he studied at the Rhythmic Music Conservatory. He began in the field of acoustic jazz, but has gradually moved towards a combination of jazz and expressive means taken from other musical genres, especially classical music. Currently he creates experimental music that is not easy to classify; it combines contemporary classical music with synthesizers and jazz improvisation. Zawadzki's first album in this style was *Between the Dusk of a Summer Night* (2017), inspired by the poetry of William Ernest Henley, where he combines the sounds of a symphony orchestra with electronics, all interspersed with his piano improvisations.

Another Polish émigré jazz musician is percussionist Kuba Gudz. While still a student at the Jazz Institute in Berlin, he became involved in numerous artistic projects in Germany and decided to stay abroad. "I had a job here. While still a student I played a lot of free, soul, and hip-hop. I settled here in this diverse musical scene and stayed for good," says Gudz.[177] He has maintained professional contacts with his Polish colleagues, playing in projects launched by Marek Konarski and Michał Martyniuk. His example clearly shows that nowadays distance is not an obstacle to artistic cooperation.

Denmark and Germany are not the only destinations for young Polish jazz musicians. Many still choose America. The opportunity to learn from the greatest jazz stars is still seen as a great opportunity. Idols previously known only from recordings become their teachers and later their artistic partners, with whom they jam and record. Many young jazz musicians have emphasized that it was a big surprise for them to discover that these great artists turn out to be ordinary people with whom one can simply chat and work together.

Other Continents

In 2005, the outstanding Polish guitarist and composer Rafał Sarnecki left Warsaw for New York. He is another musician with a non-musical education, having studied physics at Warsaw University. His love of physics eventually gave way to his passion for music (he had begun taking piano lessons at the age of eight). In the United States, Sarnecki took classes at the New School in Manhattan. Contact with American musicians changed his understanding of rhythm and, consequently, his composing. His own compositions from that period were collected on his debut album, *Songs From a New Place*, which tells an extraordinary story about an immigrant's life. Even though he had access to many American artists, while in New York City he invited his Polish colleagues (pianist Paweł Kaczmarczyk, bassist Wojciech Pulcin, and percussionist Łukasz Żyta) to work on this album, which was released in Poland in 2008. Only for his third album, *Cat's Dream*, released in 2014, did he decide to record with his own American band, with whom he had played for several years. In addition to Sarnecki, the band consisted of pianist Glenn Zaleski, saxophonist Lucas Pino, bassist Rick Rosato, and percussionist Colin Stranahan. The vocals were provided by Bogna Kicińska, whose voice was treated as another instrument. In 2018 Sarnecki recorded a new album called *Climbing Trees* with the same musicians. Polish audiences could hear it, since it came with the August 2018 issue of *Jazz Forum*. Sarnecki has returned to Warsaw for family reasons, so there is always a chance that Poles can admire his music during live performances.

One of the farthest journeys among Polish jazz musicians was undertaken by saxophonist and clarinetist Kuba Skowroński. Since 2018 he has been living in Indonesia on the island of Bali. He graduated from the Academy of Music in Katowice, then studied at the Berlin Jazz Institute. A versatile musician, he is open to different sounds and looks for new means of artistic expression. This has led to him being warmly received among Indonesian musicians, which in turn has resulted in recordings with drummer Sandy Winarta and pianist

David Manuhutu as well as performances at Indonesian jazz festivals. He records and performs with Indonesian musicians such as Indra Lesmana, Eva Celia Lesmana, Nita Aartsen, Ade Irawan, Yuri Mahatma, and Koko Harsoe; he also teaches music. In his case, the creative possibilities opened to him by the Indonesian music scene were complemented by love, his reason to remain there.

Pianist and composer Michał Martyniuk, a native of Szczecin, has lived in New Zealand for twelve years. He graduated with a degree in jazz performance from Auckland University and has played with many famous artists from Australia and New Zealand, including Tama Wipara, Lewis McCallum, Sola Rosa, Batucada Sound Machine, and Maisey Rika. Since 2014, Martyniuk has been a member of world-famous saxophonist Nathan Haines's group. Martyniuk is a versatile artist who, without giving up on perfecting his jazz technique, has become one of the most active artists on the New Zealand music scene. Working with leading performers from Auckland, he has already recorded his own jazz-club-electronic album, *After 'Ours.* In 2018 his jazz album *Nothing to Prove* was released, this time recorded not in New Zealand but in the Cavatina studio in Bielsko-Biała. Martyniuk was accompanied on this recording by the most prominent representatives of young Polish jazz, with whom he had previously toured extensively in Poland and Ukraine: Bartek Chojnacki, double bass; Skowroński, saxophone; Kuba Mizeracki, guitar; and Kuba Gudz, percussion.

***

Young Polish jazz musicians who have studied abroad, both those who remained abroad for good and those who returned, often collaborate in various projects. Regardless of where they were educated, they join a kind of community, because their approach to music is different than that of their colleagues educated in Poland. They claim that this has happened because international schools discovered what they had to offer: sensitivity, creative thinking, and expression. They were subjects of education, not material to be shaped by teachers. In them, as well as in their music, there is an elusive element that distinguishes them from other artists on the Polish jazz scene.

KNIFE IN THE WATER
1962 directed by ROMAN POLAŃSKI
Music composed by KRZYSZTOF KOMEDA

Jacek Kurek

Rock Journeys

Tracing the émigré lives and creative activities of Polish rock musicians is not an easy task. The subject is extensive and difficult to manage, demanding insightful, precise, time-consuming, and methodical research. It is also difficult to distinguish and categorize "strictly rock" pieces from within the extensive activities of numerous Polish musicians. It should also be remembered that when we say rock, we don't mean only musicians, but also sound engineers, cover designers, music producers, concert organizers, club owners, and last but not least, the audience. Therefore, below we can offer only a few clues for the subject indicated in the headline, as thorough research is still needed. Also, I will focus on musicians, without singling out composers, as in the world of rock music, a composer is most often also a performer. Moreover, my goal here is to outline the phenomenon of the emigration paths of Polish rock musicians, without limiting the subject only to the creators of specific songs.

Few Polish artists who have decided to leave the country have managed to be more successful than jazz artists such as Michał Urbaniak and Urszula Dudziak, smooth jazz/pop singer Basia Trzetrzelewska, and rock (with a nod towards jazz-rock) artist Paweł "Mąciwoda" Jastrzębski, who was a member of the Scorpions band and a collaborator with Pete Townshend, Ian Paice, Chicago bluesmen, and Polish rock and jazz stars TSA and Walk Away. In the broadly understood pop and pop-rock scene, Jerzy Grunwald has also achieved some success, mainly in Asia. It is also possible to include Polish graphic designers, specializing in the music industry, such as the author of covers, Rosław Szaybo and an artist of Polish origins, Jo Mirowski.

Artists who have recorded in the United States include Zbigniew Bernolak and Katarzyna Sobczyk and, in Germany, Karin Stanek. Among those who performed abroad we can mention Włodzimierz Wander (who owned a music club in the United States), Piotr Janczerski, Helena Majdaniec, Romuald Czystaw,[178] Joachim Rzychoń, Józef Hajdasz, and Stan Borys. After the transformations of 1989, many of them returned to Poland and some continued to perform. The generation younger than these big-beat musicians is active outside Poland as well. The percussionist with Mech and Lady Pank, Andrzej Dylewski, lives in the United States, where he owns a music studio and still performs in the Dylewski & Taylor Band. His bandmate, Robert Milewski (Robert Millord, Robert Lor), is also an active musician. Alan Sors "Baster," known from such bands as Turbo and Bajm, joined the Chicago band Mr. Blotto.[179] Izabela Trojanowska, popular in the first half of the 1980s thanks to her albums *Iza* and *Systems* [*Układy*] as well as her collaboration with Budka Suflera and Stalowy Bagaż, moved with her husband to West Berlin in 1987. In 1991, she released an album *Izabela Trojanowska* (*Independence*),[180] recorded with Western musicians and intended for the international market, although it did not meet with significant success. Guitarist Ryszard Sygitowicz, who gained popularity thanks to his first two albums with Perfect, also performed in the United States. These are only a few examples.

The leader of Scalds [Skaldowie], Andrzej Zieliński, who settled in the United States after martial law was declared in Poland, recalled:

> A decision to stay in the United States was made after dealing with many internal dilemmas. It was a difficult choice; however, I was aware that there was no interesting life for artists in my home country, where art was pushed to the background. In Poland I had already achieved everything an artist can dream of: awards at festivals, victories in competitions, Golden Records, and prestige. Besides, I have always wanted to get to know the country that is the cradle of jazz and rock. I wanted to see this music up close, to get to know its roots and perform with American musicians.[181]

At Construction Sites, in Taxis and Trucks

Although the individual fates of musical emigrants are diverse, it is obvious that a recurring theme in their biographies concerns their struggles to make a living as a musician. Many were forced to seek employment in non-artistic fields. For example, Krzysztof Klenczon was a taxi driver, Krzysztof Krawczyk replaced roofs, Jerzy Hryniewicz ran a restaurant, and Paweł Mścisławski and Janusz Maślak decided to become truck drivers. Wojciech Sowula, who was the vocalist of Turbo for a short time in 1980, worked as a transport employee in France. Elżbieta Mielczarek lives in Germany and makes a living from practicing acupuncture and Chinese medicine, although she also still performs. The members of the band Ira, while in the United States, did not leave the music field even when they worked as builders; Artur Gadowski was a jeweler by profession, Wojciech Owczarek a teletransmission equipment fitter, sometimes also a glass technician, and Piotr Sujka a gardener. Even the aforementioned Urszula Dudziak, having already achieved significant artistic success, found herself, after parting with her husband Michał Urbaniak, employed (thanks to a friend) by a company where she could only long for music while sitting behind a computer. Luckily for herself and her fans, she only worked there for a short time.[182]

Beginning with Big Beat

The origins of Polish rock (at first rock 'n' roll, enigmatically called "mocne uderzenie" in Polish, or even more strangely, big beat in English) can be found in the Rhythm and Blues band. One symbolic date is March 24, 1959, which marked the first of the group's 39 concerts. Music played by Bill Haley, Buddy Holly, Little Richard, Elvis Presley, and others soon reached the Polish People's Republic, following jazz, which in the rough conditions of the People's Republic of Poland had become a symbol or even a synonym for freedom.[183] When in 1955 Willis Conover's *Jazz Hour* and *Music USA* programs began to be broadcast on the *Voice of America*, such music could also be heard in Poland, albeit with an audio quality marred by radio crackles. At the second Jazz Festival in Sopot in 1957, American musician "Big" Bill Ramsey performed the first live rock 'n' roll concert in Poland.

Jazz, rock 'n' roll, and rock were treated with suspicion by state authorities, who saw many ideological dangers in them. After a concert on September 17, 1959 at the sold-out Torkat hall in Katowice, the authorities decided that Rhythm and Blues's popularity needed to be muted.[184] The band's musicians were forbidden from playing for audiences of more than 400 people. Without the possibility of earning enough money, Rhythm and Blues ceased to exist after only seven months.[185] Almost immediately, Franciszek Walicki directed his thoughts towards his next group, Red-Black, which he founded on July 23, 1960. His next bands were formed soon thereafter, at first in the Tri-Cities [Gdańsk, Gdynia, Sopot], where sailors willingly sold jazz and rock 'n' roll music records. In the 1950s, European port cities had become a kind of transfer hub for fans of music released on American vinyl records, which were often unavailable on the European continent, especially in the "people's democracies."

Thus, from the very beginning, jazz and rock music, associated in Poland with freedom, clearly directed the attention of performers to the West. Many of them were aware of the lack of perspective and the poor treatment of their profession in Poland, so whenever there was an opportunity to leave the country, they did, either by performing abroad or by accepting lucrative contracts for profitable, but not necessarily prestigious, positions as musicians on ships. They formed a social and professional group that enjoyed the privileges that could be obtained through the opportunities associated with concert tours. Through their more frequent contacts with the West, they became personally acquainted with the conditions of capitalist life and made the personal connections necessary for continuing their careers abroad. Thus, rock in Poland (as well as jazz) has obviously been linked to emigration and its related hopes for, if not world fame, then at least material wealth. The music itself was often negatively impacted by such decisions, however. Even if these artists continued to perform, they often abandoned their former ambitions, taking into account instead the so-called utilitarian dimension, which was purely (or at best primarily) commercial.

An important category of Polish musicians who left Poland includes those forced to do so by the anti-Semitic campaign of 1968. The aforementioned guitarist of Impulses [Impulsy], Aleksander Wołodarski, later a renowned Swedish architect, as well as Natan Walden, the guitarist of Teenagers [Nastolatki], both did so (and both also played with Watercolors [Akwarele]). Walden left not because he suffered persecution himself, but because his family experienced it. Beginning in 1969, he lived in New York, then moved to Sweden and remained an active musician in many groups.[186] Tomasz Jaśkiewicz recalled:

> I didn't know about the role of the Warsaw Gdańsk Railway Station [from where trains with people forced to leave the country departed in 1968]. I didn't know then that it had become a symbol. It was only from the descriptions and memories of the Jews who left Poland that I realized the scale of this hideous process. Sometime later I was in Copenhagen, in a crowded club where everyone spoke Polish. Then I realized that the Jews who were forced to leave were seeking familiar company there, since they did not yet feel at home in Scandinavia.[187]

It seems symbolic that members of the first rock 'n' roll band, Rhythm and Blues, were among the emigrants. Bogusław Wyrobek (d. 1997) had been discovered earlier by bandleader and talent scout Zygmunt Wichary. Wichary was a pianist who developed a rock 'n' roll section in his band; he also discovered Katarzyna Bovery. Wyrobek was banned from playing in Poland the same year as Wichary's tragic death, 1966.[188] So he decided to emigrate to Scandinavia, where he played in clubs with his wife Hanna Rek and the Hanna Rek Band. Another vocalist from Rhythm and Blues, Wasyl Micha, known as Michaj Burano (Romani for "Tempest"), also worked with the Red-Black and Blue-Black [Niebiesko-Czarni] bands. With the latter group, he visited France, where he performed in the Olympia theater in Paris. They were the first artists from behind the Iron Curtain to appear on this stage. Burano recorded for RCA as Steve Luca. In 1968 he returned to Poland, but after a short period with the band Burano and Leske Rom, he left for France again, where he performed under another pseudonym, John Mike Arlow. At the 1972 Tokyo Festival he was awarded second prize, ahead of Julio Iglesias. In 1975 he went to Los Angeles, where he established the Arlow Land label. His last performance in Poland was in 1986.

Many musicians associated with the rock 'n' roll bands of the 1960s left Poland. Krzysztof Klenczon, together with his wife Alicja and daughter Karolina, left for the United States in 1973, wishing, as he claimed, to live in a free country and offer a better future for his daughter. His decision to give up his career in Poland was facilitated by the knowledge that Alicja had family abroad, so they would not need to start from scratch. Years later, he admitted that ambition also played a role: "Here in Poland I reached the top, but there was only the ceiling above me."[189]

Labyrinth of Freedom

The 1960s–1980s brought the creation and development of many, sometimes only ephemeral, rock groups in Poland. These years were also marked by the constant struggle of artists with authorities, who tried to disavow their work and/or use it for propaganda purposes. Governmental agencies tried various methods to accomplish this, including interpretations of folk music (of often dubious artistic quality) on albums, banning concerts, printing slander in the press, and making it difficult to publish albums. They apparently were also robbed of their income by the state (concerts abroad were made possible only by going through Pagart, the state Polish Artistic Agency enterprise). Many times requests for passports were rejected, security officers were sent to accompany musicians on international tours, and songs were used without permission. Musicians were forced to perform during events celebrating the socialist system. The timing of album releases was also often delayed (e.g., due to the lack of materials for embossing or paper for printing covers).[190]

All this influenced many artists' decisions. Therefore, the attitude of the state authorities towards rock musicians should be seen as the primary reason for both the departure of these artists during the years of the Polish People's Republic and their return after 1990. When they left Poland, they were looking for freedom and improved living conditions. Tomasz Lipiński, the co-founder of Crisis Brigade [Brygada Kryzys], characterized the situation in Poland at the end of the 1970s:

> We were a generation without prospects, because life in the country was actually conditioned by one's political attitude. Any career involved belonging to a party or one of the regime's youth organizations. To do this, you didn't have to be a Communist, but a total opportunist, an ass. I did not sign up for this. You could either emigrate or live outside of society.[191]

It should be noted, however, that despite the difficulties piling up in the country, combined with the opportunities for career development abroad, many people did not take advantage of these possibilities, although Czesław Niemen and SBB, the most successful Polish rock musicians in the 1970s, did. It was their conscious artistic declaration, a choice they made knowing its consequences. Niemen performed and recorded in Italy, where he spent over a year, spread over several trips.[192] He released albums in Germany and the United States. However, he never paid attention to his international career. SBB drummer Jerzy Piotrowski left for the United States after the breakup of the group and an episode with the band Kombi. After years abroad, he returned to be enthusiastically welcomed on stage with both SBB and other rock bands. Not many people remember that even Irek Dudek, the founder of the Rawa Blues festival in Katowice, tried to work from a distance, in the Netherlands, for several years.

It is probably not possible to describe all the reasons that prompted musicians to leave Poland during the Communist era. Jerzy Grunwald admits that he left in order to improve his technique and develop his musical skills, but here political factors were not insignificant either. According to a decision made by the Ministry of Culture, in order to perform on stage he had to first take a state exam (even though he was already a recognized artist and a winner of contests held by the *Panorama* and *Na przełaj* weeklies in 1972). Grunwald never applied to take the exam. He left the country and his emigration paths led him to the United States, Singapore, and Sweden.

Is It Still Rock?

A separate issue is the aforementioned attempt to evaluate the emigration output of Polish rock artists. Unfortunately, many who had recorded significant albums in rock 'n' roll or strictly rock music in Poland gave this activity up after leaving the country. It often happened that Polish rock musicians in exile stopped playing rock when performing on ships or in hotels and clubs. Instead, they played music that was devoid of its original features and values, except that it was useful in the places where it was performed. It is hard to say whether it was a matter of necessity to earn money (the requirement of the moment) or, paradoxically, to give up such rock ideals as rebellion. How do you rebel in a situation of relative stability and freedom? Another thing is that, as Tomasz Jaśkiewicz wrote, as a rock guitarist he was not really a rebel, and he believed the same was true of many people from his surroundings. He recalled:

> I don't believe in the big-beat musicians who fought against the regime. At least not consciously. We didn't even call them 'commies'. Of course, you can somehow say what we did generally move towards freedom. Certainly, our

songs could be interpreted that way. The real rebellion against the system came much later, with the wave of punk, with Moscow [Moskwa], Axe [Siekiera], Deserter [Dezerter] and Proletariat [Proletaryat], but in '68 there were no such artistic objections, for various reasons.[193]

Certainly, connections between Poland and rock emigrants were of a diverse nature. Some of them (Krzysztof Krawczyk, Helena Majdaniec, Bogusław Wyrobek, Tadeusz Prokop,[194] Kazimierz Cwynar, Ryszard Sygitowicz, Roman Wojciechowski "Pazur," and Józef Hajdasz[195]) ultimately returned to Poland. Others, like Krzysztof Klenczon (d. 1981), remained abroad, longing for Poland and intending to return, but these plans were carried out only upon their deaths. Many artists, like Urszula Dudziak, Stan Borys, Andrzej Zieliński, Zbigniew Bernolak, and Janusz Hryniewicz have homes in Poland and abroad. Others remained abroad, while some, including the aforementioned Jerzy Grunwald, have announced their return, but have not moved yet.

Many contemporary Polish musicians work abroad while also maintaining contact with their homeland. In 2019, Silesian guitarist Czesław Kazimierek released his well-received album *Time* in England and he was working on his third album while this article was being written.[196] Jarmila Xymena Górna (Gorna), a graduate of the Karol Szymanowski Music Academy in Katowice, has lived in London since 1990. As a student, she established the folk band Savoy. In 2018, she released an album in England with an Aramaic title, *Aspaklaria*, inspired by Hebrew mysticism.[197]

Numerous Polish rock musicians live and work in Germany, including Jan Błędowski, the violinist of the band Krzak, harmonica soloist Jan Sczepański (his *b-injecton* album was recorded with the participation of German musicians and Jan Błędowski), and pianist and guitarist Zdzisław Marcinkiewicz, who graduated from the Wrocław Academy of Music and left Poland in the 1980s. He accompanied the piano duo Marek and Michel and the Romanian band Phenix, among others. In 2003 in Germany, he released the progressive album *Fortune Memories* under the name of Special Experiment. The highly acclaimed Beata Kossowska, a harmonica player, lives in Berlin (she performs with, among others, United Blues Experience with Wofgang Bernreuther and Rudi Bayer and in a duo with Eberhard Klunker). Stanisław Wenglorz, who has been associated with the bands Bards [Bardowie], Scalds [Skaldowie], Prompter's Booth [Budka Suflera] and ZOO, also continues to live in Germany. He is the author of two solo albums recorded with the considerable help of Ryszard Sygitowicz, which were released in Poland in 1982–1986. The second one was released after he moved abroad. In exile, he has been involved in organizing concerts. Kazimierz Cwynar (who has played with, among others, Trend [Nurt], Romuald and Roman, Test, Porter Band, and Steel Baggage [Stalowy Bagaż]) left for Germany in 1984. He has played in Sunny Band, Top Selection, and Ted und Die Fremden. In 2009, he returned to Wrocław and now runs an equestrian center with his wife.

In the Audience

Rock in exile, however, also has another image. Not only have artists emigrated, but also their fans. That is why the biographies of many émigré musicians (including Józef Hajdasz, Stan Borys, Zbigniew Bernolak, Piotr Janczerski, Krzysztof Krawczyk, and bands such as Perfect, Scalds, Red Guitars [Czerwone Gitary], etc.) include topics about concerts in Polish clubs and for the Polish diaspora. A large number of respected Polish performers from all music genres (from Under the Shed [Pod Budą] and Grzegorz Turnau to the Wawele ensemble) have found, and still find, a haven in such venues.

The Polish diaspora has also had a different impact on Polish artists. In December 1981, an interview with Czesław Niemen was broadcast during the "TV Daily Journal," conducted by Barbara Pietkiewicz. The musician's statements were manipulated in order to suggest that he supported the imposition of martial law, which was obviously absurd. As a result of this event, he was boycotted in many circles. Audiences even disrupted his concerts in Berlin and Sweden; there are recordings of Niemen asking for the audiences' understanding. Niemen was strongly impacted by this and, for some time, suffered a creative block.[198] These episodes show that Polish audiences gathering in Scandinavian or American clubs in the 1980s were extremely sensitive to political themes.

It is also worth raising yet another question—one deserving of an in-depth study. In their own way, some foreign musicians (Eastern and Western alike, and not only rockers) are also emigrants who decided to settle in Poland. These include John Porter, José Torres, Igor Czerniawski, Alosza Awdiejew, Ray Wilson, and Nigel Kennedy. The first four of them began their careers in the era of the Polish People's Republic.

This summary points out that Polish rock in exile is as fascinating a subject as it is complex. It requires, as we said earlier, fundamental and methodical research that yields more than just biographical information. It is difficult to grasp as a whole, especially with regard to gathering and evaluating artistic output. This attempt at a systematic approach to "émigré rock" reveals dramatic stories of people entangled in the history of their country, searching for their way, trying to save their ideals, but also discovering how to find their own ground and support their families. These people had to make difficult, ambiguous choices as true, authentic people who shared the fate of many compatriots, and not only in the twentieth century.

Instead of **Ending**

Aleksandra Bilińska

Composing as an Autobiography

In some sense, every sort of writing is an autobiography.
Jerzy Łukosz

Autobiography, biography's slightly younger sister, has been popular since the beginning of its existence as a literary genre situated within the broader field of non-fiction. As such, autobiography can take various epistolary forms. Following the concept proposed by Małgorzata Czermińska, we can distinguish three basic perspectives in the realm of autobiography: an extroverted demeanor of testimony, resembling pure non-fiction; an introverted attitude of confession, which is less objective and more focused on inner experiences; and a position of challenge addressed to the reader, who becomes drawn into the writing as it emerges (this mindset appears in Witold Gombrowicz's *Diary*, published on an ongoing basis during the author's lifetime and being a sort of internal conversation conducted by the author with the reader, provoking them to ask questions and seek answers).[199]

Thanks to Andrzej Chłopecki, the term "life-writing" has been accepted in Polish music literature. He used it in reference to the young composer Aleksander Nowak: "A distinctive quality and a special trait of at least several significant works by Aleksander Nowak is their particular kind of 'life-writing.'"[200] The term "life-writing" as a key notion in reference to the works of Edward Stachura has been promoted by Henryk Bereza, although the awareness of creating as being synonymous with one's life has certainly been acknowledged since the beginning of creativity itself. We can be sure that it gained a new meaning during a meeting with Stachura, when Bereza famously said: "Surely, Stachura's life is life-writing. His writing is synonymous with life, one results from another, one is the other, it is unity, it is indivisible, it is a complete whole."[201] Naturally, a question about narrative identity emerges, both because of Bereza's remarks and because of the many extant publications and presentations that have looked at autobiography as a literary genre: Does write-living exist as well? Can autobiography, considered within the world of music composition, convey an actual vision of one's life, thoughts, moods, and emotions? Can it offer interesting results in a form of a work that aims for an illusion, an idealizing image, or the writing of one's life in a better perspective? Certainly it can be the result of a structure consisting of associations, aporia, fulgurations, and debris.

Maybe a good musical work can also emerge due to forgetting, which brings out new qualities and new approaches. Paul Ricoeur explained this as follows:

> Forgetting is not only the misfortune of a lack of memory, but also a strategy of creating a story. In order to tell something, you have to forget a lot in order to spare the small part that creates meaning. I believe that kindness towards

> myself is a form of trusting that I have the ability to compose a story that takes into account the process of forgetting, of being kind, and not only to myself.[202]

The narrative identity and the issue of the narrative itself naturally brings us to the problem of form. Composing or writing consists, after all, of ordering and arranging, of selecting and putting together what at times are remnants of utterances, fleeting memories, and impressions. So what would the form be in the case of a composed autobiography, or an autobiography put into the form of music? A narrative identity changes the subject and its being, which in the case of a musical work can take on an increasingly metaphysical and morphologically changed sonic form that, in turn, as a sound gesture, a rhetorical figure, can be perceived in various ways depending on many contexts. In terms of literature, it is difficult to expand a single event into a narrative sequence of a story. The same may apply to a musical work, in which the same event is included as a symbolic sonic gesture. At this point, we should ask whether a musical work, based on sound matter, brings us closer to a real and objective vision of events, or, as in the case of a literary work (and maybe even more so), moves the listener into ever more distant spaces marked by a fictionalization of objective events that are outlined solely by a musical gesture. What many researchers of the phenomenon of autobiography have in common is a vision of a subject that is sincere, whether we are dealing with a memory, fragments of memory, a diary, or an autobiographical novel. However, sometimes we also find statements that offer an interesting contrast. Witold Gombrowicz, when asked about the status of the subject of his own *Diaries*, replied:

> Sincerity? As a writer, it is what I fear most. In literature, naïve, straightforward sincerity leads nowhere. This is one of the dynamic struggles of art: the more artificial we are, the closer we come to frankness. Artificiality allows the artist to approach shameful truths. As for my diary…have you ever read a 'sincere' diary? The 'sincere' diary is the most mendacious diary, because sincerity is not of this world. And, in the long run, what a bore sincerity is! It is ineffective![203]

Between a Memory and a Diary

While still on the topic of literary works, we must also mention Bohumil Hrabal and his oeuvre, which was the work of a "recorder of reality" whose language breathed the truth of his time with the freshness of live situations as well as those observed from the outside.[204] Another autobiographical masterpiece is Roland Barthes's book under the very telling title *Roland Barthes*. This work reveals, above all, the phenomenon of a return to childhood, which is subjected to a certain kind of vivisection. It is an attempt to look at oneself as if in the mirror of a distant time. More importantly, Barthes gives up narrative continuity in favor of capturing important moments, points, and fragments. He builds stories from pleasures, from liberated diffractions, distractions, messages, and strong stimuli. While the fascinated reader may vividly follow Hrabal's routes, feeling drawn into a path that is at once a memory lane, an essay, and a kind of life-writing, then, following Barthes, one will come across exceptional states, condensation points, springboards and launching pads, while experiencing changeability in an inconsistent narrative.[205] Life according to Hrabal seems to be an extroverted story told by an introvert, while according to Barthes, it is a composition or a montage. Scraps and fragmentary reflections create a story about humans as a sort of captured moment, which seems to be completely natural for the author of the *Empire of Signs*. Wiesław Myśliwski even predicts that:

> The end of literature would have to occur only with the end of humankind, because the need to tell others about ourselves is our existential need. Perhaps human beings invented words in order to express their amazement with themselves and the world, without expecting that with this first word, they discover their humanity.[206]

Let's try to look at composers' works from this perspective, viewing composition as a composed autobiography (also taking into account related literary genres) that provides a new perspective of a work and its meaning.

Frédéric Chopin's much quoted words from a letter to his friend Wojciech Grzymała—"I can barely remember how they sing back home"[207]—almost seem to define a national-folkloristic trend as being synonymous with the memories present in the works of many émigré Polish artists. A necessary task here is to look at compositional output rooted in folklore as a memory—as a moment captured from childhood or simply as a remembrance from one's pre-emigration period. Each recollection—an image of the past recalled as a retrospective, a reminder, or a reference—can be combined with a dance gesture, especially from mazurkas, polonaises, etc. Memory is characterized by situational and temporal uniqueness; it might be fragmented and isolated from situational context or it might be concentrated on emotions or, less often, it could be based solely on an objective view. Such are the mazurkas of Frédéric Chopin, Roman Maciejewski, and Aleksander Tansman, or works inspired by memories of folklore, such as those by Michał Kondracki, Antoni Szałowski, Ludomir Michał Rogowski, and Michał Spisak, or those that recall Silesia, as in the works of Witold Szalonek. Miniature forms sometimes capture strongly condensed emotions or, at other times, just a simple, frenetic, capricious, or melancholic dance gesture.

Compositions that oscillate between being a memory and a diary can be found in Roman Berger's oeuvre. The composer reaches for motives typical of both Slovak and Polish folklore. His works are often dedicated to the memory of people who are prominent and important to him. The epic nature of these particular compositions allows us to look at them as a diary. Diaries, which, unlike memoirs, are a record of current events, are often devoid of description and interpretative context. They can also take an intimate form, however, in which the author's emotions and experiences are expressed. In Berger's case, examples of these include compositions such as *Elegy in memoriam Ján Rúčka* (1969), which is an electroacoustic composition for tape, *Memento After the Death of Miroslav Filip* [*Memento po śmierci Miroslava Filipa*] for orchestra (1973), *Adagio for Ján Branny* [*Adagio dla Jana Brannego*] for violin and piano (1987), and *Requiem da Camera – with a Theme by Witold Lutosławski* for violin, cello, and piano (1998), in which a true story about a man is intertwined with the same person's personal reflections.

As in the case of Roman Berger, Miłosz Magin's works also oscillate between memory and diary. The Polish element is present in retrospectives, heard in the piano miniatures *Petite suite polonaise* for piano (1974), *Images de Pologne* for piano (1982), and *Miniatures polonaises* for piano (1982), as well as in larger compositions such as *Polish Suite* [*Suita polska*] for orchestra (1966). His works written after 1989, which include a *Clarinet Concerto* (1990) and *Piano Concerto No. 4* (1998), constitute a kind of commentary on notes in a diary that mention the changes taking place in his homeland, which have been observed from a distance. These observations concern the events of 1989 in Poland that resulted in the country's political transformation, including the Round Table and the first partially free parliamentary elections. Magin's period of emigration and creative freedom caused him to consider incorporating Polish national and folklore material into his music, a compositional direction that seemed to be even stronger in later years. Aleksander Tansman's work can also be considered to be reminiscent of a diary, one in which he records his numerous travels, places of residence, and memories.

Observing and recalling native culture fit here into Ricoeur's remarks about forgetting, which were cited above, and which bring a different sensation to new creations. Being kind towards one's own forgetting, as Paul Ricoeur points out, makes it possible to combine a variety of musical materials and gestures. In the case of Tansman, for example, this led to his combining neotonal harmonies rooted in jazz with Polish folk melodies or with autonomous folklore-like material. This occurred in almost all of the composer's solo guitar and piano works, in his symphonies, especially the fourth one, and in other orchestral works such as *Quatre danses polonaises* (1931) and *Rapsodie polonaise pour orchestre* (1940).

Forgetting and persisting, saving and capturing important memories which are then transformed—these are what link the works of Alexander Tansman with Ludomir Michał Rogowski and Julian Fontana. The sounds of Polish music combined with these composers' signature styles, which had been gradually transformed during their stays in exile through, for example, new compositional techniques and a fascination with the folklore of their new home, often brought surprising results. Rogowski's oeuvre remained in the Slavic cultural sphere, assimilating new elements of eastern cultures. In Fontana's music, typically Polish gestures and images were linked to the music of cultures as distant as the Caribbean Sea region, especially Cuban and African-American, which the composer became familiar with during his stay in the United States. The rhythm and spirit of mazurkas and traits of polonaises can be heard in Fontana's *La Havanne, fantasie sur des motifs américains et espagnols* for piano, op. 10 (1845) and *Souvenirs de l'île de Cuba. Deux fantaisies… dédiées à Camille et Léocadie* for piano, op. 12 (1847). These folk influences can be heard in the three versions of Tansman's *Sonatine transatlantique* (for piano, for two pianos, and for orchestra, all 1930), and also in Rogowski's solo piano works, *Phantasmagories* [*Fantasmagorie*] for voice and chamber orchestra (1920), and *Impressions from Dubrovnik* for orchestra (1950).

Elżbieta Sikora's works can be also perceived as a record of current events, a reaction to an existing situation, or a travel diary. They serve as an invitation to listen and become interested in a particular character or chosen moment in her life; at times she creates an atmosphere that could evoke important events, or rather memories of them. This is the case with a composition from *The Head of Orpheus* [*Głowa Orfeusza*] series titled *Janek Wiśniewski-December Poland* (*The Head of Orpheus III*) [*Janek Wiśniewski-Grudzień-Polska (Głowa Orfeusza III*)] for tape (1982–1983) and also with *Lisbon: Tram 28* for saxophone and tape (1999). Sikora managed to create an extraordinarily impressionistic, colorful, subtly expressive, lyrical, and yet also personal atmosphere. In the first of these pieces, such an impression emerged from the drama of martial law observed by the author from afar, from the perspective of an émigré. In the second work, this was created by penetrating into the solipsistic and hermetic world of Fernando Pessoa's prose. An equally unusual internal world that was somewhat broken, but also motoric and lyrical was created in the excellent *String Quartet No. 3 "In memoriam Ursula"* (1999). This was composed in memory of the composer's niece, who died in an accident.

Examples of intimate diaries would be Chopin's preludes and scherzos, which can be seen as shorter or longer stories about one's own experiences, about emotional states that accompany travels, and about changes of surroundings. These very personal and intimate moments capture the difficult states of his worsening disease. A specific type of intimate journal—a record of her internal emigration—can be found in the works of Barbara Buczkówna. The third and final stage of her oeuvre was filled with eleven pieces intended for smaller ensembles. Written in the 1980s during the period of martial law, the timing of their composition overlapped with her increasing personal problems. The composer learned about her incurable disease, which forced her to focus on its complicated treatment. This period brought forth the most personal, autobiographical, and intimate compositions, especially the 1982 *Desunion* for soprano and double bass (intended to be performed by soprano singer simultaneously playing the double bass). The title indicates a division between body and soul: a dying body affected by a devastating disease, which is contrasted to the lyrical soprano's rendition of the soul destined for immortality. Her 1984 *Motet* for instruments, spoken word, baritone, and tape reflects a deeper yet gradual descent into the darkness of life. A rather dark and reflective tone is created by the music, which merges with the lyrics selected by the author: fragments of Rilke's *Duino Elegies* and poetry by Ted Hughes and Sylvia Plath. Another intimate journal that relates the successive stages of a disease was preserved in the work of Roman Maciejewski. A serious digestive illness imposed many changes in his life. His art seems to remain in a certain context of being, lasting, living, and creating. One senses joy, a need for contact with nature, contemplation, and meditation. His work, even broadly understood, seems to comprise a memo in the journal of life and its transformations. One example of this is his monumental *Requiem: Missa pro defunctis* for soloists, choir, and symphonic orchestra (1944–1959).

A memoir, as opposed to a diary, tells about past events from the perspective of time. It may be only a story about events, but it can also be filled with one's own reflections on them. Mikołaj Piotr Górecki's compositions have the nature of a memoir. His melancholy, lyrical, elegiac sound language, which is sometimes gloomy and sometimes dynamic, is used to create a thread that links his music from his time in Poland to his American life. Recurrent themes of Polish poetry emphasize the memoir-like character of his art. We notice this in their ever-present Polish and Slavic tone, even though the composer has lived and worked in the United States for many years. The composer uses classical and universal texts by Polish poets along with lyrical instrumental genres to comment on his personal and external realities. Some examples of this are *Guest, Sit Under My Leaf* [*Gościu, siądź pod mym liściem*] for a cappella choir, set to poems by Jan Kochanowski (2000), *Three Short Recitatives* [*Trzy krótkie recytatywy*] for soprano, violin, viola, and cello, with words by Jarosław Iwaszkiewicz (2001), *Bright Radiances* [*Jasności promieniste*], a small mysterium for soprano and string orchestra set to the words of Czesław Miłosz (2012), *Nocturne I* [*Nokturn*] for orchestra (2011), and *Elegy* [*Elegia*] for solo cello and string orchestra (2014).

Life-Writing

Life-writing, or a "stachuriad," is a term that is ambiguous and not easy to define. However, following Stachura's vision of writing, life-writing would be telling a story about one's own life, creating an idealized version of one's own experiences in conditions similar to the actual ones. Sometimes a novel's protagonist becomes a character who implements what was the author's actual desire, which either never became reality or turned out differently than expected. This kind of life-writing can be found in the work of Hanna Kulenty. Her work would probably look the same regardless of where she lived. Kulenty's life-writing stems from observing nature, movement, mobility, trances, and primal phenomena. Her creativity stems from a Neo-Platonic vision of Plotinus, becoming—in the case of an emerging work and its source or inspiration—existence itself as well as its expansion. Existence continues and emerges at the same time; from it, successive beings and emanations of existence arise. Thus, the work and its emergence become an emanating form. The main protagonists of this narrative are time and movement, which determine the entire story and give it meaning. Thus, the subject of this story is implicit.

We can situate the works of André Tchaikowsky and Szymon Laks between personal life-writing and autobiographical poems. Both composers were war survivors who were passionate about poetry and composed within an individual, hermeneutical world, far from the obligatory trends of the external music world. For both men, their works involved building a new, better, and nobler reality, in which the protagonist-composer's alter ego operated. In the case of Tchaikowsky, the best examples of this are, among others, the opera *The Merchant of Venice* [*Kupiec Wenecki*] (1982), his song cycle *Seven Sonnets of Shakespeare* [*Siedem sonetów Szekspira*] (1967) and, especially, his chamber works and pieces written for his favorite instrument, the piano. In the case of Laks, such pieces include *Five Songs to Poems by Julian Tuwim* [*Pięć pieśni do wierszy Juliana Tuwima*] for voice and piano (1936–1938, 1961–1962), *Elegy of Jewish Towns* [*Elegia żydowskich miasteczek*] for voice and piano (1961), *Four Songs to Words by Tadeusz Śliwiak* [*Cztery pieśni do słów Tadeusza Śliwiaka*] for voice and piano (1967), his string quartets, and all of his chamber music.

Life-writing that involves creating a new character in a new space and reality can undoubtedly be found in the work of Roman Haubenstock-Ramati. His musical protagonist lives and moves in a completely novel shape and structure marked by the presence of the composer in the emigrant environment of Austria. The composer called his new forms mobiles, or dynamically closed forms resembling the kinetic sculptures of Alexander Calder. He became one of the most important precursors of music graphics, developing his own system of musical signs. One of the most vivid examples and interpretations of his own life-writing is his opera *America*, set to Franz Kafka's words (1962–1964), and his various series of mobiles for chamber ensembles: *Miroirs* for various combinations of pianos (1984), *Pluriel* for combinations of string instruments (1991), and *Nouvoletta* for flute and other instrumental combinations (1992).

Just as in Haubenstock-Ramati's work, the sonic protagonist of Witold Szalonek's compositions lives in his own individualized space. Apart from recurrent themes linked to Silesian folklore, Szalonek's sonic world is dominated by multiphonic sounds as well as individual sounds, or, in other words, acoustic-physical phenomena. Aside from his early period and a few examples of folklore-inspired compositions, practically his entire oeuvre is filled with works emerging from his studies on timbre, color, and sound complexity.

The real musical "stachuriad" was Zbigniew Karkowski. His sound language defies definition. It is independent; it is a creation assembled by combining a variety of techniques, genres, and styles. It reflects a kind of living and composing that has been inscribed by existing and residing in different cultures and places in the world. On the other hand, it is an observation of the world as a universal place devoid of differences. In order to capture the essence of Zbigniew Karkowski's life and creation, we need to refer directly to Edward Stachura, as nobody could have done it better:

> Truly, and regardless of other things, this is an incredible, wonderful adventure. This is life, my life.[208]

> One has to write.... About what? Everything. Let's write about poetry then. Because everything is poetry, and everyone is a poet.... Everything is poetry, and at least a written poem is poetry; everyone is a poet, and the least poet is someone who writes poems.[209]

Zbigniew Karkowski concludes:

> I left Europe many years ago, and one of the reasons for this was that I didn't want to live and work in a creative milieu relying on government subsidies (which is very common in Europe). I wanted to be independent and earn without institutional support, because I believe that one cannot have an entirely free mind if you are constantly dependent on something. And you cannot make good, strong things without a free mind.[210]

Lyrical Quality

An autobiographical poem: lyrical or epic, certainly subjective, lacking a narrative, building sequences of events in a free manner. This term seems to describe, to some extent, any composition. However, taking a closer look, an autobiographical poem simultaneously links to a kind of creative work characterized by a certain unity of its aesthetic dimension, by constant progress, and by a development that lacks impetuous, revolutionary turns. It is an independent musical identity, an autobiography told in lyrical gestures, sounds, and arbitrarily selected instruments to which the composer assigns the role of the main protagonist; these are the characteristics of Zbigniew Bargielski's compositions. Andrzej Chłopecki summarized Bargielski's creative idiom:

> It is clear that Bargielski's work continually evolves. But this evolution takes a circular form, expanding its aesthetic dimension, becoming richer in nuance, but not in stages....The composer did not experience an acute crisis of aesthetic orientation (like Penderecki) or a more veiled, but still obvious one (like Lutosławski). If there is any threshold in his work, it is probably indicated by his *Violin Concerto* from 1976. The intense, lyrical quality of this composition, not affected by the viruses of new simplicity or new romanticism (which attacked Polish music in that symbolic year), is a discreet sign of Bargielski's sensitivity to a shift of the Zeitgeist. Bargielski's music emerged from that aesthetic storm unharmed.[211]

In Bargielski's case, stability, constancy, and creative consistency refer both to his "Polish" period and his stay in exile. An axis of creativity seen as a constant, linear development and the lyrical moments of an autobiographical poem having a sonic protagonist can be found in (apart from the *Violin Concerto* mentioned by Chłopecki) *The Valley of Bright White Bones* [*Dolina bielejących kości*], version I for instrumental ensemble and percussion (1977), *Stilleben mit Rose* for wind instruments and percussion (1977), *The Valley of Bright White Bones,* version II for improvised piano, instrumental ensemble, and percussion (1977–1993), his string quartets, *Nocturne in Blue* [*Nokturn w błękicie*] for violin and string orchestra (1981), *Garden of Passion* [*Ogród namiętności*] for soprano, bass clarinet (and alto saxophone), percussion, and accordion (1985), *Slapstick* for chamber orchestra (1997), *Nocturne in Red and Blue* [*Nokturn w czerwieni i błękicie*] for violin and string orchestra (2006), and *Mysterium of Space* [*Misterium przestrzeni*] for symphony orchestra, choir, and electronic tape (2010).

An essay is a non-fiction genre characterized by subjectivism and reflectiveness. It serves as an opportunity for an author to offer his or her own reflections, personal points of view, and opinions on the designated topic. An essay often remains non-conclusive and provides a space for further discussion. It is a hybrid genre. This description evokes associations with the music of Marta Ptaszyńska and Joanna Bruzdowicz. For both composers, art and their own personal reflections about it are important. Art remains in correlation or full integration with itself. Art comments on what is existing and changeable. It is also characterized by a certain universalism. According to Zbigniew Granat, the work of Marta Ptaszyńska, in an ideological and aesthetic sense, is Polish and international at the same time. For Granat, the composer combines different elements of diverse origin: "Temporal, geographical, and cultural areas...are similar in terms of content expressed by a human being, because they stem from common ways of experiencing the world."[212]

One example of this is her *Conductus – A Ceremonial for Winds* (1982), dedicated to Pope John Paul II. Other examples of Polish elements in her work include the old Polish anthem *Mother of God* [*Bogurodzica*] in her cantata *Polish Letters* [*Listy polskie*] (1988), dedicated to the Polish diaspora, and minor motivic references in *Fanfare for Peace* (1993), commissioned by the Cincinnati Symphony Orchestra for its centenary. International influences appear in her 1985 *Marimba Concerto,* inspired by Surrealist paintings; *Siderals* for two percussion quintets and light projection (1974) inspired by paintings by Paul Klee; *Linear Constructions in Space* [*Linearne konstrukcje w przestrzeni*] for percussion sextet (1998), influenced by the works of Piet Mondrian; and *Pianophonie*, a cycle of etudes for piano (2004) inspired by the works of Vassily Kandinsky, Paul Klee, Georges Seurat and other artists.

In the case of Joanna Bruzdowicz, stage works are important, for, in some ways, they indicate her views on the moral and ideological condition of humankind. *Penal Colony* [*Kolonia karna*] (1967), based on a story by Franz Kafka, *Women of Troy* [*Trojanki*] (1972), based on Euripides, and *Gates of Paradise* [*Bramy Raju*] (1980–1981), based on Jerzy Andrzejewski's work, form a personal commentary on Poland's reality as seen from the perspective of an émigré. Her works for film can also be considered a kind of sound essay comparable, for example, to the scores written by Wojciech Kilar to Krzysztof Zanussi's films. Such an essay is a kind of autonomous, personal conclusion, an intertextual, digressive reflection or counter-emotion. Joanna Bruzdowicz's film music never becomes a mere illustration or a way to fill the screen; it is an independent entity, an autonomous work presenting its own conclusion, and an independent sonic story. Such an approach to the function of film music is shared also by Kaczmarek.

A musical position between diary and essay can be seen as a feature of composers such as Roman Palester and Andrzej Panufnik. Both composers were intellectuals, erudite people who were devoted to science and art, engaged in cultural activities, and wrote deeply expressive works saturated with emotion and intellectual power. In the case of Palester, his musical work blends perfectly with his writings, which include his autobiography, correspondence, and radio programs. Panufnik's works are slightly more emotionally saturated than Palester's. They form a lively commentary on the history of Poland in the last century. In his statements and interviews, the word "homeland" appears frequently along with a sense of Polish identity and a need to take a stance on social, political, and religious issues. This spirit fills practically his entire oeuvre, including such masterpieces as *Sinfonia Sacra* (1963), commissioned by the Kosciuszko Foundation for the millennium of Polish statehood and Christianity in Poland, and the *Bassoon Concerto* (1984–1985), written in response to the martyrdom of Father Jerzy Popiełuszko.

***

In conclusion, let's return to the opening words of this essay: "In some sense, every sort of writing is an autobiography."[213] This is an undisputable fact. The act of creation is inscribed in the life and activities of each artist, but questions then arise: How do we interpret this work? How does it relate to the life of a particular artist? What is the relationship between these two phenomena? Does the emotional or intellectual factor prevail? In the case of émigré composers, what is more important: the "Polish issue" and a sense of Polish identity or an autonomous language and self-expression? Sound as a psychological and physical phenomenon, not burdened by the semantic properties of the written word, has a much greater chance of enabling an artist to create a significantly richer, more distinctive, and more sophisticated experience that presents a better version of their own conditions. However, it should be remembered that composers still approach the written word with respect and commitment; they take advantage of it and willingly compose pieces in which they give new meanings to literary texts. All in all, this creates a mirror in which one's entire creative personality is viewed. Thus an autobiography is recorded through composition.

Granica
Państwa

Piotr Jakubowski

We Keep Wandering: On Existential Migration

From an anthropological and historical point of view, we are—we, humanity—much more predisposed to move than to remain in one place. If the history of humans, as a species, were to last one day, the idea to settle in one place would appear at 11 minutes past 11 p.m. This idea was connected to a revolutionary observation that a seed placed in soil grows later into a plant. Over time, this created a shift from a hunter-gatherer economy towards farming, and from a nomadic life style into a sedentary one. A new form of symbolic attachment to earth as "mother," "the giver of life," the source of food, and the basis of existence remained in place for thousands of years, before this same land was also thought of as a territory, a politicized element to which rights can be claimed not only by our immediate group (clan, tribe, village), but also by our imagined community.[214]

The transition from hunter-gatherer to an agricultural lifestyle did not mean that people ceased to wander. In addition to material conditions, at least one key aspect must be taken into account here—that there is a cognitive selflessness, a curiosity about the world, a tormenting desire to discover what is behind every new horizon encountered along one's way. Such expeditions inevitably involve risk and uncertainty. Numerous dangers can exist in unknown areas, and locals, as well as other wanderers encountered on the road, do not necessarily have to be friendly. However, the hopes for possible gains—cognitive, existential, material—have proven to be many times stronger than any fear.

In the course of implementing increasingly advanced forms of political organization, one result of which is the current division of the world into nation-state territories,[215] migratory movements began to acquire increasingly strict rules and regulations. Today's dominant practice of dividing the world (or actually the land) into areas (habitats) taken by particular nations also translates into a common perception of the structure of our planet. Akhil Gupta and James Ferguson write:

> The distinctiveness of societies, nations, and states is predicated on a seemingly unproblematic division of space, on the fact that they occupy 'naturally' discontinuous spaces.... The representation of the world as a collection of 'countries', as on most world maps [political], is seen as a space naturally divided into different national societies, each 'rooted' in its proper place.[216]

The idea of a border is the fundamental rule of this division.

We encounter borders and boundaries at every step—the boundaries of districts, housing areas, and cities; the skin is the boundary of our body; we talk about the boundaries of our endurance or tolerance; specific boundary devices such as doors, windows, and gates are commonplace; but the boundary with the greatest threat to "our" integrity, sovereignty, and security (or at least this is commonly claimed to be so) is the border of the nation-state. It is therefore these places that require special surveillance, control, and regulation by political and legal systems. Each border is a historical and political construction that undergoes a kind of naturalization. To illustrate the fictitious nature of borders, we can refer to Africa, divided by colonizers into territories whose lines (after independence) often run "across" spaces inhabited by a single ethnic group, but, just as often, they include two or more such groups that do not think of themselves as representing a single entity (which has led to many violent wars, treated *nomen omen*, as "domestic" battles).

Experiencing Borders

For the first time in my life, I crossed the border during a trip to the Beskid mountains with my parents and younger brother. When we reached the top of Czantoria Mountain, a small, concrete post appeared before our eyes. Behind it stretched another country. There was no line drawn on the ground, no fences, walls, wires, or gates—only this post, which could be freely bypassed, climbed, and jumped. You could stand with one leg in Poland and the other in the Czech Republic. Thanks to the introduction of the Schengen zone, we now have an opportunity to experience the (lack of) borders in a similar way when travelling by car or train within the European Union. The fact that we are in another country is announced by your mobile device, as well as by slightly different-looking road signs, town and street names, and advertising signs in foreign languages. How easy it is to forget how lucky we are. "A state border is a tricky device," Seyla Benhabib reminds us: "If you find yourself on the wrong side, you can immediately turn from a citizen into a foreigner, devoid of rights."[217]

Let's confront our border experiences with the stories told by Alaa and Hussan, two refugees from Syria, who, after many unsuccessful attempts to get to Europe, finally managed to travel by car from Italy to Germany. Their "chauffeur" is Wolfgang Bauer, author of the book *Crossing the Sea: With Syrians on the Exodus to Europe*:

> We count down the distance posts. 240 kilometers, then 210... 110... 50... 22... 9, and suddenly the border disappears. We do not know when we crossed it. There was no barrier, no line in the place where Italy changes to the Republic of Austria.
> – Was that the border? – asks Alaa, confused.[218]

After the previous experiences of this young Syrian, the idea that a border could be simply crossed, unnoticed, seems almost unreal.

Patrick Kingsley, a journalist with *The Guardian*, went on a journey of several years along the migratory routes from Africa and the Middle East to Europe. He claimed that within one week, he "crossed nine borders, while at the same time as many as 1,300 died trying to cross just one of them."[219]

The same border can reveal different faces—an almost imaginary point or a barrier impossible to cross—depending on whether one belongs to the "right" or "wrong side of life" (notions introduced by Artur Domosławski).[220] This stems from the fact that a border is an element of the world in which existence and politics are indivisibly intertwined and human rights are understood as citizens' rights.[221] A border divides more than just natural space, changing it into a discontinuous system of political territories. It separates not only the citizens of one state from those of another one, but it also has the power to reveal more subtle divisions—between those who remain within the law and those who are outside or whose status is unclear, between the welcome and unwelcome, between those who are needed and those seen as "human garbage."[222] Crossing a border updates the status of an individual in the system of nation-states and borders; it changes the rules of membership and the conditions for possible secession.

Political and legal coordinates affect not only an individual on the move, but also the nature of the movement itself. Emigration is part of a system that entails both organizing the various practices concerning relocation, or actually crossing borders (i.e., from one country to another) and, at the same time, inscribing the movement of a body or bodies into a specific legal context. Every emigration is at the same time an immigration, if we look at it from the perspective of the so-called host country. The prefixes "e-" and "i-" indicate the direction of migration, which includes the process of moving (for a longer or potentially permanent period of time) from one place to another, where the minimum unit of "distance" is indicated by towns or cities (we are not talking about migration from one district of a given city to another), and the most implicit one, the nation-state. This is how the *Dictionary of the Polish Language* describes it: "[migration is] the movement of people to new places of settlement, especially to other countries."[223]

While this definition refers to the very fact of movement and the prefixes give it direction, it is the adjectives that determine its causes. So, one basic division distinguishes between political and economic (labor) migration. A special case that includes the former, but goes beyond it at the same time, is the status of a refugee, inscribed in the international legal code after mass escapes of people following the catastrophes of war and political unrest in the first half of the twentieth century (Armenian genocide, repression of political opponents after the October Revolution, two world wars). Of course, the phenomenon itself occurred much earlier than the date it was included in the supra- and international legal order, but it was only population movements on such a scale that made displacement an issue to be tackled on a global level. In 1950, the office of the United Nations High Commissioner for Refugees was established; a year later the *Convention Relating to the Status of Refugees* (known as the Geneva Convention) came in being, defining a refugee as a person who, "owing to a well-founded fear of being persecuted for reasons of race, religion, nationality, political convictions, or membership in a particular social group, was forced to leave the country of his nationality and is unable or, owing to such fear, is unwilling to avail himself of the protection of that country."[224]

In an excerpt from this definition—"forced to leave…"—we can find the starting point for another dividing line for migration, this time embracing the idea of leaving one's place of residence in order to look for, as Pope Francis said, "a better future."[225] Thus, migration is divided into voluntary and forced, and these categories are treated in opposition to one another, as disjointed alternatives, not as two extremes of a highly complex spectrum. The strict principles of Aristotle's logic therefore make it clear that everyone is either a forced or a voluntary migrant. A migrant cannot be this and that at the same time, nor can a migrant be neither this nor that, *tertium non datur*. But is there ever a situation of absolute coercion in life that does not allow for even the slightest form of opposition, or, on the contrary, a full act of free will?[226]

This division prompts certain legal consequences. The criterion of coercion draws a demarcation line between refugee and migrant. In addition to the legal situation, the public perception of each category should also be taken into account. While a refugee, by default, is a victim, someone who has experienced harassment and persecution and therefore deserves assistance in the name of ethical bonds with universalist claims, the migrant, most often an economic one (the term itself refers to material motives, usually not respected), simply wants to find a place where he will live a better, more prosperous life, where he will have better chances and prospects (but not at our expense...?).

Homines Viatores (People of the Road)

The division of people on the move into migrants and refugees has been strongly criticized by Artur Domosławski. As he has written, "differentiating and selecting migrants can, unfortunately, be useful in political disputes and the race for power."[227] This division does not pass closer scrutiny, however. Situations of certain people refuse to fit within the narrow definitions of an 'economic migrant' or a 'refugee.'"[228] Judy Fudge, a lawyer from the University of Kent, seconds this opinion:

> The stark dichotomy between 'refugee' and 'economic migrant' masks the reality that many people fall between those two extremes. Today, the reasons why people cross borders are highly complex and hardly fit the definitions of the 1951 convention on refugees. People who fall outside the internationally recognized definition of a refugee, but are nevertheless fleeing extreme poverty or lack of life chances, are as much 'survival' as 'economic' migrants.[229]

These quoted excerpts show an indelible gap between the order of life and legal constraints. At the level of established law, the diversity and the ambiguity of everything that makes up our life experience must be reduced to abstract, generalized categories. There is little room for much nuance, ambiguity, or ambivalence. On the subject of migration and how we perceive and treat people on the move as well as newcomers, a critical awareness of the purely formal and inevitably reductive nature of legal regulations is crucial. This can be a starting point for not equating these two dimensions—existential and lawful—and for not confusing abstract legal categories with real human beings.

In 2015, there were more than 244 million migrants worldwide (that is, one out of thirty living humans either permanently or temporarily moved to or settled down in a place other than their city or country of origin).[230] A comparison of data from previous years shows a clear upward trend in this regard, so it is reasonable to assume that today the number is even higher. And while it is easy for us to accept the global flow of capital and cultural patterns, the movement of people does not arouse particular enthusiasm.

We will never know the life stories of even a small percentage of those almost a quarter of a billion people who decided to leave their place of origin and take the risk of going towards the unknown. Migration researchers agree that this process cannot be stopped, it can only be managed sensibly. The so-called migration crisis of the second decade of the twenty-first century is only a prelude to the mass movements of crowds of people that await us in the future. Instead of erecting walls and fences and enclosing ourselves in national strongholds, it is necessary to hold a fair public debate, to raise intercultural competencies, and finally to implement sensible integration policies. This refers to systemic and institutional levels. On the level of everyday interpersonal relations, on the other hand, it is crucial to cultivate attitudes of openness and empathy towards those whose various life circumstances have brought them to the same city, under the same sky. As a 22-year-old Chechen woman living in Białystok said (in a book published by Anna Konik): "The earth is turning and you cannot tell what will happen the next day. If you were in our place, what would you do?"[231]

Hopefully, one of the many benefits from reading this book on Polish emigrant composers will be a realization that Poles were, are, and will be existential migrants. Thanks to the development of technology, new means of transportation and communication, and a growing prevalence of supranational structures over those of the nation-state, moving between one country or continent and another is easier today than ever before. For many, however, it still carries the risk of losing everything they have, including life. The perception of each of them—of each of us—as an existential migrant, that is, someone who, for various reasons, more or less serious, more or less conscious, has decided to set out on the road and seek a place where he or she can live better, more easily, or simply differently, becomes an increasingly urgent challenge in the name of the most broadly understood human solidarity.

The experience of a community of contemporary *homines viatores* (people of the road) or "flights," as Olga Tokarczuk has put it, is the first step towards the realization of Kant's idea of "perpetual peace."[232] This is perhaps a utopian goal, but certainly one worth pursuing. It was a philosopher from Königsberg who argued for the right

> that all people are entitled to, that they could present themselves to society in accordance with the concept of joint ownership of the earth's surface, where, as on a globe, they cannot infinitely disperse and hence must finally tolerate the presence of each other. Originally, no one had more right than another to a particular part of the earth.[233]

These words should also be remembered today, in the twenty-first century, in an era of mass migrations on an unprecedented scale, in the face of unrest but also the opportunities that come with it.

Part II

Composers' Profiles

In Other Words,
Marlena Wieczorek Asks,
Experts Respond

Zbigniew Bargielski

Date and place of birth:
21 January 1937, Łomża.

Date and place of emigration:
1967, Austria (Klagenfurt – Graz – Vienna).

Return to Poland:
Yes, gradually since October 2002.

Key quote

We don't want to, and perhaps we can't, remain in awareness of an impending doom. Since we have begun to exist, destroying us once and for all would be ridiculous…for there must be, after all, a regularity, logic, and aim to our existence, a hope that bringing us onto the human scene has more than a mere existential dimension. We are looking for the cause and effect of our presence, hoping that our discovery could help understand the meaning of birth, existence, and death.[234]

Activities before emigration

He had been composing since he was 15. When he was 19, he made his debut as a composer. The Lublin Philharmonic, Andrzej Cwojdziński conducting, performed his *Christmas Carol Suite I* [*Suita kolędowa I*] for symphonic orchestra. Bargielski also had interests outside of music. In October 1953 he enrolled in a chemistry program at Lublin's Marie Curie-Skłodowska University and from 1954–1957 he studied law at the same university. He abandoned that program in favor of composition classes at Warsaw's State Higher School of Music, which he attended from 1958–1962 (the music imperative had prevailed!). Simultaneously, he had been composing music for theater and was involved in the Polish Students Association. (As a manager of summer student camps in Mielno, he bravely proposed changes to higher education in music, which were met with disapproval from the Higher School's administration and led to his suspension.) He eventually received his diploma in 1964 at the State Higher School of Music in Katowice. He contributed to various magazines (*Przegląd kulturalny*, *Kurier Polski*, etc.), worked as a speaker at the National Philharmonic in Warsaw, and was involved in the Polish Composers' Union as a secretary of the Warsaw branch.

In 1965, as the winner of the Polish Composers' Union's Young Composers Competition in Warsaw (first prize for *Parades* for symphonic orchestra, 1964), he was awarded a one-year scholarship in Paris for the 1966–1967 academic year. He enrolled at the Écoles d'art américaines Conservatoire de musique – École des Beaux-Arts to study composition with Nadia Boulanger. This proved to be an important step in his composing career.

After emigration

He mostly composed, but he also looked for other sources of income. As a result, he became employed as a piano teacher at a music school in Bruck an der Mur, Austria. He also continued his education, taking classes for two semesters at the Hochschule für Musik (today Universität für Musik und darstellende Kunst) in Graz from 1971–1972 to expand his skills on percussion, which was his instrumental specialty. In 1986, he received a scholarship from the DAAD program in Darmstadt.

Over the course of several years, his position in the Austrian composing community grew, as confirmed by his membership of the Austrian Composers Association, his receipt of several important local awards and commissions, and the selection of his work *Epitaphium* for two violins to represent Austria at the prestigious ISCM festival in Oslo in 1987 (the composer has dual citizenship). Renowned performers have expressed interest in his works and he has also benefitted from monographic concerts of his pieces. Bargielski's compositions are also represented in Austrian music literature. More than 140 of his works have been written outside of Poland; by comparison, about 50 were composed in his native country. The composer includes his most important pieces among those written abroad: the quasi-Mass *Songs of the Sun* [*Sonnenlieder*] (1983), the oratorio *In No Man's Land* [*Im Niemandsland*] (1989), *Requiem* for symphonic orchestra (1992), as well as the outstanding *Violin Concerto* (1975).

Differences between the old and new realities

These differences refer primarily to socio-political realities. In the area of art, Bargielski has not noticed any differences. He enjoyed full freedom of expression in Poland as well as in Austria and has been able to communicate his own views on art (except during his studies in Poland with Perkowski, which led to a short-term creative crisis). Interestingly, Bargielski has claimed that the reception of his music in Austria was something special and the musical community there was very friendly.

Reason for leaving Poland

His decision to emigrate was prompted by the fact that his wife, a violinist, was employed with the symphonic orchestra in Klagenfurt, Austria. Bargielski joined her after his Paris scholarship ended. In 1967, their daughter Konstancja was born. His determination to stay in Austria permanently was motivated by the onset of martial law in Poland. The day before it began, the composer arrived in Poland for professional reasons; because his passport was seized, he was unable to return to Austria for several months.

Contact with Poland after emigration

His early years in Austria were difficult for the composer and led him to attempt to work in both countries. His temporary stays in Poland were related to performances, contributions to *Ruch Muzyczny* and employment in the Bydgoszcz branch of the Music Academy in Łódź, which began in October 1976. This situation did not last long, since working two weeks in Poland and two in Austria proved to be impossible to maintain long-term.

The impulse to return to Poland came from the Feliks Nowowiejski Academy of Music in Bydgoszcz, which invited him to work there in 2002. Bargielski's friend Adrianna Poniecka-Piekutowska played an important role in this decision, for she encouraged him to consider an academic position in Poland. Bargielski also mentioned others who helped him establish new contacts in his homeland, which eventually convinced him to return. First, Zofia Jaźwińska recorded a two-hour-long interview with him for Polish Radio. This marked the first significant gesture towards Bargielski from Poland. Second, Andrzej Chłopecki was a great help for him professionally. While Bargielski was still living abroad, Chłopecki had commissioned *Trigonalia* for guitar, accordion, percussion, and chamber orchestra (1994) on behalf of Polish Radio. This composition received an award from the UNESCO International Composers' Tribune in Paris in 1995. Chłopecki also helped arrange the Polish transmission of the first performance of *In No Man's Land* from Graz and the first Polish performance of the second part of this exceptional composition in 2012 in Wrocław. We can say that since his return to Poland, Bargielski has worked tirelessly to shape his well-deserved position in the Polish musical environment.

Influence of the new home on the composer's music

In an aesthetic sense, there was none, according to the composer. In fact, in Bargielski's case, we can even speak of an aesthetic *constans*, which does not mean routine or rut, but rather the consistency of his compositional style. In terms of musical inspiration, new impulses did occur, however. There was also a sense of a gradual "catching up," and at the same time, a continual re-evaluation of his own music.

Awareness of the composer's music in both countries

Not unexpectedly, since Bargielski's return to Poland, interest in his work in Austria has decreased, yet it has hardly disappeared. Austrian institutions still remember this remarkable artist, as proven by the organization of monographic concerts in Vienna and Graz and the release of recordings of his works. In Poland, the composer is gradually achieving prominence. Bargielski's music is now deservedly recognized, as demonstrated through increasing commissions, performances, publishing, discographies, and writings.

Composer's personality

He is independent, marked by a creative imperative, and often remains in a state of permanent anxiety. When he is not creating music, he writes poetry. An important feature of his personality is the feeling of "remaining unsatisfied" after completing each composition, with a constant need to do "something new." He does not give up any available means of musical impact, but instead constantly broadens their scope. His compositions of the last decade demonstrate this. In the *Schizophonia* piano quintet (2012), he elevates the status of the melody (a quasi-chorale) while setting up collisions with ambivalent neo-avant-garde structures. In other pieces, such as *Domino* for flute, violin, and viola (2017), or *anilo-vi klänge* for flute, clarinet, violin, viola, cello, percussion, and piano (2018), he places texture, color, and movement in the foreground. In *anilo-vi,* he introduces unusual elements of acting. In *Fonoplasticon*, a piano sextet for flute, oboe, clarinet, bassoon, horn, and piano (2016), his musical sense of humor can be heard.

Bargielski's creative independence is proven by the fact that long-term exposure to Austrian (Germanic) culture not only left no significant impact on his artistic worldview and attitude, but quite the contrary, he remained true to his identity, to his own (genetic!) preferences, ideals, and aesthetic choices, which are related to Mediterranean (Romance) culture. These features can be noticed on various levels of his musical *métier*: logic, clarity of structure, musical sense of humor, positive mood (similar to French *sérénité*), lyrical finesse, and a sensual vulnerability to sound, timbre, and nuance.

Remarkable anecdote or biographical fact

True stories:

- Warsaw, State Higher School of Music, 1959: Witold Rudziński told Bargielski directly after an exam, "Professor Perkowski applied to remove you from the course," (immediately adding) "but don't worry, if you would like, I'll be glad to include you in my class!" [quote from Z. Bargielski].
- Warsaw, after many years: a concert at the Chamber Hall of the National Philharmonic included the fifth of Zbigniew Bargielski's *Five Sonnets* [*Pięć Sonetów*] for viola, performed by Stefan Kamasa. During the intermission, Perkowski approached Bargielski and said "I am sorry, I have judged you wrongly as a composer" [quote from Z. Bargielski].

Respondent's Top Choices

- **Favorite work:** many of them: *Violin Concerto* (1975), *Trigonalia* (1994), *String Quartets* (III–V; 1985–1986, 1994, 2001), *Brief an Milena* (2005), *Noc-Dzień* [*Night-Day*] song cycle (1995), *Hierophany* (1996), *Fonoplasticon* (2016).
- **Best work:** *In No Man's Land* (1988–1989).
- **Composition still waiting to be discovered:** *Violin Concerto* (1976), even though it has been recorded with Wanda Wiłkomirska as soloist and published by Polish Music Publishers. One can only regret that violinists do not know such a great composition, which should belong to the basic repertoire of young talented violinists.

Respondent: Violetta Przech

Roman Berger

Date and place of birth:
9 August 1930, Cieszyn.

Date and place of death:
22 December 2020, Bratislava.

Date and place of emigration:
1952, Czechoslovakia (Bratislava).

Return to Poland:
He did not return.

Key quote

An authentic expression strives towards integrating the definite with the Infinite, towards a 'proof' that what is definite has meaning as long as it can work as a medium for the Infinite. This is, in my opinion, the essence of creativity—the endless discovery of the horizons of the Infinite dimensions of Space, and the perspective of the Universe. Fascination in the processes of perception stems from this essence. This is the message of art.[235]

Activities before emigration

He and his family were forced to emigrate to Slovakia. From 1949 until his departure, Berger studied at the State Higher Music School in Katowice, taking classes in music theory with Jan Gawlas and piano with Marta Gabryś-Furmanik. Earlier, he had taken private music lessons at a Polish school in Český Těšín.

After emigration

After emigrating, he began his studies at the Vysoka Škola Múzických Umeni in Bratislava, where he received a diploma in piano performance in 1956 and, after a break, in composition. He graduated from Dezider Kardoš's class with honors in 1965. Initially, Berger's main area of activity was piano. He devoted himself to it both as a performer and as a lecturer at the Bratislava Conservatory. Berger's first works were also written for piano. His compositional activity is inextricably linked with three other spheres: his professional career (as a sound engineer with Czechoslovak Television and as a teacher with his home university and the Institute of Art History at the Slovak Academy of Sciences), his reflections on music (he wrote a number of works in the areas of music theory and philosophy), as well as his social and community activity (during the Prague Spring he was the secretary of the Slovak Composers' Union and after 1989 he joined a team developing new concepts of artistic education at the Ministry of Education in Slovakia.) In the 1960s, he belonged to a circle of composers (alongside Ilja Zeljenka, Peter Kolman, Miro Bázlik, and Ivan Parík) who shaped the avant-garde profile of Slovak music. He was one of the pioneers of electronic music in Czechoslovakia; his graduation composition, *Transformácie* (1965), was an important voice in the pan-European artistic discussion on serialism and aleatorism. After Warsaw Pact troops invaded Czechoslovakia in 1968, he was severely repressed. He was excluded from participating in musical life and deprived of permanent employment. However, he continued his creative work, gradually rejecting the ideas of the avant-garde. Instead, he refined his means of artistic expression to create personal and expressive music that sometimes incorporated meditative features. Berger's contributions also include creating the Melos-Ethos International Festival of Contemporary Music, which was first held in Bratislava in 1991. Its name emphasizes the ethical and humanist messages of art, which are so important to the composer.

Differences between the old and new realities

Berger's emigration involved changing his residence and professional work within a *de facto* single area—the so-called Eastern Bloc, which was dependent on the Soviet Union and whose cultural policies were centrally managed. It should be remembered, however, that in Czechoslovakia there were greater pressures from the ideology of socialist realism than in Poland. The phases of political and cultural "frosts" and "thaws" were shaped differently than in Poland and the subtle relations between the "brother countries" and their respective composing associations were also an important factor affecting artistic creativity.

Reason for leaving Poland

In 1952 the Czech intelligence demanded that the composer's family leave their homeland (Zaolzie) and settle in Slovakia. This action was prompted by the pro-Polish activity of the composer's father, Father Professor Józef Berger, founder of the Polish Evangelical Church in Český Těšín and a well-known social activist. As a consequence of these repressions, the future composer's passport was seized, making it impossible for him to continue his studies in Katowice.

Contact with Poland after emigration

After his forced emigration, Berger strived, albeit unsucessfully, to continue his musical studies in Poland with Bolesław Woytowicz, never having intended to lose contact with his home country. His works bear numerous traces of Polish inspiration (he used the texts of Polish poets in his work and reacted musically to events taking place in the country), but he returned to Polish musical life slowly.

"The process of repatriation" (the composer's term) began with a meeting at the Polish Composers' Union in autumn 1984 and later manifested itself in invitations to join the juries of Henryk Wieniawski and Witold Lutosławski Composers Competitions, as well as a much delayed debut at the 1988 Warsaw Autumn Festival. Since 1996, Berger has been a member of the Kraków branch of the Polish Composers' Union; in 1999 he became an honorary member of the same union.

Influence of the new home on the composer's music

It can be assumed that Berger's work would have developed along the same paths regardless of his place of residence, since he possesses a distinctive, unrestrained artistic personality. Undoubtedly, however, external conditions had a certain influence on the shape of particular works, as demonstrated in their titles and dedications (e.g., *Elégia in memoriam Ján Rúka* and *Memento po smrti Miroslav Filipa*). Overall, as the composer himself once said in an interview, emigration gave him experiences that he would not have had if he had stayed in Poland. These shaped his creative philosophy, which was to seek "support outside of society," in the world "of infinity and mystery."[236]

Awareness of the composer's music in both countries

Since the fall of the Communist system, Roman Berger has enjoyed respect and recognition both in Slovakia and Poland. In 2012 the Polish Composers' Union awarded him its annual prize in appreciation of his "outstanding compositions and inspiring work in the field of music philosophy and theory." Berger's works have been presented at prestigious festivals and recorded on CDs (on monographic albums as well as anthologies). His music is characterized by a slow narrative that contemplates every sound, timbre, chord, and moment of silence. It remains a real challenge for both performers and listeners and is not intended, perhaps, for wide dissemination.

Composer's personality

Roman Berger is an artist and a philosopher with a strong sense of responsibility for the state of cultural awareness within society. His ideas, which stem from his vast knowledge about current trends in humanities (psychology, sociology, theology), natural sciences (mathematics, physics) and formal sciences (logic, cybernetics, systems theory), focus on emphasizing the spiritual and ethical dimensions of human creativity as a manifestation of life.

Remarkable anecdote or biographical fact

In 1979 Roman Berger completed his work on the theory of contemporary harmony entitled *Logical Basics of a General Harmonic System* [*Logické základy harmonického systemu*], which was to become the foundation of his doctoral degree. Berger tried to systematize the harmonic series according to algebra, thus creating a kind of universal musical grammar. He received very good reviews for his work, but he refused to defend the thesis because he did not want to take a mandatory exam on Marxism.

Respondent's Top Choices

- **Favorite work:** *Epitaph for Copernicus* [*Epitaf pre Mikuláša Kopernika*], electronic music (1972).
- **Best work:** *De profundis* for bass, piano, cello and live electronics (1980).
- **Composition still waiting to be discovered:** There are many of them, especially unpublished works from the early stage of his career such as *Trio* for flute, clarinet and bassoon (1962).

Respondent: Iwona Lindstedt

Wojtek (Wojciech) Blecharz

Date and place of birth:
21 June 1981, Gdynia.

Date and place of emigration:
2008–2014, United States (San Diego); 2015, Germany (Berlin).

Return to Poland:
So far, he has not returned.

Key quote

My sensitivity played an important role in a time of crisis. I moved abroad to study, I wrote music, and at some point I began to wonder: Why am I even doing this? When did it begin? Where does this sensitivity come from? It was an attempt to redefine myself as an artist. I eventually found answers. I believe I have come to terms with trauma. It will remain a part of my life somewhere deep inside, but the point is not to keep opening old wounds and fueling the drama, but to extract energy to act. I respect and accept it when I compose.[237]

Activities before emigration

Initially, he was an oboist specializing in early music and performing with the Pressus ensemble. His first works, from his years studying composition with Marian Borkowski at the Chopin University of Music in Warsaw, often included vocal and choral parts, but did not display much individuality.

After emigration

Blecharz's interests include insightful studies and contact with instruments, a withdrawal from empiricism and psychology, a strong emphasis on the performative and visual aspects of music (the so-called gestures of music), and in-depth work with the archetypes of culture. Gradually, he moved from the field of music towards theater and installations, with the bodily aspect becoming a key element both in performing and receiving music. Also of importance was his embedding of his works in specific, non-concert public spaces—in *site specific* rooms, parks, and houses. Another important aspect of Blecharz's work is his willingness to work patiently with actors, musicians, and listeners, purposely enhancing the level of communication so that together they can actively receive and co-create music.

Differences between the old and new realities

These worlds are actually different from each other. There is no comparison. The reason for his emigration was not so much a desire to go to the United States as it was a breakthrough in his personal life, indicating the end of adolescence and the beginning of maturity.

Reason for leaving Poland

Blecharz experienced a deep crisis related to graduating from the Chopin University of Music with compositional skills, but losing the purpose for which they could be used. Technique, the duplication of existing forms and materials, and a space within a specific niche of contemporary composition were no longer enough for him. He strongly felt the need to start all over again, to look at things from a different angle. He wanted to bring the music of compassion closer to life, to the human body, sensuality, and authenticity, to basic experiences and feelings. He also hoped to overcome his own trauma (related to his father's departure) and illness (asthma). His primary goal became the defining and expressing of his own musical identity.

Contact with Poland after emigration

He maintains extensive contacts. He visits regularly for social and professional reasons. He has received commissions from the Adam Mickiewicz Institute, Warsaw Autumn Festival, and the Lesser Poland Garden of Art [Małopolski Ogród Sztuki]. His cooperation with theaters has developed particularly vividly with the Warsaw's Grand Theater – Polish National Opera [Teatr Wielki – Opera Narodowa], the Variety Theater [Teatr Rozmaitości] and Universal Theater [Teatr Powszechny] in Warsaw, and the Dramatic Theater in Wałbrzych. Close contacts with vocalists, instrumentalists, and ensembles (Royal String Quartet, Maciej Frąckiewicz, Magdalena Bojanowicz, Kwadrofonik, Barbara Kinga Majewska, and Anna Radziejewska) are also a regular feature of his time in Poland. Curatorial work has proven to be an important element as well, particularly with the Install-Actions [Instalakcje] Festival at Warsaw's New Theater.

Influence of the new home on the composer's music

This influence has occured on many levels. During his doctoral work at the University of California in San Diego, his encounters with students, musicians, and lecturers from different parts of the world became key components of his own investigations. Another crucial element was his contact with psychologist Piotr Winkielman, with whom Blecharz co-taught classes on music as a metaphor for experiencing the world. His move to Berlin was preceded by a visit to the legendary Berghain club with its powerful sound system that enables a bodily, even visceral way of perceiving music.

Awareness of the composer's music in both countries

Blecharz's music is currently known in international circles, as the artist has received invitations from the United States, Germany, Poland, France, Israel, Australia, and China. The composer's personality is undoubtedly helpful here, as is his rare ability to go beyond the environment of contemporary music and music in general. Every year Blecharz's work becomes more and more popular and is presented in different places. However, it seems that most of his workshops and installations still occur in Poland.

Composer's personality

The composer combines a socially active way of life with an ability to reach out to many audiences with his ideas, opening them to new experiences and appreciation of people, and then cooperating creatively with them. His sometimes brusque extrovert character—which conceals the hidden characteristics of his personality—is revealed in his high activity on social networking sites, his constant play with his own image, and his care for his clothes and appearance. At the same time, the artist is sensitive to questioners and is able to quickly move on to the level of an in-depth or even deeply personal relationship.

Remarkable anecdote or biographical fact

Asthma prevented him from developing a career on wind instruments. This led him to take up composition. It is said that he has to get new shoes before each premiere. He wears an ever-increasing number of meaningful tattoos, which are connected to important stages of his life. He likes to work with actors and non-musicians, with whom he conducts vocal experiments, trying different ways of making sounds.

Respondent's Top Choices

- **Favorite work:** *Liminal Studies* for string quartet (2014), *Hypopnea* for accordion (2010).
- **Best work:** Opera-installation *Transcryptum* (2012) and the individual pieces from the production.
- **Composition still waiting to be discovered:** *Airlines* (2008).

Respondent: Jan Topolski

Joanna Bruzdowicz-Tittel

Date and place of birth:
17 May 1943, Warsaw.

Date and place of emigration:
1968, France (Paris); 1975–2002, Belgium; 2002, France (Céret and Taillet).

Return to Poland:
No, she lives permanently in France and visits Poland regularly.

Key quote

One cannot learn how to compose. One has to be born with this talent. We can merely learn the rules of grammar and spelling in music, to learn how to write for particular instruments and how to orchestrate without making basic mistakes. I have learned from him [Messiaen] *to hear music, voices, and noises around us in this special way.... Thanks to him, I have learned to listen to orchestral music as if it is a choir and to hear instruments as voices of nature. It was a very interesting experience and very good for me.*[238]

Activities before emigration

Joanna Bruzdowicz-Tittel grew up in a musical family. Her first compositional attempts date back to her childhood. She claims that she began composing at the age of six.[239] She graduated with honors from Kazimierz Sikorski's composition class at the State Higher School of Music in Warsaw in 1966, where she also studied piano. While still a student, she gave concerts as a pianist in Austria and Belgium.

After emigration

The young composer began her stay in France by continuing her studies in composition and musicology. In 1969 she took part in the organizational and creative work of the Groupe international de musique électroacoustique. Her activities also include music criticism and journalism. Moreover, the composer is active in institutions promoting Polish music and electroacoustic composition. She conducts master classes in the United States and France. After she went to study abroad, the composer remained there. She moved to Belgium in 1975. Since 2002 she has lived in Céret and Taillet in southern France. In 1996, she established the International Music Festival in Céret, which is dedicated to composers representing the three countries having the first democratic constitutions in the world: the United States, Poland, and France.

Differences between the old and new realities

It is difficult to point out any differences. It is much easier to see a consistent and profound development and humanism, which was already apparent at an early stage of her career. Bruzdowicz's compositional style is most fully demonstrated in her stage works and film music. Her operas are not only characterized by the highest artistic qualities, but they have also become symbolic works related to Poland's recent history. They also provide an important voice in any discussion of the moral and philosophical condition of contemporary man.

In 1967, before her emigration, the twenty-four-year-old composer composed the opera *Penal Colony* [*Kolonia Karna*], a faithful adaptation of Franz Kafka's 1914 short story. Its play of meanings and symbols and its difficult and emotional dialogue between a traveler and an officer justifying the use of the newest machine—a tool of torture used to punish prisoners—was interpreted in many ways: as a disturbing war satire, a foreshadowing of concentration camps, and even a dramatic vision of religious fanaticism. In Bruzdowicz's approach, we see, above all, the brutality and distortion of justice in an inhuman system of power. The allusion to the postwar political situation in Poland was obvious. The work was written for the opera in Prague, but the perversity of fate meant that the work was not premiered due to the Prague Spring and the invasion of Warsaw Pact troops in 1968. It was finally staged in 1972 in Tours, France. The Polish premiere did not take place until 1995, at Warsaw's Grand Theater – Polish National Opera.

In 1972, Bruzdowicz's opera *The Women of Troy*, based on a play by Euripides that tells the story of women entangled in the drama of war and enslavement, had its premiere in Paris. Euripides focused not on the phenomenon of winners and heroes, but rather on the cruelty, thoughtlessness, and looting committed by warriors, especially in the face of the weak and defenseless women of Troy. The opera contributed a voice in a discussion that had been intensifying since the 1970s—a debate on the modern presentation of the heroes and victims of war. Bruzdowicz's third important stage work was her opera *Gates of Paradise* [*Bramy raju*] (1980–1981), based on a novel by Jerzy Andrzejewski. This is another work written to an important text and under unusual conditions. While dealing with the period of Communism, Andrzejewski emphasized his lack of acceptance for fanaticism, including the religious variety. Andrzejewski was interned at the time when the opera was being written. Locked in his own apartment and supervised by Polish security services, he could not contact anyone. The composer presented a story of children embarking on a cruel crusade. The opera's premiere, planned for 1985 at the Grand Theater in Łódź, was stopped by censors. It was finally allowed to be performed on 15 November 1987 at the Grand Theater – National Opera in Warsaw.

Bruzdowicz's early works, especially those written while still in Poland, are characterized by the need for experimentation and a search for color and form. They provide examples of successful explorations of electroacoustic music and music that exists in correlation with other artistic disciplines, including the visual arts, dance, movement, and pantomime.

Reason for leaving Poland

The direct reasons for her emigration were the composition studies in Paris that she undertook from 1968–1970 after receiving a scholarship from the French government. She studied with Nadia Boulanger, Olivier Messiaen, and Pierre Schaeffer. At the same time, she began studying musicology under Jacques Chailley at the Paris Sorbonne.

Contact with Poland after emigration

The composer has maintained contact with Poland. She remains a member of the Polish Composers' Union and visits the country on a regular basis. Despite this, her work remains relatively unknown in Poland. It is performed only occasionally, while her scores are difficult to access. In 2013 the composer was awarded with the silver *Gloria Artis* Medal for Merit to Culture.

Influence of the new home on the composer's music

Her life during emigration has resulted in a vast amount of music, mainly for film, but also radio works, vocal and vocal-instrumental compositions, and an equally impressive catalog of strictly instrumental works. What is distinctive about this output is certainly the musical content and construction of narration and tension, which is inseparably connected with feelings of imagery and soundscapes and with narratives stretching between the epic and the lyrical. It would seem that such narratives would require a different, autonomous compositional form, but in Bruzdowicz's work we find a tendency to use classical frames within universal as well as more individual approaches. Bruzdowicz's instrumental music is filled with humanist content and emotions, as well as analogies to visual arts in the form of sound colors that pulse with a life akin to film imagery.

Awareness of the composer's music in both countries

The name of Joanna Bruzdowicz-Tittel is currently among the most frequently mentioned of all Polish composers in international concert halls. From the rich catalog of the composer's works performed in Poland, her stage works are the most famous and recognizable. Her outstanding film, instrumental, and vocal music remain better known outside Poland, France, and the United States.

Composer's personality

In the case of Bruzdowicz-Tittel, one striking feature of her personality is a clearly felt balance of emotions, which is also manifested in the formal and expressive equanimity of her music. The wide range of emotions and colors in her compositions seems to be the result of her careful understanding of humans as independent creatures on the path of life and at the same time as people who are part of the mystery of nature and the world.

Remarkable anecdote or biographical fact

In 1972 Joanna Bruzdowicz-Tittel received French citizenship for her contributions to French culture. This allowed her to hold the position of councilor in the city of Thaillet for three terms.

Respondent's Top Choices

- **Favorite work:** *String Quartet No. 1 "La Vita"* (1983).
- **Best work:** Operas: *Penal Colony* (1967), *Women of Troy* (1972), *Gates of Paradise* (1980–1981).
- **Composition still waiting to be discovered:** *16 Pictures from Salvador Dali's Exhibition* [*16 obrazków z wystawy Salvadora Dali*] for piano (2004).

Respondent: Aleksandra Bilińska

Andrzej Dobrowolski

Date and place of birth:
9 September 1921, Lviv.

Date and place of death:
8 August 1990, Graz.

Date and place of emigration:
1975, Austria (Graz).

Return to Poland:
He did not return.

Key quote

The problem is that his music is not easy. It is sonoristic, connected with mathematical precision and a love for classical forms as well as abstraction.[240]

Activities before emigration

During the Nazi occupation, he studied organ, clarinet, and singing at the Warsaw Conservatory. After the war he studied composition and theory at the State Higher School of Music in Kraków with Artur Malawski and Stefania Łobaczewska. From 1954–1976, he taught theory at the State Higher School of Music in Warsaw. Beginning in 1964 he also taught a composition class. He was an important figure in the Polish Radio Experimental Studio, founded in 1958. He was involved in the activities of the Polish Composers' Union—from 1954–1968 he served as its Secretary General and also belonged to the Warsaw Autumn Festival's program committee.

After emigration

After emigration Dobrowolski was primarily active as a teacher. Beginning in 1975 he was a guest lecturer at the Hochschule für Musik und darstellende Kunst in Graz (today's Universität für Musik und darstellende Kunst Graz, often abbreviated to Kunstuniversität Graz). The following year he became a professor at the same university and three years later became dean of the Faculty of Composition, Theory, and Conducting. He taught composition and electroacoustic music classes there and was also associated with the Institut für Elektronische Musik in Graz. His students included composer Bernhard Lang and others.

Differences between the old and new realities

In the 1970s the Polish People's Republic, despite its apparent prosperity, experienced political issues that hindered scientific and artistic development. Dobrowolski never joined the Polish United Workers' Party, which made it difficult for him to pursue a professional career at Warsaw's music academy. In Graz, on the other hand, where the composition department was only just developing, the composer's outstanding knowledge and skills were properly appreciated.

Reason for leaving Poland

Dobrowolski's emigration was motivated by the offer of a professorship from the Hochschule für Musik und darstellende Kunst in Graz. His departure from the country allowed Dobrowolski to develop his career freely—in Austria, he was appointed professor of composition and soon became the dean of the department.

Contact with Poland after emigration

After 1976, Dobrowolski's music continued to be frequently performed at Polish festivals such as the Warsaw Autumn and the Poznań Musical Spring.

Influence of the new home on the composer's music

Dobrowolski went to Graz as a mature and talented composer, regarded by the Austrian community as one of the most important representatives of the Polish avant-garde and a pioneer of electronic and experimental music. However, it was at the Institut für Elektronische Musik where Dobrowolski came into contact with the latest technologies, which even at the end of his life led him to use very sophisticated electronic tools in the composition process, e.g., computers and a digital FM synthesizer in one of his last works, *Passacaglia für TX 816*.

Awareness of the composer's music in both countries

In Graz, with which the composer was associated for the last fifteen years of his life, the memory of Dobrowolski is still alive and his music, which is primarily electroacoustic, is still performed. He is considered to be one of the main founders of the Graz school of composition, whose representatives include Bernhard Lang and Georg Friedrich Haas. In Poland, Dobrowolski's music is rarely heard, certainly less often than the other pioneers of Polish electroacoustic music. On the twenty-fifth anniversary of the composer's death, the Chopin University of Music in Warsaw organized a conference to celebrate his work. In both Poland and Austria, the composer is regarded as a precursor of electroacoustic music who had great influence on the development of the two experimental studios in which he worked.

Composer's personality

Dorota Szwarcman, Dobrowolski's student, remembers him as an excellent, accessible teacher. Bernhard Lang recalls his professor kindly as well. Dobrowolski's precision and diligence can be noticed in his method of working on compositions in the studio, which requires precise planning of the entire process beforehand, as well as in terms of purely instrumental music, for which insightful research on the performing possibilities of an instrument is necessary.

Remarkable anecdote or biographical fact

In 1990, in recognition of his contributions to Graz's musical life, Dobrowolski received the Johann Joseph Fux Styrian Government Music Award. Since then, the government in Graz has honored him by awarding the Dobrowolski award every three years to an outstanding local composer. In 2017 it was given to Joanna Woźny, a Polish composer living in Graz.

Respondent's Top Choices

- **Favorite work:** An interesting work in Dobrowolski's oeuvre is a non-electroacoustic one, the *Music for 3 Accordions, Harmonica, and Percussion* [*Muzyka na 3 akordeony, harmonijkę ustną i perkusję*] (1977), written for the Warsaw Accordion Trio and Zygmunt Zgraja, a harmonica virtuoso. The work is based on the idea of number three (three accordionists, three percussionists, three types of harmonica) and has a topophonic construction—the musicians are arranged in the shape of a triangle, while the soloist performs inside that space.
- **Best work:** One of Dobrowolski's last works, which uses advanced electronic tools, is *Passacaglia für TX 816* (1989). The composition, written at the Institut für Elektronische Musik, uses a 64-voice FM Yamaha TX 816 digital synthesizer and Atari computers. The microtonal, mathematically designed structure of the piece was transferred into complex threads of data and performed by a sequencer. The composition is rarely performed since it requires an extensive onstage sound system.
- **Composition still waiting to be discovered:** *String Quartet* (1989), *Symphony No. 1* (1955).

Respondent: Ewa Chorościan

Jerzy Fitelberg

Date and place of birth:
20 May 1903, Warsaw.

Date and place of death:
25 April 1951, New York.

Date and place of emigration:
1922–1932, Germany (Berlin); 1933–1939, France (Paris); 1940–1951, United States (New York; in 1947 he became an American citizen).

Return to Poland:
He did not return.

Key quote

The work of first-rate composers like Jerzy Fitelberg, whose journey into oblivion was the direct result of nothing but ideological politics, speaks for itself and deserves its rightful place in the firmament of musical art.[241]

Activities before emigration

Jerzy Fitelberg's youth had a great influence on the formation of the future composer. His father, conductor Grzegorz Fitelberg (1879–1953), worked with many orchestras in Poland (the Warsaw Philharmonic and the Polish Radio Orchestra) as well as abroad (the Vienna State Opera, Sergei Diaghilev's Russian Ballets, etc.). It was Grzegorz Fitelberg who introduced little Jerzy to the world of music. In addition, his father's musical environment and concert tours outside of Poland fostered the development of his young talent. Jerzy Fitelberg graduated from Warsaw Conservatory with degrees in piano and composition. However, feeling the need to improve his musical skills as a nineteen-year-old, in 1922 he decided to continue his studies in Berlin.

After emigration

While abroad, Fitelberg focused mostly on composing classical music, although it was not out of the question for him to also undertake other work to support himself. He was a good pianist; he also wrote reviews of concerts in Berlin for the American *Modern Music* quarterly. The fact that his works were played and appreciated by both audiences and critics is demonstrated by his numerous awards and distinctions. His music was performed by famous musicians and renowned orchestras. His biggest compositional success was *String Quartet No. 2*, honored at a competition organized by the Association of Young

Polish Musicians in Paris in 1928. The competition jury, comprised of Maurice Ravel, Florent Schmitt, Albert Roussel, and Artur Honegger, awarded first prize to 25-year-old Fitelberg. In 1936 Fitelberg also received the prestigious Elizabeth Sprague Coolidge Award for *String Quartet No. 4*. His greatest achievement, however, was the award for his entire oeuvre, granted by the American Academy of Arts and Letters in 1945.

Differences between the old and new realities

These worlds differed mainly in the possibility of cooperation with the West and contacts with the best musicians and latest artistic trends. His departure can also be interpreted as a desire to cut himself off from his father's influence and attempt to become independent. Later, in the United States, thanks to his European contacts, Fitelberg connected with a circle of musicians who went through similar paths of emigration, including conductor Artur Rodziński, composer and pianist Karol Rathaus, and violinist Stefan Frenkel.

Reason for leaving Poland

The young Fitelberg was undoubtedly attracted by the artistic possibilities of Berlin in the 1920s. While studying in the capital of the Weimar Republic, he established worldwide contacts, attended concerts, wrote reviews, eagerly listened to the radio, and sought out new music in concert programs. When Hitler came to power, however, Fitelberg's Jewish origin deprived him of the opportunity to participate in Berlin's musical life. For this reason, he left for Paris in 1933, where he spent the next few years. Fearing he would lose his life after the outbreak of the Second World War, he emigrated to the United States and settled in New York.

Contact with Poland after emigration

Fitelberg's contact with his homeland was minimal, basically limited to relationships with other Polish emigrants, yet the Polish titles of many of the songs and mazurkas he composed suggest that his native country remained on his mind. Having remained completely cut off during the war, after 1945 he re-established his links with Poland in exchanges of letters with his father, perhaps also with his friends from his youth, and through reading the Polish press. Reading the *Ruch Muzyczny*, a biweekly musical magazine, inspired his enthusiastic article in the *Modern Music* quarterly about rebuilding postwar Poland's musical environment. However, unlike his father, he never decided to return to Poland.

Influence of the new home on the composer's music

Fitelberg studied at the highly regarded Berlin Hochschule für Musik in the composition class of liberal professor Franz Schreker. His music's motoric rhythms, bold harmonic solutions, graceful melodies (sometimes in folk character), and moments of reverie and reflection immediately bring to mind the influences of neoclassicism and Stravinsky's compositions. He composed chamber works in traditional genres (serenades, etudes, caprices, and suites) for wind quintet, string quartet, and solo instruments (piano, violin, clarinet, organ), as well as symphonies, concertos, and other works (e.g., *Nocturne* for orchestra). For Fitelberg, radio was an important medium for conveying contemporary music. The orchestration of works with a view to recording them for radio was one of the topics he raised on the pages of *Modern Music*. He also dedicated his *Symphony No. 1* to Franz André, a conductor at Belgian Radio.

Awareness of the composer's music in both countries

Fitelberg's works first fell victim to Nazi censorship; later Communist policies prevented interest in them from developing in postwar Poland. The composer's premature death also contributed to the lack of promotion of his works in the context of postwar music. Abroad, even in the United States, despite his American citizenship, he was always a "foreigner." The New York Public Library has a large collection of notes and manuscripts by Fitelberg, but scant personal documentation makes it difficult to reconstruct his life. Recent recordings have contributed to the increase in Fitelberg's interest in the context of Polish composers in exile (*Poland Abroad* and *Franz Schreker's Masterclasses in Vienna and Berlin*, vol. 2, EDA Records). The Canadian ARC Ensemble has recently released a recording devoted to Fitelberg's music (Chandos 10877).

Composer's personality

Due to the lack of documents, we can only define Fitelberg's personality based on his works. His oeuvre was extensive, especially considering his premature death at the age of 48. Having lived in several countries, he spoke a number of languages (Polish, German, French, and English, the last of which he excelled at writing). He did not seem to be sentimental, instead expressing a rather practical approach to moving between countries.

Remarkable anecdote or biographical fact

He wrote three songs—*Lost Fantasies*, *Silverblue,* and *A Timely Tale*—under the pen name Steve Terry.

Respondent's Top Choices

- **Favorite work:** The *Andante* movement from an early work, *String Quartet No. 2* (1928), particularly its opening section, which uses a simple, especially contemplative cello melody.
- **Best work:** *Nocturne* for orchestra (1944), premiered with the New York Philharmonic Orchestra in 1946.
- **Composition still waiting to be discovered:** *Concertino da camera* for piano and violin (1951), commissioned by conductor Serge Koussevitzky and the last work completed by Fitelberg.

Respondent: Ewelina Boczkowska

Mikołaj Piotr Górecki

Date and place of birth:
1 February 1971, Katowice.

Date and place of emigration:
1996, Canada (Banff, Montreal); after 2001, United States (Bloomington, Indiana; Laredo, Texas).

Return to Poland:
He has not returned.

Key quote

Becoming a composer was never my intention. It simply happened.[242]

Activities before emigration

As the son of Henryk Mikołaj Górecki, he was raised in a musical environment from an early age. He started learning to play the violin early on (his father wanted him to become a violinist) and then began studying piano. Even before he graduated from the Secondary Music School in Katowice (1990), he won a composing competition—in 1988 he received first prize at the First Competition for Young Composers in Bielsko-Biała for his *Preludes* for piano. In 1994, when a student in his father's composition class at the Karol Szymanowski Academy of Music in Katowice, he was awarded third prize from the Critics' Chapter at the Second Competition for Young Composers in Kraków for his *Sonata* for clarinet and piano. In 1995 he graduated with honors and began teaching at his home university. A year later he went to study abroad, and after graduation he settled in the United States.

After emigration

After two scholarships at the Banff Centre for the Arts in Canada (1996–1997), he continued his studies at Indiana University in Bloomington (United States), where he received his doctorate in composition (2000). From 2000–2001 he lectured at McGill University in Montreal; he currently works at Laredo College in Texas. He regularly composes in various musical genres from symphonic and vocal-instrumental to chamber music. His compositions are performed in the United States as well as in Poland and other European countries.

Differences between the old and new realities

The completely different reality of America has allowed Górecki not only to break away from the circumstances of life in Poland, but also to move away from its domestic music milieu, where he was seen primarily from the perspective of his famous father's achievements. His stay abroad has helped him develop the necessary distance; without the pressure of comparison to his father, he was able to establish his own compositional idiom.

Reason for leaving Poland

When asked about the reason for leaving Poland, the composer replied briefly: "the need for peace and time."[243] In the United States, he has been able devote himself fully to his creative work (in addition to his teaching duties) and to develop his own compositional style.

Contact with Poland after emigration

In an interview, the composer said: "I've never left for good. It's simply been a good couple of years."[244] Throughout these years he remained in constant contact with Poland, both privately (visiting his family) and professionally. His works are often performed at Polish festivals and concerts, including the Katowice Festival of Premieres [Festiwal Prawykonań] in Katowice, Karol Szymanowski Music Days [Dni Muzyki Karola Szymanowskiego] in Zakopane, and concerts and recordings with the Silesian Philharmonic, the Aukso Orchestra, and others. The composer also has received commissions from the Ministry of Culture and National Heritage and writes for outstanding Polish performers, including Ewa Pobłocka, Joanna Domańska, Kaja Danczowska, Agnieszka Duczmal, and the Amadeus Orchestra.

Influence of the new home on the composer's music

Górecki claims that apart from a different sense of time and peace, his new land has not affected his music. Indeed, it seems that he has continued the style known from the works he created in Poland, which are marked by the vocal quality of their melodic lines and a mood of nostalgia and mild melancholy. His music, however, is not devoid of humor and energy in fast movements (e.g., *Trio Titanic* for clarinet, horn and piano, 2012–2013). The composer's musical language is communicative and accessible, far from experimentation and sonic extravagance; communication with the audience and conveying his emotions through music remain most important to him. A note of contemplation and reverie, often present in his music (e.g., in *Radiant Light* [*Jasności promieniste*], a small mysterium for soprano and orchestra set to the words of Czesław Miłosz, 2014), often reveals a close affinity with the music of his father. The composer does not avoid the atmosphere of nocturnes (*Concerto notturno* for violin and string orchestra, 2001; *Nocturne* for orchestra, 2011) or elegiac moods (*Elegy* [*Elegia*] for cello and string orchestra, 2015; *Sonata lamentosa* for soprano, cello, and piano to texts by Krzysztof Kamil Baczyński, 2016). He also shows a stormy nature from time to time, as in *Arioso e furioso* for guitar, string orchestra, and percussion (2014).

In terms of the lyrical layers of his works, the composer most often reaches for Polish poetry (by Jan Kochanowski, Czesław Miłosz, and Krzysztof Kamil Baczyński) and traditional religious writings (*Gloria* for mixed choir and string orchestra, 2000; *Mass* [*Msza*] for baritone, choir and orchestra, 2015). *Zan Totemico*, a composition for orchestra (2006) inspired by the pre-Columbian poetry of the Aztec, is an example of American inspirations (Central American, specifically).

Awareness of the composer's music in both countries

Górecki's music is performed in both countries. His compositions have been presented in New York, Chicago, Montreal, Victoria, Edmonton, and Washington, as well as in Katowice, Wrocław, Poznań, Bielsko-Biała, Zakopane, Łódź, and Warsaw. His music is warmly received by audiences on both sides of the Atlantic. The composer returns to Poland frequently, where he enjoys a group of friendly performers as well as a regular audience.

Composer's personality

Górecki would describe his personality as sanguine, dispassionate, and irascible, and indeed, all these elements can be found in his works, although in different doses. It seems that the composer appreciates peace and independence the most. At the same time, he displays great respect for musical traditions. Hence, he has never felt the need to break with the musical past and seek new forms of expression, because he is comfortable finding his own way among traditional idioms and musical techniques. He prefers to work methodically.

Remarkable anecdote or biographical fact

In his early youth, the composer played guitar in a rock band, hiding this fact from his parents. He has always been interested in various types of music (including entertainment), and in his compositions one can find influences of the various styles from which he has built his musical language. He adores Mozart and points to the *Symphony in G minor*, KV 550, as his favorite work. Recently the composer decided to add a middle name and now he is usually referred to as Mikołaj Piotr Górecki.

Respondent's Top Choices

- **Favorite work:** *Orpheus and Eurydice* for orchestra (2003).
- **Best work:** In the case of a composer in the heyday of his creativity, it is difficult to point out the best work of a lifetime. Certainly, one of the most important and recognized ones is the *Concerto notturno* for violin and string orchestra (2000), which enjoys huge popularity and has been performed by renowned violinists such as Krzysztof Bąkowski and Kaja Danczowska.
- **Composition still waiting to be discovered:** *Mass* for baritone, choir and orchestra (2015).

Respondent: Beata Bolesławska-Lewandowska

Roman Haubenstock-Ramati

Date and place of birth:
27 February 1919, Kraków.

Date and place of death:
3 March 1994, Vienna.

Date and place of emigration:
1950, Israel (Tel Aviv), 1957; Austria (Vienna).

Return to Poland:
He did not return.

Key quote

That which is new in our era, the spontaneity of art, connects a work of art directly to an idea. If this occurs in a musical composition that is partly or entirely developed, it is linked more or less to limited aleatorism. From the compositional point of view, spontaneity requires, or calls for, graphic notation. Such notation is based on ambiguity, because it directs or—more importantly, in my opinion—it provokes spontaneity, as happens in the case of 'musical graphics'.[245]

Activities before emigration

The early works of Roman Haubenstock, who studied with Artur Malawski in Kraków, were inspired by the music of Debussy, Ravel, and Stravinsky, among others. In turn, his fascination with the twelve-tone system, especially as seen in Anton Webern's works, developed during his studies with Józef Koffler in Lviv and significantly influenced his further creative path. His war experiences were dramatic: in 1941, he was accused of spying and imprisoned by the Soviet authorities. After receiving amnesty due to his work as a military musician, he joined Anders' Army and eventually reached Palestine; there, he adopted his Hebrew name, Ramati. In 1945, he settled in Kraków, where he joined in the reconstruction of Polish musical life. He was an editor for *Ruch Muzyczny*, where he also published articles on atonal composition and film music. He also headed the music department at Polish Radio's Kraków branch. Mostly, however, he worked on developing his own musical language, demonstrated best in the *String Trio "Ricercari,"* published in Israel.

After emigration

At the request of the Israeli government, Haubenstock-Ramati organized and ran the State Music Library. From 1954–1956 he taught composition at the Music Academy in Tel Aviv. He also continued his creative work, in an interesting way. As did many other young Israeli artists educated in Europe, he combined modern compositional means with local inspirations (e.g., in *Bénédictions* for soprano and nine instruments). However, he felt isolated from the mainstream of avant-garde music and, for that reason, took advantage of a scholarship to study in Europe in 1957. Among other places, he worked in Pierre Schaeffer's Parisian *musique concrète* studio and established contacts that enabled him to change his residency and place of work. He moved permanently to Vienna and took up a position at the Universal Edition Music Publishers. Until 1971 he was a lecturer and consultant there, where he supervised the graphic design of new music scores. He also was a professor at the Universität für Musik und darstellende Kunst from 1973–1989 and directed the Institut für Elektroakustik und Experimentelle Musik from 1976–1986. He has led numerous composition courses (including those in Darmstadt) and lectured in academic institutions around the world. It was thanks to him that in 1959, during the Donaueschingen Festival of Contemporary Music, the first exhibition of musical graphics was organized, thus displaying an art form that has aesthetic value as a visual design and does not have to be (although it may be) "translated" into music.

Differences between the old and new realities

Haubenstock-Ramati functioned not between two but actually in three different worlds. In each of them, as an artist, he had to challenge different political, social, and economic conditions that impacted his creative work. Poland in the second half of the 1940s struggled with the consequences of war devastation, while Israel, since its very beginning, has faced the consequences of a lack of proper infrastructure and industry as well as a mass influx of immigrants, as Jews arrived from all over the world. Although both in Poland and Israel, Haubenstock-Ramati was able to make a living, it was only in Austria that he gained what was essential for him—an opportunity to develop artistically, free of pressure from state cultural policy.

Reason for leaving Poland

The reasons for his emigration from Poland were exclusively artistic: the impossibility of composing what and how he wanted. The pressure of Stalinist cultural policy was unbearable for him and he strongly rejected the possibility of accepting a compromise. Artistic motivations—although not without a shadow of political influence—made him decide to move to Vienna. The internal and external problems of the young state of Israel, and especially the overly conservative attitude of its cultural community towards music as it attempted to create its own national version did not produce conditions sufficient for creative freedom, of which the composer was an ardent advocate.

Contact with Poland after emigration

In one of his letters to the Austrian musicologist Robert Schollum, Haubenstock-Ramati wrote: "Please do not assign me to the 'Polish school', because that is not appropriate! I belong to the Viennese school and I am expanding Schoenberg's and Webern's ideas towards the variability and multiplication of musical form!!" However, these emotional words are only an aesthetic declaration, perhaps inevitable given the uproar that the term "Polish school of composition" caused in the musical world of the 1960s. The composer never lost contact with his home country, as evidenced by his correspondence stored at Paul Sacher Stiftung in Basel. As a professor at the Vienna Hochschule, he trained composers who came from Poland, including Bronisław Kazimierz Przybylski, Edward Bogusławski, and Paweł Szymański. Moreover, Haubenstock-Ramati's compositions appeared regularly in the programs of the Warsaw Autumn Festival (eleven of his works were performed there between 1961 and 2000), and he visited Poland several times to assist in these premieres.

Influence of the new home on the composer's music

After 1958, Haubenstock-Ramati's most important achievement was to create the idea of a modern musical form whose framework was set by the composer, but whose actual shape was left to the performers. He called these so-called "dynamically closed forms" mobiles, by analogy to the visual arts, specifically to the sculptures of Alexander Calder (1898–1976), which are characterized by the interaction of moving parts. The process of creating this form consisted of repeating its elements and simultaneously differentiating such repetitions—in other words, a "constant changeability through constant repetition." The composer also explained this idea through the metaphor of playing cards, in which the deck means a fixed formal structure and the order of individual cards is a variable determined as they are handled. Haubenstock also searched for an adequate way to transfer these principles of construction to graphic notation, which led to the creation of a specific type of score showing a number of fields arranged in a certain area. Moreover, the composer became a precursor to the genre of musical graphics (i.e., musical works written in the form of graphic signs rather than notes), for which he developed an original, recognizable language of signs. Towards the end of his life, he turned to the idea of "imagined music," showing the essence of orchestral sound in delicate sound structures and their unique constellations, which due to their temporary nature play out more in the listener's imagination than in real time.

Awareness of the composer's music in both countries

Alongside Friedrich Cerha and György Ligeti, Haubenstock-Ramati even during his life was considered one of the most outstanding representatives of twentieth-century Austrian music and an heir of the Second Viennese School. Today, however, his output remains in the shadow of the achievements of others. He remains unknown to a wider audience, recognized only by an elite group of listeners. His music is available to a narrow circle of the initiated and is usually presented in selected forums, for example at new music festivals or on labels such as Hat Hut Records (Switzerland) and Kairos (Vienna). Considered an "Austrian composer of Polish origin" (*Grove Music Online*), he is still awaiting his rightful place in the history of twentieth-century Polish music.

Composer's personality

Accounts from Haubenstock-Ramati's friends, associates and students reveal an image of someone who was extremely modest, avoided the glamour of public life, and was charmingly discreet. As an artist, he was an example of tolerance and openness to novelty; as a teacher, he displayed succinctness, consistency, and responsibility as he passed on the art of composition to young students. He did this in a manner devoid of excessive verbal persuasion, and his teaching was based on examples of his own openness and sensitivity.

Remarkable anecdote or biographical fact

In 1991, despite a fundamental aversion to the media, Haubenstock-Ramati agreed to design the title page of the first issue of *Ton*, a newly created magazine devoted to contemporary music; he also accepted an interview request. This situation took an unexpected turn, as it was the composer who started asking questions of his interviewers. As a result, an exciting, chaotic dialogue developed, brimming with multifaceted digressions and returns to barely abandoned threads in altered conditions, all of which are reminiscent of the composer's principles for shaping music.

Respondent's Top Choices

- **Favorite work:** *Credentials or "Think, Think Lucky"* for voice and eight instruments, to a text by Samuel Beckett (1960).
- **Best work:** *America* [*Amerika*], an opera, libretto by the composer, based on Franz Kafka's book (1962–1964).
- **Composition still waiting to be discovered:** *Recitativo ed aria* (*Harpsichord Concerto*) (1954, new version 1978).

Respondent: Iwona Lindstedt

Dobromiła Jaskot

Date and place of birth:
29 May 1981, Toruń.

Date and place of emigration:
2015, Australia (Perth).

Return to Poland:
No, but she visits Poland occasionally.

Key quote

When I look back at my life, I can see that things were falling into place. I haven't experienced a struggle against various adversities in the creative field. I don't want to push my way to the front. I'm simply waiting for things to develop. Of course, I'm very motivated and passionate. This is the most important thing for me—a sense of heading in the right direction. I'm not afraid of the future. I'm prepared for anything, and I'm aware it won't always be easy.[246]

Activities before emigration

Prior to her emigration, Jaskot worked as a lecturer at the Feliks Nowowiejski Academy of Music in Bydgoszcz, where she led popular classes on electronic, film, and multimedia music. She was educated in Poland, receiving a Master's degree in composition at Poznań's Academy of Music. She also completed postgraduate studies in film music at the Music Academy in Łódź and a doctorate at the Academy of Music in Wrocław. She has received scholarships and commissions from her home country. Many of her works have also been premiered in Poland, for example, the opera *Phaedra* [*Fedra*] in 2006 at Warsaw's Grand Theater – National Opera. Her exceptionally colorful and somewhat mystical creative personality, a fascination with Eastern music and Buddhism, as well as an original musical language were shaped during her life in Poland. Her works have been performed frequently; she has also appeared on stage as a pianist, which she studied at music schools in Toruń. At the Academy of Music in Bydgoszcz, she managed the electroacoustic studio and organized concerts and workshops for composers, performers, and sound directors.

After emigration

Jaskot works as a freelance artist in Australia. She composes, performs her own works, and gives private piano lessons. Occasionally, she cooperates with universities, including the Western Australian Academy of Performing Art (a department of the Edith Cowan University) and the University of Western Australia in Perth and Monash University in Melbourne; she also works as an examiner in composition classes. She is developing other passions, which it was not possible to do in Poland—interior design is now an important part of her professional life. It is important to note that Jaskot's music can be heard increasingly often at important new music festivals such as the Bendigo International Festival of Exploratory Music (BIFEM) or Totally Huge New Music Festival (Perth). Invitations have also come from excellent performers, including the Elision Ensemble and the Argonaut Quartet, as well as artistic associations such as TURA New Music from Perth.

Differences between the old and new realities

These worlds differ primarily in their mentality—their approach to life. Australia has a more relaxed attitude towards issues that would generate problems in Poland, which undoubtedly allows Australians to pursue their own passions more independently. However, concert life, especially in the field of contemporary music, is very different than in Poland and culture in general has a different status. Grants and artistic scholarships are not as established there as in Europe or the United States; as a result, new music has to follow a much longer and more difficult path to reach Australian stages. In Perth, as in all of Western Australia, improvised music reigns, performed on the basis of arrangements between performers and composers made almost immediately before the concert. In comparison, music that is precisely noted and requires many weeks of preparation, including numerous rehearsals and polishing of every detail, remains in a somewhat less favorable position.

Reason for leaving Poland

The main reasons for Jaskot's emigration were the general professional atmosphere, the sense of a lack of prospects, and a feeling of underappreciation in Poland, which were in complete contrast to the artistic scene in Australia, where her talent and potential were properly assessed. Above all, however, it was love that prompted her to look for new prospects in Australia, for she followed Dominik Karski there.

Contact with Poland after emigration

Jaskot's contact with Poland is extensive on both artistic (commissions, performances) and personal (family, friends) levels. While she is rarely personally in Poland, thanks to her presence on concert programs, social media, and the possibilities offered by the Internet, her presence is felt strongly in her home country.

Influence of the new home on the composer's music

At the moment, it is difficult to clearly determine to what extent (if at all) her new home has influenced Jaskot's work. Before her departure from Poland, she was already fully developed as an artist. I think that the endless stretches of land in Australia are more suited to her mystical, meditative music, which often seems to create large metaphysical sonic spaces.

Awareness of the composer's music in both countries

It seems that Jaskot's music, although appreciated all over the world, is welcomed more in Poland than in Australia. It is performed and commissioned much more often in her home country, perhaps due to her numerous artistic friendships that have led to commissions and also to the different approach to contemporary music that is taken in each country. It seems that after such a short period away from Poland (five years as of 2020), it is still too early to compare the reception of this composer's music in both countries; more time is needed to gain an adequate perspective.

Composer's personality

Warmth, goodness, and kindness radiate from this artist, although she also displays certain tendencies to "cut herself off" from the world during periods of intense creativity. She always remembers her friends and close acquaintances; her cordiality and curiosity about the world make meeting with her after several years' absence seem as she had seen you only yesterday. It is worth adding that she was one of the most respected and loved lecturers among the students at the Music Academy in Bydgoszcz.

Remarkable anecdote or biographical fact

The composer loves wildlife and animals (especially domestic ones). For years she had a dog named Markiz: a wonderful, musically sensitive, extremely cheerful, and humorous Russian greyhound, whom she had dreamed of since childhood and who was a source of pride when he won awards at dog shows. Unfortunately, Markiz could not follow his guardian to Perth, so he found a new, loving home with a Czech owner. In Perth, she is accompanied by two cats; she admits they love late medieval and Renaissance music.

Respondent's Top Choices

- **Favorite work:** *Atnongara* for piano (2002), for its unique sonic mood and total "being outside of time"; it is a kind of mysterium in which the listener is confronted with the absolute.
- **Best work:** Hopefully it is still a matter of being in the future; certainly, the interactive opera *Phaedra* (2006) holds an important position in Jaskot's oeuvre.
- **Composition still waiting to be discovered:** Improvised music and the one which is not yet written.

Respondent: Małgorzata Gamrat

Jan A. P. (Andrzej Paweł) Kaczmarek

Date and place of birth:
29 April 1953, Konin.

Date and place of emigration:
1989, United States (Los Angeles).

Return to Poland:
Since about 2005, Jan A. P. Kaczmarek has been splitting his time between Poland and the United States, spending about five months each year in his homeland.

Key quote

Emigration has a very strong influence on the way one experiences Polishness.[247]

Activities before emigration

After an internship at Jerzy Grotowski's Laboratory Theater, Kaczmarek, then a law student, decided to pursue an artistic career. Grotowski's encouragement to look creatively at the surrounding world resulted in Kaczmarek's interest in music and, in particular, in Fischer's mandolin. This rare nineteenth-century instrument, somewhat similar to a zither, never entered mass production and only a few copies have survived. Kaczmarek, who already played mandolin, modified the Fischer mandolin, calling it Niewkacz, and introduced new playing techniques, thus becoming a truly uncommon musician. In 1977 Kaczmarek, together with guitarist Grzegorz Banaszyk, began cooperating with the Theater of the Eighth Day. For over two years, as the Orchestra of the Eighth Day, they prepared music for the theater's productions. As time went on, the Orchestra's activity shifted beyond the framework of theater music. In mid-1979 the Orchestra ended its cooperation with the Theater, yet retained its name, which had been made famous through numerous tours and concerts in Poland and abroad. A 1982 tour of the United States turned out to be particularly important, thanks to which the ensemble released the album *Music for the End*, recorded for Flying Fish Records, an independent label from Chicago. In Poland, this was released in 1984 as *Muzyka na koniec.* The following years brought two more albums, *At the Last Gate* (1984) and *Waiting for Halley's Comet* [*Czekając na Kometę Halleya*] (1985). The Orchestra of the Eighth Day, to the disappointment of their fans, disbanded in 1989 due to Kaczmarek's emigration.

After emigration

Today, Kaczmarek is most often associated with film music. His achievements in this field overshadow his earlier activities in Poland, including the concert music he composed at the time. Interestingly, in deciding to stay in the United States, Kaczmarek hoped to continue the artistic work with which he was associated in Poland. However, he had to face the fact that in Los Angeles the focus was on film music, with very little demand for other types of compositions. His new beginning meant that instead of writing sophisticated music linked to his artistic experiences with the Theater of the Eighth Day and the Orchestra of the Eighth Day, Kaczmarek took up composing music for low-quality horror films. With time, however, working on less prestigious productions opened opportunities to perform tasks that were much more challenging and closer to his Polish experiences. In 1992, Kaczmarek received a Drama Desk Award and an Obie Off-Broadway Theater Award for his compositions for *'Tis a Pity She's a Whore*, a play staged at New York's Public Theater by Joanne Akalaitis. The importance of these prestigious awards was reinforced by the fact that Akalaitis was known for her earlier collaboration with Philip Glass. However, his artistic success in New York did not translate into attractive film commissions; the theater in the United States is too much of a niche market to influence Hollywood, according to the composer. His real breakthrough came with Agnieszka Holland's *Total Eclipse* (1995). Kaczmarek still considers this one of his greatest achievements. Its success reinforced Kaczmarek's position as a composer of film music, which has been confirmed by his subsequent successful and well-received productions, such as scores for *Unfaithful* (2002) and *Finding Neverland* (2004).

Differences between the old and new realities

Apart from the obvious differences resulting from the different political, social, cultural, and economic realities of both countries, it is worth noting that Kaczmarek had to modify his approach to his own work after his emigration. The music he wrote in Poland, which was derived directly from the spirit of Grotowski's practices, was oriented towards the artistic, creative, intellectual, and sublime. It functioned in an off-theater space and co-existed in a folk environment alongside the music of bands such as Osjan, Jorgi Quartet [Kwartet Jorgi], and Warsaw Manta [Varsovia Manta], i.e., it was spiritual, trance-like, exploratory music. The desire to remain a composer required Kaczmarek to change his approach to issues perceived as crucial in the United States: openness, boldness, pragmatism, positive attitude, looking for new possibilities, and taking advantage of opportunities. For many years Kaczmarek was reluctant to mention his first soundtrack, the trashy horror film *Pale Blood*. Today he does so more willingly, because it proved to be significant: despite the low quality of the film, composing its soundtrack helped him enter a network of relationships, dependencies, and opportunities, which eventually led to working on *Finding Neverland* and, as a result, an Oscar award. Compared to Poland's post-Communist period of transition, mentioning the benefits in the United States of technical possibilities; access to instruments, performers, and sound libraries; cooperation with Sony Classical and other well-known music labels; budgets for recording orchestral parts; and access to the media would be stating the obvious. The United States offered Kaczmarek a possibility that he could not even dream of in his homeland during the late Polish People's Republic and the country's subsequent era of transformation.

Reason for leaving Poland

The reason for Kaczmarek's emigration was his desire to live in a country free from the absurdities of the Polish People's Republic and to develop his own career. Interestingly, the composer did not initially plan to emigrate. He made a relatively quick decision and took the opportunity to extend his stay on a State Department scholarship, eventually remaining in Los Angeles.

Contact with Poland after emigration

Kaczmarek has never lost his personal and artistic bonds with Poland. In 1993, after his emigration, he composed music for Małgorzata Łazarkiewicz's film *White Marriage* [*Białe małżeństwo*], followed by soundtracks to the films *Total Eclipse* and *Washington Square*, which were produced in the United States, but made in cooperation with one of Poland's most important directors, Agnieszka Holland. In the second half of the 1990s, Kaczmarek wrote music for television theater: *Looping*, directed by Leszik Mądzik (1997) and a documentary film dedicated to Mądzik and directed by Grzegorz Królikiewicz, *...As Little Light as Possible...* [*...Jak najmniej światła...*] (1998). Many soundtracks to international films were recorded in Poland, mainly due to Kaczmarek's collaboration with Sinfonia Varsovia. Several Polish films with Kaczmarek's music have been made in the twenty-first century (*Quo Vadis*, *Hania*, *Who never lived* [*Kto nigdy nie żył*], *Joanna*, and *The Secrets of Westerplatte* [*Tajemnice Westerplatte*]). Overall, his activity in Poland has intensified since the 1990s.

Influence of the new land on the composer's music

In an interview, Kaczmarek said that America taught him that "the impossible is possible. That if you're bound to hang, you won't be drowned. And that faith does wonders. And more directly speaking, it also taught me to be disciplined and to understand the world." Thanks to his location in the United States, Kaczmarek has become a go-to name in film music. Cooperation with the local film industry has given him the opportunity to work with outstanding musicians, orchestras, and producers. It is clear that the composer has access to resources difficult to obtain in Poland. For example, he took advantage of the budget possibilities of *The Unfaithful* and—having a choice of thousands of American musicians!—brought Leszek Możdżer from Poland to do the recording. The American film industry has given Kaczmarek a previously unknown scale of activity and international recognition, which has brought him cooperation with the film industries of Canada, Germany, Japan, and other countries.

Awareness of the composer's music in both countries

Kaczmarek said recently: "I spend five months a year in Poland. This movement is beneficial for me. I can take a look from outside. I get a different perspective." This goes hand in hand with the fact that the composer has strongly limited his film activity. For a long time, he has been writing mostly for niche, documentary productions (e.g., the Oscar-winning *Joanna* by Aneta Kopacz). He has focused instead on other activities related to music, above all the Transatlantic [Transatlantyk] festival that he founded. He also has composed music intended for live performance, such as *Emigration – Symphony Without End* [*Emigra – Symfonia bez końca*], prepared for the Emigration Museum in Gdynia. Since 2017, the composer has been an honorary member of the ZAiKS Authors' Association in Poland.

Composer's personality

Kaczmarek is a driven, expressive, and energetic artist. But this "American" attitude is only one facet of his story. In his interviews, which he eagerly gives, he reveals the face of an artist-intellectual shaped in Poland under Grotowski's influence. A shy introvert, he had to reshape himself to become a versatile, self-confident creator who knows his own worth.

Remarkable anecdote or biographical fact

There was a risk we might never have had Kaczmarek's music for *Finding Neverland.* The film's producers were reluctant at first, since they did not believe that he would be able to create the fairytale-like, subtle, joyful soundtrack that the script required. When Kaczmarek found out about it, he quickly decided to act and wrote a suitable piece, hired an orchestra and choir, recorded it, and sent it to the United States. He beat the competition, which included John Williams and James Horner. Horner had such a strong desire to take part in this production that he had declared he would compose the music for one dollar.

Respondent's Top Choices

- **Favorite work:** The Eighth Day Orchestra, LP titled *Jan A. P. Kaczmarek. Music for the End* [*Jan A. P. Kaczmarek. Muzyka na koniec*] (1984).
- **Best work:** Soundtrack to *Finding Neverland* (2004).
- **Composition still waiting to be discovered:** The Eighth Day Orchestra, LP titled *Jan A. P. Kaczmarek. Music for the End* [*Jan A. P. Kaczmarek. Muzyka na koniec*] (1984).

Respondent: Mariusz Gradowski

Jacek Kaczmarski

Date and place of birth:
22 March 1957, Warsaw.

Date and place of death:
10 April 2004, Gdańsk.

Date and place of emigration:
13 December 1981, France; 1995, Australia (Perth).

Return to Poland:
He returned to Poland on 1 May 1990 and remained there between his first and second periods of emigration.

Key quote
I was thrown into unknown waters / This song wouldn't have been made otherwise![248]

Activities before emigration
Prompted by his grandparents, Jacek Kaczmarski had been learning music since the age of seven. After a mere half a year of lessons, he composed his first piece, *Chinese Melody* [*Chińska melodia*]. In 1965 Kaczmarski enrolled in a piano class. He did not enjoy it, but it became an incentive to reach for something else. His grandmother allowed him to play an instrument closer to his heart—the guitar—only after he completed his piano practice. He was self-taught on guitar; however, the musical preparation received from his grandparents and from these music classes gave him the basic skills for building chords and melodies.

During the second year of high school, Kaczmarski translated Tim Rice's rock opera *Jesus Christ Superstar* with the intention of presenting it at school. However, its religious subject matter caused the school's vice-principal to prohibit the production. In the 1970s Kaczmarski participated in song contests, primarily student ones. He won first prize at the Student Song Festivals in Kraków in 1977 and 1978. He started working with the Under the Aegis [Pod Egidą] cabaret in 1977 and co-founded the Piosenkariat group, from which the future trio of Kaczmarski, Gintrowski, Łapiński emerged. Before martial law, they recorded three programs: *Paradise* [*Raj*] (1979), *Walls* [*Mury*] (1980), and *Museum* [*Muzeum*] (1981). Also in 1981, the fourth program, entitled *Shouting* [*Krzyk*], was recorded with Zbigniew Łapiński. He enjoyed success elsewhere in Poland as well, winning second prize (together with Przemysław Gintrowski) at the 19th National Festival of Polish Song [Krajowy Festiwal Polskiej Piosenki] in Opole for his *Epitaph for Vladimir Vysotsky* [*Epitafium dla Włodzimierza Wysockiego*].

After emigration

He undertook worldwide concert tours, whose target audience was the Polish diaspora. During the first six months of martial law, he gave numerous concerts for the Polish community in France. In 1982 he toured Europe, performing in Switzerland, Sweden, and Denmark, and in early 1983 he was in Canada and the United States. Improved conditions created better opportunities for recording music, which resulted in new releases, both official ones as well as bootleg recordings distributed in the underground (samizdat), such as *Fallen Angels* [*Strącenie Aniołów*] (1982, Stockholm), *Carmagnole* (1982, Wiesbaden), *Armor* [*Zbroja*] (1982, Paris, London), *Chicago Live* (1983, Chicago), *Litany* [*Litania*] (1986), *Cosmo-Polak* [*Kosmopolak*] (1987), and others.

Kaczmarski's move to Munich and the start of work with Radio Free Europe were transformative moments in his life as an emigrant. His job, duties, and fixed salary stabilized his life, and thanks to the radio broadcasts (including *Jacek Kaczmarski's Quarters* [*Kwadranse Jacka Kaczmarskiego*], in which he presented his works along with personal commentaries), he had constant contact with Poland and was "present" in the country. His second emigration—the Australian one—was a period in which Kaczmarski devoted himself more to family life, although he did not give up his creative work. During this time he created the programs A *Praise of Malice* [*Pochwała Łotrostwa*] (1996), *Between Us* [*Między nami*] (1998), *Two Rocks* [*Dwie Skały*] (1999), *By the Way* [*Mimochodem*] (2001), and two live albums—*Concert '97* [*Koncert '97*] (1997) and *Twenty Years Later* [*Dwadzieścia lat później*] (2000).

Differences between the old and new realities

These two worlds were as different as the reality of socialist countries was different from that of free Western nations. The distance was deepened by a lack of contact with his Polish relatives and Kaczmarski's longing for them.

Reason for leaving Poland

Emigration in 1981 was not a choice, it was a necessity. Kaczmarski was in France when martial law was announced. Overnight, he was cut off from his homeland. The road back to Poland was closed. His second emigration—to Australia—was freely made by the artist. During his first stay in that country in 1986, he fell onto his knees almost immediately after leaving the plane at the Sydney airport and shouted "This is the Promised Land! I want to live here!" He moved there permanently in 1995, motivated by the desire to get rid of the pressure of writing poetry and music on commission "for someone." He used Australia as a place where he could find tranquility and an atmosphere conducive to contemplation. It was also a kind of escape from his image as the "Bard of Solidarity."

Contact with Poland after emigration

After December 13, 1981, Kaczmarski remained in the Polish diaspora, which was particularly strong in France. He corresponded with his Polish relatives, especially his wife Ewa Inka Kadryś. One way of maintaining contact with his homeland was through the recordings of his concerts that were smuggled into Poland and dispersed there unofficially. His aforementioned work in Radio Free Europe constituted an additional expression of concern for the reality of living in Poland.

After settling in Australia, Kaczmarski visited Poland relatively often, primarily for concerts. His contact with his homeland is summed up by the announcement for the song *June Wind by the Fireplace* [*Czerwcowy wicher przy kominku*] from the *Two Rocks* program: "What remains is burning in the fireplace, drinking strong liquor, devoting oneself to poetic visions, and worrying about events in Poland."

Influence of the new home on the composer's music

The new environment surrounding his first emigration did not form a breakthrough in Jacek Kaczmarski's musical style, since he was still in the process of developing his trademark idiom. One exception was *Litany,* recorded in 1986 during a concert tour in Australia. This was the first album in the artist's output to be made with an ensemble; he returned to this practice only in 1998 for the album *Between Us*, recorded with the participation of jazz musicians.

A clear stylistic breakthrough took place after 1995, when the artist settled permanently in Australia. The harmonic layer of his songs was expanded and the guitar arrangements, especially in the *Two Rocks* program, became much more mature, sophisticated, and varied. There is no doubt that Kaczmarski's technical skills in playing the classical guitar increased during this time.

Awareness of the composer's music in both countries

The memory of Kaczmarski lives on in Poland. Festivals devoted to his work, such as *The Source Still Flows* [*Źródło wciąż bije*] and *Sentimental Metamorphoses* [*Metamorfozy Sentymentalne*] are organized, the Jacek Kaczmarski Foundation operates, and his works are often covered by pop artists (*Prayer at Sunrise* [*Modlitwa o Wschodzie Słońca*] by Kazik & Kwartet ProForma, *Drinker* [*Pijak*] by White House Records & Peja, and the album *And You Are Sowing* [*A ty siej*] by the Habakuk ensemble).

Composer's personality

It is very difficult to capture the artist's personality in several sentences. Kaczmarski has certainly been haunted by many contradictory emotions. He was aware of his weaknesses and demons and he succumbed to them at the same time. His major problem was alcoholism, which made his work in Radio Free Europe difficult and destroyed his family life. This was worsened by the instability of his character and his irresponsibility towards his relatives. In 1985 Kaczmarski went on a concert tour in South Africa the day after the birth of his child, despite being pressured not to do so. The newborn did not survive the tenth day of its life, and the father did not even show up for the funeral. He was a romantic hero, torn by great passions, taking life to the fullest. Many autobiographical threads can easily be found in his poetry, for example in the poem *Confessional* [*Konfesjonał*]:

> *I did not treat my life as a right.*
> *I treated it as my achievement,*
> *And what was not mine, I considered no one's.*
> *Taking everything without debt in mind.*
> ...

The richness of evil which I was aware of
Was only a spur in my life.
I lived with the suffering and destruction of others,
Unable to suffer and die on my own.

Remarkable anecdote or biographical fact

As an anecdote, I would like to quote the words of Stanisław Ledóchowski, Jacek Kaczmarski's friend from his student days:

> He complained a little....Sometimes he even used strong language. I remember that once, after a concert in France, he came out and spewed 'a bunch of idiots.' He was angry that they were interested only in politics, looking for political subtexts everywhere, that they weren't interested in his poetry.[249]

Respondent's Top Choices

- **Favorite work:** A difficult choice, but I decided to select *Epitaph for Eulenspiegel* [*Epitafium dla Sowizdrzała*] (1993), performed by the Kaczmarski, Gintrowski, Łapiński trio, as it conveys the best in Kaczmarski's work. A masterpiece of a poem intertwined with a musical composition from which the essence of things is extracted. Truth. And an outstanding piano performance by Zbigniew Łapiński!
- **Best work:** *Epitaph for Vladimir Vysotsky* (1982). A piece written in homage to Kaczmarski's master, Vladimir Vysotsky. The lyrics refer to the Russian poet's biography and, according to the author, his entire knowledge of the Soviet Union. Musically, it represents early Kaczmarski—a simple harmonic and melodic construction, a characteristic "galloping" guitar beat recognizable also from *The Chase* [*Obława*] (1989) and *Walls* (1978), which are Kaczmarski's best-known works, and an expressive performance, including hoarse vocals on the verge of screaming, in imitation of Vysotsky's singing.
- **Composition still waiting to be discovered:** *Rhythms* from *Between Us* (1997), an impressionistic description of a seaside landscape that imperceptibly turns into a bitter reflection on the inevitability of passing. This song is not well known, but is absolutely exceptional in Kaczmarski's oeuvre. I'm strongly impressed by the jazz arrangement made by Janusz Strobel, which corresponds perfectly with the lyrics.

Respondent: Filip Marcinkowski

Bronisław (Bronislau) Kaper

Date and place of birth:
5 February 1902, Warsaw.

Date and place of death:
26 April 1983, Los Angeles, California.

Date and place of emigration:
1927, Germany (Berlin); 1933, France (Paris); 1935, United States (Los Angeles).

Return to Poland:
He did not return.

Key quote

If you're excited by something, you'll come up with new ideas. How many women have you known in your life? Then along comes another and you love her. You've seen eyes before, legs before, but wait—there's something different about this one, something in the eyes, in the voice, a smile, an expression, something in the way she walks. It's the same with films—all you need are a few little things and off you go again.[250]

Activities before emigration

Kaper came from a wealthy Polish family with Jewish roots. He studied piano and composition at the Music Conservatory in Warsaw, as well as law at the University of Warsaw, where he was considered one of their best students. Before leaving the country, he earned his living tutoring in mathematics and Latin, among other things. At the instigation of a friend, he started composing for cabarets, thus earning extra income through royalties. His early piano pieces and songs were also popular.

After emigration

During his six years in Berlin, Kaper became known as a songwriter and film music composer. He formed a harmonious duo with songwriter Fritz Rotter, with whom he composed as many as two songs a day at the peak of his popularity. He also wrote songs for singing actors, including Richard Tauber and Jan Kiepura. Later, he continued his career in Paris, where he met Louis B. Mayer, who, delighted with his song *Ninon*, offered him a contract in Hollywood. For the next 28 years Kaper collaborated with the Metro-Goldwyn-Mayer label (MGM), writing music for over a hundred productions. In 1954 he won an Oscar for the musical *Lili*. In the 1960s, he started composing music for television.

Differences between the old and new realities

In Europe, there was little money for specialists. A composer who worked on a given film was responsible for writing both the score and the songs, then conducting his own compositions during recording. Within the structures of the studio system developing in the United States, everyone had their own narrow responsibilities, which were designed to not interfere with their colleagues' tasks. So when Kaper was hired to write songs, he did not write scores, and vice versa. Different people were responsible for orchestrating the piano sketches of his compositions and then making the recording. However, the scope of the composer's duties increased as years went by and his work became more well known.

Reason for leaving Poland

Kaper was already a successful composer when he was a student, but he decided to move to Berlin in order to develop his career among other European artists in that vibrant cultural metropolis. However, the increasing anti-Semitism and repression of art after Hitler came to power in 1933 forced him to leave Germany. While in Paris, he met Louis B. Mayer, thanks to whom he found himself in Los Angeles, where he remained until the end of his life.

Contact with Poland after emigration

Kaper considered himself an ambassador of Poland to the United States. He maintained contacts with other émigrés and with friends living in Warsaw. Polish filmmakers and musicians, including Józef Lejtes, Andrzej Krakowski, Jerzy Abratowski, and Violetta Villas were frequent guests at his villa on Bedford Drive. He was probably also visited by Roman Polański and Krzysztof Komeda. For many years, he had been friends with Artur Rubinstein, with whom he supported Julian Tuwim during the latter's forced emigration to Brazil in 1940. Kaper was eager to organize lavish parties for the Polish literary circle, including Sławomir Mrożek, Julian Stryjkowski, Stanisław Dygat, and Stefan Kisielewski. Living in Beverly Hills and driving a Cadillac, the artist was the embodiment of the American dream for many Poles.

Influence of the new home on the composer's music

Kaper had been interested in American music since he was young. He enjoyed playing pieces by George Gershwin, Jerome Kern, Vincent Youmens, and Arthur Schwartz. His work in Hollywood allowed him to compose in a style that referred to these artists as well as to late European romanticism. Kaper's music is mostly based on simple melodic ideas, which are colored by dissonant harmonies and elements of jazz improvisation. In several scores written for large symphony orchestras, the composer also uses ethnic instruments (e.g., those that are part of the gamelan, a traditional Javanese orchestra) which gave his music an exotic sound.

Awareness of the composer's music in both countries

In Poland, Kaper's name was ignored for many years for censorship reasons. Only in the 1990s was he recognized as a Polish composer again, although information about his Jewish origins was usually not discussed. In 2016, Polish jazz musicians became interested in Kaper's work. Among them were Kuba Stankiewicz (the album *The Music of Bronisław Kaper*) and Krzysztof Kaczmarczyk with the Audiofeeling Trio (*Vars & Kaper DeconstructiON*).

Kaper's personal archive, which contains sketches of his compositions, recordings of his works, private notes, documents, and photographs, including those from before he left Europe, is kept at the University of California in Los Angeles (UCLA). His compositions *Green Dolphin Street* and *Invitation* have gained the status of jazz standards and have been interpreted by such artists as Miles Davis, John Coltrane, and Pat Metheny. In 1975, an album *The Film Music of Bronislau Kaper Played by the Composer*, which presents the composer's archival piano recordings, was released by Delos.

Composer's personality

According to William F. Krasnoborski, who interviewed Kaper in 1975, the composer was an extremely sociable and open man who approached life with a great deal of optimism. At the age of over seventy, he retained his youthful enthusiasm, spontaneity, and brilliant sense of humor, often infecting his interrogator with sincere laughter that stemmed from his own self-deprecation. The artist, who seemed to be entirely Americanized, was betrayed only by his European accent.

Remarkable anecdote or biographical fact

Shortly after his arrival in the United States, Kaper composed *You're All I Need*, which was used in the romantic comedy *Escapade* (1935). The song became number one on the Lucky Strike Hits Parade, a popular radio show sponsored by the cigarette brand Lucky Strike. When Kaper (who did not speak English well yet) found out about this from his publisher, he did not know how to react—he recognized the brand, but could not understand what the connection was between his song and smoking.

Respondent's Top Choices

- **Favorite work:** *Invitation*, a song written for *A Life of her Own* (1950), later used as a theme in *Invitation* (1952).
- **Best work:** The soundtrack to *Mutiny on the Bounty* (1962), especially the love theme, *Follow Me.*
- **Composition still waiting to be discovered:** Most likely it can be found in Kaper's archive in Los Angeles.

Respondent: Agnieszka Cieślak

Jarosław Kapuściński

Date and place of birth:
12 December 1964, Warsaw.

Date and place of emigration:
1992, United States (San Diego); 1999, Germany (Karlsruhe); 2000, Canada (Montreal); 2001, United States (Stockton and, since 2008, Stanford).

Return to Poland:
He has not returned.

Key quote
My artistic message is to compose structurally integrated works in which sound and image are considered equal.[251]

Activities before emigration
At first, Jarosław Kapuściński was a pianist specializing in contemporary music. In 1987 he graduated from the State Higher School of Music in Warsaw (now the Chopin University of Music), where he studied with Jan Ekier, Bronislawa Kawalla and Szabolcs Esztényi. A year later, while on a scholarship at the Banff Center School of Fine Arts in Canada, he became interested in audiovisual art. In 1991 he completed a composition class with Włodzimierz Kotoński at the Warsaw Academy of Music, while also working at the Polish Radio Experimental Studio and the Polish Society for Contemporary Music and co-founding the Intercollegiate Art Festival (Warsaw 1986–1988). Kapuściński's early compositions indicate his interest in innovative music, such as his works for tape, a singing cellist (*Sonata in the Woods*, 1988), and amplified violin, synthesizer and tape (*Chagalliana I*, 1990). Since 1988, the focus of his interest has shifted towards audiovisual art. He has been strongly inspired by the works of abstract artists (P. Mondrian and V. Kandinsky) and the animations of Norman McLaren.

After emigration
Kapuściński left Poland as a young student artist. He improved his skills in Paris, Banff, and San Diego, working under the direction of Rand Steiger, Roger Reynolds, Brian Ferneyhough, Jōji Yuasa, and others. In 1997, at the University of California in San Diego, he earned a doctorate in composition, presenting for his graduation piece (besides his

dissertation on intermedia art) the audiovisual composition *Mudry* (1996). Most of the artist's works have been created outside of Poland. Currently, he works primarily as an intermedia artist, composer, and pianist (often performing his own works). According to Kapuściński, the key to his artistic attitude is understanding music as the logic of emotion and form. His creative stance is characterized by an attachment to traditional means of expression, while also remaining open to new technology. He often composes at the piano; almost all of his works link traditional instrumentation to an electronically controlled image. He is also an active teacher, lecturing at universities in San Diego, Stockton, and Montreal, at the branch of Stanford University in Kyoto, and in The Hague, Odense, and Shanghai. Since 2008, he has taught at Stanford University, and since 2016, he has been the Chair of the Music Department there. He also publishes academic essays on intermedia composition and traditional Japanese music.

Differences between the old and new realities

Intermedia art in Poland in the 1980s and 1990s offered only narrow possibilities, which meant that an entirely new frontier, at least in terms of technology, was waiting in the West. In America, the composer found institutions where he could develop his own compositional direction and gain access to new technologies, equipment, modern animation programs, etc. He is now recognized internationally and is a valued lecturer. Kapuściński enjoys the creative freedom of artists who, while working in the United States, are less burdened with the expectations and influences of the music community.

Reason for leaving Poland

The composition methods and technologies that Kapuściński encountered in Banff were almost inaccessible in Poland in the late 1980s and early 1990s. Since the artist wanted to continue his work on intermedia art, his decision to study abroad seemed natural. At first, the composer stayed in Paris, but later a Witold Lutosławski scholarship enabled him to study in the United States. Gradually, for personal and professional reasons, his educational trip turned into a permanent stay.

Contact with Poland after emigration

Kapuściński maintains close contact with his homeland, visiting Poland regularly and participating in its cultural life. He stresses that despite having three passports (Polish, American, and Canadian), he feels primarily Polish. The composer collaborates with the WRO Art Center [Centrum Sztuki WRO] in Wrocław, the Warsaw Autumn Festival, and the Audio-Art festival in Polish, as well as with various well-known artists, including photographer Kacper Kowalski. He is a member of the Polish Composers' Union, the Polish Society for Contemporary Music, and the Polish Association of Electroacoustic Music.

Influence of the new home on the composer's music

His new home has had a great influence on Kapuściński's work, as the composer can now be considered to be dealing with genres he became acquainted with in the West. Certainly, the greater creative freedom characteristic of the United States was of importance for the development of his individual style. In the American music community, there is a pluralism of styles, with no standards imposed by critics. Moreover, especially at Stanford, the composer gained access to advanced technologies.

Awareness of the composer's music in both countries

Kapuściński's work bypasses traditional geographical criteria. Presented in the United States, Poland, and other countries, the properties of each performance location are often decisive factors that affect how a work's audio and visual layers can be realized. The composer's works often appear at contemporary music festivals such as Warsaw Autumn, Audio Art, or Spoleto, and also at festivals dedicated to audiovisual forms (WRO) or animation (e.g., in Poznań), as well as at universities and cultural institutions (such as MOMA in New York and the Center for Contemporary Art in Warsaw). As an artist, he is recognized and valued in the communities of new music and audiovisual art, not only in Poland and the United States (mainly in California), but also in Japan, Canada, and other countries.

Composer's personality

Kapuściński's personality and work are marked by contemplation and mindfulness. These traits developed through his contact with Japanese culture, which influenced his perception of the world. Concentration, precision, and an open mind are his trademarks. Building relationships, largely through music, is also important for him, as are links between different media, as he explores what happens between image and sound. He tries to combine multiple dimensions in order to create a satisfying whole that carries an emotional load and allows a relationship with audiences and performers. Understanding and showing the richness of reality—as the composer says, "redancing" it from a musician's perspective—is the basic premise of his mature work, which is free from any modernist quality related to novelty.

Remarkable anecdote or biographical fact

During his stay at the University of California, Kapuściński became interested in Japanese culture, especially *nō* theater as an intermedia art genre, in which visual solutions are invariable and always connected with specific music. He also explored the traditions of the local court music known as *gagaku*, engaging in a project to research and popularize the phenomenon of the imperial orchestra, which has been performing the same repertoire continuously for hundreds of years.

Respondent's Top Choices

- **Favorite work:** In *Calligraphies for Ziqi* (2018), the simplicity of the piano part is especially captivating. Its visual layer, developed with a computer programming language (*Antescofo*), is comprised of the movements of the calligraphy master, whose speed is determined by the pianist while the computer "listens" and reacts. The work presents a traditional Chinese story about a relationship which, thanks to music, is not destroyed either by social differences or the passing of time.
- **Best work:** *Mondrian Variations* (1992) would seem to be the obvious choice here, with its audiovisual virtuosity, which has become the composer's trademark. However, Kapuściński emphasizes the importance of another work, namely *Where is Chopin?* (2010), in which the instrumental layer was formed using Frédéric Chopin's *Preludes,* Op. 28, which are especially significant to the composer. Literal quotations are interspersed here with modifications of pace or texture (e.g., by revealing only the part for the left hand, but with harmonic extensions); sometimes repetitions appear or the prelude is played starting from the end. The visual layer, on the other hand, consists of photos of about

150 audience members taken at various locations across the world, from Seoul to Buenos Aires. The entire work provides a view from the composer's perspective; it is also a careful contemplation of both Chopin's music and the audience's reaction. Worthy of note is the degree of unification in the piece, when the recipient's experiences harmonize with the composer's message, thus creating a close relationship.

- **Composition still waiting to be discovered:** *Side Effects* [*Efekty uboczne*] (2017), created in collaboration with photographer Kacper Kowalski. Its visual layer consists of bird's-eye view images. Each fragment is preceded by information about the coordinates of a given place, while on the screen we see, among other things, a beach with a water slide, ice flowing under a bridge, and an icebreaker. Although we observe movement, the shots remain static, which gives the impression of looking at it from a new perspective, forcing the viewer to reflect differently on it. The image displayed is accompanied by a varied, suggestive piano part.

Respondent: Kinga Krzymowska-Szacoń

Zbigniew Karkowski

Date and place of birth:
14 March 1958, Kraków.

Date and place of death:
12 December 2013, Peru.

Date and place of emigration:
1971, Sweden (Göteborg), 1994; Japan (Tokyo).

Return to Poland:
He did not return.

Key quote
The music and cultural theories developed up to now should be destroyed.[252]

Activities before emigration
He left Poland at the age of 21; any works created before then remain unknown. He studied flute at the Chopin State Music School in Kraków.

After emigration
He enrolled in university while already abroad. He took composition lessons in Göteborg and sonology classes in The Hague. In Paris, he studied with Pierre Boulez, Olivier Messiaen, and Iannis Xenakis. He often stressed that only Xenakis had taught him anything. Karkowski, an international pioneer of noise music, has worked with a Japanese producer known in contemporary music circles as Merzbow. He has recorded over sixty albums both as a solo performer and in cooperation with other artists.

Differences between the old and new realities
Karkowski has often refrained from the kind of rational, analytical approach to music that is popular in Poland. In Japanese clubs, he played *noise*, which simply connects people experiencing this harsh music, without the need for any rational reflection.

Reason for leaving Poland
Unknown. Karkowski left as a young man. He mentioned that he was surprised by how much he has traveled.

Contact with Poland after emigration

He occasionally returned to his homeland, for example, for workshops and a concert at the Electroacoustic Music Studio of the Academy of Music in Poznań (2012) or for a concert at the BWA gallery in Zielona Góra in 2009, which apparently was short but successful. Karkowski believed that thanks to the Internet and globalization, similar cultures could be experienced in most corners of the world. He was not active on the Polish contemporary music scene because he was against state funding of art.

Influence of the new home on the composer's music

Karkowski could express himself freely in underground, independent clubs. As far as other spaces are concerned, a Japanese temple inspired his album *Mutation*, by Karkowski & Aube.

Awareness of the composer's music in both countries

We can talk about Karkowski's music as it functions in the global arena (including the Internet and the *noise* scene) and within Polish contemporary music. Karkowski has been perceived for years as a legendary and exceptionally talented artist in the world of independent music. The Polish contemporary music community is slowly beginning to open up to his work but the reception of his music there is still low-key.

Composer's personality

Karkowski was a vivid, mysterious visionary. He was uncompromising and more like a punk musician than a contemporary classical composer. However, he did not identify personally with any particular music community. In fact, he maintained that he did not even make *noise* music. He was an anti-intellectual musician, fascinated by the physicality of sound and the power of its influence.

Remarkable anecdote or biographical fact

Despite his comprehensive education, Karkowski disliked speculating and theorizing about music. He often created without first having any plans and expectations. One could say that in this respect he was John Cage's Polish successor.

Respondent's Top Choices

- **Favorite work:** Xopher Davidson & Karkowski, *Processor* (2013).
- **Best work:** Karkowski & Aube, *Mutation* (1999).
- **Composition still waiting to be discovered:** *The Idiot* [*Idiota*] (year unknown), an opera.

Respondent: Wojtek Krzyżanowski

Dominik Karski

Date and place of birth:
24 June 1972, Szczebrzeszyn.

Date and place of emigration:
1991, Australia (Perth).

Return to Poland:
Yes, in 2006, but in 2015 he left again.

Key quote
The relationship between a musician and an instrument, the physicality of operating it, is the other side of sound.[253]

Activities before emigration
Before he left Poland, Dominik Karski received his musical education by studying classical guitar, not composition. He also attended an arts high school.

After emigration
Karski studied composition in Australia. He attended the University of Perth and the University of Brisbane, where he enhanced his skills under the guidance of Brian Howard and Stephen Cronin. He received his doctorate in 2012 under the supervision of Brenton Broadstock and Michael Christoforidis. He also worked with Chaya Czernowin at the Universität für Musik und darstellende Kunst in Vienna. Karski enjoyed his first compositional successes in 1998, when his piece *Floating on the River of Time* for instrumental ensemble received the ABC Young Composers Award. He was subsequently awarded the Albert H. Maggs Composition Award in 2003 for his *inward* for piccolo, bass clarinet, and piano. Since then, Karski's efforts have focused on compositions for chamber ensembles and, in a conceptual sense, on seeking inspiration in the relationships between a musician and an instrument. The composer is particularly interested in the element of articulation; it is in this area that he seeks sources for his compositions, often using amplification. In terms of form, he looks for solutions that evolve over time, using the poetics of the uncanny associated with the passing of time and its lack of precision. These features have made Karski's work interesting not only for contemporary music lovers, but also

for critics. Karski takes an active part in composition forums, such as FORUM 2000 or *Rencontres de musique nouvelle* in Canada in 2001, and in contemporary music festivals in England, Germany, Switzerland, Holland, Canada, the United States, and Poland. His most important achievements include the performances of *inward* by Ensemble Sur-Plus in Stuttgart in 2005 and *Glimmer* for alto and bass flutes at the Gaudeamus Music Week in Amsterdam in 2002. *Superb imposition* for double-bass recorder, commissioned by Swedish flutist Anna Petrini and written as part of a Kulturkontakt Nord grant, received the Nutida Sound award in 2012 in the contemporary music category.

Flutes are a distinct feature of Karski's work, such as in *Matter of Perspective* for offstage piccolo, amplified bass flute, bass clarinet, piano, violin, and cello (2000), the aforementioned *Glimmer*, the *streamforms* series, *open cluster* for bass flute (2003), *To Remain in Change* for piccolo, flute, alto flute, bass flute, and cello (2005), *pre-seed* (2009) for flute and ensemble, *wherewhowhen* for bass flute, percussion, and harpsichord, and others. Karski's catalog of works also includes one stage piece, *These People Are Only One and a Half Minutes Away from Eternity* [*Osoby te od wieczności dzieli tylko półtorej minuty*] (2013).

The artist's compositional interests are broad, yet specific. He focuses on the search for sound qualities in the aforementioned relationship between musician and instrument. Through this relationship (often using amplification), he creates a narrative that is as fluid and evolving as possible. This has essentially become his trademark.

Currently Dominik Karski is associated (as a mentor) with the Cybec 21st Century for Young Composers Program, a forum for young composers at the Melbourne Symphony Orchestra. He deals with composition independently, but also conducts English classes for scientists.

Differences between the old and new realities

There is a diverse range of music performed both in Poland and in Australia. It includes both scored and graphic music and a variety of aesthetics, from references to classicism or romanticism to avant-garde or sound art. This tendency demonstrates that the current shape of contemporary music is determined by an international environment. In both countries, the issue of financing culture is also similar. The only difference is that in Poland the infrastructure is much more extensive, which makes it easier to obtain grants, but in the area of contemporary music it also can become an obstacle. In Australia, on the other hand, it is easier to establish contacts in a less structured music environment. From an aesthetic point of view, the Australian market also focuses more on the manifestations of popular culture; reaching for unknown repertoire, which is more difficult to perceive and requires a greater level of expertise from the listener, is rare. Karski stresses that in Poland audiences are more musically aware, which offers the possibility of a conceptual preparation of concert programs.

Reason for leaving Poland

Dominik Karski emigrated with his parents, who took part in the 1991 emigration program. They applied to stay in Australia and Canada. A quicker response from Australia determined their decision.

Contact with Poland after emigration

Karski lived in Poland between 2006 and 2014. He remains in touch with the Polish music community, with both musicians and institutions. His work appears on festival concert programs and he also receives commissions from the Ministry of Culture and National Heritage. He also maintains personal contacts inside Poland.

Influence of the new home on the composer's music

The answer to this question is not easy. Karski's compositional profile was shaped in Australia, which is certainly important for his creative persona. The influences of the Australian musicians with whom Karski collaborated and the local academic community with whom he was involved during his studies have been significant as well.

Awareness of the composer's music in both countries

In Poland, his work has been presented at the Warsaw Autumn Festival and Musica Polonica Nova. He has received stipends from the Ministry of Culture and National Heritage for *pre-seed*, dedicated to Richard Craig, and for *Certainty's Flux*, written for Swedish violinist Karin Hellqvist. An important event in his career was the performance of *Superbimposition* during the Musica Electronica Nova festival in Wrocław in 2011. Cooperation with the Flute o'clock duo and the Polish label Bôłt Records resulted in an album containing all of Karski's flute compositions written before 2016; the album is titled *Karski Glimmer Flute o'clock*. His cooperation with Flute o'clock also resulted in the creation of *Streamforms V*, performed with Małgorzata Walentynowicz in October 2018. Cooperation with Ryszard Lubieniecki led to creating *Metaphysical Graffiti* for amplified, prepared accordion. In 2003 Karski received an award at the Andrzej Panufnik International Composition Competition in Kraków. His works are not only recognized by Polish musicians, but are also widely discussed by music critics. He has had similar successes in Australia, where he has had the opportunity to work with renowned Australian musicians, e.g., Elizabeth Sellars (violin), Geofrey Gartner (cello), Katheleen Gallagher (flute), Claire Edwardes and Peter Naville (percussion). His works have also been performed by such esteemed ensembles as the ELISION Ensemble, Libra Ensemble, and Ensemble Offspring. He is a respected member of the Australian music community, which is reflected in his involvement in the Cybec Program. His works are also performed at festivals in almost all of Europe, Canada, and the United States.

Composer's personality

Dominik Karski is a man of high culture and a strong work ethic. At the same time, his scientific approach to reality transfers well into his artistic pursuits. Musings on the physicality of sound as an effect of the musician's correlation with an instrument are at the center of his interests.

Remarkable anecdote or biographical fact

The composer returned to Poland during his studies in Vienna, because living in Poland and commuting to Austria proved to be more affordable than organizing his life there from scratch.

Respondent's Top Choices

- **Favorite work:** *Certainty's Flux* for amplified violin (2012).
- **Best work:** *Streamforms* for amplified bass flute (2003).
- **Composition still waiting to be discovered:** *These People are Only One and a Half Minutes Away from Eternity* (2013).

Respondent: Karol Furtak

Tadeusz Zygfryd Kassern

Date and place of birth:
19 March 1904, Lviv.

Date and place of death:
2 May 1957, New York.

Date and place of emigration:
1945, United States (New York).

Return to Poland:
He did not return.

Key quote

A human being should remain true to one principle:... To be honest in everything he does. There is usually a high price to pay for this, but there is no price that is too high for honesty.[254]

Activities before emigration

Until 1939, Kassern earned a living by working at the prestigious General Prosecutor's Office in Poznań, although he enjoyed composing above all. His works, including *Concerto for Voice and Orchestra* (awarded in 1929 at a Parisian composers' competition, where the jury included Ravel, Roussel, Honegger, and Schmitt), *Concerto for String Orchestra*, *Piano Sonatina No. 1*, *Four Copernicus Motets* [*Cztery motety Kopernikowskie*] for mixed choir, *Orava Suite* [*Suita orawska*] for men's choir and mezzo-soprano, were well received. Some of these pieces even became known as the "hits" of classical music at the time. He was also active as a music critic, publishing reviews in *Nowy Kurier*, *Dziennik Poznański*, and *Muzyka*, and as a speaker and organizer of concerts for the contemporary music section of the Poznań Music Society. At the end of 1945, he accepted a position at the Consulate General of the Republic of Poland in New York, where he concentrated on helping musicians in his war-torn country and popularizing Polish music in the United States.

After emigration

After resigning from the consulate, Kassern continued to live in New York City, where he successfully found employment as a music teacher and arranger. While he was able to cope with this work, gaining recognition in the field of composition seemed to be a daunting task, although he eventually decided to accept the challenge. He left a lot of interesting pedagogical music behind. Most importantly, he composed three operas, which were thematically very interesting and stylistically diverse; he also starting writing several more operas. One of the completed operas, *Sun-Up*, based on a drama by Lula Vollmer, was staged in New York. His pedagogical works were not only played, but also published by G. Schirmer.

Differences between the old and new realities

Interwar Poland was not an ideal country, but Kassern had a good life there. The successes he achieved in every area of activity probably brought him much satisfaction. It proved to be different in exile. In his letters to his family, he wrote that he was "fighting hard for recognition and bread, that he was working without respite, because the huge, ruthless competition forces everyone here to intensify all their efforts and do the best they can." The biggest problem for Kassern, however, was that he was stateless for many years due to the Cold War and the tightening of American immigration policy. This led him to have a nervous breakdown that ended in a suicide attempt. In September 1956, circumstances improved when the composer was finally registered as an immigrant.

Reason for leaving Poland

He left for political reasons. The demands made on Kassern by the Ministry of Foreign Affairs of the Polish People's Republic were unacceptable to him. He did not agree with the Sovietization of Poland, let alone the influence of totalitarian rule on culture or the unfair life he felt he would have to lead while working at the consulate. After severing cooperation with the Polish government, authorities "removed him from Polish culture." Almost immediately, a commission for an opera was canceled, his music was banned from concert halls, and Polish Music Publishers withdrew the scores of his works being prepared for print. In early 1951 he was expelled from the Polish Composers' Union.

Contact with Poland after emigration

After the decision to emigrate, Kassern did not break his contacts with either his loved ones or the Polish music community. He continued to correspond with his family, and it is mainly thanks to this that we know what his life in the United States was like. Contacts with the Polish music community became more extensive after the so-called political thaw took place in Poland in the mid-1950s. He started writing articles for *Ruch Muzyczny* and made plans to exchange music information and work with institutions. The artistic community in Poland, especially in Poznań, thanked him with a series of concerts of his music. According to an account by Michał Kondracki, another Polish composer in exile in New York, we know that Polish culture was a priority for Kassern.

Influence of the new home on the composer's music

Kassern's oeuvre until 1948 mostly displayed a neoclassical and folkloristic style, at a time when American composers showed more interest in expressionism and opera. In order to compete in his new home, he had to adapt to local fashions. His first opera, *The Anointed*, was a fulfillment of earlier decisions to create a musical monument dedicated to the Jews murdered during the war; it was his first piece in an expressionistic style. His next opera, *Sun-Up,* was composed in a technique reminiscent of interval structuralism; it includes places in which an American folk song emerges, meaningfully linked to the surrounding content. His third opera, the satirical *Comedy of the Dumb Wife*, reflects a return to neoclassicism. Several dozen pedagogical pieces present different tendencies, but it is worth noting that they contain quotations from both American and Polish melodies.

Awareness of the composer's music in both countries

At present, Kassern's works are rarely performed in the United States. Only a few chamber pieces appear on local stages, e.g., *Sonatina* for flute and piano and some pedagogical compositions. His works are heard much more frequently in Poland. The most important events there include the staging of *Comedy of the Dumb Wife* at the Academy of Music in Gdańsk and a production of a modified version of this opera at Poznań's Grand Theater. Also, the National Piano Competition sponsored a program in Gdańsk titled "Music performed by children – Tadeusz Kassern's compositions." There have also been monographic concerts and performances of his most famous works, including *Concerto for Voice and Orchestra*, *Concerto for String Orchestra*, and *Concerto for Double Bass and Piano*; these occurred primarily in Poznań, Gdańsk and Warsaw. More recordings and publications of this music should be a goal for the future.

Composer's personality

From letters to his friends and relatives, it appears that Kassern was a hardworking man who keenly shared his experiences and was kind to others. He emphasized the importance of culture, especially music, in social life. As an artist, he found pleasure in art, but stressed the importance of its message. The difficult conditions of his life did not kill his passion for making the most of it.

Remarkable anecdote or biographical fact

The most poignant thing in Kassern's life was his enormous commitment to culture, especially music. He remained true to this mission throughout his life, regardless of where he lived. The world expressed gratitude for this at least twice. Just before World War II, Kassern was called a luminary of Poznań's culture. To commemorate this, his portrait was placed on the wall of the Scoffer's Club at 14a Freedom Square [Plac Wolności]. He was remembered a second time during his time at the consulate in New York; after one of the many aid activities carried out by Kassern, Witold Lutosławski wrote to him, saying "You are...the archangel Gabriel among Polish musicians."

Respondent's Top Choices

- **Favorite work:** *Comedy of the Dumb Wife* (1953), an opera.
- **Best work:** *The Anointed* [*Koniec Mesjasza*] (1951), an opera.
- **Composition still waiting to be discovered:** *Sun-Up* [*Jutrzenka*] (1952), an opera.

Respondent: Violetta Kostka

Paweł Klecki (Paul Kletzky)

Date and place of birth:
21 March 1900, Łódź.

Date and place of death:
5 March 1973, Liverpool.

Date and place of emigration:
1920, Germany (Berlin); 1938, Switzerland (Lausanne, Geneva).

Return to Poland:
No, but he visited Poland as a conductor starting in 1959.

Key quote

What was Klecki's music like? Very close to the German tradition: one can hear there echoes of the neo-romanticism of Brahms or Mahler, but also modernism and expressionism. It is difficult to define the style in a strict way. It is eclectic, but also coherent.[255]

Activities before emigration

Because Klecki left Poland for Germany in order to study composition in 1920, his previous musical activity in Poland was rather humble. Before his departure, he was known as a promising violinist; at the age of 15, he joined the newly founded symphony orchestra in Łódź and enjoyed his first successes as a solo performer.

After emigration

He was most prolific as a composer between 1920 and 1943 (34 works, including three symphonies, three string quartets, many songs, piano, violin and flute concertos, and chamber compositions). After World War II, he abandoned composing in favor of conducting. As he explained, this was due to post-Holocaust trauma.

Differences between the old and new realities

In Poland, Klecki was known as a violinist. Between 1920 and 1933 in Germany, he was preoccupied mostly with composing. Between 1933 and 1943, while in exile in Italy, the Soviet Union, and Switzerland, he divided his time between composing and conducting. After World War II, he focused only on the latter activity.

Reason for leaving Poland

Klecki emigrated twice. He went first to Germany in search of better conditions for developing his career. For political reasons (he was Jewish), he left Germany in 1933 and went to Italy. In 1938, he moved again, this time to Switzerland

Contact with Poland after emigration

Klecki never lost contact with his home country. During the first stage of his emigration, when in Germany, he would visit Poland, where his works were performed sporadically. This period in Klecki's life has not been thoroughly researched yet, so we do not know how often he actually visited. He enjoyed his largest recognition, both as a composer and a conductor, in Germany. After the war (at least until 1968), he visited Poland for performances.

Influence of the new home on the composer's music

Emigration to Germany offered Klecki a chance to develop his composing skills. During the 1920s, he was recognized as part of German musical life. His chamber and symphonic music was frequently performed; in 1927, the first live performance of his compositions took place at the Berlin Philharmonic. When Hitler came to power in 1933, Klecki was no longer welcome in Germany. His music was no longer heard and his scores were destroyed, since they were classified as examples of *Entartete Musik*. He continued to compose, but in much more difficult circumstances. One of his last works is *Symphony No. 3*, composed in 1939, soon after the artist settled in Switzerland. It bears the subtitle *In memoriam*, which can be interpreted in two ways—as a farewell to the world he knew and as an homage to the victims of anti-Semitism, which eventually included many of Klecki's relatives.

Awareness of the composer's music in both countries

Klecki's oeuvre is practically absent on Polish and international stages. There have been attempts to publish his works in the United States, where performances of his work do take place, although usually only one hearing of any piece occurs. In Poland, Klecki's music is most often heard in Łódź. Pianist Adam Manijak recorded his chamber music for the DUX label (*Piano Trio* and *Violin Sonata*) and a program at the Tansman Festival included his *Flute Concerto* and other compositions. Recently, his works were performed at the National Philharmonic in Warsaw (*Preludes,* op. 4, performed by pianist Ignacy Lisiecki, and *Symphonic Variations,* op. 30, by the Warsaw Philharmonic, conducted by Łukasz Borowicz). The Polish Radio National Symphonic Orchestra has also recorded Klecki's *Symphony No. 2.* Still, performances remain infrequent and as a composer Klecki is almost unrecognized (he is much better known as a conductor).

Composer's personality

Klecki proved to be adaptable in life. He began as an orchestra violinist (and was also a successful soloist). Later he focused on composing and, even later, on conducting. His work was rooted in a post-romantic idiom; he never accepted the musical avant-garde, which for him included dodecaphonic music and compositions written after 1945. According to Jerzy Waldorff (from his account in his book *Devils and Angels* [*Diabły i anioły*]), Klecki claimed that "music beginning with dodecaphony is a great fraud that allows hundreds of conmen to flourish."

Remarkable anecdote or biographical fact

As he escaped from Italy to Switzerland, Klecki left the scores for his compositions in a briefcase in the basement of a Milan hotel. He was certain that all of his compositions had been destroyed during the war. After the war, during renovations in La Scala, the briefcase was found by chance and sent to the artist's Swiss address. He never dared to open the package. His wife did after his death. It turned out that all the scores survived.

Respondent's Top Choices

– **Favorite work:** *Symphony No. 2 in G Major*, op. 18 (1928).
– **Best work:** *Symphony No. 3 "In memoriam,"* op. 31 (1939).
– **Composition still waiting to be discovered:** three string quartets (No. 1 in A minor, op. 1, 1923; No. 2 in C minor, op. 13, 1925; No. 3 in D minor, op. 23, 1931).

Respondent: Lech Dzierżanowski

Krzysztof (Christopher) Komeda (real name: Krzysztof Trzciński)

Date and place of birth:
27 April 1931, Poznań.

Date and place of death:
23 April 1969, Warsaw.

Date and place of emigration:
1967–1969, United States (Los Angeles).

Return to Poland:
After his accident and stay at an American hospital, Komeda's wife took him back to Warsaw, where he died without regaining consciousness.

Key quote
Krzysztof was amazed, he was happy and proud. He said: Me, look, me! It's mine, mine![256]

Activities before emigration
He was a laryngologist by education, but he learned to play piano during his childhood. However, in his musical career, especially in composition, he was at least partly self-taught, gifted with outstanding talent. Komeda's career illustrates the path that Polish jazz has taken: from semi-amateur, stylistically backward attempts in the mid-1950s to his own, fully professional style in the middle of the next decade. Since his appearance at the First Jazz Festival in Sopot in 1956, Komeda gradually strengthened his position as the leading figure of modern jazz in Poland. He gained recognition as an outstanding author of film soundtracks, including Roman Polański's works (*Knife in the Water* [*Nóż w wodzie*], 1962; *The Most Beautiful Deceptions in the World* [*Najpiękniejsze oszustwa świata / Les plus belles escroqueries du monde*], 1964; *The Trap* [*Matnia*], 1966; *Dance of the Vampires*, 1967) and those of Henning Carlsen (e.g., *The Cats* [*Kocice*], 1965; *Hunger* [*Głód*], 1966). He also wrote a jazz composition in the style of the so-called *third current* (e.g., *Ballet Etudes* [*Etiudy baletowe*], 1962). His 1966 album *Astigmatic*, considered a masterpiece, is one of the most important albums in the history of Polish jazz. He also performed extensively, mainly in Scandinavia and Germany, where he recorded an album titled *Meine süsse europäische Heimat* (1967, in the famous series *Dichtung und Jazz* series curated by Joachim-Ernst Berendt).

After emigration

Komeda's stay in Hollywood in December 1967 opened up the possibility of developing an international career in film music (he had already earned recognition outside Poland, not only thanks to Polański's films and jazz, but also thanks to compositions written for Danish cinematography). In the United States, he completed music for *Rosemary's Baby* (directed by Roman Polański, 1968) and *Riot* (directed by Buzz Kulik, 1969). Taking into account a contract with Paramount Pictures that concluded in the summer of 1968 (which obliged Komeda to create music for three films a year), the planned soundtrack to *The Adventures of Gerard* [*Przygody Gerarda*] (directed by Jerzy Skolimowski, 1970), and the 1969 nominations for the Golden Globe and Grammy Awards for his famous *Lullaby from Rosemary's Baby*, one could assume he was heading for a brilliant career. Unfortunately, this was stopped by his premature death, caused by a head injury in October 1968.

Differences between the old and new realities

The reality of the American "dream factory" in which Komeda quickly immersed himself, which involved establishing good relationships not only with his new clients but also with Polish artists in exile (including Henryk Wars and his wife), was certainly different from conditions in Poland. Komeda's composing and arranging habits also required some changes, since he was now separated from musicians he had previously worked with who had possessed an ability to creatively present his music (these included Tomasz Stańko and Rune Carlsson). Also, his artistic autonomy seemed more restricted than it had been in Poland.

Reason for leaving Poland

Komeda left Poland after receiving an invitation to work on the film *Rosemary's Baby*; Polański had insisted that Komeda be involved in the project. The great success of the film and its music radically changed the position of both artists. It also seems that 1967 marked the collapse of a career formula that Komeda had developed in Communist Poland and abroad.

Contact with Poland after emigration

Despite emotional anxieties, Komeda maintained contact with his wife Zofia, an outstanding animator in the jazz community and a remarkable personality who remained in Poland. As she stated in the documentary *The Time of Komeda* [*Czas Komedy*] (directed by Robert Kaczmarek and Mariusz Kalinowski, 1994), the composer was not thinking about permanent emigration: "Krzysztof never told me that he planned to stay in America; quite the opposite." Komeda's contract with Paramount gave him the opportunity to work from anywhere in the world; the artist also continued to pay compulsory dues to Pagart (a Polish agency).

Influence of the new home on the composer's music

Komeda was an experienced and conscientious musician, in full control of all stages of the creative process (which, according to various witnesses' accounts, impressed American film producers). On the one hand, Hollywood created conditions for his work that were unattainable in Europe, while, on the other, Komeda was open to the expectations and conditions of American production. Marek Hendrykowski points out, however, that during Komeda's period of emigration, the composer did not create any autonomous jazz compositions.

Awareness of the composer's music in both countries

In the 1990s, Roman Kowal believed that Komeda "still remains the only original Polish [jazz] composer on a global scale." After twenty years, this opinion (also held by other musicians, such as Tomasz Stańko) remains valid. The composer's name is still known internationally, although his output is known only selectively.

Composer's personality

"It would seem as if this talkative, modest boy was living his quiet, humble life," noted the composer's wife. However, introversion and shyness were only a part of Komeda's personality, for he hid his extraordinary individuality and self-esteem beneath these traits. As an artist, he was organized and consistent; his international career also indicates his ability to adapt to new challenges.

Remarkable anecdote or biographical fact

Komeda created seven variants of lullabies for *Rosemary's Baby*. In her memoirs, Zofia Komeda said that all of the material was presented in front of a committee that included the composer and his wife, the head of the music department at Paramount Pictures, Henryk Wars, Roman Polański, and Sharon Tate. Two pieces were chosen, one of which (sung by Mia Farrow, the film's lead actress) became internationally famous. The remaining lullabies were lost, probably stolen while Komeda was in a coma.

Respondent's Top Choices

- **Favorite work:** The soundtrack to *Rosemary's Baby,* which is fascinating both on the screen and independently.
- **Best work:** The sound in *Rosemary's Baby* remains a great achievement of his American period; it presents an ideal of an audiovisual covenant, in which the dialogue between image and sound offers a quality that exceeds their simple summation. Komeda perfectly amplified Polański's sense of horror, pessimism, and irony, using his characteristic technique of an functional use of the initial material, which is then subjected to continuous transformations (of tempo and timbre, among other elements). In the scenes of Rosemary's satanic hallucinations, the composer does not attack the viewer with sudden strokes of horror, but rather builds a consistently ominous mood based on clusters, choral incantations, and sonoristic effects (e.g., howling).
- **Composition still waiting to be discovered:** An interesting element in Komeda's oeuvre is the slightly neglected soundtrack for *Riot* (1969). Zofia Komeda believed that her husband should not have accepted the commission for what was a B-class movie. But this film shows how flexible and absorbed he was. The opening ballad, *100 Years* (with lyrics by Robert Wells, interpreted by Bill Medley), based on ostinato bass and a counterpoint of harmonica solo, refers to the tradition of westerns and "masculine cinema." By transforming it during the scene in which Cully Briston (one of the protagonists) dreams, the composer perfectly, albeit somewhat ironically, captured the style of popular cinema. Other parts (e.g., an alarm siren) show Komeda's signature ability to create simple, non-illustrative, yet expressive and functional motifs (often of a modal or sonoristic nature), which, subjected to small variations, create a kind of second layer to the film.

Respondent: Grzegorz Piotrowski

Marzena Komsta

Date and place of birth:
7 February 1970, Gdynia.

Date and place of emigration:
November 1993, France (Lyon, Paris).

Return to Poland:
She has not returned.

Key quote

A human being is deeply dependent on their mirror image in the soul of another person, even if that soul would be nonsensical.[257]

Activities before emigration

Beginning in 1989, Komsta studied composition with Eugeniusz Głowski at the Stanisław Moniuszko Academy of Music in Gdańsk. Later she worked with Zbigniew Bagiński and Włodzimierz Kotoński at Warsaw's Academy of Music (now the Chopin University of Music). Composition was her focus of interest even before she began these classes, as shown, for example, by her *Oberek* for piano (1988). Komsta's early Polish works differ technically from those created after her departure in two meaningful ways. In her early compositions, she constructed her works according to the principle "from detail to the whole": the macroform emerged through successive phrases and themes of the composition. Secondly, due to technical limitations, there were relatively fewer electroacoustic compositions in Poland than in other countries. One important composition from this period is *For Unwanted Prometheuses* [*Niechcianym Prometeuszom*] (1991), where for the first time she reached for extramusical concepts. This composition was followed by the last piece she wrote in Poland, *Agmen* (1993), composed for the Dutch ensemble De Ereprijs. It represents a turning point in her work: before her departure, her preferred means of expression were movement, compositional energy, ostinato structures, strong contrasts, and controlled aleatorism.

After emigration

Initially, she began working at the Conservatoire national supérieur musique et danse in Lyon. The year she graduated, she was admitted to the Formation Doctorale en Musique et Musicologie du XXe siècle at the Institut de Recherche et de Coordination Acoustique/Musique (IRCAM) in Paris. A year earlier she had been awarded a scholarship from the Nadia et Lili Boulanger Foundation. Her prestigious achievements during her stay abroad also include the Villa Kuyojama prize in Kyoto, thanks to which she had the opportunity to become a resident composer. Since then (2003), she has divided her professional life between France and Japan.

Komsta continued the programmatic line initiated by *Agmen*. Extramusical reflections have become gradually more expansive, described in more and more extensive programs. However, she has emphasized that the basic feature of her works is still the aesthetic aspect of sound. Inspiration from extramusical, philosophical content serves as a starting point for the creative act, but in the perception of a work it is not a key element or even a necessary one. The composer has also departed from attaching structural importance to ostinato structures and adhering to the "general-to-detail" principle and has moved toward a deepening interest in electroacoustic works, such as in *...tu sais?* (1995), *Stelfer* (2014), and *Desire* (2005). She also uses live electronic music, incorporating techniques of simultaneous processing of sound by the computer during the performance. This occurs, for example, in *Songe XXV* (2006) and *Les Espaces de mes rêves* (2003). The composer also looks for sound values that are suggestive to the listener, for example, taking advantage of the human voice (including her own, as in compositions for tape *Stelfer* and *Desire*) or Oriental instruments, such as in *Tamashii No Soko Kara "From the Depth of the Soul"* [*Tamashii No Soko Kara "Z głębi duszy"*] for shakuhachi, a traditional bamboo flute used by Buddhist monks. At the same time, Komsta seems primarily attracted by the specificity of articulation rather than the particular instrument being used, as she applies Asian articulations to European instruments.

A search for specific sound phenomena has also inspired her to use prepared instruments and to create ephemeral compositions, such as the aforementioned *Les Espaces de mes rêves*. Such compositions are not written down or recorded; they exist only in performance. The composer performs them herself; their overriding feature is impermanence. Since Komsta's became involved with Japanese culture, her compositions have become more meditative, largely maintained in *piano* dynamics. Contrast and timbre still play an important role, but the aesthetic expressiveness of her compositions has become less aggressive.

Differences between the old and new realities

These worlds differed primarily in their technical capabilities. In Poland in the early 1990s, the equipment used by electroacoustic music studios was sometimes of a lower quality than composers' private equipment. This caused significant limitations in creativity. Moreover, the French community was more open to experimentation and innovative concepts such as spectral harmony or far-reaching transformations of sound.

Reason for leaving Poland

Komsta left Poland to study with Philippe Manoury and Denis Lorrain at the Conservatoire national supérieur musique et danse in Lyon in the Department of Composition, Acoustic, Electroacoustic and Computer Science Music. Having received a scholarship from Witold Lutosławski in November 1993, she left for France. She stresses that her departure was a conscious artistic decision.

Contact with Poland after emigration

Komsta maintains contact with Poland. She visits the country privately and professionally. Occasionally, she gives lectures at universities (e.g., at the Institute of Musicology at the Catholic University of Lublin in 2015), and receives commissions from Polish institutions, e.g., the Adam Mickiewicz Institute, for which she composed *Stelfer*. An important event connecting the artist with Poland, which was done partly for personal reasons, was her participation in recording an album titled *Olter* (2005), dedicated to the memory of Jacek Olter.

Influence of the new home on the composer's music

The influence of her new environment offered new technical possibilities in the field of electroacoustic composition. Timbre, which has always been an important feature of her work, could now be shaped through processes previously unavailable to her. This contributed to a calming of her aesthetics, as the element of movement gave way to the contemplation of timbre. Her departure prompted the creation of more difficult works; the element of virtuosity was always important for her, but after 1993 these tendencies intensified. Interestingly, this higher degree of complexity is typical for compositions written for artists from southern Europe. The influence of Japanese customs on Komsta has also been significant. As she herself says, "time flows more slowly there." This has caused a turn towards meditative aesthetics, calmer agogics, and subtler dynamics.

Awareness of the composer's music in both countries

In Poland, Komsta's work has been presented at contemporary music festivals, such as the Warsaw Autumn, the Gdańsk Meetings of Young Composers, and Musica Polonica Nova. She has also received commissions from Polish institutions and non-governmental organizations. We could clearly say that her activity has left its mark on Polish musical culture at the end of the twentieth century and the beginning of the twenty-first, as shown by the numerous references to her name in popular books and articles concerning recent Polish music. Shortly after she left, she was also nominated for the prestigious Polityka's Passport [*Paszport Polityki*] award. In France she also receives commissions, not only from institutions (e.g., Studio GRAME in Lyon), but also from the French government and directly from performers. It is worth mentioning that she was one of only two graduates per year allowed to complete her chosen area of study.

In Japan, Komsta is an ambassador for the latest French music. The composer has a permanent professional relationship with many ensembles from all over Europe. Among other things, she receives commissions for both electroacoustic and acoustic music. In Japan, on the other hand, she carries out projects that go beyond concert premieres; she collaborates with many artists from various fields and her music inspires both performances and installations.

Composer's personality

Komsta is a methodical, goal-oriented artist focused on the realization of specific concepts. Her creative process is affected by her reflection on topics related to philosophy and life as they impact both individuals and society. Moreover, it is important for her to search for specific sound qualities and to focus on the issue of musical form. Komsta is welcoming towards people and responsive to their empirical and spiritual needs. She has a positive attitude towards innovative projects and willingly cooperates with other artists (e.g., from the visual arts), musicologists, and journalists.

Remarkable anecdote or biographical fact

Komsta, while still a student in Poland, stood out from other young artists, who mostly wrote neotonal and repetitive compositions. Due to her originality, Philippe Manoury invited her to participate in his prestigious studies in France. She was granted a Witold Lutosławski scholarship for this purpose. Lutosławski was the first to notice the importance of timbre in her works.

Respondent's Top Choices

- **Favorite work:** *Desire*, a miniature for tape (2005).
- **Best work:** *Stelfer* for band and electronics (2014).
- **Composition still waiting to be discovered:** *lFdlC (le F de la C)* for piano and three pianists (1996).

Respondent: Karol Furtak

Michał Kondracki (actually Michał Kondracki-Ostoya)

Date and place of birth:
5 October 1902, Poltava.

Date and place of death:
27 February 1984, Glen Cove, New York.

Date and place of emigration:
1938, departure from Poland; 1940, Brazil (Rio de Janeiro); 1943, United States (New York).

Return to Poland:
He did not return.

Key quote

In fact, he's an incorrigible romantic. Even the classical character of his music derives from the pure spirit of romanticism, deeply rooted in the composer's psyche and fueling his creative imagination.[258]

Activities before emigration

Before leaving Poland, Michał Kondracki revealed his talent as a mature and original composer; he was one of Karol Szymanowski's most promising students. He also studied composition with Roman Statkowski and piano with Henryk Melcer-Szczawiński. In 1927, he graduated with honors from Warsaw Conservatory. Between 1926 and 1939, he wrote seventeen compositions for large ensemble, including symphonic, vocal-instrumental, and stage pieces. Kondracki's work was greatly influenced by his interest in folklore, which he creatively developed in works such as *Little Highlander Symphony* [*Mała symfonia góralska*] (1930) and *Kurpian Suite* [*Suita kurpiowska*] (1933). His later compositions, starting with his *Piano Concerto No. 2* (1935), were increasingly saturated with lyricism. Kondracki was also active in music criticism and journalism (writing for the *ABC* daily, *Kwartalnik Muzyczny*, and *Muzyka Polska*), and later in collecting folklore in the Hutsul, Podhale, and Żywiec regions of Poland. He co-founded the Polish Society for Contemporary Music and was a board member of numerous organizations, including the Karol Szymanowski Society.

After emigration

Beginning in 1940, Kondracki lived in Rio de Janeiro, composing and cooperating with the local radio station, which resulted in a series of musical programs devoted to Ignacy

Jan Paderewski. After settling in the New York area in 1943, he was primarily involved in giving piano lessons and working as the president of The Long Island Little Orchestra Society. He composed increasingly less, instead devoting himself to his great passions of nature and travel (thanks to his great erudition, he became a tour guide to the Mediterranean region).

Differences between the old and new realities

Already in the 1930s, Michał Kondracki had gained recognition as a composer. Although critics pointed out certain formal shortcomings in his works, they almost unanimously recognized him as the hope of Polish contemporary music. He received a scholarship from the French government (thanks to which he studied at the Parisian École Normale de Musique with Nadia Boulanger and Arthur Honegger) and won numerous national and international awards (including a gold medal at the World Exhibition in Paris in 1937 for his ballet *Legend, or the Fairytale of Kraków* [*Legenda, czyli baśń Krakówska*]). The musical environment in the United States remained an alien ground to the composer due to the fact that it was guided by different, more commercial priorities. That is why Kondracki became primarily a traveler, educator, and publicist in America.

Reason for leaving Poland

It is highly likely that the decision to emigrate was not an intentional one. In the summer of 1939, he embarked on a long journey. While on board a Polish merchant ship in the Mediterranean, World War II began. In 1940 he arrived in Brazil.

Contact with Poland after emigration

At the end of the 1940s, Kondracki, having resigned from his compositional career in the United States, tried to attract interest in his new works from the Polish Composers' Union and Polish Musical Publishers, albeit unsuccessfully. Thereafter, he maintained contact with the Polish music community primarily through his journalistic activities. From 1948–1949 and again from 1957–1969, as a correspondent for *Ruch Muzyczny*, he described the musical life of New York City and important artistic events in the United States. Moreover, as part of his cooperation with Voice of America's TV channel, he conducted interviews with Polish artists performing in the United States.

Influence of the new home on the composer's music

Brazilian culture, especially its freshness of melody and lively rhythms, influenced Kondracki's work in the early 1940s. His *Brazilian Dance* is one result of these inspirations. In the United States, however, he gradually withdrew from composing. He admitted that he did not count on success in a reality in which "the dollar opens all the doors, in a country that does not know any feelings of sentiment or personal or artistic considerations."[259] After 1942, he wrote only eleven pieces, the last of which, the 1958 *Anthem to Aphrodite* [*Hymn do Afrodyty*], was dedicated to his wife, Longina Kassern-Kondracka.

Awareness of the composer's music in both countries

Although in the 1930s Kondracki's works appeared quite often in the repertoire of Polish orchestras, his work was largely forgotten after World War II (for both political and practical reasons, since a large part of his output was lost). Currently, compositions such as

Soldier [*Żołnierz*], *Oberek*, and *Toccata* are sometimes included in concert programs. In the United States, Kondracki's work remains unknown, although some compositions were certainly performed during his lifetime. The few available sources indicate, for example, that the school orchestra from Long Island had his 1955 *Carol* for flute and string orchestra in its repertoire.

Composer's personality

Kondracki had a serene disposition, which clearly translated into his original, colorful, and humorous musical language. He enjoyed staying close to nature, so in the United States he chose to stay away from large urban areas. Due to his numerous travels (he visited almost all the continents), he avoided settling for a permanent job. His interests included antiquity and art history.

Remarkable anecdote or biographical fact

Kondracki was sporadically involved in film music. For example, he co-authored the music for the film *Girl Looking for Love* [*Dziewczyna szuka miłości*], directed by Romuald Gantkowski (1937). The key role in the film is played by a family of Polish émigrés who, like Kondracki in 1940, had settled in Brazil.

Respondent's Top Choices

- **Favorite work:** *Cantata ecclesiastica* for mixed choir, orchestra and organ (1937) stands out among Kondracki's works. The only religious work in the composer's oeuvre, it is sometimes described as his best composition.[260] His signature humor and energetic rhythm were replaced here by a concentrated religiosity and deep emotionality.
- **Best work:** In 1937 Kondracki wrote a two-act ballet *Legend or Fairy Tale of Kraków*, which was an adaptation of a story about the legendary sorcerer Twardowski. This piece was considered one of the best Polish ballets[261] of the time and subsequently became part of the repertoire of the Representational Polish Ballet, winning recognition among audiences in Paris, London, and New York. Kondracki's music and the stage action work together in perfect harmony. The music, supported by vivid instrumentation, illustrates themes of conflict, mystery, and fantasy.
- **Composition still waiting to be discovered:** Kondracki preferred large ensembles. He wrote mostly orchestral works, which allowed him to fully reveal his compositional artistry. Other distinctive features of Kondracki's work include a brilliant use of dynamics, humor, and a *joie de vivre*. These features can be found in the symphonic composition *Soldiers* (1932), which was honored at the 1932 Olympic composers' competition in Los Angeles and was eagerly performed by Grzegorz Fitelberg and Leopold Stokowski. In this evocative work, now completely forgotten, the composer imitates a natural acoustic phenomenon (the Doppler effect) with the use of successive key changes.

Respondent: Kinga Krzymowska-Szacoń

Abel (Adam) Korzeniowski

Date and place of birth:
18 July 1972, Kraków.

Date and place of emigration:
2006, United States (Los Angeles).

Return to Poland:
He has not returned.

Key quote

For me, film is a perfect art form which reflects our strength as a society. It shows what we can achieve by working together.[262]

Activities before emigration

Adam Korzeniowski graduated from the Academy of Music in Kraków with degrees in cello (1996) and in composition (2000), studying the latter with Krzysztof Penderecki. In 1998 he was awarded the Creative Scholarship of the Mayor of the City of Kraków in the field of composition, and between 1999 and 2001 he worked at the Academy as an assistant. Film music has always been his dream field. He has been creating music for theater performances and films since the start of his career. His first success came in 2000, when he received the Golden Lion Award at the Polish Film Festival in Gdynia for music to Jerzy Stuhr's film *Big Animal* [*Duże zwierzę*]. Korzeniowski's other honors include the Ludwik Award, donated by the Kraków theater community for his music to *Kafka*, directed by T. Wysocki, the Jańcio Wodnik Award for the soundtrack to *An Angel in Kraków* [*Anioł w Krakowie*], director Artur Więcek, and the Golden Knight award for the soundtrack to *Weather for Tomorrow*, directed by Jerzy Stuhr. His score for Fritz Lang's *Metropolis* was performed in 2004 at the Era New Horizons Film Festival with an impressive ensemble of almost 200 performers.

After emigration

After the success of *Metropolis*, Korzeniowski knew that the kind of career he dreamed of would not be available in Poland. He sent demos to various foreign music agencies, eventually receiving a response from Evolution Music Partners. In 2006, he left for Los Angeles, where he settled with his wife. His start there was not easy—his first commission, for a score to *The Half-Life of Timofee Berezin* [*Połowiczny rozpad Timofieja Berezina*] was not completed until six months after his arrival, yet it turned out to be crucial for his further career in the States. Over the next few years, he composed music for two animated films (the American movie *Terra* and the Polish film *Star of Copernicus* [*Gwiazda Kopernika*]) in addition to several short and feature films.

The score he wrote for Tom Ford's film *A Single Man* was a turning point. In 2009 he received the San Diego Film Critics' Award for it, and a year later he was nominated for a Golden Globe award for the same film. This award became his key to almost all Hollywood doors. Among other things, it resulted in a collaboration with Madonna on her film *W.E.*, whose soundtrack was also nominated for the Golden Globes (2012). His next film, *Romeo and Juliet*, brought him three IFMCA awards in 2013 (in the categories Best Soundtrack of the Year, Best Film Composer of the Year, and Best Music for Drama) and a nomination the same year for *Escape from Tomorrow* (Best Music for Fantasy/Science Fiction/Horror and Best Composition of the Year in Film Music). The soundtrack for *Penny Dreadful*, for which Korzeniowski was twice nominated for an Emmy (in 2015 and 2016) and won the BAFTA Television Craft Award (2015), was also a great success. Apart from film compositions, he has composed music for Tiffany & Co. commercials and arranged songs by Edith Piaf to be performed by Patricia Kaas.

The composer's latest achievement, music for Tom Ford's *Nocturnal Animals* (2016), brought him the IFMCA award (Best Music for Drama category) and a number of nominations (including ACCA, BAFTA, and Golden Derby).

Differences between the old and new realities

Poland is not a country that offers an easy developmental path for a composer. Its academic system offers only a classical education. Specific film music composition studies are available only at the Academy of Music in Łódź. There is still no Hollywood-style film studio with its own orchestra, which would allow one to compose and perform large symphonic scores, and commissioned work provides relatively small remuneration. In America, the situation is completely different: Film studios do not lack money for either musicians or composers, who in turn can freely develop their ideas. Success in the United States is usually associated with long-term benefits. The status of a film music composer brings a certain level of stardom, which in Poland is reserved for directors and actors.

Reason for leaving Poland

The experience of scoring the large-format version of *Metropolis* in 2004, which despite its success did not contribute to the development of the composer's career in Poland, made Korzeniowski realize that his dream of composing film music could come true only in Hollywood. The composer often stresses that artists are appreciated in America. Their work is treated as an actual profession, but it comes at a cost—art there is perceived as a business, although commercial and qualitative success often go hand in hand. In Poland, art is not considered an occupation that allows for a stable life. Korzeniowski provided an example from his own life: a bank was reluctant to offer him a loan due to his lack of permanent employment, even though his earnings exceeded the national average.

Contact with Poland after emigration

Korzeniowski is rarely seen in Poland. He attended the sixth and tenth editions of the Film Music Festival in Kraków, where in 2017 his monographic concert opened the event. At the same time, he was honored for his outstanding achievements by the Mayor of Kraków, Jacek Majchrowski, who gave him a symbolic key to the city.

Influence of the new home on the composer's music

When he arrived in the United States, Korzeniowski already had a well-developed musical style marked by subtlety, minimalist means of expression, repetition, and emotionality. These elements can be heard in his early works as well as in recent productions. We can assume that his shift in residence did not affect his music much; rather, it brought an increase in comfort and a greater range of compositional possibilities. Perhaps Korzeniowski's experiences in the United States made him stick to his chosen path, since he did not need to experiment in other directions.

Awareness of the composer's music in both countries

Korzeniowski is primarily a film music composer (with exceptions, such as the monographic concert in Kraków). The global reach of American cinema makes him recognizable everywhere his films are presented.

Composer's personality

Korzeniowski's attitude resembles his music: subtle and balanced. He is deeply concerned with aesthetics, which manifests itself not only in his music, but also in the careful selection of statements he makes. His reserved approach translates into a highly individualized compositional style and sound. Being in America has added more optimism to his views on life; he has mentioned that in Hollywood, you have to forget about the words "you can't." Instead you must focus on solutions and dedicate yourself to your work. Korzeniowski was aware of the level of competition there, so he developed an original musical language.

Remarkable anecdote or biographical fact

In primary school he became friends with Borys Lankosz (director of *Reverse*, 2009, and *Seeds of Truth*, 2015). They worked on their first films together; Lankosz was the cinematographer and director, while Korzeniowski was responsible for the music. They once bet on which of them would be the first to win an Oscar—the stakes were one dollar.

During a holiday trip to Toronto in his youth, he worked in a warehouse during the day and at night he washed dishes in a go-go club. Working a dozen or so hours a day paid off—upon his return, he was able to buy equipment for composing, including an electronic synthesizer and an Atari computer.

Respondent's Top Choices

- **Favorite work:** *Pull the Trigger* (2014) from the first season of the soundtrack to *Penny Dreadful.*
- **Best work:** Soundtrack to *A Single Man* (2009).
- **Composition still waiting to be discovered:** Korzeniowski is primarily recognized as a film music composer. The early stage of his career is an interesting period, especially his music for theater.

Respondent: Anna Wyżga

Martyna Kosecka

Date and place of birth:
18 January 1989, Gdynia.

Date and place of emigration:
2016, Iran (Tehran).

Return to Poland:
She has returned.

Key quote

In Poland, where I am only occasionally, I feel a bit unknown and unnoticed, while in Europe and Iran I can fulfil myself freely.[263]

Activities before emigration

For Kosecka, Poland is primarily a country where she received her composing education (with Krzysztof Meyer at the Academy of Music in Kraków) and took conducting classes (with Rafał Delekta at the same school and with Szymon Bywalec at the Academy of Music in Katowice). Her first performances and competition successes took place in Poland. These included her electronic composition *Theme: Music of Pressures* [*Temat: muzyka ciśnień*], presented during the 2009 Warsaw Autumn Festival. In 2013 she was a finalist at the Tadeusz Baird Composers' Competition. She was also a laureate of the fourth Zygmunt Mycielski Composers' Competition.

After emigration

After moving to Tehran, Kosecka began teaching and performing. She also organized local musical events. Together with Idin Sami Mofakham, she founded the Spectro Center for New Music and contributed to the creation of the International Festival of Contemporary Music in Tehran.

Differences between the old and new realities

Iran offers great opportunities to promote Western music precisely because its own traditions of musical education and performance as well as its contemporary music are so different from what is found in the West. Undoubtedly, this has given direction to her activities; she admits that in Poland, she would have had to consider different tactics for professional development.

Reason for leaving Poland

Better professional and financial opportunities, in addition to personal reasons.

Contact with Poland after emigration

Very good, due to electronic media and frequent travel.

Influence of the new home on the composer's music

Her new reality has allowed her to expand her musical language with Iranian scales, although they are used in a rather subtle way in her compositions. Microtonality and spectral music are among her primary musical interests.

Awareness of the composer's music in both countries

Kosecka admits that she feels rather unnoticed in Poland. In 2018, her music was included in the program of the International Kraków Composers Festival (*Passagio I* from 2014 and *Akmē* from 2015) and the Poznań Musical Spring (*Passagio I*). In 2017, important accents were the performance of *Orsi*, awarded at the Krzysztof Penderecki Composers Competition, and the premiere of *Mythos* at the laureates' concert of the Zygmunt Mycielski Composers Competition. In the area of foreign performances (in the Czech Republic, Austria, Croatia, Switzerland, Norway, Russia, Armenia, the United States, Sweden, and Finland), Kosecka's work is heard thanks to its inclusion in the repertoire of performers she has befriended (e.g., soprano Blanka Dembosz and double bass player Mateusz Loska).

Due to Kosecka's activity in Iranian music circles promoting educational and contemporary music, her works are performed there more regularly, for example, at the Tehran International Contemporary Music Festival (TCMF), as well as during a series of electronic music concerts co-created with Idin Sami Mofakham (SpectroDuo). In 2017, the independent music label Tehran Records released an album containing the composer's chamber music.

Composer's personality

Kosecka is an ambitious and exacting artist and her compositions are equally demanding for performers and listeners alike. She is tireless and meticulous in her work. This translates into her music, which is full of complicated rhythms and rich, often extreme sound effects. She is open to novelties—she draws on the richness of the cultures she has become acquainted with while travelling, and translates literary and poetic worlds, both real and distant (including fantasy ones), into sounds.

Remarkable anecdote or biographical fact

One of the first works of the young composer was *Dumka* (2006) for piano, which features traditional tonality and romantic, cinematic aesthetics. This graceful piece has enjoyed great interest for a long time, even though it emerged before she began formally studying composition. She has kept it in her official catalog of works, and it remains a YouTube favorite.

Respondent's Top Choices

- **Favorite work:** *Ápeiros* (2013), due to its study of sound.
- **Best work:** *Klothó* (2017), an opera that synthesizes the composer's pursuits so far.
- **Composition still waiting to be discovered:** *Apeiros* (2013), which has already been premiered but deserves more frequent performance.

Respondent: Emilia Stefańska

Hanna Kulenty

Date and place of birth:
18 March 1961, Białystok.

Date and place of emigration:
1992, the Netherlands (Arnhem).

Return to Poland:
Yes, but not permanently. She lives in Poland and the Netherlands.

Key quote

I feel a need to write music in which the things between the notes matter, in which metaphysics matter. My antenna is tuned to such signals.[264]

Activities before emigration

In Hanna Kulenty's biography there are turning points that divide her work into distinct periods: pre- and post-emigration. These landmarks took place in 1986, when Kulenty began her postgraduate studies in composition under Louis Andriessen at the Royal Conservatory of Music in The Hague (1986–1988), and in 1992, when she settled permanently in the Netherlands, in Arnhem. She has always been engaged in multidisciplinary creative activities, including lyric writing and especially drawing (she even planned to study at the Academy of Fine Arts). During her studies with Kotoński (1980–1986), creating her own musical graphics became her preferred form of conveying ideas. Kulenty's compositional output from before 1986 consists mainly of instrumental compositions, for which she received several prizes at international competitions (e.g., second prize at the 1985 European Young Composers' Competition in the Netherlands for her *Ad Unum* for orchestra). At the same time, she wrote her chamber opera *A Parable About Grain* [*Przypowieść o ziarnie*] (1985) and other compositions, including *A Request for Sun* [*Prośba o Słońce*] for tape (1984) and *Souvenir from a Sanatorium* for computer (1988).

After emigration

Since her departure from Poland, the composer still focuses on creating works for various instrumental combinations. She has created orchestral compositions, including solo concerti (*Viola Viva* for viola and chamber orchestra, 2013; *Trumpet Concerto No. 3*, 2014;

GG Concerto for harpsichord and string orchestra, 2009). Although after 1992 she did not write exclusively electroacoustic works, she has used electronic or electroacoustic means in her instrumental works, e.g., a cello sound system and delay effect in *Sinequam Forte A* (1994) and *Sinequam Forte B* (1994) and tape music in the stage piece *Islands* (2006). Her stage work, including two operas, *The Mother of Black Dreams* [*Matka czarnoskrzydłych snów*] (1995) and *Hoffmaniana* (2003), is one of the interesting areas of Kulenty's mature oeuvre, in which she successfully combines electronic, instrumental, and vocal sounds. As a result of her interest in vocal experiments, she has written several pieces, primarily in the late 1990s and early 2000s, including *Decimo* for choir and six voices (2000).

Differences between the old and new realities

It seems that Kulenty's work had initially been met with more enthusiasm abroad than in Poland, as evidenced by her numerous international successes. Her early compositions, written while still in her native country, may evoke associations with the work of Iannis Xenakis or György Ligeti (the composer herself admits to being inspired by their work) due to their characteristic structural complexity and multi-layered texture. Compared to the aggressive sound of works from the 1980s, such as *Symphony No. 1* (1986) and *Perpetuus* for chamber ensemble (1989), Kulenty's post-emigration oeuvre appears milder in tone. The strong dramatic overtone typical of the early period became intertwined with an introverted mode of expression, as in the lullaby *A Cradle Song* for violin, cello, and piano (1993), which was influenced by the tragedy of her daughter's death. In her later orchestral compositions and in *Violin Concerto No. 2,* we see a more lyrical type of expression, a sublime sound, and a certain seriousness resonant of new romanticism. More recently, Kulenty has approached postmodern aesthetics with her eagerness to use elements of pastiche and manipulate musical conventions and genres, as exemplified by the jazzy *Drive Blues* for piano (2000).

Reason for leaving Poland

As she admitted in an interview, Kulenty left for Holland for personal reasons. Professional considerations also played a part. While working as an independent composer, she had received many commissions for new works from Dutch institutions and ensembles. For example, the aforementioned piece *A Cradle Song* was commissioned by the Arnhem Conservatory of Music, the piece *Air* for instrumental ensemble (1991) by Orkest de Volharding, and the piece *Stretto* for flute, clarinet and guitar (1998) by De Ereprijs.

Contact with Poland after emigration

Kulenty's emigration is somewhat unusual, as she has never left Poland permanently. Since 1992, she has lived in Arnhem in the Netherlands as well as in Warsaw. She also has dual citizenship. The composer is often present for the premieres of her compositions in Poland, such as *Siesta* (2016) at the Warsaw Autumn Festival in 2016. Moreover, Kulenty has been teaching composition at the Feliks Nowowiejski Academy of Music in Bydgoszcz for several years.

Influence of the new home on the composer's music

It is difficult to point to a specific moment of radical change in style or aesthetics that could be associated with the influences of Dutch reality and culture, for at least two reasons. First, Kulenty's relationship with the Netherlands began very early on, before she moved there, and second, a significant part of her output has been created abroad. The most noticeable turn in Kulenty's work that could be related to the possible influence of Dutch music, if Andriessen's minimalism may be described this way, took place during her studies with this composer.

However, Kulenty's further transformation of her own musical language and the development of original compositional techniques (e.g., a "polyphony of arches" or a "polyphony of time dimensions") were influenced by a variety of inspirations, not exclusively Dutch, such as the philosophical ideas of the Far East. Her stay in the Netherlands has facilitated access to a variety of diverse musical influences from the entire world, which resulted, for example, in *Lysanxia* for gamelan and tape (1994).

Awareness of the composer's music in both countries

Kulenty's works can be heard nearly every year during Polish music festivals (e.g., Warsaw Autumn). They are also performed in the Netherlands (e.g., a new staging of the opera *Mother of Black Wings Dreams*, directed by Javier López Piñón in Zwitsal Fabriek in Apeldoorn in 2016). A comparable number of first performances have taken place in Poland (nearly forty as of 2017), as well as in the Netherlands (over thirty performances as of 2017). It is worth mentioning that her music has also been used in several films by Polish artists, including Łukasz Barczyk's films *The Motionless Mover* [*Nieruchomy poruszyciel*] and *The Spaniard* [*Hiszpanka*].

Composer's personality

Kulenty's identity is formed largely a result of a combination of her numerous talents in the areas of music, literature, and art. This is also reflected in her rich compositional output, in which she willingly draws on extramusical inspirations, as exemplified in the titles of her compositions. They demonstrate her interests in such diverse subjects as geometry and numbers (*Trigon* for chamber orchestra, 1989), inspired by the shape of a triangle and the number three) or painting (*Still life with a Violin* for solo violin, 1985). In terms of purely musical inspirations, a special place is occupied by dance idioms, including *Mezzo Tango* for wind ensemble (2004) and *Waltz In A* for piano (2009), and jazz (*MM-Blues* for two pianos and two drums, 1999). Kulenty's compositions are characterized by her need for intellectual inquiry and her desire to include emotional elements. The first of these features is revealed as a strictness of compositional thinking, mainly influencing the construction of each piece. The latter can be sensed in the area of sonic expression, which is full of a sensory impulsiveness that evokes an impression of spontaneity. Other recurrent themes are a respect for tradition and a need to reflect on aesthetic and philosophical problems, in particular the issue of time, as she has mentioned in numerous interviews, comments on compositions, and lectures, and to which she devoted much attention in the paper she wrote for her habilitation degree.

Remarkable anecdote or biographical fact

Relatively recently, Kulenty has become known as a literary writer. On 21 September 2017, Moonrise Press published her novel *Inverted House*, written in English, which combines surrealistic, poetic, and autobiographical themes.

Respondent's Top Choices

- **Favorite work:** *Trumpet Concerto No. 1* (2002). I value this work for its expressive qualities, which evoke a sense of constantly accumulating tension through the use of a broad palette of accelerations and decelerations. This composition does not tire listeners with an intensity of expression, but draws them into its sound, thanks to the use of a quarter-tone trumpet and the repetition of a single sound in the low register of the piano part, which is reminiscent of a distant bell.
- **Best work:** *The Mother of Black Dreams* (1995).
- **Composition still waiting to be discovered:** *Trumpet Concerto No. 3* (2014).

Respondent: Weronika Nowak

Andrzej Kwieciński

Date and place of birth:
11 June 1984, Warsaw.

Date and place of emigration:
2005, the Netherlands (The Hague).

Return to Poland:
He has not returned.

Key quote

Intuition is very important to me, but I want to control everything.[265]

Activities before emigration

Andrzej Kwieciński left Poland after graduating from secondary music school. Prior to that, he was involved primarily with education. He graduated from the Józef Elsner State Music School in Warsaw, studying singing (countertenor) with Robert Lavaty, composition with Sławomir Czarnecki, and electroacoustic music with Jan Oleszkowicz. He also participated in private composition classes with Paweł Mykietyn and Hanna Kulenty. Kwieciński began his studies in musicology at the University of Warsaw, which he abandoned after a year.

As a teenager, he took part in the Students' Music Forum. His first compositions, which were performed there, do not appear in his official catalog. His first official piece was *Umbrae* (2004), a piece influenced by his interest in spectralism, a genre that incorporates acoustic spectra in musical compositions. The basis of *Umbrae* is the spectrum of the note E, but the piece is distinguished mostly by its expressive pulsation and techniques taken from minimalism, which were similar to the work of Kwieciński's teacher at the time, Hanna Kulenty. Kwieciński admits to being inspired by the music of Mykietyn, Morton Feldman, and Tomasz Sikorski. *Opus One* [*Opus pierwsze*] turned out to be mature enough to withstand the test of time; it opens Kwieciński's monographic album recorded by the Royal String Quartet and Tomasz Januchta (Bôłt Records, 2016).

Kwieciński's early compositions were appreciated by performers and critics. The Nonstrom ensemble commissioned a piece from him, and in an issue of *Glissando* magazine (No. 3, 2005), the 21-year-old composer received as much attention as Agata Zubel or Wojciech Ziemowit Zych.

After emigration

Kwieciński began his studies at the Royal Conservatory in The Hague, where he studied with Richard Ayers, Diderik Hakma-Wagenaar, Martijn Padding, Yannis Kyriakides, and Louis Andriessen. After graduation in 2011, he devoted himself primarily to creative work and participation in composition courses.

Differences between the old and new realities

At The Hague Conservatory, unlike in Polish schools and universities, less importance was attached to theoretical or historical preparation and more emphasis was placed on practice. Regular group composition lessons were not held in the company of all students and professors, in a supposedly open atmosphere (but where critical comments could also be made). It was also easier to get in touch with instrumentalists educated in performing contemporary music.

Reason for leaving Poland

It is difficult to say whether Kwieciński's trip to Holland was intended as a permanent emigration or if it was planned as just a short stage in his life. This is how he explains his decision: "Around 2004, I realized that I had to decide where to study. I was working with Hanna Kulenty, who...suggested The Hague." He also mentioned a need for novelty, something he might have not experienced in Poland.

Contact with Poland after emigration

Kwieciński has never lost contact with his home country. He has been a beneficiary of Polish grant programs (e.g., the Witold Lutosławski Society). During the 2011–2012 artistic season, he had an artistic residency at the Łódź Philharmonic, for which he composed *Sinfonia: Luci nella notte IV*. The Ministry of Culture and National Heritage and the Institute of Music and Dance provided funding for four of his works: *Concerto: Re Maggiore*; *Non si può fuggire: Ciaccona; erschallen*; and *Un momento indugiò*. The composer's music can be regularly heard at Polish festivals such as Warsaw Autumn, Musica Polonica Nova, Festival of Premieres [Festiwal Prawykonań], Quartessence [Kwartesencja], as well as at the Polish Radio Music Salon, where a monographic concert occurred in 2016. His pieces have been performed by leading Polish instrumentalists and singers, including Barbara Kinga Majewska, Polish Radio Choir, Lutosławski Quartet, Orchestra of New Music, and Music Cooperative. Reviews, interviews, and articles dedicated to Kwieciński have appeared in *Ruch Muzyczny*, *Dwutygodnik*, *Glissando*, *MEAKULTURA.pl*, and on the Polish Radio 2 website. His *Canzon de'baci*, submitted as a Polish piece to the International Composers' Tribune, brought him victory in the category of young composers, with a recommendation in the main category and a special award from the International Music Council and Radio France. In May 2018 Kwieciński also became one of the Composers of the Month in a program organized by Polish Music Publishers.

In the Netherlands his work is performed, published, and awarded as well. Most of Kwieciński's compositions have been published by Donemus Publishers. He has won numerous awards and scholarships in Dutch competitions (including the Young Masters XXI, Gaudeamus, Dutch Masters of Culture, and a Schuurman Schimmel-van Outeren Stichting scholarship). His works have been performed, among others, at the Young Composers Meeting in Apeldoorn and the Kamermuziek Festival den Haag.

Influence of the new home on the composer's music

What has influenced Kwieciński the most is not The Hague as a city itself, but rather its music academy, the possibility of contacts with a new community, and a different style of work. He owes a lot of his development to studies with Rozalie Hirs and to the Nieuw Ensemble, in which he participated the first year of his studies.

Awareness of the composer's music in both countries

The most suitable term to describe Kwieciński's activity would be "international." The majority of his new works have had their premieres in Poland and are later published with Donemus in the Netherlands. Still, we have to note that he has had performances in Hamburg, Lisbon, and Copenhagen and has received commissions from the Ernst von Siemens Stiftung Deutschlandfunk, UNESCO International Music Council, and Radio France. He has also worked with Ensemble Resonanz from Germany, the Swiss ensemble proton, and the Portuguese Gulbenkian Orchestra. He received positive reviews of *Umbrae* in the Luxembourg publication *Pizzicato*.

Composer's personality

Andrzej Kwieciński is an open, witty, and sociable person. Friendly to his audience, he is always eager to respond to students' or researchers' questions about his works, although as a teacher he never interferes with anyone's writing, leaving them space for freedom of interpretation. He admits to having dyslexia and a mild obsessive-compulsive disorder; he enjoys order and repetition. His work is based on discipline and daily routine. The compositional process for him begins with searching for an idea, sketching forms, developing concepts for "deep layers," which often consist of one or more works of early music, and eventually building the final sound. He is often critical towards his own work, which manifests itself in writing new versions and removing many compositions from his catalog.

The composer is inspired equally by literature (William Faulkner and his multilateral narratives), painting (Jackson Pollock), Renaissance music (Gesualdo, Monteverdi, Vecchi), Baroque music (Cavalli, Rossi, Händel, Vivaldi, Buxtehude), and contemporary music (spectralists, Salvatore Sciarrino).

Remarkable anecdote or biographical fact

He originally considered studying in Italy, allegedly due to the sun and good food there, but considered The Hague (even before Hanna Kulenty's suggestion) when he heard that the Netherlands is the only country whose citizens would like to own a work of abstract art, an idea often rejected by people from other countries.

Respondent's Top Choices

- **Favorite work:** *Sinfonia: Luci nella notte IV* (2012).
- **Best work:** Probably not written yet (hopefully so!), but *Canzon de'baci* (2013), a manifesto of a stylistic breakthrough which was appreciated at the International Composers' Tribune.
- **Composition still waiting to be discovered:** Something not yet written.

Respondent: Dominika Micał

Szymon (Simon) Laks

Date and place of birth:
1 November 1901, Warsaw.

Date and place of death:
11 December 1983, Paris.

Date and place of emigration:
1926, 1945, France (Paris).
Deported from Paris to Auschwitz in 1941.

Return to Poland:
No.

Key quote

I am an exception among Polish composers, because I spent nearly three years in Auschwitz, and the things I saw and experienced there must have left a mark on my life, not only in psychological terms, but also on my art.[266]

Activities before emigration

The composer was born in 1901 to a Jewish family in Warsaw. Initially, he studied mathematics in Vilnius, but he returned to his home town in order to study composition and conducting at Warsaw Conservatory. Laks's compositional debut took place in 1924 at the Warsaw Philharmonic with the performance of his symphonic poem *Farys*.

After emigration

Laks left for Paris twice, first in 1926 in order to continue his education and again in 1945 after the American liberation of the Dachau concentration camp (prior to that he had been at the Auschwitz camp). Before World War II, together with other Polish composers fascinated with Szymanowski, he was active in the Association of Young Polish Musicians in Paris. In the 1930s, he wrote music (under a pseudonym) to Aleksander Ford's films: *Sabra* (1933) and *The Awakening* [*Przebudzenie*] (1934). He spent the early days of World War II in Paris, where he was arrested in 1941 for being a "foreign Jew." After his return to Paris in 1945, he focused on chamber music (*String Quartet No. 2*, *Eight Jewish Folk Songs* [*Osiem ludowych pieśni żydowskich*], and *Three Warsaw Polonaises* [*Trzy polonezy warszawskie*]). In 1947, he wrote a memoir about the concentration camp titled *Musiques d'un autre monde*. Later, he composed *Poem* for violin and orchestra (1954), *Symphony* for string orchestra (1964), and an opera buffa, *L'Hirondelle inattendue* (1965). In the 1970s he dedicated himself to translation (e.g., concentration camp memoirs by Krystyna Żywulska) and to political and social writing. He remained in Paris until his death at the age of 82.

Differences between the old and new realities

Laks left for Paris at a very young age. His individual musical style got a chance to crystallize under the clear influence of jazz, blues, and neoclassicism. He did not understand the Parisian fascination with Russian culture and the corresponding lack of Polish cultural influence, especially when compared to the nineteenth century and the Great Emigration. His interwar oeuvre is diverse, but adheres to neoclassicism; he wrote chamber compositions, songs, and film music. After World War II, Laks became interested in Jewish culture, writing music to lyrics by Polish-Jewish poets (Julian Tuwim and Antoni Słonimski). He also became intrigued by Polish and Jewish folklore. Paris became his new home and offered him a chance to meet his brothers, far from traumatic memories.

Reason for leaving Poland

In 1926, Laks fulfilled his goal of studying at the State Conservatory in Paris with Paul Vidal and Henri Rabaud. After the war, he did not want to remain in Poland due to his disappointment in the political situation, so he returned to Paris.

Contact with Poland after emigration

Laks was interested in politics, including the increase of Polish-Jewish tensions before the war. His activity in the Association of Young Polish Musicians in Paris and meetings with Szymanowski provided him with information about current Polish culture. After World War II, he stayed informed about political, social, and cultural events, as proven by his writings, which were in the form of prose, memoirs, and diaries. In 1949, he received an award for his *Ballad* for piano in a contest organized by the Polish Composers' Union.

After 1967 and Israel's attack on Egypt, Laks gave up composing. His disappointment in politics led him pursue a career as a critic of daily life and culture. His writings published in the 1970s and 1980s reveal his erudition and sense of observation. He provided analyses of Polish-Jewish relations and became interested in the situation of Poles under Soviet influence. In the Polish diaspora, he became recognized thanks to his *Auschwitz Games* [*Gry oświęcimskie*] (London, 1979), published in Poland by the State Museum of Auschwitz-Birkenau in 1998.

Influence of the new home on the composer's music

In his compositions, Laks combined various genres—those popular in Paris and those typical for the Polish community in that city, which meant they were mostly neoclassical. The 1930s marked the most dynamic period in his career, when he wrote chamber works, songs, and film music. After World War II, Laks was strongly influenced by his wartime experiences and its resulting trauma. Jewish themes began to emerge in his works, such as *Elegy for Jewish Towns* [*Elegia żydowskich miasteczek*] (1961) and *Five Songs to Julian Tuwim's Poems* [*Pięć pieśni do wierszy Juliana Tuwima*] (1965). He stopped composing in 1967, explaining that "writing music stopped making sense."

Awareness of the composer's music in both countries

Laks remains most famous thanks to his book titled *Auschwitz Games* [*Gry oświęcimskie*][267] (an earlier version had the French title *Musiques d'un autre monde*), whose first edition in 1948 was translated to more than a dozen languages.[268] Thanks to this, Laks is part of the Holocaust literary discourse. Several of his chamber works, such as *Suite Concertante* [*Suita concertante*] for trombone and piano or *Five Songs to Julian Tuwim's Poems* were published by Polish Music Publishers. Laks's oeuvre has been popularized by Boosey & Hawkes publishers. His most famous works include his string quartets, recorded by the Szymanowski Quartet and the Messages Quartet, and his Holocaust-themed pieces, which are mostly songs. In France, his opera *L'Hirondelle inattendue* has recently gained popularity.

Composer's personality

Laks lived for music. He had worked as a violinist, performing on a cruise ship around the world and doing live performances at silent film screenings and in cafés; he also gave music lessons. He was interested in politics and engaged in social life. After the war, he tried to rebuild his career. In his writings, he reveals himself as a sarcastic but constructive critic, not avoiding irony and humor. He corresponded with many friends, proof of which are numerous quotes from letters inserted into his published writings.

Remarkable anecdote or biographical fact

The turning point in Szymon Laks's biography was his imprisonment in the Auschwitz-Birkenau concentration camp. Given number 49543, he led the camp music band. The emotions that arose while playing Christmas carols and Polish music left a mark on his life. He later recalled:

> On Christmas Eve of 1943, I took a small group of Dutchmen to the women's hospital, where…we were supposed to play a few carols to console the sick.…We started with the traditional German carol *Silent Night, Holy Night* (among the sick there were a few German women, the rest were almost all Polish), which the audience listened to attentively. In our repertoire we still had *Sleep, Little Jesus* [*Lulajże Jezuniu*], *He Lies in the Cradle* [*W żłobie leży*], *They Came Running to Bethlehem* [*Przybieżeli do Betlejem*], and *God is Born* [*Bóg się rodzi*]. We began with the first. After a few bars, quiet weeping began to be heard from all sides, which became louder and louder as we played and finally burst out in general, uncontrolled sobbing that completely drowned out the celestial chords of the carol.…From all sides spasmodic cries, ever more numerous, ever shriller—in Polish, which I alone understood—began to roll in on me: 'Enough of this! Stop! Begone! Clear out! Let us croak in peace!'…I did not know that a carol could give so much pain.[269]

The composer's son remembered:

> Both of his brothers, who had arrived in France almost at the same time, avoided deportation, because early on they went south towards Nice. Father's sister stayed in Poland and, together with her son David, was killed in a Ger-

man concentration camp. Father was saved from death thanks to his musical knowledge: he was a violinist, later a conductor of the Auschwitz-Birkenau orchestra.[270]

Respondent's Top Choices

- **Favorite work:** *String Quartet No. 3* (1945), based on Polish folk motives, is a special piece, because it is the first work written by Laks after liberation. The composition can be read in parallel with *Auschwitz Games*, which provides a polyphonic, multithreaded testimony of a survivor. Additionally, he recalled a number of folk melodies that bring out various emotions in listeners and which evoke the power and meaning of this work.
- **Best work:** Laks considered his book *Auschwitz Games* [*Gry oświęcimskie*] (1979) to be his magnum opus. He believed that his attempt to describe his experiences was something more than building a memory or a recollection of music during the war. He said: "For this is not a book about *music*. It is a book about *music in a Nazi concentration camp*."[271]
- **Composition still waiting to be discovered:** It is worth recalling Laks's chamber works to the words by Tuwim, Jastrun, and Słonimski, as well as his piano compositions. His opera *L'Hirondelle inattendue* (1966) also waits discovery by Polish audiences.

Respondent: Piotr Krajewski

Wanda Landowska

Date and place of birth:
5 July 1879, Warsaw.

Date and place of death:
16 August 1959, Lakeville, New York.

Date and place of emigration:
1896, Germany (Berlin); 1900, France (Paris); 1913, Germany (Berlin); 1919, France (Paris); 1941, United States (New York, Lakeville).

Return to Poland:
She did not return.

Key quote
The harpsichord muse.[272]

Activities before emigration
Before Landowska left Warsaw, she began playing concerts and composed her first works.

After emigration
Landowska's oeuvre mainly consists of miniatures, but she also wrote compositions for larger ensembles and cadenzas to concertos by Mozart and Haydn. Among her first compositions published in France are the piano works *En route*, *Lied*, and *Danse polonaise* as well as *Automne* for violin and piano. Landowska's first works were mainly stylized dances; later larger pieces appeared, such as *Hebrew Poem* [*Poemat hebrajski*] for orchestra and *Serenade* for string instruments. On recordings, we can find, among others, *Le Houblon* and *Bourée d'Auvergne*.

Landowska led an active concert life and was also involved in education and research. She became famous for reviving the harpsichord as a solo instrument. Comparable to the work of Nadia Boulanger with composition students, she educated an entire generation of young harpsichordists, such as Ralph Kirkpatrick, Rafael Puyana, Aimée Van de Wiele, Isabelle Nef, Max Drischner, Erwin Jacobi, José Iturbi, Clifford Curzon, Janina Wysocka-Ochlewska, Emma Altberg, Kazimierz Flatau, and Alexis Weissenberg.

Differences between the old and new realities
Moving to the West offered better work opportunities as well as a chance to join the international musical network.

Reason for leaving Poland

She wanted to study composition with Heinrich Urban.

Contact with Poland after emigration

Landowska considered herself to be Polish. She spoke Polish, and she performed and recorded Polish music, including works by Michał Kleofas Ogiński, Adam Jarzębski, Marcin Mielczewski, Mikołaj Zieleński, Bartłomiej Pękiel, and Stanisław Sylwester Szarzyński. She also performed before Polish audiences. In 1910, she appeared at the Chopin Festival in Lviv, playing works by Polish harpsichord composers. On 6 March 1914, she performed again in Lviv, and on 3 November 1918 in Kraków. During her last visit to Poland in 1936, she played with a Warsaw orchestra and performed a recital in Lviv.

Influence of the new home on the composer's music

Expanded opportunities allowed Landowska to intensify her artistic activity. The early music revival movement was alive in Paris thanks to Schola Cantorum and promoters such as Ignaz Moscheles, François-Joseph Fétis, Amédée Méreaux, and Louise Farrenc, as well as Camille Saint-Saëns, who was still active in the early twentieth century. Other supporters of early music at that time included Paul Taffanel, Louis Diémer, and Henri Casadesus.

Landowska maintained correspondence with Francis Poulenc for more than half a century and with Alfred Cortot, with whom she began her activities at an educational-performance center in Saint-Leu-la-Fôret.

Awareness of the composer's music in both countries

Landowska's compositions never became popular in Poland or elsewhere.

Composer's personality

She was charismatic, charming, and lively—this was the image of Landowska that remained in the memory of people who had met her.

Remarkable anecdote or biographical fact

Wanda Landowska revived J. S. Bach's *Goldberg Variations* as a concert piece. She recorded the piece in 1933.

Respondent's Top Choices

- **Favorite work:** *Le Houblon* (1951).
- **Best work:** This still waits for the proper time; Landowska's oeuvre as a composer still has not been properly recognized.
- **Composition still waiting to be discovered:** *En route* (1901?).

Respondent: Dorota Relidzyńska

Roman Maciejewski

Date and place of birth:
28 February 1910, Berlin.

Date and place of death:
30 April 1998, Göteborg.

Date and place of emigration:
1934, France (Paris); 1938, Great Britain (London); 1939, Sweden (Göteborg); 1951, United States (Los Angeles); 1976, Canary Islands (La Graciosa); 1977, Sweden (Göteborg).

Return to Poland:
He did not return.

Key quote

I'm far from possessing the professional fervor typical of artists. Recently, it has been typical to come across a type of artist who does not know how to move, how to eat, or how to rest, and cares only about racing against time.... Being a composer, I try not to forget about what is most important—existence itself.[273]

Activities before emigration

He was the hope of young Polish music before World War II, an outstanding composition student who amazed the press and even Karol Szymanowski. As a pianist, his skills helped him earn money in dance schools; he even conducted a choir.

After emigration

Initially, when he travelled to Paris thanks to a scholarship, he was heavily involved in classical music. Later, in Sweden and in the United States, he created a lot of music for practical use. He wrote music for theater, e.g., for Ingmar Bergman, conducted choirs, and performed as a pianist, mainly in piano duos. He dedicated about fifteen years of his life to his magnum opus, his *Requiem*. Apart from this he also composed mazurkas.

Differences between the old and new realities

Maciejewski's world after emigration changed significantly, in part because he ceased to be artistically active and instead had to focus on purely commercial work. He changed also as a person, due to a gastric disease that threatened his life. After his recovery, he turned from being a sociable person, open to professional development, into an outsider who applied a different approach to his work. He began to believe in a return to nature, vegetarianism, yoga (not a typical choice for the 1940s), meditation, and Eastern philosophy.

Reason for leaving Poland

He received a state scholarship to go to Paris. With his Swedish wife, he travelled from Great Britain to Göteborg in order to meet his in-laws. There, the outbreak of World War II prevented him from returning to Poland. At the invitation of Artur Rubinstein, he went to live in the United States. Later, he lived in the Canary Islands, in a tent on the desert island of La Graciosa. Eventually, he found himself back in Sweden, mostly by chance, but this also gave him an opportunity to receive a pension.

Contact with Poland after emigration

Maciejewski followed life in Poland and remained in touch with his family, but visited only sporadically. An intensive social life was not in his nature. He missed his country and loved ones, as demonstrated in his letters. Throughout almost his entire life he wrote mazurkas for piano; these remain, aside from the monumental *Requiem*, his most important artistic statement and a sort of creative diary.

Influence of the new home on the composer's music

New places of residence did not expand his creative horizons significantly. His musical language remained consistent and unchanged. As he declared, "My artistic statement has to be honest and authentic. I cannot follow fashion, it is alien to me."[274]

Awareness of the composer's music in both countries

In Poland, Maciejewski has been discussed more frequently recently as his works slowly enter the concert circuit, but even his greatest achievement, the *Requiem*, still requires considerable publicity efforts. It seems that the *Requiem*'s length and ensemble size hinder performances due to the amount of funding and organization necessary to arrange them. His piano works have a better chance of being performed. Abroad, Maciejewski's music remains unknown and is performed only occasionally.

Composer's personality

It is difficult to tell what is most interesting about Maciejewski's life—his music or his personality. The aforementioned personal transformation made the composer perceive himself differently as an artist; composing remained important, but it was not more important than existence itself. Also, his approach to career, money, and time changed. This resulted in a distinctive lifestyle and the desire to write only for himself, but it also encouraged a *joie de vivre* and close contacts with nature. He admitted:

> There were periods in my life when I fell silent, because in order to express myself and my inner truth, I need to first learn about it, and the best way to know this leads, I believe, through silence and listening carefully to myself. Cutting myself off from the intensity of life helps as well. This is when one enters a sort of timelessness, which facilitates the discovery of the right approach to the time in which one lives.[275]

Remarkable anecdote or biographical fact

Maciejewski decided to leave after a long stay in the United States, which ended with a successful *Requiem* performance. He gave away his belongings and lived for several weeks in a tent in the Canary Islands, on the deserted island of La Graciosa. At some point, he decided to visit Sweden in order to apply for a pension. While walking around the familiar streets of Göteborg, he walked into a music shop and began to spontaneously play a piano. He loved its sound so much that he bought the instrument, only to realize afterwards that he did not know what to do with it. In order to solve the problem, he decided to look for an apartment, which influenced his decision to stay in Sweden.

This anecdote is typical for the composer. He did not make plans; he was not a strategist in life. His philosophy of life, his life story, and his personality were, aside from his art, the main reasons why I decided to write a book about him.[276]

Respondent's Top Choices

- **Favorite work:** *Concerto* for two pianos without orchestra (1936).
- **Best work:** *Requiem: Missa pro defunctis* (1944–1959).
- **Composition still waiting to be discovered:** *Mazurkas* for piano (1928–1990), which remain unknown, even though they should be universally recognized.

Respondent: Marlena Wieczorek

Miłosz Magin

Date and place of birth:
6 July 1929, Łódź.

Date and place of death:
4 March 1999, Bora Bora.

Date and place of emigration:
1957, Portugal (Sintra, Lisbon); 1960, France (Paris).

Return to Poland:
He did not return.

Key quote
I am often in Poland in my thoughts, I am one of those composers who draws inspiration from folk music.[277]

Activities before emigration
In the 1950s Miłosz Magin was primarily a pianist. In 1955 he earned an award at the International Chopin Piano Competition in Warsaw (Chopin's works were a regular feature of his repertoire, and he became a valued interpreter of them) and in 1957 he was a laureate of international competitions in Paris and Lisbon. He graduated with honors from the State Higher School of Music in Warsaw and began touring Europe. Together with his wife, Idalia, he founded the Polish Folk Ensemble [Polski Zespół Ludowy]. Magin's compositional output, including his earliest pieces, was dominated by piano works. Initially, the composer used modern solutions (e.g., dodecaphony), but he quickly turned towards classical and romantic traditions.

After emigration
Magin moved to Paris in the early 1960s, working at the Conservatoire Russe de Paris Serge Rachmaninoff and the Conservatoire International de Musique. At that time, he gave concerts on many continents, but did not compose much. These proportions were reversed after 1963, due to a hand injury the artist suffered in a car accident. From that moment on, he devoted himself largely to composition. He usually chose classical forms. In addition to piano works, he also liked to write for string orchestra and percussion. After his recovery, Magin returned to the piano, still intensively performing and recording, among other things, all of Chopin's works for the Decca label. In 1985, together with his

wife, he founded the International Piano Competition in his name, which is still held in Paris today and which promotes Polish music; according to Magin's concept, the competition jury is to put musicality before technical aspects of performance.

Differences between the old and new realities

As Magin expected, the West offered a richer cultural life and greater freedom than was possible in Poland. However, it also posed challenges to his marriage (his wife stressed the difficulties of adapting to her new environment).[278] Gradually, with the growing importance of the piano competition he initiated, Miłosz Magin became a valued figure in the Parisian cultural world.

Reason for leaving Poland

Among the reasons for Magin's emigration, the political situation in Poland at the time seems to be most important. For a performing pianist, the impossibility of travelling freely was burdensome. The composer's wife described the artistic situation there as "closed horizons."[279] In the late 1950s, the couple managed to obtain permission to leave Poland, which rarely happened. Initially they decided to stay in Portugal, but it did not meet their expectations, so they moved to Paris.

Contact with Poland after emigration

One has to consider the consequences of their decision to emigrate during the Communist era. For nearly fifteen years, for political reasons, Magin stayed away from Poland. His first performances in Warsaw and Żelazowa Wola took place in the 1970s and in subsequent years, the artist returned to Poland frequently; in February 1999, a few weeks before his death, he gave a recital at the Frédéric Chopin Society in Warsaw. In the early 1990s, he gave master classes, among others, at the Academy of Music in Łódź, where he also sat on the jury of the Karol Szymanowski International Competition.

Influence of the new home on the composer's music

National musical elements seem to play a major role in Magin's oeuvre. The use of Polish folklore as a source of inspiration is characteristic of even such seemingly autonomous works as his *Clarinet Concerto* (1990). While abroad, the artist began to compose more, which resulted not from his emigration but from the dramatic accident mentioned above, in which he suffered a serious hand injury.

Awareness of the composer's music in both countries

Magin's name remains more recognized in France than in the artist's homeland, largely due to the competition he founded.

It is important to note that although the composer's works do not belong to the avant-garde movement and do not fit into the style of many contemporary festivals, they are still eagerly received by listeners and performed by pianists, including the composer himself. Recordings of his music have been published by Acte Préalable and Polskie Nagrania.

Composer's personality

Music accompanied the artist from an early age, when he made several attempts at composing. He was strongly self-motivated. A patriotic trait is also clearly visible in his personality. The artist missed Poland, popularized Polish music, and always included works by Polish composers in his recitals. This bright and joyful composer kept track of the young generations of pianists from the other side of the Iron Curtain and helped facilitate their careers in the West. He was a caring and kind teacher who often opened his classes by emphasizing the positive aspects of his students' playing.

Remarkable anecdote or biographical fact

Miłosz Magin, a renowned performer of Chopin's music, missed his homeland just as Chopin had while living in Paris 120 years earlier. Magin's grave at the Père-Lachaise cemetery is located only a few steps away from his master's tomb.

Respondent's Top Choices

- **Favorite work:** *6 Miniatures polonaises* (1982). Even though these were written for children, they contain typical features of Magin's music—folklore, liveliness, and moodiness. These are Polish dances with distinctive titles such as *Nostalgia for the Homeland* [*Nostalgie du pays*].
- **Best work:** Three piano concertos play an important role in Magin's oeuvre, especially the energetic *Piano Concerto No. 2* (1964), which is full of unexpected turns, joy, and originality. Suggestive, colorful themes intersect with contrasting, reflective parts. In this concerto and in *Piano Concerto No. 3* (1970), Magin abandoned the use of the instrumental ensemble typical of that genre.
- **Composition still waiting to be discovered:** The moving *Stabat Mater* (1972) has an unexpected cast of performers, for it is an instrumental piece for string orchestra and timpani. Its simplicity of expression, depth, and mood of religious contemplation bring to mind the Polish music of the early 1970s, for example, some of the works of Henryk Mikołaj Górecki, Krzysztof Penderecki, and others.

Respondent: Kinga Krzymowska-Szacoń

Adam Makowicz (real name: Adam Matyszkowicz)

Date and place of birth:
18 August 1940, Gnojnik (Zaolzie).

Date and place of emigration:
1978, United States (New York); since the early 2000s, Canada (Toronto).

Return to Poland:
He did not return permanently, but since 1989 he has visited Poland regularly.

Key quote

When I arrived in the States, I was an original pianist to Americans, because, like Leszek Możdżer today, I linked classical music to jazz. I played jazz in a classic style, but at the time I lacked a certain feeling, something that comes naturally to Americans through dancing.[280]

Activities before emigration

He moved from his hometown of Rybnik to Katowice and then to Kraków in order to perform jazz on his beloved piano. This kind of music has fascinated him from his early school years. After spending a few months improvising on a decaying piano in the Catacombs student club, Makowicz ended up in Kraków's Helikon jazz club, where he met other Polish jazz musicians, including Wojciech Karolak, Andrzej Kurylewicz, and Tomasz Stańko. In 1960, he formed his first band, the Jazz Darings quartet, and moved to Warsaw, where his collaboration with Kurylewicz, Zbigniew Namysłowski, and the band Novi Singers began. He travelled with these musicians all over the world, from Cuba through India to New Zealand. Although he has always had a quite traditional view of jazz, at the beginning of the 1970s, thanks to his collaboration with Michał Urbaniak and Urszula Dudziak, he switched to playing a Fender electric piano for a while and absorbed the technical innovations of the time, including the application of electronics to jazz.

After emigration

Initially, Makowicz planned to go the United States for only a year. However, after his first album was released overseas, his career began to gain momentum. He gave concerts, recorded a lot, was invited to music festivals, and had the opportunity to perform with the most outstanding jazz musicians active in America at the time, including Sarah Vaughan,

George Shearing, Benny Goodman, and Herbie Hancock. Receiving a permanent resident card from the United States and then American citizenship in 1986 enabled Makowicz to perform in concert halls around the world. At the beginning of the twenty-first century, he moved to Toronto, Canada, where he has led a lively concert career and organizes artistic events with his wife, Joanna Makowicz, a producer at J.A.M. Global Arts Management.

Differences between the old and new realities

In addition to the fact that the years spent in exile in the United States ensured Makowicz's fame and financial stability, they also allowed him to develop his career on his own terms. Even before he left Poland, he knew that playing in bands was not for him; doing so taught him a lot, but did not allow him to pursue his own musical ideas. It was not until he left for the United States that he was able to develop his solo career and play the kind of jazz that was closest to him.

Reason for leaving Poland

In the 1970s, a trip to the United States was probably a dream come true for every young jazz musician who thought about developing his career outside Europe. Thanks to the help of Michał Urbaniak, Jan Byrczek, and John Hammond, Makowicz went to New York, where for a few months he played in the jazz club The Cookery, gave his first concert at Carnegie Hall, and recorded his first solo album, *Adam*, for CBS Columbia. Playing "first piano," according to his own vision of jazz music, was what he had been striving for during his years of working with other jazz bands. He managed to achieve this after his return to the United States in 1978, where he settled after a successful 1977 concert tour. He did not plan to stay permanently, but like many other artists, his return to Poland was prevented by the increasingly difficult political situation and the introduction of martial law in Poland in 1981.

Contact with Poland after emigration

After 1989, the constant fear and ongoing problems with passports and visas that many Polish citizens had experienced finally ended. Governmental policy towards Polish artists living abroad also changed, so that Makowicz was able to come to Poland again annually. Until the mid-1990s he worked with Krzesimir Dębski and orchestras all over the country and organized monographic concerts devoted to the music of Irving Berlin, Cole Porter, George Gershwin, and Jerome Kern, among others. He regularly performs solo recitals, but also willingly works with musicians specializing in classical music, intertwining classical repertoire with jazz improvisations. Since 2017, the composer has been an honorary member of the ZAiKS Authors' Association.

Influence of the new home on the composer's music

Makowicz devoted his early years in the United States to learning what real American swing was. Thanks to playing in clubs and cooperating with the "major league" of American jazz musicians, he understood what he wanted to create and play and how much power a beautifully played, swinging melody could have. He also carried out various projects at the meeting points of cultures and styles, many of which combined classical music and jazz.

Awareness of the composer's music in both countries

Makowicz's music has been known and appreciated in Poland, the United States, and Canada, where he lives now, for a long time, mainly due to his jazz interpretations of classics, especially the works of Chopin. Aside from solo recitals, he has collaborated with soloists and symphonic orchestras, which has helped secure his popularity worldwide.

Composer's personality

As a young man, he did everything possible to develop his talent and achieve his goals. His friends and musicians with whom he has worked consider him to be a positive and energetic man who even today remains a titan of energy.

Remarkable anecdote or biographical fact

After moving to Kraków, Makowicz lived for a while in the basement of a dorm where coal was stored. In the next room, the Catacombs student club was in business. An old, collapsing piano was there. Makowicz intermittently played and slept, and in the evenings he performed with other young musicians who were also fascinated with Western jazz, which was then not widely accessible in Poland.

Respondent's Top Choices

- **Favorite work:** *Winter Flowers* from the eponymous album (1978) and *Drinking Song* from *Unit* (1975).
- **Best work:** Makowicz moved overseas as a renowned pianist, but his real breakthrough was his first album released in the United States, *Adam* (1978). His album with Leszek Możdżer, *Możdżer vs. Makowicz at Carnegie Hall* (2004), was also a great success.
- **Composition still waiting to be discovered:** Several 1970s albums recorded with other Polish musicians, especially *Unit* (1975) with Tomasz Stańko, deserve rediscovery.

Respondent: Iwona Granacka

Krzysztof Meyer

Date and place of birth:
11 August 1943, Kraków.

Date and place of emigration:
1987, Germany (Cologne).

Return to Poland:
He lives in Germany, but maintains his ties with Poland.

Key quote
Using various techniques is for me only a means to compose, and it won't be an exaggeration when I say that I can enter some areas of my inner musical world with any possible technique. Regardless of how I got there, I reach the point I intended in the beginning.[281]

Activities before emigration
Krzysztof Meyer graduated with honors from the State Higher School of Music in Kraków with degrees in composition, following studies with Stanisław Wiechowicz and Krzysztof Penderecki (1965), and music theory (1966). He completed his education with Nadia Boulanger in Paris and also studied privately with Witold Lutosławski. From 1966–1987 he taught theoretical subjects at the Academy of Music in Kraków and from 2008–2013 he taught composition. He was also the assistant dean of the Academy (1972–1975) and head of the music theory department (1975–1987). From 1966–1968 he performed as a pianist with the MW2 ensemble. He took part in and received awards at various composing competitions in Poland and abroad (including the Grand Prix of Prince Pierre of Monaco in 1970). He was active in the Polish Composers' Union as a member of the Executive Board (1971–1985) and as its president (1985–1989). He also participated in the work of the Warsaw Autumn program committee from 1974–1988. In 1973 the first edition of his monograph on Dmitri Shostakovich was printed by Polish Music Publishers.

After emigration
He was employed as a professor of composition at the Hochschule für Musik in Cologne from 1987 to 2008, when he retired. He also taught contemporary music in many centers in Europe and beyond, including Austria, Brazil, France, Germany, Switzerland, Venezu-

ela, and the Soviet Union. He is a member of the Akademie der Künste in Mannheim. In addition, he was a resident composer at the Cologne Philharmonic from 1991–1992 and at the Seattle Festival in 1996. Meyer's music has been performed in many of the most important music venues, including Carnegie Hall in New York, the Berlin Philharmonic, and the Vienna Musikverein.

Differences between the old and new realities

The composer claims that in terms of academics there was no difference between the two countries (apart from the fact that he could finally teach composition in Cologne, which was impossible in Kraków for various reasons). However, in terms of participation in concert life, the differences were significant. In the West, concert life is richer. Meyer has had the opportunity to get to know and collaborate with many outstanding performers and to work in philharmonic halls or with festivals as a composer-in-resident (e.g., Cologne and Seattle). In Poland, such an opportunity arose only five years ago (at the Warsaw Philharmonic). Above all, political conditions changed with his departure. As he has said, "Almost from the very beginning of our residence in Germany, we were able to travel freely anywhere in the world, without fighting for passports, visas, etc. I do not think that with my departure, anything was taken away from me. My world did not change after leaving Poland, it expanded."

Reason for leaving Poland

A proposal to become a composition professor from the Hochschule für Musik in Cologne.

Contact with Poland after emigration

"I never felt my departure to Germany was equivalent to emigration. On the contrary, I continued to try to maintain communication with my home country." These words are taken from Meyer's autobiography, *Masters and Friends* [*Mistrzowie i przyjaciele*]. For the first two years of his stay in Cologne, he was still the president of the Polish Composers' Union (1987–1989). After his retirement, he once again taught composition and theory at the Academy of Music in Kraków; later, between 2009 and 2013, he was a professor of musicology at Adam Mickiewicz University in Poznań. During the 2013–2014 season, he was a resident composer at the National Philharmonic in Warsaw. He works constantly as a lecturer and program consultant with the Princess Daisy Ensemble Chamber Music Festival at Książ Castle. His books have also been published in Poland: an extended edition of Shostakovich's monograph (*Shostakovich* [*Szostakowicz*], Kraków 1986, which has had several foreign translations), and, together with his wife, Danuta Gwizdalanka, a two-volume monograph about Witold Lutosławski (Volume I, *The Road to Perfection* [*Droga do doskonałości*], Volume II, *The Road to Excellence* [*Droga do mistrzostwa*], Kraków 2003, 2004). He also published the aforementioned book, *Masters and Friends* (Kraków, 2011), which contains the composer's memories of his young years in Kraków and beyond.

Influence of the new home on the composer's music

Meyer believes that the influence of his new home was positive, thanks to his close acquaintances, the presence of outstanding composers (György Ligeti, Mauricio Kagel), and contacts with music publishers (Sikorski) and record companies (Naxos). However, as far as the influence on his music itself is concerned, he believes that to some extent there may have been some, because in Germany new music is nurtured differently than in Poland.

When Meyer left Poland, he was already a mature artist who followed his own path; he simply continued doing this. He also has not felt limited by any restrictions regarding instrumentation—he still writes both chamber and symphonic music.

Awareness of the composer's music in both countries

Meyer's works are performed in Poland, Germany, and other countries. Many of them are dedicated to outstanding musicians. He has received more performances abroad due to the incomparably larger music market in Germany, and, for that matter, all of Europe. For example, Meyer has said that fourteen of his compositions were performed in Poland in 2018, and twenty-seven in the West, including eleven in Germany. In general, of the works he wrote after leaving Poland, about 80 percent of them were premiered outside the Poland. Nevertheless, he has stressed that in Poland he knows many great, devoted performers who are invaluable to him. Both Naxos and DUX have released recordings of Meyer's music.

Composer's personality

Meyer has a vast knowledge of music literature, which he openly shares as a teacher and author. He has always been known as an extrovert, as the life of the party. His excellent memory has also led to uncomfortable situations; after his memoirs were published, some members of the Kraków musical community were unhappy with what had been written.

Remarkable anecdote or biographical fact

Meyer himself is an inexhaustible source of anecdotes. He placed many of them in *Masters and Friends*, which did not please everyone. This book is worth reading not only for this reason, but also because it gives a colorful picture of the era and its musical community. As he explained in the book's introduction, "I consider it an extraordinary gift from fate that I have been able to meet so many extraordinary people, who have harmoniously combined outstanding, sometimes even brilliant talents with greatness of character and righteousness of conduct," even as he clarified that not all of them could be mentioned without making the book into a lengthy saga. He maintained cordial relations with Dmitri Shostakovich and Witold Lutosławski. He felt such a bond with the former that, as he repeatedly told us (and repeated in the book), he once heard in a dream one of the themes of the Russian composer's *Fifteenth Symphony*, which was still unwritten.

During his work in Cologne, he developed friendships with György Ligeti and Maurice Kagel. Unfortunately, he has not written anything about his contacts with them so far.

Respondent's Top Choices

- **Favorite work:** An unusual choice: the opera *Cyberiad* (1970). First, because of my admiration for Stanisław Lem's work, and second, because of the sense of humor that the composer revealed in a special way in this opera.
- **Best work:** Meyer's work is diverse and versatile. It is difficult to say what his magnum opus is. It seems, however, that his entire body of chamber music (especially his string

quartets, of which there are currently fifteen), which he considers to be particularly important, could be regarded as such.

- **Composition still waiting to be discovered:** This is also difficult to define, because his work is also rich in terms of quantity. There are many works that have not yet been heard in Poland.

Respondent: Dorota Szwarcman

Eugeniusz Morawski (Eugeniusz Morawski-Dąbrowa)

Date and place of birth:
2 November 1876, Warsaw.

Date and place of death:
23 October 1948, Warsaw.

Date and place of emigration:
1908, France (Paris).

Return to Poland:
He returned to Poland in 1930, after 22 years abroad.

Key quote
There is a kind of greatness reminiscent of the pathos and monumentalism of facades with columns. There are strange, compelling, thin, froglike sounds and strikingly original instrumental combinations, a passionate exploitation of the possibilities of scale and timbre, all of which create a unique sound world with an amazing atmosphere.[282]

Activities before emigration
Before his forced departure from Warsaw, he studied composition with Zbigniew Noskowski, and also painting and sculpture. As a composer, he was not widely known among Polish critics. He and Mikalojus Konstantinas Čiurlionis planned to organize a symphonic concert of their works, which did not occur due to Morawski's arrest.

After emigration
He was active in the diaspora as an accompanist and composer of chamber music and songs. He attempted to conduct his own orchestral pieces, but only succeeded in leading premieres of three symphonic poems.

Differences between the old and new realities
His stay in Warsaw was dedicated to education and pro-independence activism. In France, he studied counterpoint with André Gedalge. He tried, with moderate success, to gain recognition among the Polish diaspora in Paris, mainly as a composer of songs, chamber music, and piano compositions. He also tried to become known among the French with his symphonic music, but had only limited success in that area. He never managed to be

fully appreciated by French critics. His stay in France was mostly an existential struggle. He became an important and influential person in Polish musical life only after his return to his native country.

Reason for leaving Poland

He was arrested and expelled from the Russian Empire in the spring of 1908 for his activity in the armed faction of the Polish Socialist Party—he was planning to assassinate a tsarist policeman.

Contact with Poland after emigration

After leaving Polish lands, he stayed in contact mostly through correspondence. Before Poland regained independence, he remained in forced exile, but later he stayed abroad voluntarily. Only in the early 1930s, thanks to writer Juliusz Kaden Bandrowski and Polish Army Lieutenant Bolesław Wieniawa-Długoszowski, did he receive an opportunity for stable employment in Poland and began considering a return.

Influence of the new home on the composer's music

He modernized his approach to music, abandoning his previous model of late romantic symphonic poems for a style closer to neoclassicism, although he always used large ensembles for his orchestral works.

Awareness of the composer's music in both countries

In France his music remains unknown, but in Poland it has enjoyed a slow rediscovery. In recent years, two monographic albums with his symphonic works and songs have been released, and in 2017 the Grand Theater – National Opera staged his ballet *Świtezianka*.

Composer's personality

He was a difficult personality who had as many enemies (mainly from the circle around Karol Szymanowski) as dedicated friends. In his youth, he was friendly with Mikalojus Konstantinas Čiurlionis; later his cohorts included Stanisław Kazuro, Piotr Rytel, and Juliusz Kaden-Bandrowski. He was known as an incorrigible womanizer. At the same time he did not care about his own composing activities. As the head of the Warsaw Music Conservatory (1932–1939), where he replaced Karol Szymanowski in a scandalous atmosphere that was exaggerated by his enemies, he was the complete opposite of his famous predecessor. Fully devoted to public activity, the school blossomed under his leadership, at the cost of ignoring his own composing. This approach had cruel consequences: about 70 percent of his unpublished scores burned in his apartment on Krakowskie Przedmieście street during the Warsaw Uprising in 1944.

Remarkable anecdote or biographical fact

His arrest on 3 November 1907 for activity in the armed faction of the Polish Socialist Party was an event that influenced his later career and his personal life. Morawski was the only Polish composer who had to deal with such grave consequences from his involvement in the pro-independence movement.

Respondent's Top Choices

- **Favorite work:** *Nevermore* (1911), a symphonic poem based on E. A. Poe's *The Raven.*
- **Best work:** If one can even tell; about 70 percent of his oeuvre burned during the Warsaw Uprising. Perhaps the *Świtezianka* ballet (1930).
- **Composition still waiting to be discovered:** The monumental ballet *Love* [*Miłość*] (1928), which lasts nearly three hours.

Respondent: Marcin Gmys

Piotr Moss

Date and place of birth:
13 May 1949, Bydgoszcz.

Date and place of emigration:
1981, France (Paris).

Return to Poland:
Yes, in August 2017.

Key quote

An outstanding orchestrator, bravely combining the sounds of various instruments, thanks to which his works, especially the orchestral ones, are rich in timbre and tone.[283]

Activities before emigration

Since the beginning of his composing activity, Piotr Moss has won numerous awards, for example, at the Polish Composers' Union's Youth Competition for his *Symphony "Charon"* (1972) and at the C. M. Weber International Composers' Competition in Dresden for *Quartetto per Quattro Violoncelli* (1978). At that time, however, the core of his work consisted predominantly of music for theater, film, and radio. In the 1970s the artist continued to study composition with Krzysztof Penderecki and Nadia Boulanger.

After emigration

The composer moved to France when he was 32. The majority of his works have been created there, including *Stances*, *Fresque*, and *Passions*. Many of them brought the composer prestigious awards and international recognition. Commentators have emphasized the colorfulness and suggestiveness of his mature work, which could have been influenced by his experiences in writing theater music. At the same time, Moss continued to write music for theaters, television, and radio, although this activity was no longer a priority. Shortly after settling in France, thanks to Professor Bronisław Horowicz, he established contact with French Radio; currently, he cooperates with the France Culture and France Musique radio stations. Since 1989, his work with Polish institutions has intensified. In 2012 he received the Grand Prix of the Two Theaters [*Dwa Teatry*] Festival in the category of theatrical plays. In 1993, he began collaborating with writer Jean-Louis Bauer, which has resulted in a number of oratorios, operas, and song cycles.

Differences between the old and new realities

Despite his young age, when Moss left Poland he was already a recognized composer. In Paris, he enjoyed greater artistic freedom and a richer cultural life than existed in Poland in the early 1980s, but he still had to rebuild his career again. Nevertheless, even at the beginning of his stay, he received commissions from French institutions. Critics also emphasize that Moss turned out to be one of the few Polish composers who has gained international recognition while working outside Poland. He has won several dozen prestigious awards, first performances of his works have taken place in renowned concert halls, and he has worked with well-known performers, including Mstislav Rostropovich, Gautier Capuçon, Jean-Claude Casadesus, Laurent Petitgirard, and Véronique Briel. After 1989 differences between the two worlds gradually blurred and the composer began to spend more time in Poland.

Reason for leaving Poland

Piotr Moss mentions political reasons as the primary cause for his emigration. Martial law, declared in 1981, kept him in France, with which he had been associated since the mid-1970s. In 1984 the composer received French citizenship.

Contact with Poland after emigration

It is worth noting that the composer himself, while remaining in close contact with the Polish music community, does not consider himself to be an émigré artist. Although for political reasons, he did not live in Poland for a few years after 1981, he still received commissions from Poland as well as from France and Germany. Since 1989 he has been working almost simultaneously in both countries, traveling between them frequently. Since 1972 he has been a member of the Polish Composers' Union.

Influence of the new home on the composer's music

His decision to stay in France in 1981, even though it was for political reasons, was linked with a kind of "new beginning" for him professionally. The composer, who had tired of his activities in many fields, including film, theater, and arranging, shifted his focus to classical music. His new home was also associated with a slightly different musical style, although it should be noted that the French environment—above all Nadia Boulanger—had already had a major influence on the composer's views and attitude since his earlier stay in Paris.

Awareness of the composer's music in both countries

Moss's compositions, commissioned by renowned ensembles and soloists from all over the world, are valued and frequently performed in France and Poland, where they appear in the programs of such festivals as the Warsaw Autumn, Festival of Premieres [Festiwal Prawykonań], the Contemporary Music Laboratory [Laboratorium Muzyki Współczesnej], the Polish Chamber Music Festival [Festiwal Polskiej Muzyki Kameralnej], and others. His works have been recorded, among others, by the DUX, Polskie Nagrania, and

BMG labels, with ensembles such as the National Polish Radio Symphony Orchestra and l'Orchestre Philharmonique de Radio France. For his work, he was awarded the French title of Officer of the Order of Literature and Art in 2016 (Officier dans l'ordre des Arts et des Lettres; in 2000 he was appointed a knight of this order). He also received a special award from Poland's Minister of Culture and National Heritage in 2009. In both countries, Piotr Moss remains a recognized creator of theater, film, and popular music and he is the author of numerous music programs for Polish and French radio.

Composer's personality

His personality has been greatly influenced by his contact with Nadia Boulanger. Thanks to her, he realized that artists are responsible for their own talents, which are also not their exclusive property. Piotr Moss emphasizes the humanistic aspect of his music, which is accessible, rooted in romanticism and neo-romanticism, and filled with expressive narratives and humor. At the same time, he remains an open-minded artist who eagerly uses modern sonoristic or aleatoric techniques as well as unusual instruments. He is also inspired by painting, including the works of Marc Chagall and Caspar David Friedrich.

The composer admits that he does not feel an inner compulsion to communicate through music. Most of his works are created through commissions that "activate hidden layers," which is why his work is so varied; the composer even compares himself to a chameleon, changing color according to the proposed subject matter. He appears to be an extremely creative and, at the same time, an accessible artist who remains in good relations with the public.

Remarkable anecdote or biographical fact

As a 15-year-old, Moss, who was fascinated with the work of Bacewicz, sent a letter to the artist. He did not know her address, so he wrote only: "Grażyna Bacewicz—composer Warsaw." Surprisingly, the letter was handed over and the recipient received an answer together with a word of encouragement to continue composing. A few years later, the young composition student began his classes at the State Higher School of Music in Warsaw under the direction of Bacewicz, who was also a famous violinist.

Respondent's Top Choices

- **Favorite work:** *Chagall, String Quartet No. 4* (2008) is inspired by the painting of Marc Chagall. In its successive fragments (which do not avoid aspects of a musical collage), this extraordinary artist evocatively and with a touch of humor depicted themes characteristic of his work, such as elements of Jewish culture, love, and circuses.
- **Best work:** In the composer's oeuvre of over three hundred works, many stand out. My choice is therefore subjective—*Cinq tableaux de Caspar David Friedrich* for orchestra (2007). This work, inspired by paintings by the German artist, was influenced by the programmatic symphonies of the nineteenth century. Its individual movements bear suggestive titles (*Fog* [*Mgła*], *Woman at Sunset* [*Kobieta o zachodzie słońca*], etc.), while at the same time they are characterized by colorful instrumentation and an unusually convincing narrative.
- **Composition still waiting to be discovered:** His commissioned works are usually quickly performed. This was true of *Rhapsody* (2003), a commission from the Lorraine

Philharmonic. It contains numerous Polish themes, such as motifs from *Bogurodzica*, polonaise rhythms in the finale, and self-quotations from his own music to Stanisław Wyspiański's play *The Wedding* [*Wesele*]. According to the composer himself, "*Rhapsody* is a kind of symphonic poem about the Polish soul."[284]

Respondent: Kinga Krzymowska-Szacoń

Ignacy Jan Paderewski

Date and place of birth:
18 November 1860, Kuryłówka.

Date and place of death:
29 June 1941, New York.

Date and place of emigration:
1882, Germany (Berlin); 1884, Austria (Vienna); 1885, France (Strasbourg, Paris); 1899, Switzerland (Riond-Bosson); 1913–1921, United States (Paso Robles, California); 1923, Switzerland (Riond-Bosson); 1940, United States (New York, Paso Robles).

Return to Poland:
He did not return permanently.

Key quote

The history of nations is made by titans of human genius. Ignacy Jan Paderewski—one of the best pianists ever, a composer, master teacher, publisher of Chopin's works, public speaker, social activist, and politician—was undoubtedly one of them.[285]

Activities before emigration

After graduating from the Music Institute in Warsaw (later the Warsaw Conservatory) in 1878, Paderewski taught piano there at the secondary school level. To add to his modest salary as a teacher, he played at parties and, with the violinist Władysław Górski, in resorts; he also gave private piano lessons. His time in Poland was devoted primarily to improving his skills on piano and making his first attempts at composing. His pieces were characterized by a Romantic spirit, strongly linked to the traditions of Chopin. Some of his songs and small pieces for piano were performed during various exhibitions. He also willingly improvised, which brought him more satisfaction than playing notated compositions. His time spent in Poland was also marked by his first family tragedies: his father was imprisoned for participating in the January Uprising of 1863 and a few months after his marriage in 1881, his first wife died.

After emigration

The first stages of his emigration consisted mostly of travels for educational and artistic development. He wanted to study composition and deepen his pianistic skills, as well as do concert tours and earn money. During this time he lived both abroad and in Poland. In 1882 he went to Berlin to study composition with Friedrich Kiel, with whom he also studied counterpoint. While there, he published his first compositions with Bote und Bock. At the same time he taught piano at the Music Institute in Warsaw, this time in the higher-level classes. In 1884 he studied composition with Heinrich Urban in Berlin and piano with Teodor Leszetycki (Theodor Leschetizky) in Vienna. In the meantime he met Tytus Chałubiński in Zakopane, performed one evening on the same bill as Helena Modrzejewska in Kraków, and visited his father in Żytomierz (Zhitomir, now in Ukraine). For one year (1885–1886) he worked at the Conservatory in Strasbourg. In 1888 he performed concerts in Paris, where he settled a year later. From there, he went on numerous concert tours, including a tour of the United States.

The second stage of his emigration—one can say this was his actual one—was to Switzerland in 1899, where, after marrying Helena Górska, he bought a palace in Riond-Bosson. His piano career proved to be an amazing success; the enthusiasm of his audiences was comparable to the admiration shown for Franz Liszt ("Lisztomania") in the 1840s. He continued to compose, although this activity remained on the margins of his concert career. His compositions were performed in various parts of the world (e.g., *Manru*, an opera, was produced in Dresden, Lviv, and New York). In 1903, he suspended his career as a pianist to devote himself to composition. Among other things, he wrote sketches for his *Symphony in B Minor*, op. 24, and his most important piano works, including the *Sonata in E Flat Minor*, op. 21. His tremendous notoriety and artistic success as a pianist allowed him to become gradually involved in the Polish push for independence (the so-called Polish issue), while his financial fortune allowed for more and more intensive social activity (through his funding of the Grunwald Monument in Kraków in 1910) and charity (with Henryk Sienkiewicz, he founded the Central Committee for Aid to War Victims in Poland in 1915). All of this was designed to draw the world's attention to Poland's problems. Beginning in 1916, he devoted himself to political activity, which culminated in his becoming Prime Minister and Foreign Minister in independent Poland in 1919. As Poland's situation stabilized, Paderewski resigned from his political functions and left for California, where he rested before returning to the concert stages in 1922, making recordings and donating part of his royalties to charity.

Differences between the old and new realities

It is difficult to talk about two specific worlds in Paderewski's case. Instead we should describe them as Poland and non-Poland (Germany, Austria, France, Switzerland, and the United States). He traveled the whole world and lived in many places. In some of them he even purchased houses, for example, in Switzerland and the United States. Each time, his new place of residence offered different possibilities than Poland had. In Berlin and Vienna, he could develop his compositional and pianistic skills. In Strasbourg, on the other hand, he developed as a teacher, even though he earned his living as a poorly paid piano teacher at the local conservatory. The United States was his dreamland, or "fairytale land," as he recalled in his *Memoirs* [*Pamiętniki*]. Switzerland, on the other hand, offered Paderewski an opportunity to rest in a quiet country manor. In the last period of his life, however, the United States seemed to be not so much a "fairytale land" as a location safe from World War II and a place where he could again contribute to the Polish cause. All of Paderewski's foreign worlds differed from Poland in that they were independent, had a much better developed artistic life, and offered touring possibilities.

Reason for leaving Poland

There were several reasons for Paderewski's emigration—as many as there were actual departures. Initially, he needed education that he could not find in Poland, so he went first to Berlin and then, thanks to financial support from Helena Modrzejewska (Modjeska), to Vienna. Another reason was also probably a desire to move away from the trauma of the death of his wife, Antonina Korsakówna, shortly after the birth of their son Alfred (the boy, suffering from polio, died in 1901). Financial considerations were also important: the sick child required considerable resources for treatment. Due to its favorable climate and relative quiet, Switzerland was an ideal place for his ill son (see the composer's *Memoirs*). It seems that settling in Switzerland and the United States for longer periods of time also resulted from his need for freedom, the desire to feel that everything is possible, and a yearning for comfort and an organized life.

Contact with Poland after emigration

Paderewski's contacts with his home country after his emigration were so close that it was sometimes difficult to separate a longer stay (which could be regarded as a temporary return) from shorter visits related to either concert tours or holidays. He was constantly visible in press reports from concerts and as an author of political speeches and texts on music. Above all, however, he was the greatest advocate for Polish independence—he made a major contribution to this cause with his fiery speeches, so much so that the President of the United States, Thomas Woodrow Wilson, set an independent Poland as a condition for world peace after World War I. Paderewski returned to Poland in December 1918 and in 1919 he took the positions of Prime Minister and Minister of Foreign Affairs. He signed the Treaty of Versailles on behalf of Poland. After his resignation from political office, he left the country, only to return quickly after the Bolsheviks attacked in 1920. Later, he was rarely in Poland, but kept in close contact; he supported young Polish musicians, teaching them and funding scholarships, and became politically involved once more in the 1930s. With Władysław Sikorski, he co-founded the Front Morges organization and, after the outbreak of World War II, he became one of the representatives of the Polish government in exile. As of 1934, he also led the editorial committee for Chopin's *Complete Works*.

Influence of the new home on the composer's music

All of his works evoke a romantic image of Poland. They incorporate references to Polish dances (polonaise, krakowiak, and mazurka) and highlander music (*Tatra album* [*Album tatrzańskie*], op. 12, *Polish Dances* [*Tańce polskie*], op. 5). Paderewski's love of his country is reflected in the titles of his compositions (*Polish Fantasy* [*Fantazja polska*], op. 19 and *Symphony in B Minor "Polonia,"* which includes a quote from *Dąbrowski's Mazurka* [*Mazurek Dąbrowskiego*]), themes (*Manru*), and musical settings of quotes from Polish poets (e.g., Asnyk and Mickiewicz). It seems that apart from perfecting his compositional skills, emigration did not significantly alter Paderewski's musical language, although it should be noted that he modernized his music somewhat through the use of increased dissonance and richer harmony. It has to be remembered, though, that he stopped composing at the beginning of the 1920s.

Awareness of the composer's music in both countries

Paderewski's work is performed internationally, although it is not part of the standard repertoire. It is heard in Poland more often than in other countries. His personality still obscures his compositional output, even though it was when composing that he was happiest. His achievements still await rediscovery and promotion.

Composer's personality

It is difficult to describe such a rich personality briefly. Let us mention some of his most exemplary features: he was generous, sociable, open to the world, hard-working, ambitious, stubborn in his aspirations, persistent, independent, self-conscious, critical, extremely emotional, committed with all his heart to what he did, and always helpful when necessary.

Remarkable anecdote or biographical fact

Anecdotes and interesting biographical facts about Paderewski can be mentioned in many ways, from his appearances in films (*Moonlight Sonata*, 1937) to his fervent interviews about Polish independence and his career as a Prime Minister, and to his fundraising for war victims and granting of scholarships to Polish musicians. He received numerous state awards from various countries (Poland, Belgium, France, Spain, Italy, and Romania) and honorary doctorates (from Yale, Oxford, Columbia, Jagiellonian University, and Warsaw University, among others). A less known story from Paderewski's life: teachers from the Music Institute Warsaw saw in the young student the material for a composer and performer who could play various instruments well (helicon, double bass, horn, trombone, trumpet, oboe, clarinet, and flute), but not...the piano.

Respondent's Top Choices

- **Favorite work:** *Minuet* from *Humoresques de concert*, op. 14 (1887), for its charm, lightness, *fin de siècle* elegance, and memories of childhood.
- **Best work:** For Paderewski, it was most likely *Symphony in B Minor "Polonia,"* op. 24 (1903–1907). It seems, however, that as his magnum opus we should instead consider his opera *Manru*, op. 20 (1893–1901), which was staged at the New York Metropolitan Opera the year after its premiere. In New York it was performed nine times. Its libretto, written by Alfred Nossig, was based on Ignacy Kraszewski's novel *A Hut Behind the Village* [*Chata za wsią*]. Its theme seems to be ideal for this book about emigration: the protagonist, a wandering Romani, was expelled from a collapsing house, which in the era of Young Poland was seen as a metaphor of the Polish homeland. This metaphor and the opera's subject reminded the composer of post-partition Poland; in other countries, such an interpretation would not be as profoundly understood as in the author's homeland.
- **Composition still waiting to be discovered:** Chamber music (such as *Romance in A Major* for violin and piano, 1881–1882), lyrical vocal pieces (*Four Songs to Adam Asnyk's poems* [*Cztery Pieśni do słów Asnyka*], op. 7, 1882–1885), charming piano miniatures (*Chants du Voyager*, 1881–1882), which remain outside the main concert repertoire, and works still unpublished, such as *Humoreska in A Major* for two oboes and two clarinets.

Respondent: Małgorzata Gamrat

Roman Palester

Date and place of birth:
28 December 1907, Śniatyń.

Date and place of death:
25 August 1989, Paris.

Date and place of emigration:
1947, France (Paris).

Return to Poland:
He did not return.

Key quote

I return with a belief that we all, regardless of where the fate has thrown us—I mean Polish artists here—do the same job. We work for Polish culture.[286]

Activities before emigration

After completing composition studies at Warsaw Conservatory, Palester made his debut at the Warsaw Philharmonic in 1931 with a performance of *Symphonic Music,* which was conducted by Grzegorz Fitelberg. Subsequent compositions, which were also performed abroad at festivals of the International Society for Contemporary Music and at the 1937 World's Fair in Paris, strengthened his position as one of Poland's most talented young artists. At the same time, he published essays in Polish music journals (*Muzyka Polska, Kwartalnik Muzyczny*) and composed music for theater and film. He was also an active member of the Polish Composers' Association and the Polish Society for Contemporary Music. He continued his activities in the first years after World War II. At that time, he was involved in the creation of Polish Music Publishers and the Polish Composers' Union and was also assistant dean and professor of composition at the State Higher School of Music in Kraków. As a composer, he was considered to be Karol Szymanowski's successor; his works such as the *Violin Concerto* (1939–1941) and *Symphony No. 2* (1941–1942) earned him deserved recognition both at home and abroad. In 1947 he and his wife decided to move to Paris, although they did not intend to sever contacts with his home country. He regularly visited Poland until 1949, when he took part in the Conference of Composers and Music Critics in Łagów, where the doctrine of socialist realism in music was proclaimed. He returned to Paris and in 1950 officially announced his decision to stay abroad. In Poland, his name was censored, his works banned from public performance, and his scores withdrawn from distribution.

After emigration

In 1951 Palester contributed two important essays to the Parisian *Kultura*, the most important journal published by Polish émigrés. These writings addressed the artist's duties towards society and the limits of creative freedom: *The Marsyas Conflict* [*Konflikt Marsjasza*] (nos. 7–8) and *Notes on Music* [*Uwagi o muzyce*] (no. 12). In the spring of 1952, he joined the editorial team of the Polish section of Radio Free Europe in Munich and worked there until 1972 as head of the cultural department. He never stopped composing, writing new pieces regularly until the end of his life. He focused on developing his own musical language, which was based on liberally treated dodecaphonic material, usually written within a framework of classical formal genres (sonata, concert, symphony, variations), but yet treated individually. In terms of style, Palester's music is closest to expressionism, although over the years it has also included clear references to neoclassicism and folklore or to aleatory and sonoristic solutions. A mature synthesis of styles is represented by works from his last period: *Viola Concerto* (1975–1978), *Fifth Symphony* (1977–1981), and the cantata *Letters to Mother* [*Listy do Matki*] (1984–1987).

Differences between the old and new realities

In the first years after the Second World War, the situation in the musical world in Poland was not yet clear—artists tried above all to rebuild institutional structures and to create possibilities for future activity. Creative freedom was a given and musicians were able to maintain contact with foreign countries without any serious problems. The situation began to change with the tightening of cultural policies by the ruling Polish Communists and the transfer of guidelines from the Soviet Union. The introduction of socialist realism as a binding aesthetic doctrine drastically limited any freedom of artistic expression. Palester, who had an established position in the country, could not stand the increasingly strained political atmosphere and in 1947 he and his wife moved to Paris, which he knew well from the interwar years. Initially, both of them maintained good contacts with the country. His wife, Barbara, worked as a representative for Polish Music Publishers, and the composer wrote, among other things, music for Polish films (including *Forbidden Songs* [*Zakazane piosenki*], *Border Street* [*Ulica graniczna*], and *Unvanquished City* [*Miasto nieujarzmione*]; at the 1950 premiere of the latter, his name was withdrawn from the credits). With time, working for Poland and living outside of the country turned out to be irreconcilable and unacceptable to Poland's Communist authorities. In exile, Palester was involved in working for Radio Free Europe, where he spent twenty years. As the head of its culture department, he kept an eye on the situation in Poland. His erudition allowed him to create excellent cultural programs and also to write accurate journalistic texts for *Kultura*. He developed and improved his own style, which was not dependent on political or environmental conditions, and created a number of important works, only some of which reached audiences in Poland.

Reason for leaving Poland

The isolation of Polish musical life from the West continued to increase, as did restrictions on creative freedom due to the gradual introduction of socialist realist doctrine in culture.

Contact with Poland after emigration

Until 1977, Roman Palester's name and music were officially banned in Poland. During that time he had no official contacts with the country, except for a brief period of political thaw after 1956, when several of his works were performed, including his *Symphony No. 4* at the 1958 Warsaw Autumn Festival. The composer also resumed contact with Polish Music Publishers at that point, but from the early 1960s onwards censorship tightened once more and further performances of his music were out of the question. Censorship against Palester intensified, because since 1952 he had worked for Radio Free Europe, which was detested by Poland's Communist regime. Therefore, even more so than in the case of Andrzej Panufnik, care was taken to ensure that his name did not appear in Polish publications. Only once the censors missed something—an interview with the composer that had been conducted in Paris by Tadeusz Kaczyński was published in *Ruch Muzyczny* (no. 20, 1964). Although it concerned purely musical matters, the editor-in-chief of the magazine, Zygmunt Mycielski, was required to offer an explanation, and it was only thanks to his adamant attitude that Kaczyński was able to keep his job.

After his ban in Poland was lifted in 1977, Palester's compositions began to appear at the Warsaw Autumn Festival. In 1983 the composer visited the country and took part in two concerts organized in Kraków. It was his only visit to Poland after his decision to emigrate was announced. In 1988 he was one of the protagonists of a musicological conference called Wrongly Present Music [Muzyka źle obecna]; he sent an essay (*Wrongly Present Truth* [*Prawda źle obecna*]) to the meeting's organizers; this essay was later published in the conference proceedings, which were edited by Krystyna Tarnawska-Kaczorowska (Warsaw, 1989). He bequeathed his estate to the Archive of Polish Composers at the Warsaw University Library.

Influence of the new home on the composer's music

While in exile, Roman Palester did not have to adapt his music to socialist realist aesthetics. He maintained his creative independence, continuing his attempt to merge his compositional style with the most important trends of the day. He never followed modern trends blindly, but tried to preserve his own individual style and choose elements that agreed with his own creative personality. There are few direct references to Polishness, although those that do exist refer mostly to Polish poets who also emigrated, including Juliusz Słowacki, Czesław Miłosz, and Krzysztof Sowiński. In the music itself, there are no references to Polish national songs or folk melodies. Palester's musical language remained in line with twentieth-century compositional trends in Europe, with a clear preference towards an expressionist trend rooted in the music of Alban Berg.

Awareness of the composer's music in both countries

Knowledge of Palester's life and music inside Poland was almost non-existent for many years. In 1999 a monograph on Roman Palester written by Zofia Helman was published, but it did not bring about a fundamental breakthrough in the reception of the composer's music. It was not until 2016 that, on the initiative of the aforementioned Archive of Polish Composers, a number of activities were undertaken to popularize the composer and his music. Since then, a website has been developed (palester.polmic.pl), CDs recorded, his autobiography and memoirs published, conferences organized, etc. However, the work of Palester is not yet fully appreciated.

Composer's personality

He was intellectual and erudite, with a vast knowledge of Polish and European culture. He was involved in social activities, including organizations in Poland (before he emigrated) and abroad (the Free Europe Council). A brilliant journalistic personality, he discussed cultural issues passionately in his broadcasts. The writings he left behind (autobiography, memoirs, correspondence, and texts of his radio programs) are also proof of his literary talent. In his compositional output, he was independent and uncompromising, following the path of his own creative explorations.

Remarkable anecdote or biographical fact

Roman Palester did not expect that his decision to stay in exile would make him disappear from view (or rather from hearing) in Poland. Years later he admitted, "it was a blow from which I never fully recovered, so I did not get it all together." At the same time, as a man of extremely high moral standards, he believed that an artist should strive for truth in art. That is why he was convinced that in making the decision to stay in France, he simply acted "as an ordinary, decent man." With time, especially after the political thaw in Poland, he painfully felt the lack of interest in his music in his native country and the omission of his name in publications. His feelings were echoed in letters to Andrzej Panufnik and Zygmunt Mycielski, among others.

Respondent's Top Choices

- **Favorite work:** *Viola Concerto* (1975–1978), a work representing a mature compositional style, a synthesis of his creative quest. It is deeply expressive and poignantly beautiful.
- **Best work:** *La Mort de Don Juan,* with a libretto according to Oskar Miłosz (1959–1961). The composer's only opera, it is expressionistic in musical language and deeply philosophical in content; in 1962 it received first prize in a competition held by the Italian section of the International Society for Contemporary Music and its performance in Brussels in 1965 was a great success.
- **Composition still waiting to be discovered:** *Concertino per clavicembalo e dieci strumenti su temi di vecchie danze polacche* (1955), an extremely interesting combination of early music stylization and innovative sound exploration. Colorful combinations of sounds, phrases, and harmony seemingly evoke echoes of Baroque music, but at the same time there are strongly "grinding" dissonances. It is a fresh and original piece.

Respondent: Beata Bolesławska-Lewandowska

Andrzej Panufnik

Date and place of birth:
24 September 1914, Warsaw.

Date and place of death:
27 October 1991, Twickenham.

Date and place of emigration:
1954, Great Britain (London).

Return to Poland:
He did not return.

Key quote

Music is an expression of emotion and feelings. My ideal is a work in which the poetic content joins with the perfection of musical craft. Poetry in itself does not decide the musical value of a work, just as craft in itself faces the threat of lifeless and dry formulas. Timeless beauty is born only out of an equilibrium of both these elements.[287]

Activities before emigration

Panufnik made his debut as a composer before World War II. During the war, he performed in Warsaw cafés in a piano duo with Witold Lutosławski and also conducted an orchestra during concerts organized by the Main Aid Council, a charity organization tolerated by the occupying power. After 1945 he was, among other things, conductor of the Kraków Philharmonic Orchestra (1945–1946) and the first artistic director of the Warsaw Philharmonic (1946). Numerous international travels between 1946 and 1948 consolidated his position as a conductor and composer. His works presented during the war, such as *Tragic Overture*, composed in 1942 and performed in 1944, and works from the late 1940s—*Lullaby* for strings and two harps (1947), *Nocturne* for orchestra (1947), *Sinfonia Rustica* (1948), and *Polish Suite (Hommage à Chopin)* [*Suita polska (Hommage à Chopin)*] for voice and piano (1949)—established Panufnik in the first rank of Polish composers. Beginning in 1948 he was the vice-president of the Polish Composers' Union. When organizing performances abroad, he was keen to promote Polish music, introducing not only his own works but also those of émigré composers such as Michał Spisak, Tadeusz Zygfryd Kassern, and Konstanty Regamey. In the late 1940s and early 1950s he was seen as "the authorities' favorite"; he composed a few mass songs and *Symphony of Peace* [*Symfonia Pokoju*], the latter using words by Jarosław Iwaszkiewicz (1951). He was also invited to participate in propaganda performances and events in the Soviet Union, Palermo, China, and elsewhere. This sort of activity drove him to a creative crisis and, eventually, the decision to emigrate.

After emigration

Between 1957 and 1959 he worked as artistic director at the City of Birmingham Symphony Orchestra (CBSO). After 1959 he decided to dedicate himself to composing and conducted only occasionally, usually his own works. Beginning in 1970 he worked with the London Symphony Orchestra, which, in addition to recording many of the composer's works, also commissioned new ones: *Concerto Festivo* (1979), *Concertino* for timpani, percussion and strings (1980), and *Cello Concerto* (1991). He composed for other renowned British music institutions (BBC, *Triangles*, 1972; Royal Philharmonic Society, *Sinfonia di Speranza*, 1986) as well as American ensembles (Boston Symphony Orchestra, *Sinfonia Votiva*, 1980–1981; New York Chamber Orchestra, *Arbor Cosmica*, 1983; Chicago Symphony Orchestra, *Symphony No. 10*, 1988). He also wrote for such artists as Yehudi Menuhin (*Violin Concerto*, 1971) and Mstislav Rostropovich (*Cello Concerto*, 1991).

Differences between the old and new reality

These worlds differed in terms of their political systems and everything associated with them. Above all, Panufnik's experiences related to the political and creative freedom differed in each country. In Poland, Panufnik enjoyed a respected position in musical circles, but his freedom as a composer became increasingly limited. The principles of socialist realism required him to write music accessible for a mass audience—more ambitious compositions were subjected to strict criticism. Accused of formalism, they were removed from concert halls—this was the fate of Panufnik's earlier works during the early 1950s, including *Nocturne* (1947), *Lullaby* (1947), and *Sinfonia Rustica* (1948). Additionally, involvement in various cultural delegations, rallies, and political events pulled him away from composing, which only increased his frustration. In Great Britain, Panufnik remained a fully independent composer and was able to develop his own, individual style. Aside from two years as artistic director at the City of Birmingham Symphony Orchestra (1957–1959), he never accepted a full-time position. Creative independence remained his most important goal. He succeed in developing his own, recognizable style and achieved a prominent position in his new homeland. In 1991, he was knighted by Queen Elizabeth II in recognition of his achievements for the musical culture of Great Britain. Since then, he has been referred to as Sir Andrzej Panufnik.

Reason for leaving Poland

They were political. Panufnik wanted to escape the web of political pressure and involvement in non-musical causes. He could not stand the increasing limitations being imposed due to the cultural policies of the Polish People's Republic. Even though he had seemed to legitimize some activities by signing official papers related to them, his dependency on the Ministry of Culture gave him an increasing sense of enslavement and prompted a growing mental and creative crisis. He eventually decided that emigration was the only possible way out. He left the country legally, on 9 July 1954, in order to record in Switzerland (for Swiss Radio), but instead of returning to Warsaw, he went to Great Britain. In London he applied for asylum and in 1961 he became a British citizen without having to renounce his Polish nationality (it was not formally required).

Contact with Poland after emigration

Panufnik's name and music were censored until 1977. During that time, he did not maintain any official contact with his home country. After the ban was lifted, Panufnik's compositions began to appear on Warsaw Autumn Festival programs and sometimes elsewhere in the country. Still, Panufnik continued to decline invitations to Poland in order to protest its Communist rule. As a result, he visited his homeland only in 1990, after the political transformation of 1989. He was a guest of honor at the Warsaw Autumn Festival, where he was welcomed with great acclaim.

Influence of the new home on the composer's music

The composer spent his first years abroad recovering mentally and trying to find his place in a new reality. Creative development could be seen only in the early 1960s. Musically, Panufnik continued his previous language, eventually developing a compositional system characterized by symmetry and geometry (as seen in his diagrams) and the use of three-note cells, which became the basis of the melodic and harmonic structure of his works. His compositional language was anchored in a strongly emotional component, shifting between quiet lyrical contemplation and dramatic turmoil. Life abroad left a strong mark on Panufnik's oeuvre—his compositions are full of references to historical and political events in his homeland. *Sinfonia Sacra* (1963) is dedicated to the millennium in 1966 of the Polish nation and Christianity in Poland, *Katyn Epitaph* [*Epitafium katyńskie*] (1967) commemorates the victims of mass murder by the NKVD (the Soviet secret police), *Sinfonia Votiva* (1980–1981), written in the early days of the Solidarity movement, is a votive offering to the Black Madonna of Częstochowa, and the *Bassoon Concerto* (1985) is dedicated to the memory of Father Jerzy Popiełuszko, murdered by the Security Service. There is no question that physical distance led to this strong presence of Polish elements and references in the composer's work. He confirmed this in his own words: "In my compositions, I try to reflect events that I personally experience. These are mostly the social, political, and religious problems of our country. This is because Poland is everything to me. My heart and my soul belong to it."[288]

Awareness of the composer's music in both countries

It is very good. Especially recently in Poland, a visible increase in performances and musical literature can be observed. It seems that after years of absence, Panufnik's name is being recognized again by Polish audiences. In Great Britain, Panufnik's music has been appreciated for a long time. It may not be performed very often, but his name remains well known in the world of music. His compositions have been recorded, often in many interpretations, by outstanding musicians. A big contribution to the promotion of this artist was made by the London Symphony Orchestra, with which he had worked for years. Today, the LSO runs a program aimed at young composers, called the Panufnik Composers Scheme.

Composer's personality

For Panufnik, composition was most important. In the first years after World War II, he had actively participated in activities aimed at rebuilding musical life in Poland and promoting Polish music internationally. However, after experiencing Stalinism, followed by his emigration, he declined any kind of political and social activity, focusing instead on creative work. His decision to give up the artistic director's position at the City of Birmingham Symphony Orchestra appears to be a significant point in his life—despite the risk of falling into poverty, he chose to focus on composing. His marriage to Camilla Jessel in 1963 and the birth of their children allowed him to put down roots in Great Britain, but he considered himself a Polish composer until the end of his life.

Remarkable anecdote or biographical fact

Panufnik is the author of music to *Warsaw Children* [*Warszawskie dzieci*], lyrics by Stanisław Ryszard Dobrowolski, which even today is frequently performed as a symbol of the Warsaw Uprising. His daughter, Roxanna Panufnik, is one of the most recognized British contemporary music composers, while his son Jem Panufnik is a graphic artist, DJ, and electronic music composer. Jem appeared in the documentary *Dad from Behind the Iron Curtain* [*Tata zza żelaznej kurtyny*] directed by Krzysztof Rzączyński (TVP Kultura, 2009). The composer's music was also used by Andrzej Wajda in his last film, *Afterimage* [*Powidoki*, 2016], which tells the life of painter Władysław Strzemiński during the Stalinist years.

Respondent's Top Choices

- **Favorite work:** *Autumn Music* [*Muzyka jesieni*] for orchestra without violins (1962). It was written in 1962, purely for his own reasons and without regard for the popular avant-garde tendencies of the time. It is characterized by a special beauty of sound and music of disturbing melancholy.
- **Best work:** *Sinfonia Sacra* (1963), a ground-breaking work in the composer's career. Commissioned by the Kosciuszko Foundation to celebrate the millennium of the Polish State and Christianity in Poland. Finished in 1963, it was created during a difficult and uncertain time for the composer. It received first prize at the Prince Rainier Composers Competition in Monaco in 1963, which gave Panufnik hope for a better future and brought increased interest in his work in Great Britain and Europe. Today, *Sinfonia Sacra* remains one of his most frequently performed compositions. In another category, *Warsaw Children* (1944) should be mentioned, a song marginal in the catalog of Panufnik's compositions, but strongly embedded in Polish memory. It remains a symbol of the Warsaw Uprising, reminding Poles every year about the fighting in Warsaw in 1944.
- **Composition still waiting to be discovered:** *Twelve Miniature Studies*, also known as *Circle of Fifths* [*Krąg kwintowy*] (1947), an outstanding series of 12 piano etudes that refers to keyboard cycles by Bach and Chopin. In terms of compositions for piano, it is an unusually interesting, colorful work that should be included in the canon of twentieth-century Polish piano repertoire.

Respondent: Beata Bolesławska-Lewandowska

Jerzy (George) Petersburski (pseudonym J. Warrens)

Date and place of birth:
20 April 1895, Warsaw.

Date and place of death:
7 October 1979, Warsaw.

Date and place of emigration:
1947, Brazil (Rio de Janeiro and São Paulo); 1949, Argentina (Buenos Aires).

Return to Poland:
Yes, he returned to Warsaw in 1968.

Key quote
We thought that we were writing tangos. No, tangos are Argentinian.[289]

Activities before emigration
Petersburski was born into a family of musicians (he took his first piano lessons from his mother) and began his artistic life at an early age. At the age of fifteen, he made his debut at the Warsaw Philharmonic playing Chopin's *Concerto in F Minor* and, while still a student, he worked as an accompanist at the Mirage [Miraż] Theater in Warsaw. After graduation, he studied at the Music Conservatory in Warsaw with Aleksander Michałowski. Four years after graduation, in 1920, he left for Vienna, where he studied piano, composition, and conducting with Arthur Schnabel. In the 1920s and 1930s he worked as a pianist, composer, and arranger for popular Warsaw cabarets (Mirage, Black Cat [Czarny Kot], Persian Eye [Perskie Oko], Qui Pro Quo, Band [Banda], and Marine Eye [Morskie Oko]). He wrote numerous songs for theater and cabaret artists, including Mieczysław Fogg, and played live music for performances by the stars of interwar Poland: Pola Negri, Hanka Ordonówna, and Aleksander Wertyński. Around 1925, with violinist Artur Gold, he founded the Gold-Petersburski ensemble, which not only became one of the most popular jazz ensembles in Poland but also gained some popularity abroad. Gold-Petersburski played in the most renowned halls in Poland, Austria, Germany, France, Switzerland, Great Britain, and Czechoslovakia. Their performances were often broadcast by Polish Radio. The calling card of the duo was the song *When Petersburski and Gold Are Playing* [*Gdy Petersburski razem z Goldem gra*]. In the 1930s, Petersburski wrote scores for Polish movies (*Seduced* [*Uwiedziona*] and *What My Husband Does at Night* [*Co mój mąż robi w nocy*],

both directed by Michał Waszyński; *Happy Thirteen* [*Szczęśliwa trzynastka*], directed by Marian Czauski; and *The Queen of the Suburbs* [*Królowa przedmieścia*], directed by Eugeniusz Bodo). He was the first Polish composer whose songs became famous abroad and the first Polish popular music artist to be awarded the Cross of Merit by President Ignacy Mościcki (1936).

After emigration

During his more than twenty years of émigré life, Petersburski remained active as an artist. For the first two years, he performed in Brazil in a piano duo with Alfred Schütz (author of the famous military song *Red Poppies at Monte Cassino* [*Czerwone Maki na Monte Cassino*]). After moving to Argentina, he collaborated with the radio station El Mundo. Together with Kazimierz Krukowski, he ran the Teatro El Nacional in Buenos Aires (1954–1962), where he staged the musical *Blue Sky Milonga* (Blue Sky was the name of the venue where he played). He continued to compose, arrange, and record songs. Two of his hits were particularly popular: a Brazilian samba-inspired *Caffetterio*, which was played during the carnival in Rio de Janeiro, and *All Roads Lead to Buenos Aires* [*Wszystkie drogi prowadzą do Buenos Aires*], a song the Argentinians liked so much that it became the signature tune of El Mundo.

Differences between the old and new realities

Petersburski recalled the hot, vibrant atmosphere of Rio de Janeiro (and its carnival) as a wonderful place from which he had many cherished memories. Despite initially difficult beginnings, he managed to achieve a pleasant and prosperous life in Argentina. In addition to the fact that he found life in the countries of South America colorful and intense, in interviews the composer emphasized the unprecedented musicality of Brazilians and Argentinians, where everyone played an instrument and even cleaners sang in voices of operatic diva quality.

Reason for leaving Poland

During the Second World War, he stayed in the Soviet Union and performed with local orchestras. In 1941, he joined Anders' Army, with which, as a sergeant of the 1st Airborne Regiment, he crossed the entire combat route in the Middle East, providing the soldiers with musical entertainment. Petersburski left for Rio de Janeiro after the army was demobilized in 1947. Brazil and Argentina, due to their favorable policy towards immigrants (no visas were required) were popular destinations for many Polish artists and scientists. Numerous generations of Polish people lived in both countries, for they had been arriving there since the late nineteenth century.

Contact with Poland after emigration

Contacts were very good. He was in constant communication with ZAiKS in connection with the recording of his works. When he visited Poland in 1967, three songs previously unknown in Poland were released: *Blue Handkerchief* [*Niebieska chusteczka*], written in the Soviet Union, *Caffeterio*, and *Crying Piano* [*Płaczące pianino*], the latter composed in Argentina after the death of his second wife.

Influence of the new home on the composer's music

In South America, Petersburski was confronted with real tangos, which led him to claim that nobody could write tangos like the Argentinians. The locals described Petersburski's tangos as beautiful and melodious, but closer to boleros, so in order to fit in better, he modified the rhythms he used. During his stay in Argentina, he also had the opportunity to work with the legend of new Argentinian tangos, Astor Piazzolla.

Awareness of the composer's music in both countries

In Poland, Petersburski's oeuvre is widely known and performed. The artist is a legend of the country's interwar music and his hits such as *The Last Sunday* [*Ta ostatnia niedziela*] or *Tango Milonga* are popular among older and younger performers. Petersburski has also made his mark on the culture of Argentina and the world, thanks to the cult melody of this tango.

Composer's personality

He was an energetic optimist, active, and hardworking, with an incredible sense of humor. A devoted husband and father.

Remarkable anecdote or biographical fact

Perhaps if he had not studied in Vienna, his musical career would not have been so spectacular. It was the eminent operetta artist Emerich Kalman, whom he met there, who encouraged the young artist to consider composing popular songs. Having heard Petersburski improvise during breaks between classes, he supposedly said "Leave the classical music behind. Entertainment is your future."

The composer's son, Jerzy Petersburski, Jr., born in 1969, is a well-known television presenter who also writes music for television commercials.

Respondent's Top Choices

- **Favorite work:** Many of Petersburski's songs are all-time favorites. My choice, however, is a slightly less popular song, *Forget-Me-Nots* [*Niezapominajki*] (1936), performed by Stefan Witas (Syrena Records, 1930s). It is a song that brings to mind the beauty and carefree nature of the interwar period, when Polish culture flourished and elegantly dressed men and women strolled down the streets of Warsaw.
- **Best work:** The position of this work in the artist's oeuvre is evidenced by the inscription on his grave: *Composer of the Global Hit Tango Milonga / Oh, Donna Clara* (1928). Its first performers were Stanisława Nowicka, Eugeniusz Bodo, Jerzy Roland, and Ludwik Sempoliński. The melody became popular abroad as *Oh, Donna Clara* with lyrics by Lohner Bedy. It was sung by Pola Negri and Al Jolson in the great Wonder Bar show on Broadway as well as by Henri Varna, king of the French musical, the British band New Vaudeville Band (1967), and the world-renowned orchestras of Joe Loss and Stanley Black. *Tango Milonga* gained its greatest popularity through the interpretations of Mieczysław Fogg and Irena Santor. Nowadays, it is enjoying a renaissance and is played in Berlin's venues as a fashionable hit from interwar times. It is also the favorite tango of Pope Francis.

- **Composition still waiting to be discovered:** Although Petersburski devoted his life to entertainment, he also composed in other genres. One such piece is *Rhapsody of the Warsaw Uprising* [*Rapsodia powstania warszawskiego*], which he performed in Cairo before General Władysław Sikorski. The piece was not recorded, but Petersburski himself mentioned it and played fragments of it in a program from Andrzej Jaroszewski's series *Nestors of Polish Song* [*Nestorzy polskiej piosenki*] (16 June 1973). Today, the only trace of this composition is an archival recording of the radio broadcast. The *Rhapsody* has a three-part structure; in the middle part you can hear mazurka rhythms and motifs from various compositions of Chopin.

Respondent: Magdalena Nowicka-Ciecierska

Prasqual (Tomasz Praszczałek)

Date and place of birth:
2 December 1981, Jelenia Góra.

Date and place of emigration:
2005, Germany (Cologne).

Return to Poland:
He has not returned.

Key quote

Innovation and modernity are important elements of art, but for me music is timeless, or rather beyond time.…I'm increasingly interested in developing visions that I have been dreaming about, perhaps since the very beginning of my life.[290]

Activities before emigration

He is an Academy of Music in Poznań graduate. During his studies he was active in the Youth Circle of the Polish Composers' Union. He took part in numerous competitions and composition courses (among others, those led by Peter Eötvös and Brian Ferneyhough). He is also a music critic and organizer of musical events. He writes primarily chamber music and is interested in spectral techniques.

After emigration

He is not connected to any institution, but instead acts as a freelancer. His work is financed mainly through scholarships and programs such as Poland's Composers' Commissions [Zamówienia kompozytorskie]. He also works as a teacher, giving private piano lessons. Since 2018, he has lectured on sound art at the Ruhr-Universität in Bochum.

Differences between the old and new realities

It is difficult to compare both periods of the composer's activity. The first one, related to his stay in Poland, should be considered as "youthful." Only after his departure did the composer enter a mature phase. A composer of the younger generation, he is aware of participating in global culture and does not respect national borders. He lives in Cologne and considers himself a Polish composer, but does not manifest this affiliation in any way.

His musical identity is shaped by drawing on various cultures, traditions, and patterns, including those that are non-European. His artistic activities differ from those of other Polish composers in terms of their formal dimensions, shaping of sound, and subject matter. In Germany, on the other hand, Prasqual remains somewhat in the shadow of current trends. As he claims,

> My compositions are somewhat to the side of current trends in the new music scene, which is driven by Stefan Prins and Johannes Kreidler. Instead of criticizing current culture, I focus on mythology, archetypes, and universal themes. In some sense, however, these are political works, mostly because of what they do not talk about, what they knowingly avoid.[291]

Reason for leaving Poland

After graduating from the Poznań Academy of Music, Prasqual was offered a part-time job as an assistant at his home university. However, the composer did not agree with the proposed conditions, believing they would prevent him from further artistic and personal development. Having received a prestigious DAAD scholarship in 2005, he and his wife Agnieszka went to Cologne, where he perfected his compositional skills during postgraduate studies with York Höller. At the same time, he also studied piano with Klaus Oldemeyer, conducting with Rüdiger Bohn, and electronic composition with Hans Ulrich Humpert.

Contact with Poland after emigration

The composer regularly visits his homeland, both for professional and family reasons. Since 2011, he has often received commissions from Polish musical institutions, including the Polish Dance Theater, the Grand Theater – National Opera, the Wrocław Opera, and the Polish National Opera.

Influence of the new home on the composer's music

His stay in Germany has enabled Prasqual to participate in many significant artistic events. He has had the opportunity to become acquainted with both the latest compositions and the canons of musical literature, all presented in superb performances. He has mentioned several times that a key experience for him was the weeks-long series of rehearsals for the world premiere of the *Sonntag* opera in Cologne in 2011. This became an intense entry into the world of Stockhausen's music, which was accompanied by Prasqual's discovery that it was possible to create musical utopias. These experiences confirmed his belief that he should care not only about the score's content, but also its precise realization. After referring to these German models, he has convinced Polish performers of his own works to be more open and flexible in terms of performance techniques.

His stay in Cologne also facilitated his contacts not only with the music of the master from Kürten (Stockhausen), but also with the composer himself. In an interview with Krzysztof Kwiatkowski, Prasqual recalled:

> In Germany, I became acquainted with the music and figure of Karlheinz Stockhausen, who greatly influenced me. Shortly before his death, I decided

> to show him my works. He liked them very much; we wrote to each other for several months. Of course, early Stockhausen's works are discussed in Poland, but confronting such a personality and listening to live performances of *Inori*, *Mantra*, and the opera *Sonntag aus Licht* are events that provide a tremendous stimulus for development. They support visions, offer the courage needed to fulfil them, and really give wings to them. Very rarely have I experienced similar moments in Poland.[292]

Stockhausen's personality and creative attitude strongly influenced Prasqual's way of thinking about music. After the performance of his opera *Ophelia*, Prasqual strongly revised his approach to the form of a work. He turned towards monumental pieces, which he calls musical architectures. Since then, sound has been the focus of his interest. Spatial movement and variable arrangements create and transform acoustic space, creating the illusion of a three-dimensional work—a sculpture or an architectural construction—rather than a traditionally understood musical composition. This shift of focus to a multidimensional aspect affected Prasqual's compositional actions and techniques; he now considers himself a sound architect.

Awareness of the composer's music in both countries

The composer rarely writes for the sake of writing. Most of his works have been performed in either Germany or Poland and are the result of commissions. Certain compositions have also been recorded and are available on the YouTube or SoundCloud platforms. *Architecture of Light* was also released as a DVD by Requiem Records.

Composer's personality

The composer is extraordinarily erudite, familiar with international literature, philosophy, religions, and ethics. His deep fascination with Stockhausen's music and personality, which had a significant impact on the development of his work and private life, still continues. In an interview with Monika Pasiecznik, he wittily stressed that "I have devoured something of Stockhausen's personality myself."[293]

Remarkable anecdote or biographical fact

Prasqual's strong personality manifests itself in various ways. He can point accurately to musicians' critical remarks about the premieres of his works; he also emphasizes his own individual style of dress, hairstyle, and behavior. He remains uncompromising in his artistic choices. During the premiere of his opera *Ophelia* at Poznań's Grand Theater, he went against the decision of director Monika Dobrowlańska and, despite the results of the dress rehearsal, he presented a different ending of the piece to the audience, one which was shortened. In doing so, he remained faithful to his artistic concept.

Respondent's Top Choices

- **Favorite work:** The composer often deals with the mystery of death, heard in such compositions as *Salto Mortale* (2007), *Mother Nature Come to Daddy* (2003), *Viola Concerto* (2005), *Ophelia* (2005–2011), and *Five Chants from the Cage* [*Pięć śpiewów z klatki*] (2013–2014). This topic also appears in *YMORH* for 22 musicians (2010). This composition, dedicated to the memory of Jarosław Mianowski and Beata Raczyńska, was inspired by Joenne Greenberg's *I Never Promised You a Rose Garden*. It was commissioned by Deutschlandfunk Cologne and premiered on 11 April 2011 in Cologne.

- **Best work:** It is difficult to talk about one's work of a lifetime in relation to a living composer. So far, the most advanced, complex, and demanding piece of Prasqual's work is the *Orlando* tetralogy, planned as an opera cycle. In 2011, after the success of *Ophelia*, the composer began working on his next piece. He intended to write an opera whose protagonist was Virginia Woolf's Orlando, an almost mystical, eternal character who broke all social conventions and overcame gender and time barriers. Gradually, however, by exploring the novel's themes and complementing them with subsequent inspirations, the concept of the work evolved into a tetralogy, which includes four architecture-works: *Architecture of Darkness* [*Architektura ciemności*], *Architecture of Love* [*Architektura miłości*], *Architecture of Light [Architektura światła*], and *Architecture of Eternity* [*Architektura wieczności*]. Orlando's story became only a pretext for reflection on time, space, ritual, cosmogony, and eschatology. So far, only the third part of the cycle has been completed.
- **Composition still waiting to be discovered:** Many of Prasqual's projects are waiting to be discovered. They can offer a glimpse into his surprising and not entirely predictable imagination.

Respondent: Maria Majewska-Mocek

Marta Ptaszyńska

Date and place of birth:
29 July 1943, Włochy near Warsaw.

Date and place of emigration:
22 September 1972, United States (Cleveland).

Return to Poland:
No, the composer lives in the US, but visits Poland frequently.

Key quote

I think with sound. I see an image, and I can hear it. Lots of things translate to sound for me.[294]

Activities before emigration

The artist was entirely dedicated to her musical activities involving percussion and composing. She boasts three Master of Arts diplomas (1967–1968) from the Faculty of Theory of Music and the Faculty of Composition at Warsaw's Academy of Music and from the percussion studio at Poznań's Academy of Music. She has performed at the Warsaw Autumn Festival and worked with many orchestras and ensembles, including Stanisław Rachoń's radio orchestra, the National Philharmonic, Zygmunt Krauze's Music Workshop, the Mazowsze ensemble, and Jerzy Zgodziński's percussion ensemble in Poznań. She also studied composition privately with Witold Lutosławski. When not composing or performing, she was preoccupied with writing her thesis and working in the Youth Circle of the Polish Composers' Union as its president (1965–1970). In the autumn of 1969 Ptaszyńska left for France to study with Nadia Boulanger, which she did for two years. Her new life in Paris stunned her with its richness of culture and history, from which she sought to draw as much as she could, including meetings not only with Boulanger, but also with Olivier Messiaen.

After emigration

First, the composer completed her education. Only two years after her arrival in the United States, she received an Artist Diploma in composition and percussion from the Cleveland Institute of Music. In addition to her own creative work, she has been, and still is, a teacher. The list of institutions where she has taught is impressive. While studying in

Cleveland, she taught composition at Bennington College in Vermont; later, after moving to San Francisco with her husband, she worked at the University of California in Berkeley (1977–1978) and in Santa Barbara (1979–1981). She also worked at Indiana University in Bloomington (1983–1984), Northwestern University in Evanston, Illinois (1991–1994 and 1995–1997) and the Cincinnati College Conservatory of Music in Ohio. Since 1998 she has been a professor at the University of Chicago. Since the beginning of her stay in the United States, she has been active in promoting Polish music, primarily as a co-founder and vice-president of the American Society for Polish Music in New York, and contributing to the organization of many concerts and festivals, including at the Lincoln Center in New York (1991, 1993) and the *Poland – Music, Poetry, Nation* conference at the University of Chicago (2001). Currently, she works with the CONTEMPO festival, organizing concerts of Polish contemporary composers in Chicago.

Differences between the old and new realities

Marta Ptaszynska's lifestyle has not changed radically since she left Poland—she has always been focused on her work as a composer and a percussionist. America provided her with an opportunity to fulfil a dream, but only when it came to perfecting her percussion skills. She was in contact with the best musicians from the Cleveland Orchestra, with whom she performed several times and for whom she wrote *Spectri Scontri*, first performed in 1973. However, everyday reality brought disappointment due to the city's monotonous landscape, through which one can travel only by car or bus and where walking is a dangerous activity. This unpleasant impression changed when the composer moved from Cleveland to San Francisco. In America, she also encountered a completely different lifestyle:

> After my arrival in the United States in 1972, I experienced a cultural shock. It was such a completely different world! Even leaving aside everyday forms of life, which were still diametrically different from what was in Poland at that time, I was mostly alien to the mentality of people. It was surprisingly uncomplicated.[295]

Reason for leaving Poland

The idea to go to the United States emerged from Ptaszyńska's fascination with the American technique of percussion playing, which is unequalled in the world. Even before she arrived, she became a member of the Percussive Arts Society (PAS), the largest organization for percussionists worldwide. Later, from 1981–1984, she was a member of the society's board of directors. She left Poland in 1972 at the invitation of the Cleveland Institute of Music, which gave her a scholarship.

Contact with Poland after emigration

Ptaszyńska divides her time between Poland and America. She teaches in Chicago, but spends the rest of her time in Warsaw, where she writes her compositions.

Influence of the new home on the composer's music

During her time in San Francisco, the composer became interested in Eastern culture and philosophy and she began to do yoga and participate in meditations in Berkeley's tea garden. This led her to an attempt to portray in her music the perception of time according to Zen philosophy, which, in turn, inspired the composition of *Un grand sommeil noir* for female voice, flute, and harp.

Awareness of the composer's music in both countries

Ptaszyńska's compositions are often performed at concerts and festivals of contemporary music, as well as at percussion competitions in Poland and the United States. In March 2016, the world premiere of the *Symphony for 104 Percussionists* took place in Poznań and a year later, in Chicago, *Voice of the Winds* for one hundred percussionists was performed for the first time. Her *Piano Concerto* was premiered in Kalisz in autumn 2017. Her works have been published in both countries, by Polish Music Publishers and Theodore Presser Publications; they have also been released on Polish and foreign labels, including Polskie Nagrania, Olympia, Pro Viva, Bayers, Chandos, Dux, and Universal CD Accord.

Composer's personality

She's energetic, she's happy, she talks fast and a lot, but also charms people with her modest attitude.

Remarkable anecdote or biographical fact

Ptaszyńska has a specific gift—her synesthetic, visual hearing. She perceives music as colors; while looking at an image, she can hear sound. As she has admitted in interviews, these phenomena are the result of her emotional musical experiences and are reflected in a specific element of her compositions, namely harmony. She shares this phenomenon with Olivier Messiaen, but they do not envision the same colors for the same phenomena; for example, if some musical structure appeared to Ptaszyńska in light green, Messiaen would see it in blue. Debussy's music, commonly associated with the impressionist palette, appears to Ptaszyńska in shades of brown. As a child, the artist was also able to levitate, as described in the book *Music is the most perfect language* [*Muzyka to język najdoskonalszy*].

Respondent's Top Choices

- **Favorite work:** *Marimba Concerto* (1985), especially its second movement, "Eye of Silence" [Oko ciszy]. This music affirms the beauty of the world, brings positive energy, and encourages contemplation and relaxation. This movement is Ptaszyńska's musical illustration of Max Ernst's famous painting. In the music, she shows the beauty of marimba timbres.

  P.S., If I were a child, I would not hesitate to answer this question: *Mr Marimba* [*Pan Marimba*]!
- **Best work:** It's hard to select one for a living composer who is still writing new pieces. Looking at Ptaszyńska's impressive output to date, many great works have gained recognition. I will select one: the *Holocaust Memorial Cantata* (1991), written in commemoration of the victims of the twentieth century. It is a moving piece that cannot leave anybody indifferent.
- **Composition still waiting to be discovered:** *The Last Waltz in Vienna* (2001), a piece for three accordions written for the Motion Trio. Definitely worth discovering, and not only by accordion lovers!

Respondent: Magdalena Nowicka-Ciecierska

Karol Rathaus

Date and place of birth:
16 September 1895, Tarnopol.

Date of death:
21 November 1954, New York.

Date and place of emigration:
1920, Germany (Berlin); 1932, France (Paris); 1934, Great Britain (London); 1938, United States (New York).

Return to Poland:
He did not return.

Key quote

My problem is that I'm an independent, but ignored composer who has a very individual approach.[296]

Activities before emigration

He studied composition in Vienna (1913–1915, 1919–1920) and Berlin (1920–1923) and history at the University of Vienna (he received his Ph.D. in 1922 after defending a thesis about Romuald Traugutt and the January Uprising). The peak of his popularity occurred between 1922 and 1932. Initially perceived as an extremely modern composer (critic Walter Schrenk called him "one of the greatest hopes of new music"), eventually he softened his musical language. The composer's scores were released by such important publishers as Universal Edition. We should mention his ballets *Der letzte Pierrot* (1927) and *Le Lion amoureux* (commissioned by Ballet Russes, 1937) and a five-act opera, *Fremde Erde* (1930), which was popular during the interwar period. Aside from his concert and stage works, he was also a successful film music composer (he gained fame thanks to *Der Mörder Dimitri Karamasoff*, directed by Fedor Ozep).

After emigration

Rathaus initially tried his luck in Hollywood, but the approach to film music there was different than in Europe and both the lack of cooperation between directors and composers and the idea of treating film music as being less prestigious discouraged him. He accepted a job as a lecturer at the Aaron Copland School of Music at Queens College, City University of New York, where he taught theory and composition for the rest of his life. He also maintained links with the Polish diaspora and composed pieces they commissioned.

Differences between the old and new realities

Emigrating to the United States saved his life, but in his new country (he identified himself as both a Polish and an American citizen), he never became as significant a figure as he had been in Europe before the war. Regardless, like many musician-refugees who ended up in American academia, he contributed to the promotion of European musical traditions in his new home.

Reason for leaving Poland

After his studies in Vienna and Berlin, he worked in Germany, where his talent blossomed and he was highly respected. However, the rise of anti-Semitism in Germany forced him to leave. His long journey through Paris (1932–1933), London (1934–1938), and Los Angeles (1938–1940) eventually ended in New York (1940–1954).

Contact with Poland after emigration

Rathaus visited Europe after World War II, but never came to Poland again.

Influence of the new home on the composer's music

Life as an emigrant during the war years reinforced his identity as a person of Polish origin, as proven by the influence of folklore in his works from that period and in his choice of forms, lyrics, and titles. An especially popular piece was *Polonaise Symphonique* (1943), commissioned by conductor Artur Rodziński and played by a radio station in New York "to brace the hearts." Also popular were *Mazurka* and *Polish Polka* [*Polska polka*] for piano (1941) and *Three Polish Dances* [*Trzy polskie tańce*] (1942). In contrast, in his earlier compositions, he had avoided folk themes and used German lyrics, his primary language during his student days and his first years of work. In later years, Rathaus became a supporter of the Zionist movement; he composed music for two documentaries from 1945 and 1946—*Gateway to Freedom* [also known as *Histadrut*] and *Song of Israel* [*Pieśń Izraela*]). He demonstrated his appreciation for his new country by setting some of his music to the words of American poets.

Awareness of the composer's music in both countries

After the composer's death, the Karol Rathaus Memorial Association was founded and a building at Queens College CUNY was named after him. His compositions are regularly played at the college's music department, where he was its first dean. Two monographic albums have also been released by Composers Recordings Inc. (1988) and Koch (1998). In Poland, his works were almost never played during the Communist period and after 1989 the situation improved only slightly. The first album of his pieces was published in 2001 (string quartets, Acte Préalable) and more recently a recording of chamber music appeared in 2017 (DUX).

Composer's personality

He was cautious, reserved, liked, and respected by co-workers and students.

Remarkable anecdote or biographical fact

At the end of the academic year, Rathaus would organize a party with fireworks for his students in the garden of his home in Queens. He was remembered as an excellent musician and an outstanding teacher.

Respondent's Top Choices

- **Favorite work:** *After Domenico Scarlatti,* op. 56, for piano (1946).
- **Best work:** *Symphony No. 2,* op. 7 (1924), the most radical work in terms of tonality.
- **Composition still waiting to be discovered:** *Trio Serenade* for violin, cello and piano, op. 69 (1953).

Respondent: Jolanta Guzy-Pasiak

Konstanty (Constantin) Regamey

Date and place of birth:
28 January 1907, Kyiv.

Date and place of death:
27 December 1982, Lausanne.

Date and place of emigration:
1944, Switzerland (Lausanne).

Return to Poland:
He did not return.

Key quote

Obviously I am Swiss. I have a Swiss name and nobody questions it. I hold important positions there. At the same time, in the field of music, it is difficult for me not to consider myself Polish.[297]

Activities before emigration

After settling in Warsaw in 1920, he took private lessons in music theory, counterpoint, and harmony with composer Felicjan Szopski, and continued his piano lessons with eminent pianists Józef Turczyński and Antoni Dobkiewicz. At the age of 15, he worked as an accompanist at Maria Sobolewska's singing school. Via letters, his father gave him advice on composing. Suddenly, however, their contact was lost forever: In 1938 Konstanty Ferdinand was the victim of a Stalinist political murder.[298]

After receiving a master's degree in Oriental Studies Warsaw University in 1931, followed by a year's stay in Paris, Regamey taught classes in Indian Studies his home university. His educational career developed rapidly; he received a Ph.D. in Indian philology and the comparative grammar of Indo-European languages in 1935 and his habilitation degree in 1938.[299] The second half of the 1930s was also a time when Regamey's activity in the field of music criticism and aesthetics flourished, even though Regamey had not formally studied these subjects. At the time, he was considered Poland's finest music critic, at least according to an opinion formulated by Stefan Kisielewski, his frequent polemicist. He gained considerable authority as a promoter of new music. Starting in 1936, he headed the editorial board of the *Biuletyn Muzyki Współczesnej*, published by the Polish Society for Contemporary Music. His *Content and Form in Music* [*Treść i forma w muzyce*] (1933) is considered to be one of the most valuable achievements of Polish aesthetic thought from that time. In it, he brought Stanisław Ignacy Witkiewicz's theory of Pure Form to the field of music aesthetics, explaining it in an innovative way. From 1937 until the outbreak of war, Regamey was the vice-president of the Polish Society for Contemporary Music and a member of the committee qualifying works by Polish composers for festivals of the International Society for Contemporary Music. For the last year before the outbreak of the war, he was editor-in-chief of *Muzyka Polska*. He was also a member of the Polish Oriental Studies Society.

After emigration

Beginning in 1945, Regamey lectured on Orientalism (initially also Slavic Studies) at the University of Lausanne and the University of Freiburg, simultaneously composing and writing texts about music.[300] One of the more sensational episodes in his postwar life was helping Andrzej Panufnik escape from Poland. At the same time he played an increasingly important role in Switzerland's musical life. The recognition and authority that he enjoyed is confirmed by the fact that he was elected president of the Swiss Musicians Union. He also chaired the Swiss section of the International Society for Contemporary Music (1963–1968), became a member of the ISCM's Executive Committee (1969–1973), and then remained a high-profile member of both groups. In 1956 he initiated a ten-year UNESCO project to promote understanding between the musical cultures of East and West. He was the founder and first chairperson of the Swiss Music Council (1964–1968). One of his closest friends was Paul Sacher, who performed and promoted his work.

Differences between the old and new realities

These worlds differed in almost every area, just as Switzerland is different from Poland. In both places, Regamey was a kind of meteorite who brightened musical life with his extraordinarily creative personality.

Reason for leaving Poland

In September 1919, during the cruel civil war, Regamey left Kyiv with his mother (his parents were divorced). Their route as refugees led through Crimea, Romania, and Lviv. As a thirteen-year-old along the way to Varna, he gave concerts that included his own compositions. In May 1920, they arrived in Warsaw, where, apart from his secondary school education, he continued to write music.

He spent the Warsaw Uprising in the city, staying in an apartment at Szustra Street until 27 September 1944. After the capitulation, he was transported (29 September - 16 October 1944) to the camp in Pruszków and then to the Stutthof camps in the Grabówek district of Gdynia and in Kelsterbach, near Frankfurt am Main (5–16 October 1944). After that, he was released in order to obtain documents from the Swiss deputy in Berlin, which allowed him to leave for Switzerland, where, together with his mother and wife, he arrived about 20 November 1944.

Contact with Poland after emigration

He remained in close contact with the Polish music community, exchanging letters with Witold Lutosławski and others. In March 1947 he arrived in Kraków as part of Don Suisse, a Swiss program that assisted war victims in Poland and elsewhere. He also became a member of the Polish Composers' Union. His works were performed at the Warsaw Autumn Festival and published by Polish Music Publishers. In 1959, the Warsaw Autumn Festival was the site of the world premiere of *Cinq études* and the following year Polish Music Publishers published his small book about Witold Małcużyński. Aside from that, he published articles, mostly polemical analyses of the situation of contemporary music, in Switzerland and Poland.

Influence of the new home on the composer's music

His works from the 1940s are based on more traditional compositional procedures, although they also display a type of thematic work characteristic of dodecaphonic technique and bear a number of innovative achievements, especially in terms of form and orchestral color. Regamey's first entirely dodecaphonic work was his *Music for Strings* [*Muzyka na smyczki*] (1951–1953). At the same time, this piece marks the beginning of his tendency to use serialist techniques more consistently. This found its most extreme expression in his *Don Robott* opera (1958–1965). This "neotonal dodecaphony" became the structural principle of a supra-stylist synthesis. In 1955, Regamey described his music as a kind of combination of traditional, new, and archaic elements (*novation et passéisme*) taken from the past as well as from contemporary experiments; for him, this was the result of applying the principle of creative freedom.

Openness to the world and the possibility to travel were, it seems, factors that influenced his music. He was strongly connected to Tibetan culture and also discovered Indian music. In 1959 he traveled around the world for three months. In Honolulu, he took part in a conference of philosophers from the East and West, where he met Zen Daisetsu Teitaro Suzuki, the author of works on Buddhism. During this time, he increasingly aimed at merging serial technique, aleatorism, quarter-tonality, and modalism with elements of traditional tonality, developing the principle of "ultrapantonalism." The stylistic pluralism of Regamey's later work resulted from his search for simultaneous effects of contrast and integration. These differed from collage techniques or even polystylistic qualities, which emphasize a heterogeneity of collected elements. He described this later, saying,

> In reality, I practice total freedom, taking advantage of everything from medieval forms to aleatoric compositions....I have now come to a certain type of pluralism (which my adversaries call 'eclecticism'!). However, I believe that eclecticism is not a flaw, as long as it is coherent. Bach or Monteverdi, after all, offered good examples of eclecticism. But no one would try to claim that Bach is not coherent....I fully support that kind of eclecticism! I mean, creativity is an expression of freedom. And the choice of a certain style, the choice of a certain school seems to me to be a great limitation. Creativity should reveal the composer's personality. This is all that matters. Does it matter whether it is eclectic or not?[301]

Awareness of the composer's music in both countries

Few of Regamey's compositions exist in recorded form. There is only the *Quintet* (1944), composed in occupied Warsaw, which in recent years has been released on Ebony Band and in the Poland Abroad series and has gained some popularity.

Composer's personality

He was universally liked, even adored. His unquestionably special personality was noticed by such great artists as Witold Lutosławski, who described him as such:

> A tall dark-haired man with dark, burning eyes and a penetrating gaze, a man of an unbelievable intellect. Talking to him was an extraordinary pleasure, because this amazing speaker was always thinking ahead, anticipating the questioner's thoughts, so that going through all the stages of a discussion wasn't necessary. The speed of communicating with him on even the most intricate issues, in comparison with the majority of people, was like flying a jet compared to driving an ordinary taxi. He was an expert in Sanskrit and Indian culture and a full professor at Warsaw University who spoke several dozen languages. He was a man whose brilliant musical talents allowed him to read any score smoothly on the piano. He did not need to practice because his fingers and brain seemed function together with such naturalness and ease, as if it was the most ordinary part of his everyday life. He was a brilliant and splendid music critic, a seasoned polemicist, and an advocate of progressive musical thought. This is how Konstanty Regamey was when I knew him in Warsaw in the 1930s.[302]

Remarkable anecdote or biographical fact

Regamey remembered that during the Nazi occupation, he led several parallel lives in the underground resistance movement, using a number of identities, although he offered only general information about this period. He explained his motivation for staying in Poland in 1939:

> Why did I stay in this hell, when I had a passport from a neutral country that would allow me to leave Poland without difficulty? I had a wife, family, and friends, many of whom died after arrest and torture. I would be ashamed to leave. I spent happy years in this country. I made a career and it would be disloyal for me to leave Poland at a time when life was becoming so difficult and dangerous. All the more so because I had a Swiss passport that gave me benefits: I risked less than the Poles, although, admittedly, people were often killed on the street for no reason at all! Thanks to my passport, I was able to put a document on my door certifying that I was a Swiss citizen, representing a nation that did not take part in the war. Until the Warsaw Uprising, the Gestapo respected this document. This allowed me to provide shelter to people, many of them leaders of the Polish resistance.[303]

Respondent's Top Choices

- **Favorite work:** *Seven Songs to Words of Omar Khayyam* [*Siedem pieśni do słów Imara Chajjama*] for bass-baritone and chamber orchestra (1942) and *Cinq études* for female voice and piano or small orchestra (1955–1956).
- **Best work:** opera *Don Robott* (1959-1965) to Erwin Tauber's libretto, which is only partially completed.
- **Composition still waiting to be discovered:** *Mio, mein Mio* (1973), a fairy tale in two acts with a prologue to Gerda Bächla's libretto, based on Astrid Lindgren's book.

Respondent: Katarzyna Naliwajek

Ludomir Michał Rogowski

Date and place of birth:
3 October 1881, Lublin.

Date and place of death:
13 March 1954, Dubrovnik.

Date and place of emigration:
1918, Croatia (Dubrovnik).

Return to Poland:
He did not return.

Key quote
An artist is nothing more than a medium, a liaison expressing the truths and the words of infinity, a pencil which should be well attuned, subordinate to the will of the great, eternal Artist.[304]

Activities before emigration
After studying in Warsaw, Leipzig, Munich, Rome, and Paris, he worked in Vilnius (1908–1911), where he founded a symphonic orchestra (together with Konstanty Gałkowski from Russia) and the Lute [Lutnia] choir at the Polish Music Society, an organization that aimed to promote Polish music. He also composed music for the plays staged at Ihnat Bujnicki's theater and arranged folk songs for the choir he conducted. He was famous for his composition of the unofficial Belarusian anthem *Who's Coming*, written to the words of Yanka Kupala (1909).

He spent World War I in France, in Paris and the Côte d'Azur, composing and performing on piano, leading a Polish choir, conducting concerts of his own music in aristocratic salons (including Natalie Clifford Barney's), and directing concerts organized by the Polish Artists Society in Paris and the Polish Circle in Nice. He came into contact with eminent personalities such as Anatole France, Gabriele d'Annunzio, Isadora Duncan, and other representatives of the European art world. After Poland regained independence, he was active in the areas of performance and journalism in Warsaw, as he strived to raise the musical level of society and promote national and Slavic music.

After emigration

In 1926 he left Poland for Dubrovnik, then belonging to the Kingdom of Serbs, Croats and Slovenes (later Yugoslavia, now Croatia), where he gained recognition and developed his own conception of pan-Slavic music (1926–1954). He remained in southern Europe for the rest of his life. He conducted choirs at the Catholic and Orthodox churches in Dubrovnik and also gave vocal lessons. He composed operas, ballets, symphonies, chamber music, and solo and choral songs—more than a hundred works, of which only a small portion have been published. His *idée fixe* was to form a Slavic brotherhood, an ideal that he proclaimed through art and journalistic activities.

Differences between the old and new realities

After Poland regained independence, Rogowski was active in Warsaw, an important cultural center. At that time he was one of Poland's leading composers; he was also known as a publicist and organizer of concert life. After moving to the provincial town of Dubrovnik, he lost the opportunity to exchange professional experiences and draw inspiration from other artists. Instead, he focused on developing his own concept of pan-Slavic music. He also worked with choral ensembles.

Reason for leaving Poland

The daily struggle for a position in the musical world frustrated Rogowski, who believed that art should attract attention on its own, without anyone needing to advertise it. His growing disillusionment with the relationships in the artistic world of interwar Warsaw made Rogowski flee to a provincial city in southern Europe, where he could enjoy his serenity and, moreover, the warm climate that was beneficial to his health. Rogowski, arriving in Dubrovnik at the age of 45, already had a reputation as an outstanding composer and conductor, which he owed to his performances in Poland, France, Monte Carlo, and Belgium. Having such a well-known artist in Dubrovnik (the Czech composer Josef Vlach-Vrutický was also there) was a big event and a source of pride for residents. As a reward for composing a mysterium of St. Blaise (the patron saint of Dubrovnik), the town's authorities offered him a free apartment in the former Benedictine monastery of St. James, thus contributing to his decision to stay in "Slavic Athens."

Contact with Poland after emigration

He made short visits to Poland before World War II; thereafter, contacts were limited to correspondence with artists and friends who sometimes visited him in his Yugoslavian hermitage.

Influence of the new home on the composer's music

The traditions and music of Dalmatia, as well as the area of the former Yugoslavia in general, were used by Rogowski in his work not only as new sources of inspiration, but also as expressions of his enthusiasm for the idea of Slavic brotherhood. In his mature works, the composer merged elements of Polish, Croatian, and Serbian music.

Awareness of the composer's music in both countries

Rogowski's compositions are a permanent part of the repertoire of the Dubrovnik Philharmonic; they are also performed during the summer international festival held every year in that city. A recording of his symphonic music was released in Croatia (Cantus, 2011). In Poland, his songs and piano miniatures are played; a recording devoted entirely to his vocal music was released in 2017 (DUX).

Composer's personality

He was a dreamer, an introvert, and a romantic who preferred faithfulness to his ideals over financial gain. He was commonly perceived as eccentric, due to his behavior and manner of dressing (he wore a very long black coat as a kind of artist's uniform, even during warm days in Dubrovnik).

Remarkable anecdote or biographical fact

Rogowski, despite his small posture and rather plain appearance, enjoyed a great deal of interest from women, both during his less than ten-year marriage to Ludwika Nawroczyńska and later when he was adored by his vocal female students.

Respondent's Top Choices

- **Favorite work:** *Fantasmagories* for female voice (without text) and chamber orchestra (1920), due to its original musical language and orchestration, including its instrumental treatment of the human voice.
- **Best work:** *Symphony No. 2 "Joyous"* (1936), the first work in which the composer fully reaffirmed his vision of national music, using sound materials of folk and oriental origins.
- **Composition still waiting to be discovered:** The monumental vocal-instrumental mysterium *Miracle of St. Blaise* [*Čudo svetog Vlaha*] for solo voices, choir, and orchestra (1927), dedicated to the patron saint of Dubrovnik. This piece contains local literary and musical themes; for some time it was considered to be the town's unofficial anthem. The work's premiere was attended by more than 300 artists. It was a great success, thanks to which the Polish composer gained recognition in Dubrovnik. The piece is now considered lost, although a fragment of the first movement has recently been found.

Respondent: Jolanta Guzy-Pasiak

Roman Ryterband

Date and place of birth:
2 August 1914, Łódź.

Date and place of death:
17 November 1979, Palm Springs, United States.

Date and place of emigration:
1939, Switzerland (Bern); 1955, Canada (Montreal); 1960, United States (Chicago, and since 1967, Palm Springs).

Return to Poland:
Ryterband returned to Poland for a short period in 1946 in order to find his missing relatives.

Key quote

People of the world in which we are compelled to live are unfortunately separated by a great deal of differences. These differences certainly make the world and our life colorful and sparkling, but overplayed they produce discord, unrest, and suffering. Believing in the high mission of the arts, and in music as the most sublime international language, I have ever since preached understanding among people by means of this universal idiom. I trust that my share might contribute to getting a bit closer toward the ideals of harmony, happiness, and mutual respect—ideals pursued by the people of our great country since its inception and by mankind in general.[305]

Activities before emigration

Ryterband spent the first 25 years of his life in Poland. He came from a wealthy Jewish family of lawyers and musicians from Łódź. At an early age he learned to play the piano, make music with his family, and create his first compositions. He took piano lessons at Helena Kijeńska's Conservatory in Łódź. Due to his father's pressure (he was a lawyer), he also graduated from Warsaw University. The 1930s were filled with composing, conducting, and extensive concert tours in Poland and abroad.

After emigration

Ryterband lived in Bern, Switzerland until 1955. There, he completed his musical studies and obtained his Ph.D. in musicology, at the same time performing, composing, and working as a teacher and conductor. In Switzerland he also met his future wife, Clarissa de Lazzari, started a family, and in 1954 was granted Swiss citizenship. At the same time, however, he began to think about moving to America. He went to Montreal in 1955; after another five years, he went to Chicago, eventually spending the last twelve years of his life in Palm Springs, California.

Differences between the old and new realities

The young, extremely talented musician and composer left Poland on the eve of World War II, not knowing that in the blink of an eye, it would not be his home for many years. Living in exile—first in Switzerland, then in Canada and the United States—allowed him to develop an international career, continue his education, establish valuable contacts, and provide a stable financial situation for himself and his family.

Reason for leaving Poland

Ryterband was on a tour of Western European countries when war broke out in September 1939. He managed to reach Switzerland on one of the last trains before the border was closed. The country that gave him shelter in such urgent circumstances became home to the composer and his family for the next fifteen years.

Contact with Poland after emigration

Although Ryterband never returned to Poland, at all stages of his artistic activity and in all the countries where he lived, he was active in Polish communities and engaged in initiatives related to Polish culture. He led Polish community choirs, organized concerts, and worked with Polish artists.

Influence of the new home on the composer's music

Learning about various languages and cultures was the composer's great passion. Thanks to his studies and academic activities in Bern, Ryterband had the opportunity to deepen his ethnomusicological interests. He conducted research in the folk music of various cultures and nations, including Slavic, Swiss, Italian, and African-American, whose elements he later used in his own works. Ryterband, both as a musician and composer, was extremely open to collaborating with other artists and experimenting with various genres and instrumental ensembles. There was always room in his work for classical compositions, religious works, and popular music.

Awareness of the composer's music in both countries

Ryterband's oeuvre still remains largely unknown, especially in Poland. The preserved manuscripts and documents of the composer were donated by his family to the Polish Music Center at the University of Southern California in Los Angeles, which aims to preserve and popularize the achievements of Polish composers. Some of his compositions can also be found in Harvard University's Houghton Library and Moldenhauer Collections. It is thanks to the great involvement of the composer's family that his works are performed more frequently and his lesser known compositions have been recorded and published.

Composer's personality

He was a man who, in his private and artistic lives, expressed courage, enthusiasm, and curiosity about the world. His artistic activity in many areas, as well as his involvement in various cultural initiatives everywhere where he lived, prove that he enjoyed new things and was always ready for different challenges.

Remarkable anecdote or biographical fact

Jakub, Roman Ryterband's uncle, was the first violinist of the Łódź Philharmonic. When Abram, the father of the young composer, found out about Jakub's economic problems, he tried everything to discourage his son from continuing his musical education. The young pianist never abandoned his greatest passion but he eventually fulfilled his father's wish and graduated in law from Warsaw University.

Respondent's Top Choices

- **Favorite work:** *Suite Polonaise (Ten Regional Dances)* (1944) for piano (the orchestral version has never been performed) and *Sonata Breve* for violin and harp (1961).
- **Best work:** *Suite Polonaise* for piano and its orchestral version (1977, arranged by Tadeusz Dobrzański), which was dedicated to Pope John Paul II and Poles around the world.
- **Composition still waiting to be discovered:** the symphonic poem *Vida Heroica* (1953).

Respondents: Iwona Granacka and Diana Eisele (Roman Ryterband's daughter)

Zbigniew Seifert

Date and place of birth:
7 June 1946, Kraków.

Date and place of death:
15 February 1979, Buffalo (United States).

Date and place of emigration:
1973, Germany; 1976, United States.

Return to Poland:
He returned to Poland in 1978 for a special tour.

Key quote

There was no such violinist before—he's our national treasure.[306]

Activities before emigration

He was always strongly associated with Kraków's jazz community. While only sixteen, he created his own quartet, with which he began to conquer the Polish jazz scene. His excellent compositions and outstanding improvisation skills were noticed by Tomasz Stańko, who invited Seifert to join his quintet in 1968 (and with whom he played until 1973). While he was in Stańko's band, he discovered how to play jazz violin, which eventually replaced the saxophone in his performances.

After emigration

Going to Germany had great influence on the development of his career. In 1973 he began working with the Austrian saxophonist Hans Koller. In 1974 he recorded an album with German pianist Jasper van't Hof. During the same year, Seifert composed and recorded *Concerto for Improvisational Violin, Rhythm Section, and Orchestra*. Later, he made his first recording—the album *Solo Violin*, which contains excellent compositions and Seifert's own virtuoso improvisations. His move to the United States resulted in a contract with the Capitol label. His most significant albums include *Zbigniew Seifert*, *Violin* (with the Oregon band), *Passion*, and one of the most important records in the history of jazz, *Man of the Light*.

Differences between the old and new realities

Seifert's career gained momentum when he went abroad. It allowed him to work with the finest artists from Europe and the United States. Seifert said that emigration offered him what he expected: many contacts, musical experience, and freedom. He became an independent and recognizable musician.

Reason for leaving Poland

Seifert left Poland primarily to develop his career. The violinist received an offer from the Austrian saxophonist Hans Koller. Thanks to a special invitation sent from Germany to the Pagart Polish Artistic Agency, he was able to leave without difficulties and soon got used to living in the West.

Contact with Poland after emigration

In 1978 Seifert returned to Kraków. Special concerts were organized for a wide audience. These concerts were recorded and posthumously released on the Kilimanjaro concert album. During these performances, Seifert was accompanied by Kraków musicians: Jarosław Śmietana, guitar; Janusz Grzywacz, piano; Zbigniew Wegehaupt, double bass; and Mieczysław Górka, percussion. Unfortunately, as Seifert explained in an interview attached to the album, this line-up of musicians was not quite optimal. The Polish players differed quite a bit from those with whom he had made his previous records. He said that it was hard for him to play with the Kraków band, but he also emphasized that this was the result of a lack of experience among the city's jazz musicians. These were his last performances in Poland. Later, Zbigniew Seifert left again for the United States.

Influence of the new home on the composer's music

Seifert's music blossomed. The music of John Coltrane and McCoy Tyner had a big impact on his own work. On the *Man of the Light* album, which offers world-class, mainstream jazz at the highest level, he fully expressed his personal musical language.

Awareness of the composer's music in both countries

Zbigniew Seifert, one of the most important jazz violinists in the world, inspired many musicians. The Zbigniew Seifert Foundation established in Poland promotes his music and publishes scores and previously unreleased recordings. Every two years the Zbigniew Seifert International Jazz Violin Competition for violinists, violists, and jazz cellists is also organized.

Composer's personality

He was trained as a classical violinist from an early age, but his love of jazz music allowed him to develop the unconventional combination of improvisation and traditional violin playing. His love of John Coltrane's music helped him transfer Coltrane's style to violin. He said that he offered his heart and his strength to jazz. He was not afraid of new challenges. He lived intensely, even when he already aware that he suffered from cancer. Apart from his love for jazz, he liked the life of a jazz musician. He avoided schemes and routines in his life, while expressing optimism and a sense of humor.

Remarkable anecdote or biographical fact

There is an anecdote saying that Zbyszek did not like to wear his watch while playing violin. At a concert in Germany, he took off his watch and put it in front of him. He closed his eyes and started playing solo. When he opened his eyes, the watch was gone. I think that if it were not for Zbigniew's early death, we would have heard him on a recording with McCoy Tyner.

Respondent's Top Choices

- **Favorite work:** *City of Spring* (1976?)
- **Best work:** *Man of the Light* (1977?)
- **Composition still waiting to be discovered:** *Jazz Concerto* [*Koncert jazzowy*] for violin, symphony orchestra and rhythm group.

Respondent: Tomasz Chyła

Elżbieta Sikora

Date and place of birth:
20 October 1943, Lviv.

Date and place of emigration:
1981, France (Paris).

Return to Poland:
She has not returned.

Key quote
We don't know when the first sound was made. We discuss the birth of music, yet sound is in the dolphin's song, the lion's roar, the rabbit's squeak, the highlander's call…and in the noise made by cars.[307]

Activities before emigration
She graduated from the Department of Sound Engineering (studying with Antoni Karuzas) at the State Higher School of Music in Warsaw (currently the Chopin University of Music). After a two-year stay in France, she returned to Warsaw, where she studied composition with Tadeusz Baird and Zbigniew Rudziński, again at the State Higher School of Music. During her university years, she, Krzysztof Knittel, and Wojciech Michniewski founded the KEW ensemble (the acronym consists of the first letters of names Krzysztof, Elżbieta, and Wojciech). In 1979 in Warsaw, the premiere of her one-act opera *Ariadne* [*Ariadna*] took place. This composition was recorded the same year by Polskie Nagrania Muza.

After emigration
The artist's first stay in Paris in 1968 lasted two years, during which she studied with Pierre Schaeffer and François Bayle. In 1981 the composer moved permanently to Paris where, having received a scholarship from the French government, she took a computer music course at the Institut de Recherche et de Coordination Acoustique/Musique (IRCAM) and then studied composition with Betsy Jolas (1982–1983). Thanks to a scholarship from the Kosciuszko Foundation, in 1983–1984 she worked under the direction of John Chowning, the American composer and inventor of FM synthesis, at the Center for Computer

Research for Music and Acoustics (CCRMA) at Stanford University. From 1985–1999, she lectured on electroacoustic composition at the conservatory and the school of fine arts in Angoulême.

Differences between the old and new realities

Sikora left Poland during the Communist era, so going to a vibrant France at the end of the 1960s proved to be an unusual cultural experience that was related both to the specific atmosphere of Paris and its greater creative freedom. In 1968 she left her home country with a diploma in sound engineering, but in order to make a living in Paris, she was initially forced to reach for various part-time activities, such as working at a gas station.

Reason for leaving Poland

In one of her interviews, the composer explained that one reason for her departure was her fascination with French culture, which she shared with her family.[308] Sikora first went to Paris in 1968 to study with the most important pioneers of electroacoustic music. She had already planned to stay in France with her husband, director Krzysztof Rogulski. He was banned from leaving Poland in 1970 for making a politically inappropriate documentary, which prompted Sikora to return to Poland. She left for Paris again in 1981; after martial law was imposed in Poland, she decided to stay abroad permanently.

Contact with Poland after emigration

The composer visits Poland frequently and participates in its musical life. In 1999 she received her doctorate in composition from the Academy of Music in Wrocław. From 2011 to 2017, she directed the Musica Electronica Nova festival in Wrocław.

Influence of the new home on the composer's music

Sikora went to Paris for a specific purpose—to study electroacoustic music. There, she gained not only contacts with the most important artists of this genre, which was important for her creative development, but also access to advanced technical equipment. The artist still regards France as one of the main centers of electroacoustic music.

Awareness of the composer's music in both countries

Sikora's music is appreciated in both countries, although paradoxically, as the artist admits in one of her statements, in France she is still treated as a Polish composer, while in Poland her work is perceived as French.[309] In both countries, Sikora's music is often performed at festivals, and the artist has been awarded two of the most important state honors in Polish and French cultural heritage: the Knight's Cross of the Order of Merit in Poland and the Chevalier de l'Ordre des Arts et des Lettres in France.

Composer's personality

Sikora is perceived as an excellent organizer, as evidenced by the programs of the Musica Electronica Nova festival in Wrocław when she was its director. One sign of her great strength of character was her willingness to leave her homeland to study in France. It is no coincidence that the composer wanted a strong, outstanding woman as the heroine of her latest opera; she found one in the person of Maria Curie-Skłodowska.

Remarkable anecdote or biographical fact

One anecdote illustrating the composer's sonic fascinations is related to her electroacoustic piece called *Grain de sable* for the studio in Bourges. The composition is based on the sounds of different types of glass (including bottles and light bulbs) being broken. To make the recordings, Sikora located the site where glass from giant containers was to be poured into trucks and got the truck driver to agree to let her record the sounds. She owes her interest in unusual sounds to Pierre Schaeffer's lectures; this curiosity is still present in her work.

Respondent's Top Choices

- **Favorite work:** An interesting example of her early work on tape is *Voyage II* [*Podróż II*] (1976), commissioned by the Polish Radio Experimental Studio. The composition's sound layer, in which echoes of electronically processed instruments and whispers reverberate, fits into the compositional trend of sonorism, which in the mid-1970s was rarely practiced. However, the contemplative, almost minimalist form of the piece still yields fresh and interesting sounds despite its technological age.
- **Best work:** One of her most important premieres in recent years was *Madame Curie*, an opera staged in 2011 at the UNESCO Hall in Paris. Electronics add color to the orchestral sound; some of the acoustic instruments she used are guitar and accordion. The work's libretto is based on the life of the Polish Nobel Prize winner—a strong, independent figure who, like Sikora, emigrated to France and bound her life to that country.
- **Composition still waiting to be discovered:** The radio opera *Derrière son double* (1983), written for French Radio, remains her least known work in the opera genre. It was commissioned by the then-head of the Atelier de Création Radiophonique, Alain Trutat. The almost thirty-minute composition, using Jean-Pierre Duprey's libretto, was written for soprano, baritone, four actors, string quartet, flute, and percussion.

Respondent: Ewa Chorościan

Stanisław Skrowaczewski

Date and place of birth:
3 October 1923, Lviv.

Date of death:
21 February 2017, St. Louis Park, Minnesota.

Date and place of emigration:
1960, United States (Minneapolis).

Return to Poland:
He did not return.

Key quote

When I received an offer to go to America, I was happy. It was a different world. I stopped arguing and worrying and focused on music instead. After some time, I realized how abnormal the atmosphere surrounding my work in Poland was. Now I know that I used to feel as if I was standing upside down and everyone else tried to prove that it was a perfectly natural position. I had to leave Poland in order to be able to see this all from a distance.[310]

Activities before emigration

After World War II, Stanislaw Skrowaczewski went from Lviv to Kraków, where he continued his education at the State Higher School of Music, studying composition with Roman Palester and conducting with Walerian Bierdiajew. In 1946 he became director of the Wrocław Philharmonic; a year later he went to study composition in Paris with Nadia Boulanger. During his stay in Paris, he and three of his fellow composers—Maurice Ohana, Pierre de La Forest Divonne, and Alain Bermat—founded the Zodiaque ensemble, whose aim was to discover beauty in new music. In 1949 he returned to Poland and was appointed artistic director of the Silesian Philharmonic. From 1954–1956 he conducted the Kraków Philharmonic and from 1956–1959 he was employed as a conductor of the National Philharmonic in Warsaw.

His own compositions included *Night Music* [*Muzyka nocą*] (1949) and *Symphony for Strings* (1947–1949), which were important works at that time. In 1953, he won second prize at the International String Quartet Competition in Liège for his *Third String Quartet*, and in 1956 his *Symphonic Suite* received a gold medal at a Moscow composers' competition.

Also in 1956 Skrowaczewski won the International Conducting Competition in Rome, after which he was invited by George Szell to work in the United States. He made his debut there in 1958 with the Philadelphia Orchestra. A year later he visited the United States again, conducting orchestras in New York, Philadelphia, and Cincinnati. In 1960 he accepted an offer to become the artistic director of the Minneapolis Symphony Orchestra and settled in the United States permanently.

After emigration

He spent nineteen years working as a conductor with the Minneapolis Symphony Orchestra (now the Minnesota Orchestra). In his repertoire, he included works by Polish composers, among them Szymanowski, Lutosławski, Penderecki, Bacewicz, Baird, Palester, and Panufnik. While he was the orchestra's director, he refrained from programming his own compositions. In 1995, he composed *Passacaglia immaginaria*, one of his most important works, after receiving a commission from the orchestra.

Due to his intense conducting career and constant work as artistic director of the Minneapolis orchestra, Skrowaczewski's compositional work was pushed into the background. At the request of the orchestra's musicians, he composed an *English Horn Concerto* in 1969 and *Ricercari Notturni* for saxophone or clarinet and orchestra in 1977. His full return to composing occurred later, in the 1980s and 1990s, when he wrote his most important works: *Violin Concerto* (1985), *Symphony* (2003), and the aforementioned *Passacaglia immaginaria* (1995).

Differences between the old and new realities

The Polish People's Republic in the 1950s, with all of its political limitations, and the United States in the same era represented two radically different worlds. The freedom of the Western world gave Skrowaczewski the opportunity to develop his conducting career internationally, without having to face Poland's sometimes absurd political and cultural constraints.

Reason for leaving Poland

Skrowaczewski wanted to develop an international conducting career, but travel restrictions and other policies implemented by Poland's Communist government significantly limited his plans. Poland's government made it difficult for Skrowaczewski to travel abroad and take part in international activities. His wife, whose father before World War II owned a well-known health resort, Truskawiec Zdrój near Drohobycz, experienced complications as well. They both accepted their departure from Poland with relief. As the artist recalled:

> We left together, but with great difficulty. They did not want to give us passports. Luckily, by chance the Prime Minister appeared at a meeting of the Polish Composers' Union. One of my friends asked him why he would not let me leave the country: 'Why won't they give him a passport?' The Prime Minister was surprised and had the passports issued immediately. This happened three hours before our planned departure. We packed within an hour. We left Poland with one suitcase. We lost everything else that was in our apartment.[311]

Contact with Poland after emigration

After settling in the United States, the artist visited Poland only after 21 years. After that, he was invited back regularly to conduct concerts in various parts of the country. Towards the end of his life he came to Poland at least once a year, primarily conducting symphonies by his beloved Anton Bruckner. He sometimes included his own compositions in these programs. He was always welcomed in Poland, with his performances selling out. He received numerous awards for his artistic activity: In 1999 he received the Commander's Cross with Star of the Order of Polonia Restituta and in 2014 the Grand Cross of the Order of Polonia Restituta. In 2002 he accepted the title of First Guest Conductor of the National Polish Radio Symphony Orchestra in Katowice. In 2004 he received an honorary doctorate from the Academy of Music in Wrocław and in 2012 the Karol Szymanowski Academy of Music in Katowice honored him with the same degree. He became an honorary member of the Polish Composers' Union in 2005. In 2009 in Katowice, he received the "Diamond Baton," an award granted by Polish Radio's Executive Board, and in 2015 the Polish music community awarded him the honorary award of the Coryphaeus of Polish Music for his lifetime achievements.

Influence of the new home on the composer's music

Emigration did not seem to have a major impact on Skrowaczewski's musical output, except for the fact that he suspended his composing career for many years due to his need to concentrate on conducting. Undoubtedly, his excellent knowledge of the orchestra and its individual instruments was conducive to his compositional work. His own pieces are always precisely written down and "friendly" to performers, even if their texture is dense and their musical language inspired by dodecaphonic techniques and polyphony (e.g., *Passacaglia immaginaria*). In his compositions, a distinct "romantic" gesture is communicated through an emotional depth of expression reminiscent of late nineteenth-century works, which is combined with a remarkable sonic imagination, all achieved while maintaining a clarity of construction and logic of musical narration.

Awareness of the composer's music in both countries

Skrowaczewski's music is poorly known in Poland and the United States. He is primarily esteemed as a conductor, especially as an unrivalled interpreter of Bruckner's symphonies. As a conductor, he has been universally praised, as evidenced by excellent reviews, hundreds of recordings, and honorary doctorates awarded by the universities of St. Paul and Minnesota and the New England Conservatory of Music, among others. He received commissions for new compositions, often from musicians with whom he worked. He usually conducted his own pieces himself, but his music remains in the shadow of his conducting career.

Composer's personality

He was a very warm and modest man with a great working discipline. Devoted to his wife and family, he enjoyed composing at home. He admitted that after a busy concert season he had to take a break from music, preferably by walking in the mountains or skiing. Only after such a "reset" was he able to resume composing.

Remarkable anecdote or biographical fact

Skrowaczewski led an active conducting career for over seventy years, amassing a record of public performances comparable to that of Leopold Stokowski. Many of the composer's early works (including the Liège-awarded *Third String Quartet*) went missing after the family departed Poland, since they left most of their belongings in that country.

Respondent's Top Choices

- **Favorite work:** *Passacaglia immaginaria* for orchestra (1995).
- **Best work:** *Symphony* (2003).
- **Composition still waiting to be discovered:** Most of the composer's oeuvre awaits discovery, starting with his early compositions, the *Symphony for Strings* (1947–1949) and the orchestral variations titled *Night Music* (1949).

Respondent: Beata Bolesławska-Lewandowska

Bettina Skrzypczak

Date and place of birth:
25 January 1963, Poznań.

Date and place of emigration:
1988, Switzerland (Riehen).

Return to Poland:
She lives in Switzerland and regularly visits Poland.

Key quote

At the center of my attention are issues concerning the boundaries of musical aesthetics and philosophy, such as transcendence in art, the question of chaos (mainly in the approach of early Romantic German philosophers), points of tangency between science and art (the work of Iannis Xenakis and one's own reflection in Eulerian composition), and relationships between music and visual arts (such as in the case of Alberto Giacometti).[312]

Activities before emigration

Bettina Skrzypczak was born in Poznań in 1963. She completed her education in the same city, studying composition (with Andrzej Koszewski) and music theory at the Ignacy Jan Paderewski Academy of Music. Immediately after graduating, she decided to continue her studies abroad. While still in Poland, she made her compositional debut with two very good, fresh-sounding works, *ABC* for tape (1986) and *What is Black What is White* for two percussionists (1987). Her 1991 work, *String Quartet No. 2,* brought her international fame; the piece received a prize at the UNESCO International Composers Tribune in Paris. The distinctive features of her compositional style could already be heard in her earliest works. Formally, these pieces are often one-movement compositions with a quite striking internal division. Fluctuations of tension and timbre that align with asymmetrical lines, arcs, and structures are key features of this music.

After emigration

For further studies, Skrzypczak chose the Hochschule für Musik in Basel, where she studied composition with Rudolf Kelterborn and electronic music with Thomas Kessler. At the same time, she also studied musicology at the University of Freiburg.

Differences between the old and new realities

Skrzypczak belongs to a group of artists whose clear, individual style could be observed early on. Her studies and experiences abroad allowed her creativity to flourish. In Switzerland, she took up teaching and developed her compositional skills.

Reason for leaving Poland

An important reason for emigrating was the desire to continue her studies in the field of electronic music. These efforts became a starting point for developing her own individual interest in the area of timbre, with which she experimented in orchestral works and other pieces.

Contact with Poland after emigration

Skrzypczak's oeuvre has been presented in Poland on many occasions, including at the Warsaw Autumn Festival. She has divided her time between Switzerland and Poland, in terms of both composing as well as teaching. Since 2002 she has been a professor with Hochschule Luzern – Musik in Switzerland, and since 2010, a visiting professor at the Feliks Nowowiejski Academy of Music in Bydgoszcz. In her own teaching, she has succeeded at conveying her experiences as a composer as well as the knowledge she has gained from meeting eminent figures. About her work with students, the composer has said:

> I focus primarily on teaching composition. I strive to develop students as comprehensively as possible….I consider it a particular pedagogical challenge to support students on their compositional path without imposing any aesthetic models on them. Inspired by the practical aspect of teaching, in Lucerne I introduced a topic called 'Modern Instrumentation and Its Application in Practice'. Important elements of this subject include cooperating with instrumental teachers and experts representing such areas as acoustics and sound engineering, presenting acoustical phenomena in a practical way (e.g., the specifics of instrumental sounds and their application in practice, the analysis of the properties of individual instruments using electronic means), studying timbre and performance techniques (based on students' own etudes), and conducting live workshops during which students' compositions are performed and discussed.[313]

Skrzypczak also teaches topics in the humanities at the Hochschule Luzern – Musik, with an emphasis on music aesthetics and philosophy. She has also introduced a course called "Composing at School," which is a methodical preparation of future music school teachers.

Influence of the new home on the composer's music

Studying electronic music with Thomas Kessler and perfecting her creative skills during computer and live-electronics courses have yielded excellent results, not only in her purely electronic music but also in her instrumental compositions. One development has been her use of microtonality and unconventional ways of using acoustic instruments and the human voice. In her creative process, she precedes her actual composing with a period of experimentation during which she works and improvises with musicians. Skrzypczak is also fascinated by contemporary and traditional musical rhetoric as well as the issue of time, which she considers important for the development of form. The use of rich combinations of timbre and dynamics, as well as a characteristic arranging of the orchestra into groups introduces listeners to a polyphony of complex sonic layers.

An excellent balance between experimentation, improvisation, and empirical experience can be observed in the compositions she has created in Switzerland. What is important to her in the first moment of creation is movement and emotions, and in a later stage, the organization and rationalization of ideas and feelings, which are ultimately subjected to critical examination. Perhaps the composer's tendency to compose asymmetrical one-movement pieces developed from these experiences. These works, in turn, are the result of various inspirations. This is the case, for example, in the composition *SN 1993 J*, whose title is the catalog number of a supernova. Figures, strands, and uneven lines are the result of viewing the latest photos of the supernova; for obvious reasons, they cannot convey reality. They are only a presumption, hence the blurred lines and points of the music. *Vier Figuren* was inspired by Albert Giacometti's sculptures. It contains a sense of delight with detail and also with its often elusive, veiled entirety. The piece was inspired by four of Giacometti's sculptures: *Great Head*, *Walking Man II*, *Great Woman III*, and *Great Woman IV*. Each of them constitutes a specific central axis, a point of reference, hence there are three groups of instruments. The fourth sculpture, and at the same time all of them, are represented by the listeners. We experience migrating groups of sounds and a kind of three-dimensional plane. The listener can feel as if the sound was approaching or moving away from them or as if it was approaching one of the sculptures. Skrzypczak's creative attitude is characterized primarily by a deep sense of humanism and a love of art and science alike. In her work, both directly and as sources of inspiration, she draws on texts by such artists and researchers as Leonardo da Vinci, Jorge Luis Borges, Boethius, and Leonhard Euler. She has also been inspired by the visual works of the sculptor Alberto Giacometti and the supernova *Sn 1993 J*. As the composer herself stresses: "the artist and scientist share a common goal, which is to seek the truth."[314]

Awareness of the composer's music in both countries

Despite the presence of Skrzypczak's works on the Polish contemporary music circuit, the composer seems to be much more recognizable outside her home country. She constantly receives commissions for compositions that are performed by outstanding ensembles at renowned festivals around the world.

Composer's personality

Her personality is decidedly sincere, experimental, and oriented towards experience, with an interest in life and continual education. She is independent, non-conformist, and combines empirical experience with intuition.

Remarkable anecdote or biographical fact

In 2004, at Skrzypczak's initiative, the Ensemble Boswil für Neue Musik was created. She had a number of duties with this ensemble. From the very beginning, she was its artistic director, but that is not all she did. One can even claim that establishing the ensemble was a fulfilment of her dream to create a group in which it was possible to conduct ongoing experiments with timbre. The group's work reflects a harmonious combination of artistic and educational fascination and needs. The composer and her students all share an extraordinary opportunity to verify her ideas and her formal and sonic solutions.

Respondent's Top Choices

- **Favorite work:** *Vier figuren* for an ensemble of 18 musicians in three groups (2001).
- **Best work:** At present, it seems that the epitome of her experiences can be heard in *anomaly Lunae media* for soprano, baritone, and 15 instruments in three groups (2007).
- **Composition still waiting to be discovered:** *Miroirs* for mezzo-soprano and chamber ensemble (2000).

Respondent: Aleksandra Bilińska

Cezary Skubiszewski

Date and place of birth:
10 December 1948, Warsaw.

Date and place of emigration:
1974, Australia (Melbourne).

Return to Poland:
He has not returned.

Key quote
I believe that I am still on the road to self-discovery. Each task is a great challenge for me.[315]

Activities before emigration
He learned to play the piano. His discovery of Ray Charles was a breakthrough moment for him. He created a band with Aleksandr Bem and Janusz Zieliński, but did not plan to become a professional musician. He also played with Jerzy Bryl, Maciej Lipiński, Jerzy Wiernik, and Marek Doliński in a band initially called Viruses [Wirusy], then Deceased [Denaty] and finally ACB.

After emigration
In Australia he studied veterinary medicine at Melbourne University, but after a few years he returned to composing, creating the soundtrack for the series *Sky Trackers* (1994), and, before that, writing so-called serious music (*Home at Last*, 1981). In the mid-1990s Skubiszewski collaborated with director Jerzy Domaradzki, also an immigrant. The result of this meeting was *Lilian's Story* [*Historia Liliany*], for which he was nominated for an Australian Film Institute award.

Differences between the old and new realities
The political and economic situation in Poland made Skubiszewski's artistic development impossible. Australia gave him more opportunities.

Reason for leaving Poland
These reasons were related to both financial and professional matters. Although Skubiszewski has mentioned that his decision to emigrate was influenced by "political stuffiness," moving to Australia also allowed him to develop his composing career.

Contact with Poland after emigration

Skubiszewski works with Polish directors. In the early 2010s, he began to have more frequent professional contacts with Poland. In 2012 he wrote the soundtrack for Wiktor Skrzynecki's film *Felix, Net, Nika and the Theoretically Impossible Catastrophe* [*Felix, Net i Nika oraz teoretycznie niemożliwa katastrofa*], in 2014 he collaborated with Michał Otłowski on the score to *Jeziorak*, and in 2015 he composed the soundtrack to Krzysztof Łukaszewicz's *Karbala*. In addition, his music for Lawrence Johnston's film *Night* was recorded by the National Polish Radio Symphony Orchestra in Katowice.

Influence of the new home on the composer's music

In Poland, Skubiszewski played popular music and jazz. In Australia, along with beginning his career as a film composer, he began to write orchestral music, including pieces inspired by classical music. Still, he did not give up jazz and rock entirely.

Awareness of the composer's music in both countries

Skubiszewski is highly regarded in Australia. Twice he has been awarded the so-called Australian Oscar, i.e., the Australian Film Institute Award (today the Australian Academy of Film Art). He is known for his many cinema and television productions. In Poland, he is definitely less recognized, but worth promoting.

Composer's personality

He says about himself: "My system is that I simply put my head down and get to work." He is known for his diligence and his ability to make bold and difficult decisions, exemplified by emigrating to Australia and leaving veterinary studies for music.

Remarkable anecdote or biographical fact

While working on *The Sound of One Hand Clapping* [*Oklaski jednej dłoni*], Skubiszewski met the members of the Irish ensemble Riverdance, who were touring Australia. They agreed to play the music for Skubiszewski's new film, but stipulated, with a great sense of humor, that it should not contain Irish music. During a party one evening, Eimear Quinn sang in front of the guests. Her performance impressed Skubiszewski; after brief negotiations, she also agreed to perform a piece of his music for the same film. There was a problem, however—she and the company had to leave for additional touring the next day. Skubiszewski did not waste any time. Overnight, he composed a song for her, which they recorded the following morning.

Respondent's Top Choices

- **Favorite work:** *The Sound of One Hand Clapping*, directed by Richard Flanagan (1998), soundtrack.
- **Best work:** *The Red Dog* [*Przygody Rudego*], directed by Kriv Stenders (2011), soundtrack.
- **Composition still waiting to be discovered:** *La Spagnola*, directed by Steve Jacobs (2001), soundtrack.

Respondent: Grzegorz Dąbrowski

■

Michał Spisak

Date and place of birth:
14 September 1914, Dąbrowa Górnicza.

Date and place of death:
28 January 1965, Paris.

Date and place of emigration:
1937, France (Paris).

Return to Poland:
He did not return.

Key quote
You know that the meaning of my life is music alone. If even one bar, one second of my music gives someone pleasure, it will be a great source of joy for me.[316]

Activities before emigration
Spisak left Poland at the beginning of his creative career. Between 1933 and 1937 he studied violin with Józef Cetner and composition with Aleksander Brachocki; he also took private lessons with Kazimierz Sikorski at the Silesian Music Conservatory in Katowice. During this time, he worked as a violinist and created his first compositions. In recognition of his achievements, he received a scholarship to study in Paris in 1937.

After emigration
Spisak's attitude as a composer was shaped during his studies with the Nadia Boulanger; he became one of the most important representatives of neoclassicism. He was active in the Association of Young Polish Musicians in Paris, which promoted Polish music in France (he was successively its secretary, vice-president, and president). He maintained contacts with numerous Polish musicians who lived in Paris on artistic scholarships (including Grażyna Bacewicz). He spent the war years in Voiron, composing frequently. After the war, he returned to Paris, where he continued his dynamic creative activity, which was met with recognition and awards at international competitions, including the Queen Elisabeth of Belgium Music Competition in Brussels (for *Serenade* for orchestra, 1953, and *Concerto Giocoso* for chamber orchestra, 1957).

Differences between the old and new realities

France became a second homeland for Spisak. As a result of his studies with Boulanger and her many professional connections, he was presented with many opportunities to develop his compositional skills, broaden his creative skills, and present his works. In Paris, then the European capital of new music, he was able to become acquainted with the most up-to-date trends in composition and performance, which were later reflected in his own work.

Reason for leaving Poland

He received a scholarship for his high academic achievements at the Silesian Music Conservatory.

Contact with Poland after emigration

The composer always spoke fondly of his home country; he maintained relationships with his friends there, as evidenced by correspondence that has been preserved. He was involved in promoting Polish music and artists in France. In Poland, unfortunately, he felt that he was not sufficiently appreciated. He never managed to come back for good, but he was a permanent guest of the Warsaw Autumn Festival from 1957 until his death.

Influence of the new home on the composer's music

His stay in France solidified his compositional style. His studies with Boulanger and his fascination with Stravinsky's music (especially his second, neoclassical period) made him one of the most important representatives of Polish neoclassicism. He enjoyed reaching for forms and genres characteristic of past centuries. The narrative element in his works is transparent and its instrumentation extremely colorful.

Awareness of the composer's music in both countries

Spisak's music is still waiting to be discovered, although interest in his works is clearly growing, as seen by the wide range of concerts that have taken place in recent years. The International Michał Spisak Music Competition in Dąbrowa Górnicza, held since 2007, has played an important role in promoting his life and works. The Euterpe publishing company, to which the composer's heir transferred the rights to his estate, has also helped to promote his music. A number of mementos of the composer's legacy, donated by Spisak's wife, Andrée Thibault, can be found in the Polish Library in Paris.

Composer's personality

Spisak was perceived as an extremely modest and good person, distinguished by an extraordinary fortitude and affirmation of life despite many difficulties and adversities (he suffered from polio in his childhood, which caused paralysis of his legs). The composer's friends and biographers stress, however, that suffering is absent in his music, which instead is full of rhythmic pulsation, clearly perceptible joy, and a passion for life and creation.

Remarkable anecdote or biographical fact

Spisak's name has become famous also in the world of sports: he won a competition for an official Olympic anthem. This composition (for mixed choir and orchestra, using the text of Pindar's ode) beat 392 (!) other pieces; it was performed at the opening of the Olympic Winter Games in Cortina d'Ampezzo and at the Summer Games in Melbourne, both in 1956.

Respondent's Top Choices

- **Favorite work:** *Concerto Giocoso* for chamber orchestra (1957).
- **Best work:** In terms of publicity, the *Olympic Anthem*; for artistry, *Concerto Giocoso* (1957).
- **Composition still waiting to be discovered:** *Concertino* for clarinet and orchestra (1940–1941). The Polish Library in Paris has recently found a copy of the autograph score.

Respondent: Agnieszka Nowok-Zych

Tomasz Stańko

Date and place of birth:
11 July 1942, Rzeszów.

Date and place of death:
29 July 2018, Warsaw.

Date and place of emigration:
2008, United States (New York).

Return to Poland:
He visited Warsaw frequently.

Key quote

I move around the sonic sphere. I use the skills of a composer, but frequently I feel more like a painter or a poet…. Jazz is becoming closer and closer to classical music every year, and is gaining technical refinement, but remains primarily improvisational.[317]

Activities before emigration

By the time he settled down in New York, Stańko had already enjoyed a wonderful half-century career as a soloist, bandleader, and world-famous composer. He had recorded and released forty records under his name, the last eight of which were released on ECM.

After emigration

The artist continued his career with great success, above all, but not exclusively, leading his new band, the Tomasz Stańko New York Quartet. Musicians from the top echelons of the New York scene—to which he himself also belonged—participated. He recorded three additional albums for ECM and regularly performed in New York, elsewhere in the United States, and around the world, including Poland and elsewhere in Europe. He spoke about his artistic activity in America:

> Each of my albums is reviewed by the *New York Times* and others, and that helps to form opinions. People in New York read these reviews. And I haven't had bad reviews. My song *Suspended Night/Variation VII* was included in a jazz anthology created by the world's largest educational and research complex, the Smithsonian Institute in the United States. Of the more than 100 pieces included in that collection, only a handful are recordings by Europeans. The idea behind this publication was to present the greatest legends

and innovators in the history of jazz. For over ten years I have been listed in *Downbeat* magazine as one of the top ten trumpeters in the world. That's what I'm telling you now, that it's not honors that are important for me, but music. I love concerts. I have rooms in New York City where they're always waiting for me. Birdland, Jazz Standard, Merkin Hall...[318]

Differences between the old and new realities

The differences between the two worlds are best explained by the artist himself:

> New York City is today's Babylon. Above all, it shows how hellishly important tolerance is for mankind—it is important for our private, selfish gain. It is a city consisting of emigrants, and because every nation is good at something, it creates a fantastic mix. On the streets of New York City, one can sense an atmosphere of tolerance.[319]

> In New York City, the music vibrates and mixes so much that sometimes people walk down one street and have the impression that they have come across some musical tower of Babel. But, you know, I still hear jazz. Maybe it's a kind of perversion. I go into a regular bar and they are playing Coltrane, Rollins, or old Miles Davis. All famous jazz records. That makes me realize that this is the country of this music. Jazz is an everyday art in America and as it becomes more and more sophisticated, it attracts an increasingly sophisticated audience. That's why all jazzmen are rushing to New York....It's easy to find inspiration here. There has always been a focal point on earth: ancient Ur, Babylon, Athens, Rome, or Alexandria. New York City is the focal point of today's world, where China and other Eastern cultures meet African ones; everything in this melting pot is mixing together. This city is vibrating, pulsating, and one automatically feels energy growing inside. Every morning in Central Park, I go Nordic walking. There's traffic there around six o'clock in the morning, and there's a crowd of people running before seven o'clock. Everybody has that energy.[320]

Reason for leaving Poland

For Tomasz Stańko, as for all jazz musicians and fans, New York was the Holy Land, the land of Armstrong, Ellington, Parker, Monk, Davis, and Coltrane, as well as the Promised Land, the place of the final test of talent and craft. Tomasz Stańko himself expressed this conviction in the following way:

> For me it was the center of the universe....But I do not like it when someone says 'I dreamed of New York', because I did not dream of New York, I simply walked in this direction step by step, believing that an opportunity would come, a moment, in a stroke of luck, I would land here for good. I believe that if you want something very much, you will achieve it, despite the logs and unfavorable circumstances thrown at your feet. One should be able to grab onto happiness, to touch it and know what it is. For me it was the rhythm of this city....I reached it quite late, almost 30 years after my first visit, but I eventually got there.[321]

Contact with Poland after emigration

He often returned to Warsaw, which remained his main residence and was where he spent a lot of time. He did not emigrate in the traditional sense of the word, but rather maintained an increasingly popular way of living and working in two places, such as the east and west coasts of the United States, or New York and London. Stańko did not in any way restrict his activity in Poland or in the Polish music scene, where he performed with his quartets from both New York and Poland, the latter of which he had essentially dissolved after settling in New York. He also performed with other combinations of Polish musicians and remained the artistic director of the Jazz Autumn Festival in Bielsko-Biała. Since 2016 the composer had been an honorary member of the ZAiKS Association of Authors.

Influence of the new home on the composer's music

Living in New York provided a decisive, energetic impulse for Stańko that yielded new inspirations and references, although the essence of his work did not change much. The material for his first album written in New York, *Dark Eyes* (2009), was slightly different from his previous ones, mostly because it was intended for a different lineup of instruments, a quintet with guitar and bass guitar. On his next two albums, Stańko returned to his old formula of using an acoustic quartet. The music on these albums sounds like a continuation of previous recordings with the same line-up of instruments, although with a different set of musicians.

Awareness of the composer's music in both countries

Stańko is an icon of modern jazz on both sides of the Atlantic.

Composer's personality

Stańko considered himself to be a monad, a single unit. He was definitely self-motivated. He did not respect anyone else's superiority, but he did not impose his own, either. In his ensembles and artistic projects, he did not control, but he reigned. He was an innovator, but of an evolutionary, not revolutionary kind. He did not like risk, so he avoided it. He handled all obligations meticulously, especially those involving other people, and he reciprocated favors. He did not judge others. For the last dozen or so years or so of his life, he carefully monitored his health and physical condition.

Remarkable anecdote or biographical fact

Stańko was an outstanding aesthete and art connoisseur. He collected antique, Persian, and other oriental carpets and rugs. His collection was appreciated by experts in the field.

Respondent's Top Choices

- **Favorite work:** The main theme from the film *Farewell to Maria* [*Pożegnanie z Marią*] (1993).
- **Best work:** His last recording, *December Avenue* (ECM, 2017). Stańko considered this album to be a fulfillment of his artistic mission. He even wondered if it should be his final album.
- **Composition still waiting to be discovered:** *Twet* (Polskie Nagrania, 1975).

Respondent: Tomasz Tłuczkiewicz

Zygmunt (Sigismond) Stojowski

Date and place of birth:
8 April 1870, Strzelce near Kielce.

Date and place of death:
5 November 1946, New York.

Date and place of emigration:
1887, France (Paris); 1905, United States (New York).

Return to Poland:
He did not return.

Key quote

We practitioners are a bit like this Frenchman who never guessed what prose was, even though he had been speaking it his entire life. We are involuntary critics, because we have to notice, distinguish, and select before we begin to transfer and communicate the divine particles that form our dreams.[322]

Activities before emigration

Before Stojowski left Poland, which occurred when he was seventeen, he received some education in Kraków, mainly learning piano from Alfred Kołaczkowski and Henryk Bobiński and composition from Władysław Żeleński.

After emigration

He studied composition with Léo Delibes and piano with Louis Diémer. The most important thing, however, turned out to be regular piano lessons with Paderewski, with whom Stojowski became friends; he had studied with him since 1891 and was one of only four pianists who graduated from Paderewski's "school." In 1939, he was granted American citizenship. After graduation, he developed an impressive piano career in both hemispheres. With time, he became more and more occupied with teaching. Among other things, in New York he headed the piano department at the Institute of Musical Art, which years later was incorporated into the Juilliard School of Music.

Differences between the old and new realities

From a compositional point of view, his stay in France opened Stojowski up to Wagner's music, which was then popular on the Seine, as well as to newer currents, especially impressionism. However, until the end the artist remained fundamentally a late Romantic.

Reason for leaving Poland

He wanted to advance his skills and build an international career, which was practically impossible on Polish soil.

Contact with Poland after emigration

Stojowski never returned to Poland, but he visited several times while on tour.

Influence of the new home on the composer's music

It was not a shocking change; it seems, however, that the composer owed the most to his studies in Kraków and Paris. In the latter city, he had been somewhat influenced by Debussy's music.

Awareness of the composer's music in both countries

His music is not well known in either Poland or the United States. Paradoxically, in recent years most recordings of his compositions have been done in the United Kingdom, where albums containing his solo piano works and both piano concertos, with Jonathan Plowright as soloist, have been released.

Composer's personality

He was a balanced and kind man. He was regarded as an excellent piano teacher and achieved much in this field, especially after he settled in New York. As a composer, he did not appreciate the radical currents gaining more and more popularity at the beginning of the twentieth century—he remained a moderate conservative.

Remarkable anecdote or biographical fact

In 1918, Stojowski rejected a proposal to join the first government of the Second Republic of Poland, an offer extended by Paderewski, his mentor and the country's first prime minister. Stojowski preferred to teach.

Respondent's Top Choices

- **Favorite work:** *Piano Concerto in F sharp Minor,* op. 3 (1890), a composition for his diploma thesis.
- **Best work:** *Piano Concerto No. 2 in A Major,* op. 32 (1898).
- **Composition still waiting to be discovered:** *Symphony in D Minor* (1910), probably inspired by Shakespeare's *Hamlet* (we still do not have a public recording of this work).

Respondent: Marcin Gmys

Stanisław Syrewicz

Date and place of birth:
22 August 1946, Azov, Russia.

Date and place of emigration:
1981, France (Paris).

Return to Poland:
Stanisław Syrewicz lives permanently in Paris, London, and Warsaw.

Key quote

I divide my work into pieces for pure pleasure and for fulfillment of commissions. I have to complete these tasks, but I always do this without sacrifice. This is why I always look for a good restaurant close to a good recording studio.[323]

Activities before emigration

Stanisław Syrewicz graduated from the Academy of Music in Warsaw with a degree in piano and from the Directing Department of the Warsaw Theater Academy. In 1978 his musical, *State of Emergency* [*Stan wyjątkowy*], was premiered at Gdynia's Music Theater. He directed Domenico Scarlatti's *Narciso* at the Grand Theater in Warsaw and Ernest Bryll's Singspiel *Through the Mountains, Through the Clouds* [*Po górach, po chmurach*] at the Adam Mickiewicz Theater. Before his emigration, Syrewicz worked primarily as a composer for theater, composing music for over thirty productions. In 1976 he wrote the soundtrack to his first TV film, *Bewitching Eyes* [*Oczy uroczne*], directed by Piotr Szulkin. Before leaving Poland, he was involved in the Polish-British co-production *Sherlock Holmes and Doctor Watson* (1980).

After emigration

In 1982 Syrewicz signed a lucrative contract with Island Records, which gave him the opportunity to compose songs for Marianne Faithfull, Diane Keaton, and Jon Anderson and to work with The Rolling Stones. This contract also indirectly influenced the start of his career in composing for film. The first foreign film for which Syrewicz wrote the music was *The Holcroft Covenant*, based on Robert Ludlum's novel (1985).

Differences between the old and new realities

In Poland behind the Iron Curtain, opportunities for development were very limited. Syrewicz recalls that: "Nothing was happening on television at that time. There was absolutely no cultural activity and there was only vinegar on the store shelves."[324] The series *Sherlock Holmes and Doctor Watson* provided him with a window to the world, however. On the other side of the Iron Curtain, Syrewicz quite quickly got a chance to develop a career. At the beginning of his stay in Paris, he worked as an accompanist in a ballet school and as a live musician in cafés. However, his talent was quickly recognized and he began his international career in music.

Reason for leaving Poland

Syrewicz emigrated because martial law was imposed in Poland. He stayed temporarily in Paris, not yet thinking about leaving his home country permanently. He said that martial law was a direct reason for his emigration, but not the only one. Thanks to his work with the *Sherlock Holmes* series, he was able to build his own house in Poland, but during the composer's absence, it burned down. "I lost it, and with it, practically all of my belongings—music, scores, notes....There was nothing to return to."[325]

Contact with Poland after emigration

It was only in exile that Syrewicz's career as a film composer began in earnest. At the same time, he received proposals from Poland, which Syrewicz willingly accepted and takes advantage of even today. In total, he has composed about seventy soundtracks for cinema and television films, including for such Polish productions as *March Almonds* [*Marcowe migdały*] (1989), *The Complaint* [*Skarga*] (1991), *Sabina* (1998), *Love on the Catwalk* [*Miłość na wybiegu*] (2009), and *The House by the Backwater* [*Dom nad rozlewiskiem*] (2009). He also collaborates with Poles who are active abroad, for example, on *Ferdydurke* (1991) directed by Jerzy Skolimowski, and *L'Amour Braque* [*Narwana miłość*] (1985), directed by Andrzej Żuławski. Syrewicz currently divides his time between three countries: Poland, France, and the United Kingdom.

Influence of the new home on the composer's music

Above all, the composer has found many possibilities in film music, where he can perfect his language in both commercial and niche productions. His contract with Island Records has also resulted in, as the composer claims, countless songs.

Awareness of the composer's music in both countries

Syrewicz still works with the Polish film industry. Recently, he composed music for the popular series *Guesthouse by the Backwater* [*Pensjonat nad Rozlewiskiem*] (Polish Television, 2018). In 2012, the Film Music Festival in Łódź included a concert devoted exclusively to his work.

Composer's personality

He is hard-working, but approaches his work from a distance. As he says himself: "I have been writing film music for 35 years. The most important thing is not to do anything against yourself and not to treat it as a chore. This is why I always look for a good restaurant close to a good recording studio."[326]

Remarkable anecdote or biographical fact

Syrewicz recalled the announcement of martial law and his decision to stay in Paris:

> Many things surprised us, but on the other hand, it was a typical turn of history. We knew that something was coming, we just didn't know how or if we would come out of it safely. Tension was so great that we knew that something had to happen. At the end of 1981, Solidarity was supposed to have its own radio and TV broadcasts, so a competition for the so-called 'jingle' was announced, and I won this contest. I still have a copy of the reservation for my return flight from Paris to Warsaw on...December 13th, because we were just about to record this jingle. But the planes stopped flying. Staying in Paris was, then, not a conscious decision to leave Poland. We had a hard time trying to find ourselves in the chaos that had arisen.[327]

Respondent's Top Choices

- **Favorite work:** Music for *Ferdydurke* directed by Jerzy Skolimowski (Poland/France/United Kingdom, 1991).
- **Best work:** Songs: *Once in a Lifetime* [its Polish title was *To nie ja byłam Ewą*] to Jacek Cygan's lyrics, sung by Edyta Górniak, who took second place at the 1994 Eurovision Song Contest in Dublin; *Everyone Can Sing* [*Śpiewać każdy może*] to Jonasz Kofta's lyrics (an unforgettable interpretation by Jerzy Stuhr occurred during the Polish Song Festival in Opole, 1977).
- **Composition still waiting to be discovered:** Music for *The Clandestine Marriage*, directed by Christopher Miles (United Kingdom, 1999).

Respondent: Grzegorz Dąbrowski

Witold Szalonek

Date and place of birth:
2 March 1927, Czechowice-Dziedzice.

Date and place of death:
12 October 2001, Berlin.

Date and place of emigration:
1973, Federal Republic of Germany (West Berlin).

Return to Poland:
He regularly visited Poland.

Key quote

For me, sonorism seems to be a logical manifestation of shaping musical thought by taking advantage of the completely singular quality of particular sound generators….The thing is to convey the assumed content by sound only, by things perceived by our sense of hearing, through the timbre of a sound. Timbre is the identifying characteristic of an instrument. Sonorism is the soul of an instrument, heard through music.[328]

Activities before emigration

Szalonek debuted at the Warsaw Autumn Festival in 1959, where excerpts of his *Confessions* for choir and spoken word were performed. He quickly gained a reputation as one of the most radical proponents of experimental music. He was particularly interested in the new sound possibilities of woodwind instruments. With the help of other musicians, he persistently sought the possibility of extracting so-called combined sounds from these instruments, i.e., producing the basic sound and its aliquot(s) simultaneously, which is possible thanks to employing appropriate ways of holding and blowing the instrument. These sounds became the basis of Szalonek's music, which is extremely intriguing and endowed with a unique sonic aura. Theoretical results of these experiments were included by the composer in his essay *On the Unused Sonoristic Values of Woodwinds*, published in 1972. Szalonek lectured at the State Higher School of Music in Katowice, from which he had graduated. Starting in 1967 he also taught composition there. Before leaving for Berlin, he was also involved in music criticism, cultural journalism in the Silesian press, and popularizing contemporary music on the radio. He also conducted amateur choirs, thus participating in the local Silesian singing tradition.

After emigration

Szalonek's main activity was pedagogical work. In West Berlin, at the local Academy of Art (Hochschule der Künste), he established a composition class centered around avant-garde ideas and unconventional ways of thinking, which attracted a multilingual crowd of young students of sound art. He also promoted his own country's music and its most outstanding representatives. For example, he co-founded the local Karol Szymanowski Society and, at the Academy, he organized concerts dedicated to Polish music, which included works by Kazimierz Serocki and neoclassical repertoire from the first half of the twentieth century.

Differences between the old and new realities

Although he took part in similar activities in Poland and Germany, Szalonek worked in two different worlds. Although Edward Gierek's decade in Polish twentieth-century history was characterized by apparent liberalism, the state apparatus refused to withdraw its policies of repression, censorship, and social indoctrination. However, after the ratification by the Bundestag (on May 17, 1972) of the Polish-West German agreement "on the basis of the normalization of mutual relations," cultural and scientific exchanges between Poland and West Germany became possible. Szalonek was one of the beneficiaries of this change. From the rather conservative musical environment of the Katowice university and the realities of a centrally controlled state, the composer found himself on the other side of the Berlin wall, in the "free world," which for Poles was synonymous with prestige and financial stability.

Reason for leaving Poland

In 1972 Szalonek was appointed dean of the Katowice Academy of Music. However, he did not accept this position, since the organizational and personal demands he made were unacceptable to the Katowice authorities who supervised the university. As a gesture of disillusionment and disappointment, Szalonek entered a competition for the position of professor of composition at the Hochschule für Musik und Darstellende Kunst in West Berlin (now the Universität der Künste Berlin). He defeated Erhard Karkoschka and Helmut Lachenmann, among others. At the end of 1973, he became a professor at the Berlin Academy, succeeding Boris Blacher, the famous composition teacher. He remained in this position until his retirement in 1992.

Contact with Poland after emigration

Settling in West Berlin did not lead to a break in contacts with Poland. Until the early 1980s he also worked in Katowice, teaching composition and musical analysis. Every two weeks he traveled the Berlin–Katowice route to meet with Polish students. Although Berlin remained his permanent residence, he maintained regular contacts with Poland. Among his German friends, he defined himself as a "Polish Silesian." After his death, the composer's ashes were placed, according to his wishes, next to his parents' grave in the cemetery in Bytom-Łagiewniki.

Influence of the new home on the composer's music

Szalonek's emigration experience created a critical turning point in his life and work. The composer paid for it by experiencing a profound homesickness for his country, for Silesia, and for the family and friends he left behind. He felt isolated, which negatively impacted his creative work as well as his physical and mental condition. Endowed with an uncompromising, individualistic personality and, at the same time, devoid of desirable diplomatic talents, Szalonek was painfully affected by the fact that in both Polish and German musical circles, his creative achievements (which were often ahead of the times, especially concerning ideas about perception and performance) were not properly appreciated. This undoubtedly had consequences. In the long run, his emigration led him to retreat from radical avant-garde aesthetics and return to traditional values in music. It also resulted in attempts to redefine his own cultural identity and national affiliation. Living in a state of suspension between Silesia and Berlin prompted the composer to become a eulogist for "small homelands" on the one hand and, on the other hand, to permeate his music with testimonies of "obvious Polishness"—quotes or allusions to Chopin and references to the sound of bells or the motifs of Tatra folklore.

Awareness of the composer's music in both countries

Although Szalonek is considered one of the most original composers (not only Polish) of the second half of the twentieth century, his music is rarely performed, recorded, or published. In fact, he is known only to a small group of enthusiasts. The first monographic recording of his music was released only in 2004. The broadest perspective of his work is provided by the recordings of the Warsaw Autumn Festival Chronicle. In recent years, the artist's output has been promoted through the Szalonek Decade [Dekada Szalonka] project (co-financed by the Foundation for Polish-German Cooperation) and a number of commemorative concerts. Today, Szalonek's name is linked to an international composition competition and a square in Bytom-Łagiewniki is named after him. However, all this is not enough for his work to have found a worthy place not only in the Polish and German music scenes, but also in music history. Therefore, the most urgent issue seems to be to create a dedicated website and publish a monograph on his career (the one prepared by Daniel Cichy as part of his doctoral dissertation has not yet appeared in print).

Composer's personality

One interesting feature of Szalonek's personality was the respect he showed his students. He treated them not so much as students but as partners, as he always kept in mind Wojciech Żywny's relationship with Frédéric Chopin. His humility in the face of aesthetic differences as well as ethnic and cultural distinctions was greatly appreciated by the international group of young artists in his composition class. He was a great speaker—his lectures, sparkling with intellect and wit, always attracted crowds of young listeners.

Remarkable anecdote or biographical fact

The reason for his particular interest in the sound effects extracted from woodwind instruments remains unknown. However, the composer admitted that during his school days, his attention had been drawn to "the strange timbre of 'accidental' sounds, so-called 'squawks' produced to the delight of listeners by untrained students of woodwind instruments." Used consciously, they permanently penetrated the aural fabric of his sonoristic compositions and became his trademark.

Respondent's Top Choices

- **Favorite work:** *Improvisations sonoristiques* for clarinet, trombone, cello, and piano (1968).
- **Best work:** *Symphony of Rituals* [*Symfonia rytuałów*] for string quartet (1991–1996).
- **Composition still waiting to be discovered:** *Hautbois mon amour* for solo oboe, two harps, timpani, and string orchestra (1999).

Respondent: Iwona Lindstedt

Antoni Szałowski

Date and place of birth:
21 April 1907, Warsaw.

Date and place of death:
21 March 1973, Paris.

Date and place of emigration:
1931, France (Paris).

Return to Poland:
He did not return.

Key quote
His music is…crystal clear, precise, and definitely finished.[329]

Activities before emigration
Antoni Szałowski took his first steps in violin playing under the supervision of his father, Bonifacy Szałowski, a violinist and professor at the Warsaw Music Conservatory. Antoni began his education at the same school in 1919, at the age of twelve. He took piano lessons from Ignacy Przyłagowski and, beginning with the 1924–1925 academic year, he studied with Paweł Lewiecki. At the start of the academic year 1927–1928, he resigned from piano as a major subject and took up composition studies with Kazimierz Sikorski. He graduated with honors in 1930. Under Sikorski's direction, he completed the following works: *Two Songs* for voice with orchestra (1927), *Symphonic Variations*, *Prelude* for violin and piano, *Mazurka* for piano, *String Quartet No. 1* (1928), *Capriccio* for orchestra (1928–1929) and *Piano Concerto* (1929–30). During his studies, he enjoyed recognition from teachers and favorable reviews from critics. At the age of merely 22, he was able to boast about the performance of his *Symphonic Variations*, which Grzegorz Fitelberg included in a Warsaw Philharmonic concert program in 1929 alongside Karol Szymanowski's *Symphony No. 2* and Richard Strauss's symphonic poem *The Life of a Hero*.

After emigration
After arriving in Paris in 1931, Szałowski began composition studies with Nadia Boulanger. He also joined the ranks of the Association of Young Polish Musicians, which gave its members artistic, moral, and material support and provided assistance in musical education, concert organization, and the popularization of Polish music abroad. Szałowski

was successively secretary, vice-president and, from 1938, president of this Association. His greatest success of the interwar years was being awarded a Gold Medal at the 1937 World's Fair in Paris for his *Overture* (1936). This was recognized by Florent Schmitt, an eminent critic and valued composer, as the greatest event of the 1936–1937 season, alongside the premiere of Bartók's *Music for Strings, Percussion and Celesta*. After the outbreak of World War II, Szałowski volunteered for the Polish Army in France but, due to his poor eyesight, he was transferred to the reserves. He returned to Paris in late 1945.

The first six postwar years were the most fruitful period for the popularity of Szałowski's music, but his living situation, as was the case for many other composers in exile, was very difficult. Szałowski's works were presented at international contemporary music festivals. During the postwar period, he composed a number of orchestral and chamber pieces, most of them commissioned by French Radio, with which he had begun working immediately after the war. His orchestral compositions were presented in Paris and other locations by, among others, Paweł Klecki, Nadia Boulanger, Andrzej Panufnik, Grzegorz Fitelberg, and Mateusz Gliński. Solo and chamber pieces were played by Polish and international musicians, including Grażyna Bacewicz and Wacław Niemczyk. In 1956, during the Congress of Polish Culture Abroad, Szałowski's *Violin Concerto*, dedicated to his father, was presented. A gala concert at the Palais des Beaux-Arts in Brussels, where his *Suite* for orchestra was performed in the presence of Queen Elisabeth of Belgium (1953), was also of great importance. In 1960 Szałowski received first prize from French Radio and Television for his radio ballet *La Femme têtue*, with a libretto by Jean Lescure. This piece was honored as the organization's best music commission in the 1958–1959 season. In 1972 he received the Alfred Jurzykowski Foundation's New York Music Award (for 1971).

Differences between the old and new realities

The French capital was the most important center of the musical world in the first half of the twentieth century. It was here that new initiatives were created, creative attitudes were born, the greatest authorities and individuals were concentrated, and the most important artistic disputes took place. The need for rapprochement with the Parisian milieu was repeatedly stressed by Karol Szymanowski, who claimed that a true and insightful understanding of the music created there was one of the key conditions for the development of Polish music. Interwar Warsaw lacked this favorable atmosphere for creativity, new inspirations, and concert life; hence, Szałowski went to Paris in order to perfect his compositional skills, as well as to actively participate in these musical adventures. After the Second World War, he stayed in Paris because he wanted to continue composing in an unrestricted way.

Reason for leaving Poland

Szałowski did not "escape" from Poland but, as he often emphasized, he simply remained in Paris after his studies. The idea of giving up contact with the European milieu and his chances for developing a brilliant career was difficult to envision for the young artist, who at that time was considered by Parisian critics to be one of his generation's most talented musicians. Unfortunately, World War II not only brutally interrupted the development of cultural life, but also marked the end of that era. After his return to Paris, Szałowski tried to find himself in the new postwar reality, but as an emigrant and refugee, he could no longer count on special favors. Neither could he expect understanding in his home country, which was overwhelmed by a wave of socialist realism.

Contact with Poland after emigration

After leaving for Paris, Szałowski came to Poland only once, in 1938. A number of concerts were organized at that time. Most attention was paid to his *Overture*. A year later this piece was included in the program of the 1939 International Society for Contemporary Music Festival, held in Warsaw and Kraków. After 1949, when Polish culture was paralyzed by the process of Stalinization, music created by Poles abroad was silenced. This censorship included Szałowski's music. His removal from the Polish Composers' Union in the early 1950s was a source of deep disappointment. After the political and cultural breakthrough of 1956, Szałowski's interwar works were included in the programs of the first and third Warsaw Autumn Festivals (*Overture*, *Trio* for oboe, clarinet, and bassoon). In 1962 the Warsaw Opera premiered his ballet *The Enchanted Inn* [*Zaczarowana oberża*] (1945), but with a libretto changed without the composer's consent. This once again undermined Szałowski's relationship with the Polish music community. In terms of Szałowski's larger compositions, Polish audiences could hear *Aria* and *Toccata* for chamber orchestra (1962), *Concerto* for reed trio and orchestra (1962), and *Suite* for orchestra (1963). The Polish premiere of his last composition, *Six Sketches* for chamber orchestra (1972), took place during the 1976 Poznań Musical Spring.

Influence of the new home on the composer's music

Szałowski preferred the possibility of free, unrestricted creativity over success. Having found the optimal way to express his creative intentions, he tried to compose carefully constructed music, although his fidelity to neoclassical aesthetics, once a source of fame, now placed him in the shadows. Szałowski's closest friend, Zygmunt Mycielski, recalled that "Antoni did not care about fashion or what anyone was doing next to him; he sometimes joked about it, but without bitterness."

Awareness of the composer's music in both countries

Szałowski's compositions are rarely heard on concert stages. Of his orchestral works, the interwar *Overture* is most often played in Poland. Several compositions were also performed in Poland during festivals such as the Warsaw Music Meetings and the Emigrants [Emigranci] Music Festival organized by Polish Radio. At the New Music and Architecture [Nova Muzyka i Architektura] Festival, a concert version of the ballet *Enchanted Inn*, *Sonatina* for clarinet and piano, *Concertino* for string orchestra, *Music* for strings, and *Aria and Burlesque* for cello and piano were presented. Outside of Poland, Szałowski is primarily known as the author of the *Overture* and *Sonatina* for clarinet and piano.

Composer's personality

Mycielski said about Szałowski that:

> He was an outsider, tiptoeing, as if he were only passing through the real world. As if he were made of glass, as if he were transparent, unrealistic and, in the most ordinary sense of the word, unpractical. And yet, he com-

> bined this helplessness and fear with stubbornness, which can only be called a strength of artistic convictions.[330]

Szałowski's personality fostered the development of his artistic talent and, at the same time, made it difficult for him to achieve success in life. He mastered the craft of composing perfectly. He was gifted with imagination, fantasy, intuition, and the ability to reason logically, and at the same time he was charming. He was persistent, firm, and confident in his creative activity. As a human being, however, he did not try to fit into his musical community. He did not follow current fashions, he remained secretive and rather indifferent to what was going on around him, and he did not attach much importance to his possible place in music history.

Remarkable anecdote or biographical fact

Szałowski was one of Nadia Boulanger's most faithful students. The famous "Princesse de la Musique," as Boulanger was called, not only facilitated the improvement of his compositional craft, but also helped advance his further artistic career. To Szałowski, Boulanger was a great authority. He was encouraged by every word she said, every positive comment she made about new compositions, and every sign of interest in him as a person. Nadia, despite frequent demonstrations of friendship and concern for her student, did not, however, praise his cooperation with French Radio. Her disapproval of this Parisian institution was ideologically based. The managerial positions at French Radio were held by members of the Resistance, while she represented the so-called "old France." That is why when, in 1960 Szałowski received the first French Radio and Television Award for his radio ballet *La Femme têtue* (and was the first non-French composer to be so honored), Nadia's commentary did not include any word of praise. During a meeting, Szałowski approached her and, hoping for a flattering comment, asked if she had heard of his success. Boulanger then answered briefly: "Yes, my dear, I heard."

Respondent's Top Choices

- **Favorite work:** It is difficult to select one. There is certainly the *Overture* (1936), as well as the *Violin Concerto* (1954), *String Quartet No. 3* (1936), and *Aria and Toccata* for string orchestra (1957). Interesting examples of musical illustration are the ballet *Enchanted Inn* (1945) and the symphonic poem *Lazarus Brought Back to Life*, based on Giotto's fresco (1960).
- **Best work:** Given the qualities of the work and its reception, *Overture* for symphony orchestra (1936).
- **Composition still waiting to be discovered:** I think the *Enchanted Inn* ballet (1945) is unique in this context. Performed only once, with the libretto modified without the composer's consent, it seems that staging the work in its original form would represent a symbolic payback. Its sonic layers, full of sophisticated colors and harmony, with interesting illustrative effects and musical symbolism, perfectly correspond to the elegance and joy of life conveyed in the work's subject.

Respondent: Elżbieta Szczurko

Jagoda Szmytka

Date and place of birth:
15 January 1982, Legnica.

Date and place of emigration:
2010, Germany/Europe; the composer has traveled a lot and it is difficult to name just one location.

Return to Poland:
So far not, although she visits Poland frequently.

Key quote

Art and music should be a manifestation of reality and life. I live in the present and my work is completely focused on 'here and now', where life is happening.[331]

Activities before emigration

Jagoda Szmytka is an artist of many talents who, during her studies, faced a difficult decision about her possible specialization (music, painting, theater direction, art, music theory, or philosophy). Fortunately, her imagination was not restricted by this dilemma, which was caused by an outdated system of educating artists and theoreticians that sought to limit career choices. Szmytka immediately began to compose music for listening, watching, and thinking, such as her *per._o*, a piece "at the limit" of art that was performed in Wrocław at the Musica Polonica Nova festival in 2008.

After emigration

Going first to Austria and then to Germany turned out to be beneficial from the point of view of Szmytka's career and artistic development, for there is currently no contemporary music scene as rich, varied, and inspiring as in the German-speaking countries. Contacts with the most eminent representatives of the postwar avant-garde, including those in both older and younger generations, a good network of support institutions and new music festivals, and intensive contact with contemporary art created conditions that allowed Szmytka to develop and implement many original and interdisciplinary artistic ideas—in other words, to use all of her talents and interests.

Differences between the old and new realities

The contemporary music scene in Poland is shaped around several major festivals, such as Warsaw Autumn or Musica Electronica Nova. The vast majority of these are organized by the Polish Composers' Union. Small, independent entities such as foundations or artistic associations have limited opportunities for financing projects outside this mainstream. Ten years ago, there were no open competitions for public funding of experimental music projects. There was also no commissioning program, a system important for composers in particular. To this day, there are no programs to assist in developing contemporary music performance ensembles, which are crucial for new composition. In Poland, more importance is given to national priorities, which then determine the interests of institutions and grant-givers. This situation strongly shapes the scene of new music in Poland and distinguishes it from the German scene, which is better funded, more strongly institutionalized, offers more space for experimentation, and is also more international.

Reason for leaving Poland

The direct reason for Szmytka's departure was a desire to continue the studies that she undertook first in Graz with Beat Furrer and Pierluigi Billone and then in Karlsruhe with Wolfgang Rihm. Above all, she was driven by her search for a distinct creative vision, the need to be constantly on the move, and the desire to constantly expand her horizons or, as the artist herself calls it, to "compose herself." The migration of artists has had a positive dimension in her case, and its advantages have been appreciated by various institutions supporting artists.

Contact with Poland after emigration

Szmytka maintains constant contact with Poland. Her music is performed at various Polish festivals of contemporary music, among other events. She comes to Poland as an artist well established in the international environment of contemporary music and art. Szmytka has received many awards, including the Staubach Honorarium and Stipendienpreis in Darmstadt (2014) and a Deutscher Musikautorenpreis from GEMA (2016). She has worked for many years as a resident artist at the Zentrum für Kunst und Medien Karlsruhe. Her pieces have been played and commissioned by festivals and institutions such as Internationale Ferienkurse für Neue Musik Darmstadt, Lucerne Festival, Festival d'Aix-en-Provence, Wien Modern, Huddersfield Contemporary Music Festival, Ultraschall in Berlin, Eclat in Stuttgart, Tonhalle Düsseldorf, Deutschlandfunk in Cologne, Royaumont in Paris, Grand Theater – National Opera in Warsaw, Warsaw Autumn Festival, Codes in Lublin, and Musica Polonica Nova in Wrocław. Her music has also been played by Ensemble Garage, Ensemble Interface, ensemble recherche, European Workshop for Contemporary Music, IEMA, E-MEX Ensemble, leise dröhnung, Kwartludium, Ensemble l'arsenale, Ensemble Besides, and the Kronos Quartet.

Influence of the new home on the composer's music

I think that, in her case, new surroundings were crucial for the development and implementation of new artistic ideas. Her numerous travels, residencies, and commissions from music festivals, galleries, and museums all over Europe form a strong creative stimulus, while scholarships, Germany's lush musical and artistic scene, and contacts with people from all over the world—including the best performers—provide a network of support that is more difficult to obtain in Poland. Szmytka has also emphasized that in Germany and Switzerland she has found understanding for her artistic ideas, which has motivated her to continue her constant exploration of new ideas.

Awareness of the composer's music in both countries

Currently, Szmytka is well recognized in the contemporary music community. Her work has been presented at the most important new music forums in the world. Furthermore, many radio broadcasts and monographic articles in the foreign press have been devoted to her, which has increased the recognition of her music.

Composer's personality

Szmytka presents a strong personality, extraordinary intellect, and perfect artistic intuition, which has led her towards Internet culture, trans-media art, and, broadly understood, the boundaries between music and other arts. She draws inspiring themes from these areas in a creative and intellectual manner. I believe that she thoroughly reflects upon everything she does. She works strategically. Recently, she has been working as a performer and a curator as she constantly expands her field of activity and redefines the role of an artist.

Remarkable anecdote or biographical fact

Szmytka's road to composing was complex. After completing secondary music school (she played flute), she studied art history and, a year later, music theory. She also considered theatrical directing and visual arts (she was always painting and creating visual objects). Eventually, after a few years, she decided to study composing, ignoring the sarcasm of her composer friends, and later enriched her studies with philosophy. Thus, she received a thorough education in the humanities.

Respondent's Top Choices

- **Favorite work:** Chamber works such as *inane prattle* (2013) and *electrifier memories of bloody cherries* (2011), multimedia compositions such as *¿i? study of who where when* (2010), and contextual music such as *GAMEBOY* (2014).
- **Best work:** It is yet to emerge.
- **Composition still waiting to be discovered:** Recent transmedia works and performances, such as the *LOST* series (2015), *DIY or DIE* (2017), *LIFE* (2016–2017), *box of presence (everybody can be present)* (2016), *box of happiness* (2018), *JUSTICE* (2018), and *Voilà, that's my life* (2016).

Respondent: Monika Pasiecznik

Michał Talma-Sutt

Date and place of birth:
16 August 1969, Łódź.

Date and place of emigration:
2001, Germany (Berlin).

Return to Poland:
He has not returned.

Key quote
I have always been interested in working on form.[332]

Activities before emigration
In the late 1980s and early 1990s, Michał Talma-Sutt wrote mainly piano pieces. At the same time, he studied piano and composition at the Music Academy in Łódź. After graduation, he remained affiliated with his home university, leading, among other things, courses in electronic music at its computer studio. In the 1990s he created his first works for tape, including *What Nostradamus Has Kept Only for Himself*, which in 1998 received an award at the International Rostrum of Electroacoustic Music in Vienna. *Light and Shade*, which was created a little later, won first prize there in 2000. The composer has also created music for theater projects and films created at the Łódź Film School.

After emigration
Most of the composer's mature works were created after he left Poland. These include multimedia projects (*Soundscape One*, version II) and works for instruments and computers or multi-channel sound projection (*Cellotronicum*, *Strings'0'tronics*, *DUO*, and others). His recent works have been connected with dance. Talma-Sutt has also worked with Berlin theaters, for example, Studio am Salzufer. Recently, he has been involved in commercial music for films, radio plays, etc. He also teaches piano and has participated in cultural and political projects such as Polenbegeisterungswelle.

Differences between the old and new realities

Poland in the 1990s was a country of dynamic changes, but the availability of new technologies and the popularity of electroacoustic music in the country remained limited. The musical avant-garde is more deeply rooted in the music of Poland's western neighbors and its reception in those countries is also somewhat different. Pieces written by Talma-Sutt before his departure from Poland are mostly juvenilia, in which the electronic aspect is sometimes limited by the possibilities of the available equipment. Although some characteristic features (first of all, their attention to form) seem to be a constant theme of his work, elements such as a desire for synthesis and balance between instruments and electronics or his current fascination with the additional dimension of stage movement appear only in his mature works.

Reason for leaving Poland

The reasons why Talma-Sutt decided to emigrate were both personal and artistic. In the 1990s, the artist had already taken part in courses in computer music courses, e.g., at IRCAM in Paris (1995–1996) as well as in Karlsruhe (1999–2000). He also studied composition in Stuttgart with Ulirch Süße (1998–2001). In 2001 he settled in Berlin.

Contact with Poland after emigration

Due to his numerous contacts and the fact that he lives across the border from Poland, Talma-Sutt has remained active in Polish musical life, especially in the communities of Łódź and Wrocław. He remains a member of the Polish Composers' Union (he even was president of the union's Wrocław branch). In 2007 he worked as the artistic director of the Musica Electronica Nova festival in Wrocław. He collaborates with well-known composers, e.g., Krzysztof Knittel, the ElettroVoce duo (Agata Zubel and Cezary Duchnowski), and artists from the Format Zero Artistic Association, which brings together independent contemporary artists.

Influence of the new home on the composer's music

Berlin is a center of contemporary art in Europe. The variety of cultural events and the reception of new music there clearly influence the work of the artistic community. When we also consider the wider access to new technologies in a country like Germany, we can now understand that Talma-Sutt's new environment influenced the development of his mature work. It should be remembered, however, that the direction of this development was clearly outlined during his time in Łódź.

Awareness of the composer's music in both countries

In Poland, Talma-Sutt's compositions have been presented on numerous occasions, such as at the Warsaw Autumn Festival, Musica Electronica Nova and Musica Polonica Nova in Wrocław, or the Festival of Polish Music in Kraków. In 2014, the artist's monographic recording was released as part of the *Polish Music Today* series. His works are also performed in Germany (mainly in Berlin), both during various electronic music festivals and in shows combining acoustic music, electronic music, and dance. Such combinations are currently of great interest to the composer.

Composer's personality

Talma-Sutt constantly looks for innovative solutions, especially in the area of form, the creation of sonic and visual visions, and the interaction of acoustic and electronic elements. He is fascinated by the artistic possibilities of technology but, at the same time, he doesn't limit himself to electroacoustic music.

His attitude to art has been influenced by the work of Hermann Hesse and Eastern philosophy. He considers issues of freedom and responsibility to be basic problems of art; in his opinion, the creative process is connected with the question of the mystery of existence, so art should not be called a purely intellectual activity. He does not deny that music is a means of communication, but he also believes that the slogan "art for all" is utopian in nature. Not believing in the existence of objective music, he seeks viewers who are moved by his creations.

Remarkable anecdote or biographical fact

When asked what he finds fascinating about electronic music, the composer answered: "It's magic. It is thanks to this medium that one can really enchant listeners while experimenting with new colors, new sounds, and sometimes unbelievable things. I like it very much."[333]

Respondent's Top Choices

- **Favorite work:** *Avalon's Gates* for flute and computer (1997), written for Dorota Imienińska and premiered during the 1997 Warsaw Autumn Festival. This piece is unusually varied and surprising. Its tension-building virtuosity is interwoven with quasi-meditative sections that link the composition together and shape the form convincingly, as the composer intended.
- **Best work:** *Cellotronicum* for cello and computer (2002), written for Andrzej Bauer. The piece was premiered at the 2003 Warsaw Autumn Festival as part of a project promoting music for solo cello and electronic media. One critic, Daniel Cichy, considered it to be one of the best new Polish works, while another, Adam Suprynowicz, praised its poignant, colorful sounds that blend easily with the sound of the cello. The computer processes the cello sounds that are absorbed by the microphone, adding an automated layer of "live electronics."
- **Composition still waiting to be discovered:** His electroacoustic works are quite well known. The work entitled *Sphinx's Games* for solo flute (1996), performed at the Cité des Arts in Paris in 1996, is certainly worth mentioning. This piece is a challenge for critics due to its hidden quotations and reworking of episodes that are arranged as variations. Most importantly—it is colorful and interesting.

Respondent: Kinga Krzymowska-Szacoń

Aleksander (Alexandre) Tansman

Date and place of birth:
11 June 1897, Łódź.

Date of death:
15 November 1986, Paris.

Date and place of emigration:
1919, France (a citizen since 1938, Paris); 1941 United States (Los Angeles); 1946, France (Paris).

Return to Poland:
He never returned permanently; he went to Poland six times for short tours (1932, 1936, 1967, 1978, 1979, and 1980).

Key quote

Music, the pure and absolute art, does not reach only the senses of hearing and intellect, but also, or rather primarily, the heart.[334]

Activities before emigration

Aleksander Tansman left Poland when he was only 22. He spent only his childhood and early youth in Poland, so it is difficult to talk about any actual artistic activity. He studied first in his hometown of Łódź, taking classes in piano, harmony, and counterpoint, among other things, then in Warsaw starting in 1917. There he studied privately, learning counterpoint with Piotr Rytel and composition with Henryk Melcer-Szczawiński; he also studied law at Warsaw University. During World War I, while in Łódź, he played harp in an orchestra; for him, this provided the best "school for instrumentation." In 1916 Łódź was the site of the first performance of *Serenade* for strings, which was warmly welcomed by the local press and the public. In 1919 he took part in the first composition competition in independent Poland, receiving three awards, including the Grand Prix for *Romance* for violin and piano. As the winner of that competition, he was able to present his compositions to the Warsaw public. The negative reception of this music contributed to his decision to leave the country in autumn 1919.

After emigration

Initially, Tansman sought his luck in various jobs (at a parcel-sorting plant and as a bank clerk). In 1920 he got to know Maurice Ravel, who opened doors to the musical world—the young Pole's compositions were then performed in numerous halls in Paris. After that, Tansman was able to make a living in his chosen profession—he composed, performed all over Europe, and sometimes taught and wrote about Polish music. Paris at that time was the capital of culture, where the composer learned about the most important directions of twentieth-century art. He also developed his own musical language and artistic persona. With time, he also conquered the United States, where he first appeared in 1927 and became friends with Charlie Chaplin and George Gershwin. During World War II, which he spent mainly in Hollywood, he wrote film music to Julien Duvivier's *Flesh and Fantasy* (1942) and Gregory Ratoff's *Paris Underground* (1945), which received the first Oscar nomination ever given to a Polish composer. Additionally, he was able to dedicate himself to family life, bringing up two daughters (Mirellie and Marianne) with his wife, pianist Colette Cras. After the war, the Tansman family returned to France, where the composer continued to support himself and his family by composing, creating not only symphonic works but also music for radio plays. With time, he gained more and more international recognition and was even elected in 1977 to the Académie Royale de Belgique in Brussels, where he took the place vacated by Dmitri Shostakovich. He was also increasingly appreciated in Poland; in 1983 he became an honorary member of the Polish Composers' Union and received the medal "Meritorious for Polish Culture," and in 1986 he was given an honorary doctorate from the Academy of Music in Łódź.

Differences between the old and new realities

These two worlds differed primarily in their attitude and artistic possibilities. In Paris, Tansman was able to find and follow his own path. The city was the artistic capital of both traditional and avant-garde music; it was also a place where all creative experiments were vividly commented on by the press and the public. In musical terms, Warsaw at that time had not yet come out of the nineteenth century and so was firmly rooted in late Romantic traditions. Its attitude to artistic novelty was more conservative. Poland also had different problems to resolve than France—its main focus was to rebuild the nation after decades of partitions and war.

Reason for leaving Poland

These included a feeling of artistic loneliness, a lack of understanding of Tansman's artistic explorations by Warsaw's musical community, and a desire to learn about the latest musical trends of his time.

Contact with Poland after emigration

Tansman's contact with Poland after his emigration was limited, but quite positive. The composer came to Poland for two tours before World War II, in 1932 and 1936, visiting Warsaw, Łódź, and Kraków. During this time he developed friendships and acquaintances with Polish artists, wrote about Polish music for French magazines, and even published an essay about his work in Mateusz Gliński's newly created periodical, *Muzyka*, in 1925. Poland and Poles were constantly present in his reflections, as evidenced by the artist's correspondence, his publications, and his concert activities. After the war, he came to Poland four times, in 1967, 1978, 1979, and 1980. During the first of these trips, he established contact with Janusz Cegiełła, who became the greatest advocate of Tansman's music in Poland. The composer gave interviews for Polish magazines (mainly for *Ruch Muzyczny*), wrote music commissioned by Polish Radio (e.g., the *Second Sinfonietta* in 1978), and took part in concerts promoting his own work. He also received a number of honors, which influenced his affinity for the country. Until the end of his life, he was always interested in the situation in Poland and in Polish artists, whom he supported whenever possible.

Influence of the new home on the composer's music

Contact with the most important artists and musical directions at that time allowed the composer's personality and technique to flourish and, consequently, helped him pursue an international career. After arriving in France, Tansman spread his wings and discovered a purpose in life. In his compositions, he filtered Polish sensitivity through French moderation and precision and made full use of the latest artistic achievements.

Awareness of the composer's music in both countries

It seems that in Poland his music becomes more and more known every year. Numerous concerts feature his music and the Aleksander Tansman International Festival and Competition of Musical Personalities takes place in Łódź. In France, on the other hand, there is less awareness of his music and he seems to be considered a niche composer, associated mostly with music for children (which makes him popular among educators). His music can be heard mainly at concerts for special events, often organized at the initiative of Polish artists and institutions and the Les Amis d'Alexandre Tansman society led by his daughters (http://www.alexandre-tansman.com).

Composer's personality

Tansman was a cheerful and successful man, full of life, a bit afraid of failure, and somewhat of a mythomaniac. He was a kind and open-minded person, extremely quick to make contacts; sometimes he made friends too quickly, which led to misunderstandings. Occasionally, Tansman declared someone was his great "friend," but while the person in question recognized Tansman's name, he (or she) did not know much about him (such was his relationship with Karol Szymanowski).

Remarkable anecdote or biographical fact

One of the most interesting events in Tansman's life was his journey around the world from 1932–1933, which began in France and wandered through the United States, Hawaii, Japan, China, the Philippines, Singapore, Indonesia (Java, Bali, Sumatra), Ceylon, India, Yemen, Egypt, and the Balearic Islands. The composer brought a camera along, which allowed him to capture adventures worthy of a feature film, for example, his stay in Bali with Walter Spies, his meeting with Gandhi, and his visit to a Japanese temple in Niko. Apart from a few film shots from this journey, there are also musical memories, including *Le Tour du monde en miniature* (1933) and a report, entitled *Quelques impressions d'un voyage autour du monde*, published in *Archives Internationales de la Danse*.

Respondent's Top Choices

- **Favorite work:** *Piano Sonata No. 5* (1955).
- **Best work:** A magnificent opera (lyrical fresco), which the composer regarded as his most important work: *Sabbataï Zévi, le Faux Messie* (1957–1958, libretto by Nathan Bistritzky).
- **Composition still waiting to be discovered:** The opera *Le Roi qui jouait le fou* (1948, libretto by René Laporte).

Respondent: Małgorzata Gamrat

André Tchaikowsky (Andrzej Czajkowski)

Date and place of birth:
1 November 1935, Warsaw.

Date of death:
26 June 1982, Oxford.

Date and place of emigration:
1948–1951, France (Paris); 1956, United Kingdom.

Return to Poland:
No, he never visited Poland after he left.

Key quote

His life could be summed up in one phrase: 'The daily task of being human'.[335]

Activities before emigration

Tchaikowsky was born only four years before Germany invaded Poland, so most of his childhood was spent in the Warsaw Ghetto and then in hiding until the end of the war. He studied piano in Łódź and then Paris (1948–1950) before returning to Poland to continue his music studies in Warsaw. In 1955 he was awarded eighth place in the Chopin International Piano Competition and in 1956 he earned third place at the Queen Elisabeth of Belgium Competition (after Vladimir Ashkenazy and John Browning).

After emigration

He toured the world as a pianist until his death in 1982 and divided his time between playing piano and composition. He first lived in France and Belgium, then London, and finally near Oxford.

Differences between the old and new realities

After leaving Poland, he travelled extensively, giving concerts around the world, learning new repertoire, and composing when possible. It also meant resolving the pain of his childhood, accepting that he was Jewish and homosexual and trying to find both peace in himself and a place he could finally call home.

Reason for leaving Poland

Tchaikowsky started touring after his success at the Queen Elisabeth competition and never returned.

Contact with Poland after emigration

He kept in touch with a few friends, but his most significant contact was with Halina Janowska. Their correspondence was published in English as *My Guardian Demon: Letters of Andrzej Tchaikowsky and Halina Janowska 1956–1982* (London: Smith-Gordon, 2015) and in Polish as *…mój diabeł stróż: listy Andrzeja Czajkowskiego i Haliny Janowskiej* (Warsaw: WAB, 2011).

Influence of the new home on the composer's music

Tchaikowsky as a composer was both an individualist and a cosmopolitan. His music was deeply personal, not affected by external events. He found inspiration in international literature and poetry and also drew on his own musical experiences. Because he spent most of his life outside of Poland, it is difficult to say how leaving his country of birth affected him. Perhaps he would have set his songs to texts of Polish poets or found a topic for his opera in Polish literature or history, but because he was erudite and a polyglot from an early age, I would argue that his interests would have always remained international.

Awareness of the composer's music in both countries

His work is still not fully recognized, but with the world premiere of his opera *The Merchant of Venice*, this process has begun. Some of his other compositions have been performed and recorded in the last five years and it is hoped that more musicians will choose his works for their programs. He is respected as a composer and I believe that if more people learned about him as a person, they would also become interested in his music. He should be valued as one of the most talented pianists of his generation. With the recent release of his recordings by Sony, that is now more possible than ever.

Composer's personality

Tchaikowsky is not someone whose personality can be easily summarized since he was such a complex man. He had a wonderful (if at times not necessarily kind) sense of humor as well as astonishing literary talent, erudition, and memory. A brilliant musician, he also spoke many languages. As a Holocaust survivor, it was difficult for him to make friends, even though people loved his company. He loved being alone, yet was terrified of being lonely. His search for love and acceptance made him many enemies, but for anyone who met him, he always remained a person impossible to forget. He was a ray of sunshine who never managed to pierce his own darkness.

Remarkable anecdote or biographical fact

He had an excellent sense of humor and was never lost for words. Once, a well-known professor of piano in Warsaw criticized his playing of Chopin's *Piano Concerto in F Minor*. Tchaikowsky told the professor that he was critical only because he was jealous that he could not play the piece himself.

Respondent's Top Choices

- **Favorite work:** *Seven Sonnets of Shakespeare* (1967).
- **Best work:** *The Merchant of Venice* (1982).
- **Composition still waiting to be discovered:** *Concerto Classico* for violin and orchestra (1962–1964).

Respondent: Anastasia Belina

Ewa Trębacz

Date and place of birth:
11 November 1973, Kraków.

Date and place of emigration:
2004, United States (Seattle).

Return to Poland:
The composer visits Poland frequently.

Key quote

Art is a place where I somehow live. It is a place with which I can identify more strongly than with any physical or geographical location. It is also a place of my own, where I am free and I enjoy nearly unlimited freedom.[336]

Activities before emigration

In 2000, Ewa Trębacz graduated from the Academy of Music in Kraków with a degree in composition, having studied with Bogusław Schaeffer, and from the University of Economics in Kraków with a degree in computer science. Her first compositions, characterized by a clear individualistic line, come from this period. One of the most interesting is *Il Fonte Adamantino* (1996–2002) for string quartet and vocal ensemble. This piece was inspired by vocal improvisations performed by Olga Szwajgier. In this early composition, Ewa Trębacz paid attention to timbre and, even more, to space. It has a classical formal framework, but improvisation can be found in its individual parts. This practice became characteristic of the young composer; she does not give up using classical formal structures, but fills them with a very modern sound.

After emigration

In 2004, Ewa Trębacz became one of the first doctoral students in the field of new media at the Center for Digital Art and Experimental Media (DXARTS) at the University of Seattle (Washington, United States). She studied computer composition with Richard Karpen and Juan Pampin. She received her doctoral degree in 2010, with a dissertation based on an audiovisual work titled *Errai* for three-dimensional audiovisual space, light animation, soprano, and horn (2009).

Differences between the old and new realities

Trębacz symbolically summarized her need for change and further exploration of her creative skills in her commentary written to *Alethea* for orchestra (2000), the first piece she composed in "suspended time," which was completed after graduating from the Kraków and Seattle universities:

> The year 2000 is, for me personally, a breakthrough year marking the beginning of my independence as an artist. Independence can be understood as self-reliance, but also as a lack of permanent affiliation to any institution or center. At that time, this pushed me into the position of an outsider and made me decide to emigrate. Today, from the perspective of a dozen or so years, this piece sounds to me like music for a film that was never made. Its compositional techniques and sonic language represent a radical simplification compared to the music I wrote while still a student in Kraków. On the other hand, this apparent step 'backwards' became for me the beginning of my individual explorations.[337]

The simplification of compositional means and sonic language mentioned by the composer became necessary in order for her to be able to penetrate far more deeply into the essence of sound and to draw attention to what has become more important to her since then—space. The fundamental change between these two worlds revolved around the shifting of the young artist's attention from the world of acoustic instruments supported by new technologies towards a sound dominated by the latest technological solutions. This is undoubtedly connected with the specialized studies undertaken by the composer at her American university. In Poland, her composition classes had been aimed at developing a slightly more traditional creative technique.

Reason for leaving Poland

Further studies were needed, primarily in the field of new media, including "ambisonics" (a three-dimensional sound recording and projection technique) and computerized spatial animation. Moreover, audiovisual compositions using the latest technological solutions remain in the sphere of her interest.

Contact with Poland after emigration

Trębacz constantly visits Poland. Her work, although known, should be performed in her home country more often, for she is one of its best young composers.

Influence of the new home on the composer's music

The creative skill set which Trębacz has been using since she moved to the United States is cutting-edge. She constantly investigates the latest technological achievements in support of her creative process. She does not just admire the effects of sound color and spatial distribution, but also uses new means to create a coherent and full musical narrative enclosed in a formal framework. In the case of such compositions as *Spinning Zone* for percussion trio and electronic media (2002) or *Minotaur* for horn and surround sound (2005), we can observe various processes of variation, often created by computer transformations. In the case of *Spinning Zone*, we can hear the arch-like form of the narrative, while *Minotaur* is a cycle of variations in which listeners can follow a sonic image, hypothetically participating in the Minotaur's journey through three-dimensional space.

Transformations of sonic structure in terms of absolute pitch, sound, and space contribute to the innovative quality of her work, particularly in the area of compositional structure. Andrzej Chłopecki drew attention to Trębacz's combination of the most modern technological solutions with traditional forms, defining her composition *things lost, things invisible* for ambisonic space and orchestra as "a concerto grosso for computer that uses a new generation of technologies"; he added that one of the soloists in this piece was the acoustic space.[338]

The composer herself wrote in her commentary to this piece:

> The symphonic orchestra, divided into groups, is contrasted with an electronic layer realized with ambisonic technology and using a multi-layered system of loudspeakers. The majority of musicians have the autonomy of a soloist, whose artistic freedom must be combined with an awareness of presence in a particular acoustic space, especially when this awareness amounts to being lost. I recorded its source material in one of the most unique acoustic environments in the United States, the Dan Harpole Cistern in Fort Worden, Washington. This legendary space has a 45-second reverberation and its architecture makes the sound travel along bizarre trajectories.[339]

Awareness of the composer's music in both countries

Trębacz's works have been performed in thirty countries around the world. They are undoubtedly heard more frequently in American concert halls than in Poland. In 2018 the composer received the prestigious Listen Up! Music by Women award from the Allied Arts Foundation in Seattle. The aim of this foundation is to support outstanding female composers. In Poland, her compositions have been performed at major festivals such as the Warsaw Autumn and Kraków Composers' Days (currently called the International Festival of Kraków Composers).

Composer's personality

Trębacz is characterized above all by patience and emotional balance. Furthermore, she possesses the quality of perseverance, which can be understood here as a need to return to similar issues in order to verify them and work through them once more. Equally important features are innovation and originality of thinking.

Remarkable anecdote or biographical fact

The composer has been climbing high mountains for many years and can boast considerable achievements in this field.

Respondent's Top Choices

- **Favorite work:** *Minotaur* for horn and surround sound (2005).
- **Best work:** *Errai* for three-dimensional audiovisual space, light animation, soprano, and horn (2009).
- **Composition still waiting to be discovered:** *Ligeia* for soprano, band and surround sound (2016).

Respondent: Aleksandra Bilińska

Michał Urbaniak

Date and place of birth:
22 January 1943, Warsaw.

Date and place of emigration:
1965–1969, Sweden, Norway; 1973, United States (New York).

Return to Poland:
He returns to Poland to play concerts and for his Urbanator Days workshops.

Key quote
I have been, and I still am, playing New York.[340]

Activities before emigration
He started his musical education in the violin class at the Music School in Łódź, but due to his fascination with jazz music, he also learned to play saxophone. At the age of eighteen, he moved to Warsaw, where he began studying with Tadeusz Wroński at the State Higher School of Music. He played both violin and saxophone during this time. In 1961 he performed at the Jazz Jamboree Festival with Zbigniew Namysłowski's band. In 1962, he completed his first concert tour in the United States with Andrzej Trzaskowski's band, the Wreckers. The years 1962–1965 were marked by his collaboration with Krzysztof Komeda's quintet. In 1969, after his return from Sweden, he formed his own group, the Michał Urbaniak Constellation, with whom he recorded three albums: *Paratyphus B*, *Inactin*, and *Super Constellation*.

After emigration
In 1965 he toured with Krzysztof Komeda's Quintet in Scandinavia. When the tour was over, he decided to stay in Sweden with his future wife Urszula Dudziak and also with Wojtek Karolak. He made recordings there and worked with local musicians. Urbaniak has mentioned that such a long stay in this part of Europe was not a good idea. Together with Urszula they returned to Poland after just two years, but then their car was stolen and they had to start all over again. After arriving in the United States, Urbaniak signed a contract with the Columbia label and in 1974 his *Fusion* album was released. In subsequent years, the violinist released two albums in the United States, *Atma* and *Fusion III*. For

both recordings, jazz was combined with Polish folk music, samples of which Urbaniak had brought with him to the States. These albums were received with great enthusiasm by listeners and critics. Their success greatly influenced the rapid development of his American career.

Differences between the old and new realities

According to Urbaniak, jazz in Europe is treated more intellectually than in the States. In America, he found out that you don't have to read notes in order to be a brilliant musician. You have to love music and celebrate it.

Reason for leaving Poland

The violinist has been in love with the United States since he first went there on a two-month tour with Trzaskowski's band. His goal was to move to New York. He was fascinated by the company of American musicians. He wanted to absorb this music from the inside, playing with jazz musicians every day. He believed in the theory that since he is a jazzman, his homeland is the United States, the cradle of this music.

Contact with Poland after emigration

Urbaniak returns to Poland frequently. For many years he has travelled around Poland as part of the Urbanator Days workshop project for young musicians. He also works with many Polish musicians. He wrote the music for Polish films such as Krzysztof Krauze's *Debt* [*Dług*] (1999) and Andrzej Czeczot's *Eden* (2002). Since 2018, the composer has been an honorary member of the ZAiKS Association of Authors.

Influence of the new home on the composer's music

In an ideal manner, Urbaniak combines Slavic music, which he brought from Poland to the United States, with elements of American jazz, which he learned on the spot. His compositions and manner of playing represented something new for Americans, which helped advance his career. He signed a contract with one of the most famous labels in the world, Columbia Records. In the United States, he had the opportunity to play with world-class jazz musicians such as Miles Davis, Marcus Miller, Chick Corea, and Herbie Hancock.

Awareness of the composer's music in both countries

To this day, Urbaniak's albums are among the most important jazz albums in Poland and around the world. His compositions and performances demonstrate that there are no barriers in improvised music and that the violin does not belong exclusively to the world of classical music.

Composer's personality

As a musician, he constantly strives to achieve his goals. Since his first stay in the United States in 1961, he knew that his home would be there and that he would be able to develop his own distinctive musical language there. He has always spent a lot of time composing and playing violin and saxophone.

Remarkable anecdote or biographical fact

Urbaniak is the only musician from Poland who has recorded an album with the jazz legend Miles Davis. You can hear him on the album *Tutu*. It is said that during his stay in Sweden, together with Wojciech Karolak, these two men deceived their wives by saying if they worked abroad, they would earn enough money for new apartments. The truth was that they were collecting money to buy Hammond organs.

Respondent's Top Choices

- **Favorite work:** *Inactin* (1971).
- **Best work:** *Chinatown* (1975).
- **Composition still waiting to be discovered:** *Atma Tomorrow* (1974).

Respondent: Tomasz Chyła

Henryk Wars
(Henry Vars, real name: Henryk Warszawski)

Date and place of birth:
29 December 1902, Warsaw.

Date of death:
1 September 1977, Los Angeles.

Date and place of emigration:
1947, United States (Los Angeles).

Return to Poland:
He did not return.

Key quote
The assimilation period took me a Biblical seven years.[341]

Activities before emigration
He came from a musical family and spent part of his childhood in France. From 1919–1925 he studied composition and conducting at Warsaw Conservatory with Roman Statkowski, Emil Młynarski, and Henryk Melcer. After graduation, he began working with Warsaw cabarets such as Marine Eye [Morskie Oko] and the Syrena Record label. In 1928 he composed a piece that the *New York Times* considered to be the first Polish jazz composition. After 1929 he was involved with the cinematography field. He created music for about fifty interwar Polish films (among others, *Spy in a Mask* [*Szpieg w masce*], directed by Mieczysław Krawicz, 1933; *Love Maneuvers* [*Manewry miłosne*], directed by Jan Nowina-Przybylski and Konrad Tom, 1935; *Upstairs* [*Piętro wyżej*], directed by Leon Trystan, 1937; and *Forgotten Melody* [*Zapomniana melodia*], directed by Konrad Tom and Jan Fethke, 1938). These included timeless hits such as *Love Will Forgive You Anything* [*Miłość ci wszystko wybaczy*], *Sex Appeal*, and *You Won't Forget Me Anymore* [*Już nie zapomnisz mnie*].

After emigration
He moved to Hollywood in 1947 from Italy, where he had been a member of Anders' Army. As he said, "In those lean years, I could only assure people that I was a film music composer."[342] It was only in the early 1950s that he returned to work on films (*Chained for Life*, directed by Harry L. Fraser, 1952), initially as an arranger, copyist, and composer

working within the so-called "team composing" structure. Wars's greatest successes were the soundtrack to two films and the *Flipper* series (directed by James B. Clark, 1963; *Flipper's New Adventure*, directed by Leon Benson, 1964; *Flipper*, directed by Ricou Browning and others, 1964–1966). Wars also continued to compose songs that appeared in the repertoire of Doris Day, Brenda Lee, and Margaret Whiting.

Differences between the old and new realities

In interwar Poland, Wars enjoyed lasting success. Everyone knew and sang his melodies. Vocal stars, with Hanka Ordonówna at the forefront, pleaded with him to be asked to sing his songs. The composer's position in Hollywood was quite different and, initially, very difficult. The recommendations of Ira Gershwin and Arthur Rubinstein proved ineffective in his new reality. The presence of many first-rate European composers in the United States created fierce competition. Wars also had difficulties acclimating to the American style of film music, so that he found it hard to use the greatest assets of his craft, including his gift for creating excellent melodies. Eventually, however, he managed to return to the profession in the full sense of the word, although he never achieved a position comparable to what he had achieved in Poland.

Reason for leaving Poland

During World War II, he joined Anders' Army with the group Tea-Jazz, which he had founded in Lviv with Eugeniusz Bodo and Kazimierz Krukowski. As part of that experience, he led a band called Polish Parade, making Polish songs famous on the military fronts of Europe and the Middle East. Wars was prompted to stay abroad by news of the fate of Anders' soldiers in postwar Poland.

Contact with Poland after emigration

After the war, Wars visited Poland only once, in 1967. Several of his works were recorded at that time, including the jazz suite *Manhattan Impressions* and his *Piano Concerto*. Leading singers, including Irena Santor and Rena Rolska, recalled the composer's interwar hits, released in 1972 on *Henryk Wars' Unforgettable Hits* [*Niezapomniane Przeboje Henryka Warsa*], which also included his American hit song *Over and Over*, sung by Anna German.

Influence of the new home on the composer's music

Wars's first lean years in the United States brought forth symphonic music that lay unknown for decades. These pieces demonstrate the composer's considerable ambitions, especially in terms of form and instrumentation. They are both a testimony to his fascination with European classics and a record of his creative contacts with American music. As a composer of Hollywood film music, Wars developed his instrumentation skills; his previous works for Polish cinematography were admittedly more melodious and memorable, but at the same time a bit coarse technically.

Awareness of the composer's music in both countries

In Poland, Wars is known as one of the most important composers of popular song and his best songs continually reappear in new interpretations. Wars's second image, as a talented composer of large symphonic forms, is also being discovered. In the United States, he is a partly forgotten, marginalized artist, and his fame lasts mainly thanks to the activities of the Polish community there.

Composer's personality

Wars, as we can judge from his life and achievements, was a working man and a professional. Under no historical circumstances or social or financial conditions did he ever give up trying to continue his work.

Remarkable anecdote or biographical fact

From 1947–1950, the most difficult period of his emigration, Wars wrote symphonic works (including *Symphony No. 1* and *Piano Concerto*), which testify to his fascination with Ravel's music and his desire to compose so-called "serious" works. Until 2002, these lay forgotten in the garage of his Brentwood house. The composer's scores were sorted out by Marek Żebrowski, a Polish pianist living in Los Angeles, who also arranged for their performance.

Respondent's Top Choices

- **Favorite work:** Full of charm and humor, the unpretentious soundtrack to two cinema films and over fifty episodes of the television series *Flipper* (1963) shows that Wars finally mastered the musical conventions of classical Hollywood cinema, in this case productions suitable for family and adventure cinema. Wars's music to *Flipper*, perfectly written, may not be as melodious as his songs, but it does attract attention with its dramatic nerve, yet a minimum of intrusive illustrations.
- **Best work:** His best work—besides his interwar songs, which already belong to the Polish so-called "national songbook"—seems to be the four-movement *Symphony No. 1*, probably written around 1948. Wars showed himself to be a follower of the romantic and modernist line of programmatic music and a symphonic master who did not strictly adhere to the traditional sonata cycle. The concept of the *Symphony*, which has quite a dense score, revolves around its narrative, which offers a multiplicity of expressive actions. Its multi-phase form is based on the order of various kinds of sounds and textures, which display, along with certain themes (e.g., the clarinet in the second movement), the use of specific leitmotifs, just as in film music. In its entirety, the *Symphony* is like a split piece; like Wars's life, it is related to European traditions, to the music of Ravel and Scriabin, and also to the American idiom of music (especially in the last two movements).
- **Composition still waiting to be discovered:** His American soundtracks are waiting to be rediscovered. Their interpretation and evaluation in the context of classic Hollywood film would reveal the true meaning of the "American Wars [Vars]."

Respondent: Grzegorz Piotrowski

Mieczysław Weinberg
(Mieczysław Wajnberg, Moishe Vainberg)

Date and place of birth:
8 December 1919, Warsaw.

Date of death:
26 February 1996, Moscow.

Date and place of emigration:
1939, Soviet Union (1939, Minsk; 1941, Tashkent; 1943, Moscow).

Return to Poland:
He did not return.

Key quote

Weinberg was a composer of three nations, hence we can find special cultural values in his music.[343]

Activities before emigration

Before leaving Poland, Weinberg studied as a pianist at the Warsaw Conservatory, performed, and made his first attempts at composition. Since his childhood, he had worked with his father, who was active as a musician in Warsaw's Jewish theaters.

After emigration

Mieczysław Weinberg was active as a pianist and composer, not only in classical music, but also in film and even for the circus. It should be noted that in this case the concepts of assimilation and adaptation seems to be more relevant than emigration.

Differences between the old and new realities

How did interwar Warsaw and Soviet Moscow differ? In all aspects. Weinberg, a Polish-Jewish artist functioning at the intersection of two cultures, expanded his musical identity by incorporating elements of Russian-Soviet culture. His experience was shaped by the requirements of socialist realism, by living through the terrors of Stalinism, and by his friendships with many prominent figures of Soviet cultural life, especially Dmitri Shostakovich.

Reason for leaving Poland

Weinberg had to escape the Nazis in order to save his life. Had he stayed in Poland, he probably would have died in the Holocaust, just as his entire family did.

Contact with Poland after emigration

Weinberg's contacts with Poland were sporadic. He regularly read Polish literature and any available Polish magazines and also met with Poles visiting the Soviet Union, including Krzysztof Penderecki and Krzysztof Meyer. He visited Poland, more specifically the Warsaw Autumn Festival, as a Soviet delegate in 1966.

Influence of the new home on the composer's music

His compositional studies in the Soviet Union and his artistic activity in that country had a decisive influence on his music. Aesthetically, he was close to Shostakovich, although his own voice remained clear and personal within twentieth-century music. The circle of musicians and performers with whom he was involved also influenced him significantly, as did his work with Soviet cinematography and the corresponding need to fulfil its specific aesthetic needs. Nevertheless, many references to Poland could be found in Weinberg's work—through the texts of Polish poets, allusions to Polish folk music, and quotations from Chopin's works.

Awareness of the composer's music in both countries

Currently, Weinberg's work is being rediscovered around the world. In Russia (and to a large extent beyond), he is presented as the third great Soviet composer, after Shostakovich and Prokofiev. In Poland, he is considered a great, but unjustly forgotten artist of three cultures: Polish, Russian, and Jewish. The world premiere of his opera *The Passenger* [*Pasażerka*] in Bregenz in 2010, which was organized by David Pountney in cooperation with the Adam Mickiewicz Institute and the Grand Theater – National Opera in Warsaw, was a pivotal moment in the renaissance of his work.

Composer's personality

People who knew Weinberg remember him as a modest, friendly, and rather quiet man, who listened to his questioners with a mysterious smile on his face.

Remarkable anecdote or biographical fact

Weinberg was famous for the extraordinary creative ease he experienced as a composer. During a forum held in Bregenz in 2010 on the occasion of the premiere of *The Passenger*, Russian musicologist Mikhail Bialik told the following anecdote: According to gossip circulating around Moscow, Weinberg was very sick, so sick that he could not get out of bed. After a few days, one of his friends continued to worry about the composer's health. In response to his concerns, he heard: "But it's all right! Although he is still not getting out of bed, he is finishing a new sonata."

Respondent's Top Choices

- **Favorite work:** *Symphony No. 8 "Polish Flowers"* [*Symfonia nr 8 "Kwiaty Polskie"*] (1964).
- **Best work:** *The Passenger*, libretto by Alexander Medvedev, based on motives from Zofia Posmysz's novel (1967–1968).
- **Composition still waiting to be discovered:** *Symphony No. 2* (1991).

Respondent: Aleksander Laskowski

Krzysztof Wołek

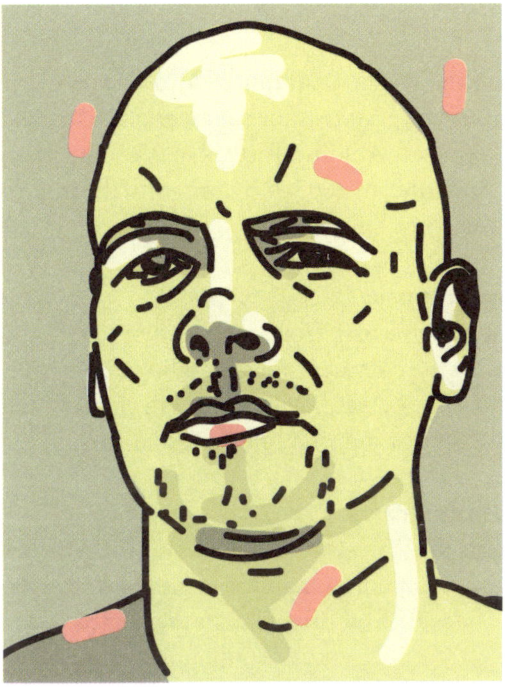

Date and place of birth:
14 April 1976, Bytom.

Date and place of emigration:
2000–2001, the Netherlands (Amsterdam); 2001, United States (Chicago).

Return to Poland:
He did not return.

Key quote

I believe that time in music, as in life, is relative.[344]

Activities before emigration

Before leaving the country, he graduated from the Chopin Music School in Bytom, having studied in its percussion class. In 1999 he studied composition with Edward Bogusławski at the Karol Szymanowski Music Academy in Katowice.

After emigration

After his stay in Amsterdam, where he studied with Louis Andriessen, Martijn Padding, and Gilius van Bergiek, he left for the United States to continue his education. He received his doctorate in computer music from the University of Chicago in 2007, studying with Marta Ptaszyńska and Howard Sandroff. He has created many electronic compositions, such as *Zero Gained* for no-input mixer (2016), and electroacoustic works, which combine acoustic instruments with live electronics.

Differences between the old and new realities

In the United States, the composer gained access to better technology. He became the head of the Computer Music Studio at the University of Louisville and is currently Professor of Composition and Director of the Electronic Music Studio at the same school.

Reason for leaving Poland

He wanted to broaden his horizons and continue his education in electroacoustic music.

Contact with Poland after emigration

He is a member of the Program Committee for the Warsaw Autumn Festival. He regularly visits Poland, where his works have been performed. *Elements* for chamber orchestra and live electronics, for example, was heard at the Warsaw Autumn Festival in 2009 and *Ins of Outs* and *Outs of Ins* for two computers, was presented in 2007 in Bytom, with the improvisational elements performed by the composer.

Influence of the new home on the composer's music

In the United States, the composer has met many artists from various disciplines and successfully collaborated with many of them. At the computer music studio in Louisville, he has access to the most modern equipment. Wołek creates works for both classical and electronic instruments; he is also the author of operas and multimedia installations.

Awareness of the composer's music in both countries

In Poland, Wołek's music is regularly performed at the Warsaw Autumn Festival, the Wrocław Music Theater Capitol, the National Polish Radio Symphony Orchestra in Katowice, the National Forum of Music in Wrocław, and the Codes Festival in Lublin. In the United States, the composer plays an important role in the electroacoustic music community. From 2010–2015 he was the director of the University of Louisville New Music Festival. He works with many associations in Poland and abroad; among others, he has been an organizer and jury member for the prestigious Charles Grawemeyer Composition Competition in Louisville. Wołek's interdisciplinary interests have enriched the concerts and projects he has organized, in which musicians, visual artists, and dancers have participated.

Composer's personality

Wołek is interested in science, robotics, and visual arts. In his opinion, it is important to be ready for new perceptual experiences. With regard to music, he seeks to reflect the present times in his own work.

Remarkable anecdote or biographical fact

Despite his love of strict forms, Wołek does not avoid improvisation. He skillfully combines composed music with an electroacoustic layer that is created live during performance. He also likes music installations and projects that combine various fields of art.

Respondent's Top Choices

- **Favorite work:** *Un Claro del Tiempo* for soprano, flute, piano and electronic (2008).
- **Best work:** *Nici*, a chamber opera based on Stanisław Lem's short story *How the World Was Saved* [*Jak ocalał świat*] (2016).
- **Composition still waiting to be discovered:** *Bouncing*, an audiovisual installation (2012).

Respondent: Wojtek Krzyżanowski

Andrzej Zieliński

Date and place of birth:
5 October 1944, Gdów.

Date and place of emigration:
April 1981, United States (New York).

Return to Poland:
In the mid-1990s, Andrzej Zieliński began visiting Poland, where he now spends most of his time, primarily in Kraków and Zakopane.

Key quote

I'm a wandering man, I cannot stay in one place. It must be an émigré's disease.[345]

Activities before emigration

With his younger brother Jacek, he established the Scalds [Skaldowie] band in 1965, for which he has composed most of his music. Among other pieces, there are hits such as *Bunny* [*Króliczek*], *Everything Tells Me Someone Fell in Love with Me* [*Wszystko mi mówi, że mnie ktoś pokochał*], *The Sleigh Runs Off* [*Z kopyta kulig rwie*], *The Lovely Cellist* [*Prześliczna wiolonczelistka*], and *You're on Cloud Nine* [*Cała jesteś w skowronkach*]; these use lyrics by famous poets such as Leszek A. Moczulski, Agnieszka Osiecka, and Wojciech Młynarski. His pre-emigration musical oeuvre includes several suites recorded with Scalds: *Krivan, Krivan* [*Krywań, Krywań*], *The Creation of the World, Part Two* [*Stworzenia świata część druga*], *The Magical Journey* [*Podróż magiczna*], and *Winter Fairytale* [*Zimowa bajka*]. *Krivan, Krivan* was a brave attempt at entering the world of expanded arrangements of works inspired by progressive rock.[346] Today, the composition is considered to be the band's greatest achievement, and its recording is believed to be one of the milestones of Polish rock music. Zieliński has also composed music for other artists, including *The Carriage Ballad* [*Ballada wagonowa*] for Maryla Rodowicz.

After emigration

After emigration, he traveled across the United States with American bands and musicians. As he said for *Dziennik Polonijny*, "I lived on the road, but I liked it then. I wanted to be a 'musical cowboy.'"[347] His status as a musician was demonstrated when New York's

Daily News called him the "Polish Lennon" in an article about European artists living in New York.[348]

Differences between the old and new realities

In December 1981, martial law was imposed in Poland. By contrast, the United States, where Zieliński was then living, was a democratic country with great tolerance for political and creative freedom.

Reason for leaving Poland

The Scalds band found out about the introduction of martial law in Poland during its tour of the United States. This political turn of events in his home country reinforced his decision to stay abroad. He also said that his dream had always been to play in America with American musicians.

Contact with Poland after emigration

During the early 1990s, Zieliński, living in New York, began to play occasionally with the reactivated Scalds ensemble. He joined the band for good in 1994.

Influence of the new home on the composer's music

As Zieliński has emphasized, performing with American artists was a tremendous experience that enhanced his later work.

Awareness of the composer's music in both countries

The reactivated Scalds band still performs and releases new albums. Zieliński has written music for the albums *Harmony of the World* [*Harmonia świata*] (2006), *Silence Screams* [*Cisza krzyczy*] (2007), and *As Years Go By* [*Z biegiem lat*] (2010). The latter contains songs composed from 1972–1980, which were supposed to be included on the band's twelfth album. Due to their tour of the United States, when Zieliński decided not to return to Poland, the album was never released. In 2000, he recorded a solo album in Poland, *Starting All Over Again* [*Znów od zera*].

Composer's personality

Zieliński, as a "proper" rock musician, still wears long hair. He explains, "my brother Jacek and I have such strong hair thanks to our Highlander mom." He adds that he can't imagine himself with a different haircut: "It is as if you cut Robert Plant's hair [the lead vocalist for Led Zeppelin]. Nobody would recognize him."[349]

Remarkable anecdote or biographical fact

In 1968, during the Opole Song Festival, the Scalds band was obliged by the enthusiastic audience to play five encores of *Everything Tells Me Someone Fell in Love with Me*, thus establishing a festival record.[350]

Respondent's Top Choices

- **Favorite work:** *Bunny* [*Króliczek*] (1969), a song to Agnieszka Osiecka's witty lyrics, formally complex but simple in expression.
- **Best work:** *Everything Tells Me Someone Fell in Love with Me* [*Wszystko mi mówi, że mnie*

ktoś pokochał] (1968), written to Wojciech Młynarski's lyrics. With this song, Skaldowie established a record of festival encores. The song is still popular today and was also used in an advertising campaign for a Polish juice product.

- **Composition still waiting to be discovered:** *I Will Find You Tomorrow* [*Jutro odnajdę ciebie*] (1967), a song written for Jerzy Passendorfer's film *The Big Beat* [*Mocne uderzenie*] (1967). Lyrical and beautiful music, today it remains somewhat forgotten.

Respondent: Anna Kruszyńska

References

Appendix: List of Composers Abroad (1918–2018)

Legend:

→ direction

* learn more about the composer in part II: *Composers' Profiles: In Other Words, Marlena Wieczorek Asks, Experts Respond*

A

Jarosław Abramow-Newerly (b. 17 May 1933) → Canada
Jerzy Gabriel Abratowski (22 April 1929 – 1 February 1989) → United States
Isidor Yulyevich Achron (24 November 1892 – 12 May 1948) → United States
Antonina Adamowska-Szumowska (22 February 1868 – 16 August 1938) → United States
Józef Adamowski (4 July 1862 – 8 May 1930) → United States
Tymoteusz (Timothee) Adamowski (24 March 1858 – 18 April 1943) → United States
Kari Amirian (actually Karolina Amirian; also known as Kari) (b. 1985) → Great Britain
George Andreani (actually Joseph Kumok) (28 February 1901 – 2 April 1979) → Argentina
Apostolis (Apostolos) Anthimos (b. 25 September 1954) → Greece
Katarzyna Arnhold (b. 4 August 1968) → Netherlands
Tomasz Arnold (b. 18 May 1990) → United States
Grażyna Auguścik (b. 17 August 1955) → United States

B

Marcin Banasik (b. 16 December 1982) → China
Zbigniew Bargielski* (b. 21 January 1937) → Austria
Józef Beer (7 May 1908 – 23 November 1987) → Switzerland → France
Roman Berger* (9 August 1930 – 22 December 2020) → Slovakia
Marek Biliński (b. 17 May 1953) → Kuwait
Zbigniew Bizoń (b. 30 March 1942) → Sweden
Wojtek (Wojciech) Blecharz* (b. 21 June 1981) → United States → Germany
Jerzy Bojanowski (18 June 1893 – 10 September 1983) → United States
Stan Borys (actually Stanisław Guzek) (b. 3 September 1941) → United States → Canada → United States
Aleksander Brachocki (17 January 1897 – 5 January 1948) → United States
Joanna Bruzdowicz-Tittel* (b. 17 May 1943) → Belgium → France
Andrzej Brzeski (25 March 1944 – 19 October 2010) → Sweden → Norway
Szymon Brzóska (b. 22 January 1981) → Belgium
Magdalena Buchwald (b. 10 March 1972) → Germany
Juliusz Bujalski (b. 4 October 1953) → United States

C

Jakub Ciupiński (b. 11 May 1981) → United States
Edward Czerny (11 June 1917 – 16 February 2003) → Germany
Tomasz Czyżewski (b. 28 July 1964) → United States

D

Monika Dalach (b. 19 July 1993) → Great Britain
Władysław Daniłowski (also known as Walter Dana) (26 April 1902 – 4 March 2000) → Italy → United States
Andrzej Dobrowolski* (9 September 1921 – 8 August 1990) → Austria
Adam Dołżycki (24 December 1886 – 9 September 1972) → Germany
Jacek Domagała (b. 19 August 1947) → Germany
Edward G. Domański (b. 12 March 1942) → Canada
Błażej Dowlasz (b. 29 May 1978) → Germany
Jan Drzewiecki (18 June 1938 – 28 November 2006) → Norway
Ireneusz Dudek (b. 7 May 1951) → Netherlands
Urszula Bogumiła Dudziak (b. 22 October 1943) → United States
Andrzej Dutkiewicz (b. 30 September 1942) → United States
Roman Dyląg (b. 22 February 1938) → Sweden → Switzerland
Andrzej Paweł Dziubek (also known as Andrej Nebb) (b. 14 June 1954) → Czechoslovakia → Austria → Norway

E

Władysław Walter Eiger (7 February 1907 – 11 May 1991) → France → United States

F

Adam FALKIEWICZ (4 January 1980 – 21 May 2007) → Netherlands
Stanisław FERSZKO (Shmuel Fershko) (26 February 1914 – 30 July 1990) → Austria → Palestine → United States
Piotr FIGIEL (13 April 1940 – 22 December 2011) → Germany
Jerzy FITELBERG* (20 May 1903 – 25 April 1951) → Germany → France → United States
Zbigniew FORYŚ (b. 3 March 1957) → Germany
Ignacy FRIEDMAN (actually Salomon Izaak Freudman) (13 February 1882 – 26 January 1948) → Germany → Denmark → Italy → Australia
Julian FRONT (12 November 1897 – December 1964) → Israel
Nina FUKUOKA (b. 22 June 1988) → Belgium → Japan

G

Aleksander GABRYŚ (b. 22 October 1974) → Switzerland
Cezariusz GADZINA (b. 13 August 1966) → Belgium
Izabelle (Wiesława) GARR (b. 1953) → France
Szymon "Pimpon" GĄSIOREK (b. 3 January 1993) → Denmark
Artur GELBRUN (11 July 1913 – 23 December 1985) → Israel
Bartłomiej GLINIAK (b. 25 December 1973) → Germany → United States
Mateusz GLIŃSKI (6 April 1892 – 2 January 1976) → Italy → United States → Canada
Czesław GŁADKOWSKI (20 July 1940 – 8 December 2002) → France
Katarzyna GŁOWICKA (Katarina / Kasia Glowicka) (b. 12 October 1977) → Netherlands
Marcin Dominik GŁUCH (b. 7 May 1973) → Sweden
Leopold GODOWSKI (13 February 1870 – 21 November 1938) → United States → Canada
Wojciech GOGOLEWSKI (b. 21 September 1953) → Germany
Henryk GOLD (3 September 1899 – 6 July 1977) → United States
Beata E. GOLEC (b. 29 June 1981) → United States
Jarosław GOŁEMBIOWSKI (b.10 February 1958) → United States
Mikołaj Piotr GÓRECKI* (b. 1 February 1971) → United States
Jarmila Xymena GÓRNA (Gorna) → Great Britain
Mieszko GÓRSKI (b. 8 February 1953) → United States
Irek (Ireneusz) GRABOWSKI (22 March 1966 – 19 August 2010) → Belgium → Qatar
Alfred GRADSTEIN (30 October 1904 – 29 September 1954) → France
Allan GRAY (actually Józef Żmigrod) (23 February 1902 – 10 September 1973) → Great Britain
Piotr GRELLA-MOŻEJKO (b. 15 March 1961) → Canada
Walter (Władysław) GRIGAITIS (1880? – 1957) → United States
Jerzy GRUNWALD (also known as George & G) (b. 7 April 1950) → United States → Sweden
Kuba (Jakub) GUDZ (b. 15 November 1992) → Germany
Włodzimierz (Wlodek) GULGOWSKI (b. 13 February 1944) → Sweden

H

Roman HAUBENSTOCK-RAMATI* (27 February 1919 – 3 March 1994) → Israel → Austria
Michał HOCHMAN (b. 4 March 1944) → United States

Józef Hofman (Hofmann) (20 January 1876 – 16 February 1957) → Germany → United States
Zbigniew Hołdys (b. 19 December 1951) → United States
Bronisław Horowicz (28 July 1910 – 10 July 2005) → France
Jerzy Hryniewicz (b. 1947) → Sweden
Edward Hulewicz (b. 22 November 1937) → United States

J

Dagmara Jack (b. 29 February 1984) → Germany → United States
Jan Janca (b. 1 June 1933) → Germany → France → Germany
Jan Janikowski (16 May 1926 – 28 May 1990) → United States
Natalia Janotha (8 June 1856 – 9 June 1932) → Great Britain → Netherlands
Tadeusz Jarecki (1 January 1889 – 2 May 1956) → United States
Dawid Jarzyński (b. 24 December 1984) → Switzerland
Dobromiła Jaskot* (b. 29 May 1981) → Australia
Anna Jastrzębska (b. 11 August 1950) → Norway
Barbara Jaźwińska (b. 14 May 1950) → United States

K

Jan Andrzej Paweł (Jan A. P.) Kaczmarek* (b. 29 April 1953) → United States
Jacek Kaczmarski* (22 March 1957 – 10 April 2004) → France → United States → Australia
Józef Kamiński (17 November 1903 – 14 October 1972) → Palestine → Israel
Bronisław (Bronislau) Kaper* (5 February 1902 – 26 April 1983) → United States
Jarosław Kapuściński* (b. 12 December 1964) → United States
Zygmunt Karasiński (2 May 1898 – 20 April 1973) → Denmark
Aleksander Karczyński (20 February 1882 – 23 December 1973) → United States
Zbigniew Karkowski* (14 March 1958 – 12 December 2013) → Sweden → Japan
Dominik Karski* (b. 24 June 1972) → Australia
Tadeusz Zygfryd Kassern* (19 March 1904 – 2 May 1957) → United States
Bernard Kawka (Kafka) (b. 16 July 1943) → United States
Maciej Kądziela (b. 3 April 1990) → Denmark
Paweł Klecki* (Paul Kletzky) (21 March 1900 – 5 March 1973) → Germany → Italy → Soviet Union → Switzerland → Great Britain
Krzysztof Klenczon (14 January 1942 – 7 April 1981) → United States
Rachel Knobler (10 June 1924 – 31 December 2017) → Germany
Mieczysław Koliński (5 September 1901 – 7 May 1981) → Germany → Belgium → United States → Canada
Jerzy Kołaczkowski (23 September 1907 – 19 December 1995) → Hungary → France → Great Britain
Krzysztof (Christopher) Komeda* (actually Krzysztof Trzciński) (27 April 1931 – 23 April 1969) → United States
Magdalena Komiażyk (b. 2 October 1945) → Italy
Marzena Komsta* (b. 7 February 1970) → France
Adrian Konarski (b. 7 February 1975) → Great Britain

Michał KONDRACKI* (actually Michał Kondracki-Ostoya) (5 October 1902 – 27 February 1984) → France → Brazil → United States
Piotr Paweł (Peter Paul) KOPROWSKI (b. 24 August 1947) → France → Canada
Abel (Adam) KORZENIOWSKI* (b. 18 July 1972) → United States
Martyna KOSECKA* (b. 18 January 1989) → Iran
Maciej KOSSOWSKI (b. 11 February 1937) → United States
Liliana KOSTRZEWA (b. 22 September 1984) → France
Sławomir KOWALEWSKI (b. 25 February 1946) → United States
Zbigniew KRUCZEK (b. 1952) → Belgium
Hanna KULENTY* (b. 18 March 1961) → Netherlands
Eryk KULM (b. 16 March 1952) → United States
Szymon KURAN (16 December 1955 – 7 August 2005) → Iceland
Dobrochna Daria KWIATKOWSKA (b. 7 May 1969) → Canada
Andrzej KWIECIŃSKI* (b. 14 June 1984) → Netherlands

L

Piotr LACHERT (5 September 1938 – 18 September 2018) → Italy → Belgium
Szymon LAKS* (1 November 1901 – 11 December 1983) → France
Jerzy LALEWICZ (21 August 1876 – 1 December 1951) → Brazil
Paul LAMKOFF (actually Peter Lampcovici) (14 December 1888 – 11 March 1953) → United States
Stanisław LANDAU (Stanley Laudan) (about 1912 – 1992) → Great Britain
Wanda LANDOWSKA* (5 July 1879 – 16 August 1959) → France → United States
Mikołaj LASKOWSKI (b. 14 October 1988) → Netherlands → Germany
Marian LICHTMAN (b. 30 March 1947) → Denmark
Borys Grzegorz LOMANI (11 April 1893 – 11 July 1975) → Brazil

Ł

Feliks ŁABUŃSKI (27 December 1892 – 8 April 1979) → France → United States
Wiktor ŁABUŃSKI (14 April 1895 – 26 January 1974) → United States
Antoni ŁAZARKIEWICZ (actually Antoni Komasa-Łazarkiewicz) (b. 12 February 1980) → Germany
Jędrzej ŁAGODZIŃSKI (b. 27 October 1996) → Denmark

M

Roman MACIEJEWSKI* (28 February 1910 – 30 April 1998) → Sweden → United States → Sweden
Miłosz MAGIN* (6 July 1929 – 4 March 1999) → Portugal → France
Krzysztof MAJCHRZAK (b. 6 January 1954) → France
Tadeusz MAJERSKI (29 June 1888 – 16 October 1963) → Soviet Union
Adam MAKOWICZ* (actually Adam Matyszkowicz) b. 18 August 1940) → United States
Anna MAŁEK (b. 23 September 1977) → Spain → Austria
Julia MARCELL (actually Julia Górniewicz) (b. 20 April 1982) → Germany
Czesław MAREK (16 September 1891 – 17 July 1985) → Austria → Czech Republic → Switzerland
Jan MARKOWSKI (14 March 1913 – 12 April 1980) → Great Britain → Germany

Michał Martyniuk (b. 7 January 1988) → New Zealand
Alfred Melodysta (Fred Melodyst, actually Alfred Fred Melodist) (24 November 1894 – 1960) → France → Israel
Krzysztof Meyer* (b. 11 August 1943) → Germany
Mirosław Męczyński (d. 28 May 2018) → Germany
Bronisław Mirski (Nek Mirskey) (actually Bronisław Moszkowicz) (21 September 1887 – 19 February 1927) → United States
Aleksandra Mońko-Allen (b. 19 June 1976) → United States
Eugeniusz Morawski-Dąbrowa* (2 November 1876 – 23 October 1948) → France
Piotr Moss* (b. 13 May 1949) → France
Maurycy (Moritz) Moszkowski (23 August 1854 – 4 March 1925) → Germany → France
Gabriela Moyseowicz (b. 4 May 1944) → Germany
Robert Muczynski (19 March 1929 – 25 May 2010) → United States
Artur Muller (20 October 1893 – 4 August 1960) → Brazil

N

Andrzej Nikodemowicz (2 January 1925 – 28 January 2017) → Soviet Union
Aleksander Nowacki (b. 21 August 1944) → Austria → Switzerland → Germany
Ewelina Nowicka (b. 26 October 1982) → Germany

O

Karol Obara (b. 4 February 1976) → Germany
Kazimierz Jerzy Oberfeld (also known as Georges Grandchamp) (16 November 1903 – 23/24 January 1945) → France
Edward Olearczyk (4 March 1915 – 9 September 1994) → Israel
Henryk Opieński (13 January 1870 – 21 January 1942) → Switzerland

P

Henryk Pachulski (4 October 1859 – 2 March 1921) → Russia
Ignacy Jan Paderewski* (6 November 1860 – 29 June 1941) → Germany → Austria → France → Switzerland → United States
Jerzy (George) Pakulski (5 October 1932 – 27 December 2004) → South Africa
Roman Palester* (28 December 1907 – 25 August 1989) → France
Zbigniew Paleta (b. 13 May 1942) → Mexico
Andrzej Panufnik* (24 September 1914 – 27 October 1991) → Great Britain
Stanisław Leon Paszke (6 November 1894 – 28 July 1974) → Germany
Marcin Pączkowski (Paczkowski) (b. 1983) → United States
Jerzy Petersburski* (24 April 1895 – 7 October 1979) → Brazil → Argentina
Ludo Phillip (Philip / Philipp) (1901 – 1970) → United States
Grzegorz Pieniek (b. 18 November 1982) → Austria
Kamil Piotrowicz (7 August 1992) → Denmark
Jan Pogány (actually Jan Maślankiewicz-Pogány) (b. 23 June 1960) → Germany
Jakub Polaczyk (b. 8 March 1983) → United States
Prasqual (Tomasz Praszczałek)* (b. 2 December 1981) → Germany
Bogdan Precz (27 May 1960 – 24 July 1996) → Spain
Zbigniew Preisner (b. 20 May 1955) → Switzerland

Marta PTASZYŃSKA* (b. 29 November 1943) → United States

R

Jacek RABIŃSKI (b. 15 December 1956) → Germany
Piotr RADKO (b. 29 April 1957) → Germany
Maciej RADZIEJEWSKI (b. 9 October 1951) → United States
Jan RADZYŃSKI (b. 1950) → Israel → United States
Karol RATHAUS* (16 September 1895 – 21 November 1954) → Germany → France → Great Britain → United States
Konstanty (Constantin) REGAMEY* (28 January 1907 – 27 December 1982) → Switzerland
Vitold REK (actually Witold Eugeniusz Szczurek) (b. 18 October 1955) → Germany
Wiesław RENTOWSKI (b. 22 February 1953) → United States
Fred RICH (actually Frederic Ephram Rich) (31 January 1898 – 8 September 1956) → United States
Mirosław ROGALA (b. 25 April 1954) → United States
Ludomir Michał ROGOWSKI* (3 October 1881 – 13 March 1954) → Croatia
Józef ROSENSTOCK (27 January 1895 – 17 October 1985) → Germany → United States
Maurycy ROSENTHAL (18 December 1862 – 3 September 1946) → United States
Adolf (Adi, Edi, Eddi) ROSNER (actually Adolph Ignatievich Rosner) (26 May 1910 – 8 August 1976) → Soviet Union → Germany
Jerzy (George) ROSNER (12 January 1909 – 15 August 2002) → United States
Wiesław RUCIŃSKI (also known as Jan Castor) (27 June 1954 – 21 April 2016) → Australia → United States
Anna (Ania) RYBACKA (b. 24 April 1986) → Denmark
Roman RYTERBAND* (2 August 1914 – 3 November 1979) → Switzerland → Canada → United States

S

Jerzy SAPIEJEWSKI (b. 20 March 1945) → United States
Rafał SARNECKI (b. 11 December 1982) → United States
Paul SAWTELL (Sawatzki) (3 February 1906 – 1 August 1971) → United States
Alfred SCHULZ (Schütz) (2 July 1910 – 21 October 1999) → Brazil → Germany
Zbigniew SEIFERT* (6 June 1946 – 15 February 1979) → United States
Władysław (Vladislav) "Adzik" SENDECKI (b. 17 January 1955) → Germany
Ryszard SIELICKI (actually Ryszard Berlinson) (3 March 1916 – 21 December 2005) → Soviet Union
Elżbieta SIKORA* (b. 20 October 1943) → France
Zygmunt SINGER (30 June 1876 – 29 January 1958) → France
Kuba (Jakub) SKOWROŃSKI (b. 1988) → Indonesia
Stanisław SKROWACZEWSKI* (3 October 1923 – 21 February 2017) → United States
Bettina SKRZYPCZAK* (b. 25 January 1962) → Switzerland
Cezary SKUBISZEWSKI* (b. 10 December 1948) → Australia
Tomasz SKWERES (b. 3 April 1984) → Austria
Jacek SOBIERAJ (b. 5 March 1958) → Canada
Adam SOŁTYS (4 July 1890 – 6 July 1968) → Soviet Union

Waldemar Sorychta (b. 1967) → Germany
Michał Spisak* (14 September 1914 – 29 January 1965) → France
Anna Stachurska (b. 1987) → United States
Tomasz Stańko* (11 July 1942 – 29 July 2018) → United States
Joanna Stępalska-Spix (b. 4 September 1967) → Germany
Zygmunt (Sigismond) Stojowski* (actually Zygmunt Denis Antoni Jordan de Stojowski) (14 May 1870 – 6 November 1946) → United States
Mieczysław Surzyński (22 December 1866 – 11 September 1924) → Germany
Paweł Sydor (b. 26 October 1970) → United States
Stanisław Syrewicz* (b. 22 August 1946) → France
Witold Szalonek* (2 March 1927 – 12 October 2001) → Germany
Antoni Szałowski* (21 April 1907 – 21 March 1973) → France
Jagoda Szmytka* (b. 15 January 1982) → Germany
Bronisław Szulc (24 December 1881 – 17 July 1955) → Palestina → Israel
Józef Szulc (1893 – unknown) → Germany → France → Switzerland → Egypt
Józef Zygmunt Szulc (also known as Jan Sulima) (4 April 1875 – 10 April 1956) → France
Leon Szulc (1880 – 1958) → Israel
Katarzyna Szwed (b. 27 April 1980) → Netherlands → Great Britain

Ś

Tomasz Śpiewak (12 September 1936 – 7 February 2017) → Australia
Kalina Świątnicka (b. 29 April 1988) → France

T

Michał Talma-Sutt* (b. 16 August 1969) → Germany
Aleksander Tansman* (11 June 1897 – 15 November 1986) → France → United States → France
Stanisław Victor de Tarczyński (7 April 1882 – 18 June 1952) → Australia
Michał Taube (13 March 1890 – 23 February 1972) → Palestine → Israel
André Tchaikowsky* (Andrzej Czajkowski, actually Robert Krauthammer) (1 November 1935 – 26 June 1982) → Great Britain
Zofia Terné (actually Wiera Chajter) (3 February 1909 – 17 August 1987) → Great Britain
Kasper T. Toeplitz (b. 29 April 1960) → France
Ewa Trębacz* (b. 11 November 1973) → United States
Seweryn Turel (actually Seweryn Turteltaub) (9 November 1907 – 1954) → France → United States
Artur Tuźnik (b. 15 March 1989) → Denmark
Andrzej Tylczyński (1 January 1925 – 11 July 2009) → Netherlands
Edi Tyrmand (1917 – 2008) → Soviet Union

U

Michał Urbaniak* (b. 22 January 1943) → United States

W

Ignacy Waghalter (15 March 1882 – 7 April 1949) → Germany → United States
Henryk Wagner (1922 – 2000) → Soviet Union
Agnieszka Ewa Waligórska-Sirén (b. 19 September 1942) → Finland
Włodzimierz Wander (19 April 1939 – 29 November 2020) → United States
Henryk Wars* (Henry Vars; actually Henryk Warszawski / Warszowski; pseudonym Fraska) (29 December 1902 – 1 September 1977) → United States
Mieczysław Weinberg* (Mieczysław Wajnberg, Moishe Vainberg) (8 December 1919 – 26 February 1996) → Soviet Union
Iwo (Ivo) Wesby (Ignatz Singer; actually Iwo Singer) (2 March 1902 – 24 September 1961) → United States
Olga Widawska-Kotulecki (b. 25 January 1967) → Germany
Adam Wiernik (4 January 1916 – 18 September 2006) → Sweden
Kuba Więcek (b. 29 October 1994) → Denmark
Mirosław Wójcik (b. 26 March 1942) Finland → Sweden
Jan Wojewódka (2 January 1919 – 11 January 1992) → United States
Bronisław Wolfsthal (22 July 1883 – 5 September 1944) → Austria → Germany
Krzysztof Wołek* (b. 14 April 1976) → United States
Radek Wośko (b. 23 August 1984) → Denmark
Joanna Woźny (b. 27 July 1973) → Austria
Zdzisław Wysocki (b. 18 July 1944) → Austria

Z

Franciszek Zachara (10 December 1898 – 2 February 1966) → United States
Roman Zajączek (1927 – 1986) → Germany
Barbara Zakrzewska (b. 1 January 1946) → United States
Rafał Zalech (b. 1988) → Austria
Sebastian Zawadzki (b. 14 October 1991) → Denmark
Andrzej Zieliński* (b. 5 October 1944) → United States
Jarosław Zieliński (31 March 1847 – 25 February 1922) → United States
Sawel Zilberts (7 November 1881 – 25 April 1949) → United States
Zbigniew Zuchowicz (b. 5 July 1965) → Iceland → Norway

Ż

Leszek Żądło (b. 4 April 1945) → Germany
Marek Żebrowski (b. 5 May 1953) → United States

OH, DONNA CLARA

TANGO MILONGA

Notes

Notes

1. *This Is How it Usually Begins* [Bo to się zwykle tak zaczyna] is the title of a song (and the first line of its chorus) written by two Polish émigrés: Julian Front, who went to Palestine during World War II and to Israel after the war, and Stanisław Ferszko, who settled in 1938 in Palestine and in 1952 moved to the United States. The song, which remains popular, has been performed by many famous artists, including Mieczysław Fogg, Bohdan Łazuka, Wiera Gran, and Maciej Maleńczuk. This slow foxtrot succinctly and accurately portrays the subject's helplessness in the face of random events that can turn one's life upside down, as often happened in the lives of the heroes of this book. See *Bo to się zwykle tak zaczyna*, lyrics by Jerzy Ryba (pseudonyms Jerry, H. Lir) and Emanuel Schlechter, music by Julian Front and Stanisław Ferszko (1934).
2. Marek Podhajski, ed., *Polish Music. Polish Composers 1918–2010* (Gdańsk: Akademia Muzyczna im. Stanisława Moniuszki; Lublin: Katolicki Uniwerstet Lubelski Jana Pawła II, 2013).
3. For more information, see Danuta Gwizdalanka, "Unknown Facts from Mieczysław Wajnberg's Biography," https://culture.pl/en/article/unknown-facts-from-mieczyslaw-wajnbergs-biography [accessed 10 December 2020]. Gwizdalanka is also the author of the first Polish monograph about this composer.
4. He was entitled to Polish citizenship because of his father's Polish origins and ownership of a property in Ustyluh (in Polish, Uściług), but he was deterred by bureaucratic barriers. In the 1980s, Andrzej Borejko (Andrey Boreyko) also did not receive Polish citizenship. The son of a Pole, he was born in St. Petersburg (then Leningrad) and, at the time, was the head of the Poznań Philharmonic. Before the deadline expired, he left Poland; today he is a valued German conductor of Russian origin. Speeding up these regulatory procedures was a privilege reserved for athletes.
5. Katarzyna Morawska, "Średniowiecze 1320–1500," in *Historia muzyki polskiej*, ed. Józef Michał Chomiński, Krystyna Wilkowska-Chomińska (Kraków: Polskie Wydawnictwo Muzyczne, 1998), vol. I, part 2, 82.
6. The problem of musicians' immigration has been discussed in detail in Alina Żórawska-Witkowska, "Eighteenth-Century Warsaw: Periphery, Keystone, (and) Centre of European Musical Culture," in *Music Migration in the Early Modern Age: Centres and Peripheries – People, Works, Styles, Paths of Dissemination and Influence* (Warsaw: Liber Pro Arte, 2016), 33–52; Barbara Przybyszewska-Jarmińska, "Music Repertory in the Seventeenth-Century Commonwealth of Poland and Lithuania. Import, Production, Export," in *Music Migration in the Early Modern Age*, 161–170.
7. Zofia Helman, "Muzycy i muzyka polska w Paryżu w okresie międzywojennym," *Muzyka* 1972, no. 2, 82.
8. Magdalena Dziadek, "(Nie)gościnny Wiedeń," *Opcje. Kwartalnik Kulturalny* 2015, no. 3 (100), http://opcje.net.pl/magdalena-dziadek--niegoscinny-wieden/ [accessed 18 August 2018].
9. An extensive overview of the presence of Polish music and musicians has been presented by Karol Bula, *Polnische Komponisten und Musiker in Berliner Musikleben zwischen 1871 und 1914* (Sinzig: Studio, 2004).
10. Karol Szymanowski, *Korespondencja. T. 1. 1903–1919*, ed. Teresa Chylińska (Kraków: Polskie Wydawnictwo Muzyczne, 1982), 68.
11. Paul Krzywicki, *From Paderewski to Penderecki: The Polish Musician in Philadelphia* (Philadelphia: Lulu, 2016).
12. Aleksander Janta-Połczynski, *A History of Nineteenth Century American-Polish Music* (New York: Kościuszko Foundation, 1982, 1992).
13. Anders' Army was the informal name of the Polish Armed Forces in the Soviet Union from 1941–1942, under the command of General Władysław Anders. In March 1942, a formal agreement between the British, Polish, and Soviets allowed the army to be evacuated from the Soviet Union; it then moved through Iran to Palestine. There, under British command, many of its soldiers joined the Polish II Corps and went on to fight in Italy against the Nazis.
14. Roman Palester, "Konflikt Marsjasza," *Kultura* (Paris) 1951, nos. 7–8, 15–16.
15. Jagoda Jędrychowska [Jędrychowska was a pseudonym used by Kazimiera Kijowska], *Widzieć Polskę z oddalenia* (Paris: Editions Spotkania, 1988), 77.
16. Jędrychowska, *Widzieć Polskę*, 84.
17. Other examples include Piotr Koprowski, who in 1971 left for Canada after completing studies in Paris; Marek Żebrowski, who has lived in the United States since 1973; Gabriela Moyseowicz, in West Berlin since 1974; Joanna Bruzdowicz, in Belgium since 1975; Anna Jastrzębska, in Norway since 1976 (her piece *Teleks to Poland* was performed in 1983 during the Nobel Peace Prize award ceremony for Lech Walesa); Isabelle (Wiesława) Garr, in Paris since 1979; and Piotr Moss and Elżbieta Sikora, in Paris since 1981.
18. During a period of increased anti-Semitism between 1871 and World War I, about half a million Jews left Russia, largely

due to pogroms. In comparison, a quarter-million people left the Austrian partition for economic reasons.

19. Leon Markiewicz, *Michał Spisak 1914–1965* (Dąbrowa Górnicza: Muzeum Miejskie "Sztygarka," 2005), 257.
20. Władysław T. Miodunka, "Emigracja – w poszukiwaniu wolności, chleba i wiedzy," in *Polska. Eseje o stuleciu* (Olszanica: Wydawnictwo Bosz, 2018), 215.
21. Czesław Miłosz, Tomas Venclova, *Dialog o Wilnie*, quoted in *Muzyka źle obecna*, ed. Krystyna Tarnawska-Kaczorowska (Warsaw: Polish Composers' Union, 1989), vol. 1, 19.
22. Danuta Gwizdalanka, *Mieczysław Wajnberg: kompozytor z trzech światów* (Poznań: Teatr Wielki im. Stanisława Moniuszki, 2013), 17.
23. Haubenstock-Ramati returned to Kraków after the war, but emigrated in 1950, first to Israel, then to Paris (thanks to a scholarship), and eventually to Vienna.
24. Janusz Krassowski, "Schütz (Szyc), Alfred," in Podhajski, ed., *Polish Music. Polish Composers 1918–2010*, 1102.
25. Janusz Krassowski, "Gold, Artur; Gold, Henryk," in Podhajski, ed., *Polish Music. Polish Composers 1918–2010*, 488–489.
26. Roman Palester, "Prawda źle obecna," in *Muzyka źle obecna*, vol. 1, 33.
27. Letter from 17 March 1961, quoted in Beata Bolesławska-Lewandowska, "Emigracyjne drogi Romana Palestra i Andrzeja Panufnika," *Roczniki Kulturoznawcze* 2017, vol. 8, no. 2, 167, https://www.kul.pl/files/1490/rk/rk8_2_2017/06-Boleseawska-Lewandowska_Corr.pdf [accessed 2 January 2021].
28. Violetta Kostka, "Kassern, Tadeusz," in Podhajski, ed., *Polish Music. Polish Composers 1918–2010*, 584.
29. Palester, "Prawda źle obecna," 31.
30. We have to remember that Szałowski felt rejected by the composers' community in Poland after 1945, which under socialist realism refused to accept émigré composers, whom the government considered "enemies of the people's state."
31. Anna S. Dębowska, "Elżbieta Sikora: Zawód kompozytora nie ma płci. Sylwetka autorki opery 'Madame Curie'," *Wysokie obcasy* 20 May 2017, http://www.wysokieobcasy.pl/wysokie-obcasy/7,127763,21825971,elzbieta-sikora-zawod-kompozytora-nie-ma-plci-sylwetka.html [accessed 30 November 2017].
32. Anna Iwanicka-Nijakowska, "Bojanowski, Jerzy," in Marek Podhajski, ed., *Polish Music. Polish Composers 1918–2010,* 356–357.
33. Dorota Szwarcman's email to Marlena Wieczorek, 9 September 2017.
34. Jacek Marczyński wrote: "When he finished his education by winning a gold medal in Paris, the Polish authorities started to persuade him to return. Andrzej Czajkowski, then 16 years old, was offered luxurious conditions: studies in Warsaw, an apartment in the Muranów district, invitations to concerts. He arrived and quickly became a star, delighting all with his talent and beauty but also shocking all with his unconventional ways. At a student costume ball, he appeared disguised as Carmen. He looked so attractive that a party dignitary asked him to dance, thinking she was a young singer. Andrzej danced, without correcting the mistake." Jacek Marczyński, "Kim był Andrzej Czajkowski," *Rzeczpospolita* 13 July 2013, http://www.rp.pl/artykul/1029161-Kim-byl-Andrzej-Czajkowski.html [accessed 30 November 2017].
35. Marlena Wieczorek in conversation with Maja Trochimczyk, Facebook, 10 December 2017.
36. Klaudia Skrężyna, "Mroczna historia z małego miasteczka," *Dziennik Polski* 1 September 2012, http://www.dziennikpolski24.pl/artykul/3175742,mroczna-historia-z-malego-miasteczka,2,id,t,sa.html [accessed 30 November 2017].
37. Quote from the documentary *Ludmila* [*Ludmiła*], directed by Bohdan Kezik, 2006.
38. Letter from Roman Maciejewski to his parents, 2 August 1948, Avidingsgatan 6, Göteborg, Archive of the National Library in Warsaw.
39. Letter from Roman Maciejewski to Wacław Gaziński, 7 August 2017, Rymdtorget 61/III, Göteborg, National Library in Warsaw.
40. Janusz Krassowski, "Kaczmarek, Jan A. P.," in Marek Podhajski, ed., *Polish Music. Polish Composers 1918–2010,* 578.
41. Jan Kalinowski, Marek Szlezer, "Andrzej Panufnik. Życie twórcy w przybranej ojczyźnie. Wywiad z Lady Camillą Panufnik," in *Polscy kompozytorzy emigracyjni. Szkice i interpretacje*, eds. Herbert Oleschko, Piotr Papla (Kraków: Akademia Muzyczna, 2014), 15.
42. Beata Bolesławska-Lewandowska, "Emigracyjne drogi Romana Palestra i Andrzeja Panufnika," 171.
43. Palester, "Prawda źle obecna," 34.
44. Quoted in Tadeusz Kaczyński, *Andrzej Panufnik i jego muzyka* (Warsaw: Polskie Wydawnictwo Naukowe, 1974), 85–86.
45. Letter from Roman Maciejewski to Zygmunt Maciejewski, probably 16 December 1947, Avidingsgatan 6, Giiteborg. Archive of the National Library in Warsaw.
46. Palester, "Prawda źle obecna," 34.

47. Jan Kalinowski, Marek Szlezer, "Andrzej Panufnik. Życie twórcy w przybranej ojczyźnie," 18.
48. Marlena Wieczorek in conversation with Maja Trochimczyk, Facebook, 10 December 2017.
49. Ewa Chorościan, "'Po zbudowaniu silnej oraz przyjaznej relacji z polskimi wykonawcami, krytykami, muzykami, nie ma siły, która by te relacje zakończyła' – wywiad z Dobromiłą Jaskot i Dominikiem Karskim," *MEAKULTURA* 2017, no. 272, http://meakultura.pl/artykul/po-zbudowaniu-silnej-oraz-przyjaznej-relacji-z-polskimi-wykonawcami-krytykami-muzykami-nie-ma-sily-ktora-by-te-relacje-zakonczyla-wywiad-z-dobromila-jaskot-i-dominikiem-karskim-1887 [accessed 29 July 2018].
50. Adam Michnik, "Dialog," *Tygodnik Powszechny* 16 July 1995, no. 29, http://www.dialog.org/dialog_pl/michn01.html [accessed 30 May 2018].
51. Jolanta Guzy-Pasiak, "Emigracja w perspektywie postkolonialnej. Wybrane problemy twórczości polskich kompozytorów emigracyjnych: Karola Rathausa i Ludomira Michała Rogowskiego," *Res Facta Nova* 2011, no. 12 (21), 177–185.
52. Tadeusz Kaczyński, "Zgubione pokolenie. W 50. rocznicę powstania Stowarzyszenia Młodych Muzyków Polaków w Paryżu," *Ruch Muzyczny* 1977, no. 5, 3–4.
53. Andrzej Sakson, "Migracje – fenomen XX i XXI wieku," *Przegląd Zachodni* 2009, no. 2, 11–19.
54. "Polonia, emigracja i Polacy w świecie," in *Encyklopedia PWN*, online version, https://encyklopedia.pwn.pl/haslo/Polonia-emigracja-i-Polacy-w-swiecie;3959692.html [accessed 23 September 2017].
55. J. Paweł Gieorgica, "Stany Zjednoczone Ameryki jako kierunek emigracji Polaków. Współczesne uwarunkowania," *Pogranicze: Studia społeczne* vol. 23, 2014, 277–298.
56. Stephen Castles, Mark J. Miller, *The Age of Migration. International Population Movements in the Modern World* (New York: Macmillan, 1993).
57. Sakson, "Migracje – fenomen."
58. Robert P. Morgan, *Twentieth-Century Music* (New York, London: W. W. Norton, 1991), vol. 1: *Beyond Tonality: From 1900 to World War I;* vol. 2: *Reconstruction and New Systems: Between the Wars;* vol. 3: *Innovation and Fragmentation: The World after World War II.*
59. One recent publication is Zbigniew Judycki, *Polscy muzycy w świecie. Słownik biograficzny* (Warsaw: Fundacja Polonia Semper Fidelis, 2015).
60. A full list of émigré composers can be found in the Appendix.
61. Zofia Helman, "Muzyka na obczyźnie," in *Między Polską a światem. Kultura emigracyjna po 1939 roku*, ed. Marta Fik (Warsaw: Wydawnictwo Krąg, 1992), 225.
62. Krystyna Tarnawska-Kaczorowska, ed., *Muzyka źle obecna* (Warsaw: Polish Composers' Union, 1989), vols. 1–2. In Zofia Helman's *Neoklasycyzm w muzyce polskiej XX wieku* (Kraków: Polskie Wydawnictwo Muzyczne, 1985), the names of Aleksander Tansman, Szymon Laks, Michał Spisak, and Antoni Szałowski were mentioned and thus included in the written history of Polish music.
63. Leszek Polony, "Spotkanie z Romanem Palestrem," *Tygodnik Powszechny* 1983, no. 42.
64. Beata Bolesławska-Lewandowska, *Zygmunt Mycielski – Andrzej Panufnik: Korespondencja. Część 1: Lata 1949–1969* (Warsaw: Instytut Sztuki, Polska Akademia Nauk, 2016) and *Część 2: Lata 1970–1987* (Warsaw: Instytut Sztuki, Polska Akademia Nauk, 2018).
65. Helman, *Neoklasycyzm w muzyce polskiej*, 16.
66. Reiner Cadenbach described the style of Fitelberg's work in his American years: "When asked about the points of reference for Fitelberg at that time, one can say that his method of composing should be placed somewhere between a highly energetic tension known from Stravinsky's music, a focus on the linear and harmonic multifacetedness of Hindemith, and the melodic color of contemporary French music (e.g., Milhaud), with its tendency for grotesqueness and satire." Reiner Cadenbach, "Jerzy Fitelberg," in *Franz Schreker, Schüler in Berlin: Biographische Beiträge und Dokumente*, eds. Dietmar Schenk, Markus Böggemann, and Reiner Cadenbach (Berlin: Universität der Künste, 2005), 26.
67. Beata Bolesławska-Lewandowska, "Folklor," in http://www.panufnik.polmic.pl/index.php/pl/kregi-inspiracji/folklor [accessed 18 September 2018].
68. Szymon Laks, René Coudy, *Musiques d'un autre monde* (Paris: Mercure de France, 1948).
69. Anna Skulska, "Weinberg odkrywany. Wywiad z Danutą Gwizdalanką," *Muzyka w Mieście* 2014, no. 8, http://mwm.nfm.wroclaw.pl/articles/305-Weinberg-odkrywany [accessed 4 October 2018].
70. Violetta Kostka, *Tadeusz Zygfryd Kassern, Indywidualne odmiany stylów muzycznych XX wieku* (Poznań: Rytmos, 2011).
71. Roman Maciejewski, Warsaw Autumn Festival program book, 1960, 29–30.

72. A contemporary view on this phenomenon can be found in the writings of German researcher Ruth Seehaber. See Ruth Seehaber, "The Construction of the 'Polish School': Self-Perception and Foreign Perception of Polish Contemporary Music between 1956 and 1976," in Eva Mantzourani, ed., *Polish Music since 1945* (Kraków: Musica Iagellonica, 2013), 49–55.

73. Janusz Cegiełła, *Szkice do autoportretu polskiej muzyki współczesnej* (Kraków: Polskie Wydawnictwo Muzyczne, 1976), 160.

74. Sonorism is a term coined by Józef Michał Chomiński. It defines a compositional technique that values tone and sound at the expense of traditional elements such as melody or harmony. Józef M. Chomiński, "Z zagadnień techniki kompozytorskiej XX wieku," *Muzyka* 1956, no. 3, 23–48.

75. Roman Berger, "Polska szkoła kompozytorska: Fakt? Mit? Wizja? Projekt?," *Dysonanse* 1998, no. 2.

76. Maciej Jabłoński, ed., *Krzysztof Meyer: Do i od kompozytora* (Poznań: Ars Nova, 1994), 92.

77. Interview with Elżbieta Sikora, "Muzyka naszych czasów," *Muzyka w Mieście* 2015, no. 5, http://mwm.nfm.wroclaw.pl/articles/433-muzyka-naszych-czasow [accessed 15 September 2018].

78. Karol Rathaus, "Problemy muzyczne w filmie dźwiękowym," *Muzyka* 1931, no. 10, 409.

79. "Najwybitniejsze utwory pięćdziesięciolecia," in *Muzyka polska 1945–1995*, eds. Krzysztof Droba, Teresa Malecka, Krzysztof Szwajgier (Kraków: Akademia Muzyczna, 1998), 337–381.

80. Tarnawska-Kaczorowska, ed., *Muzyka źle obecna*, vols. 1–2.

81. Roman Palester, "Prawda źle obecna," in *Muzyka źle obecna*, vol. 1, 31.

82. Adam Rieger, "Rozmowa z Konstantym Regameyem," *Ruch Muzyczny* 1947, nos. 7–8, 15–20.

83. On 20 September 1960 the work was performed for the first time by Halina Łukomska, Krystyna Szostek-Radkowa, Kazimierz Pustelak, and Edward Pawlak, with the Polish Radio and Television Choir in Kraków conducted by the composer.

84. Michał Kondracki, "List z USA," *Ruch Muzyczny* 1961, no. 15, 13.

85. Zofia Helman, *Roman Palester. Twórca i dzieło* (Kraków: Musica Iagellonica, 1999).

86. http://palester.polmic.pl. The same series includes a website dedicated to Andrzej Panufnik, http://panufnik.polmic.pl.

87. *Roman Palester (1907–1989): Muzyka kameralna i fortepianowa*, Jakub Tchorzewski – piano, Duo Viennese (Paweł Zalejski and Monika Hager-Zalejski, violin), Warner Music Poland 2016, 01902 9 58749 3 3. The album includes "Polish Dance" from the ballet *Song of the Earth* for violin and piano, *Preludes* for piano, *Duos* for two violins, *Etudes* for piano, *Sonata* for two violins and piano.

88. Roman Palester, *Słuch absolutny. Niedokończona autobiografia i listy z lat wojny*, ed. Zofia Helman (Kraków: Polskie Wydawnictwo Muzyczne, 2017).

89. Helman, *Roman Palester,* 337.

90. See Andrzej Panufnik, *Composing Myself* (London: Methuen, 1987); Beata Bolesławska, *The Life and Works of Andrzej Panufnik (1914–1991)* (Farnham: Ashgate, 2015).

91. For a detailed index of events during the centenary of Andrzej Panufnik's birthday, see Beata Bolesławska-Lewandowska, *Aneks do Raportu o obecności muzyki Andrzeja Panufnika w Polsce i na świecie* (Warsaw: Instytut Muzyki i Tańca, 2015). http://imit.org.pl/uploads/materials/files/Aneks_do_raportu_o_obecnosci_muzyki_andrzeja_panufnika_w_polsce_i_na_swiecie.pdf.

92. Janusz Cegiełła, *Dziecko szczęścia: Aleksander Tansman i jego czasy* (Warsaw: Państwowy Instytut Wydawniczy, 1986, 1992).

93. Detailed information about this series is available at http://www.eda-records.com/129-0-Poland-Abroad.html [accessed 18 September 2018].

94. *André Tchaikowsky. Music for Piano*, CD14, Toccata Classics TOCC 0204, 2013.

95. *Dream Lake: Witold Lutosławski. Chantefleurs et Chantefables. Andrzej Czajkowski. Seven Shakespeare Sonnets*, Agata Zubel, soprano; Joonas Ahonen, piano, ACD 216, CD Accord 2015.

96. "Pięciolinia bardzo absorbuje," *Ruch Muzyczny* 1989, no. 26, 4–6.

97. Jabłoński, ed., *Krzysztof Meyer: Do i od kompozytora.*

98. Władysław Malinowski, "Meyer – dziesięć lat podwójnej obecności," *Ruch Muzyczny* 1997, no. 13, 8.

99. Piotr Lachert, "Miłość nieodwzajemniona," *Ruch Muzyczny* 1995, no. 10, 32–33.

100. Józef Kański, "Jubileuszowy wieczór Miłosza Magina," *Ruch Muzyczny* 1991, no. 12, 3.

101. "Polskiej muzyki współczesnej persona non grata," *Ruch Muzyczny* 1997, no. 5, 14.

102. "Festiwal Witolda Szalonka?" *Ruch Muzyczny* 1995, no. 2, p. 3.

103. Lilianna Manuela Moll, *Witold Szalonek. Katalog tematyczny dzieł. Teksty o muzyce* (Katowice: Akademia Muzyczna, 2002).

104. Jacek Skolmowski, "Człowiek, którego nie było," *Dwutygodnik* 2014, no. 1. www.dwutygodnik.com/artykul/4995-czlowiek-ktorego-nie-bylo.html [accessed 31 July 2017].

105. Ewa Kowalska-Zając, *Oblicza awangardy: Roman Haubenstock-Ramati* (Łódź: Akademia Muzyczna, 2001).

106. Kostka, *Tadeusz Zygfryd Kassern.*

107. Marlena Wieczorek, *Roman Maciejewski: kompozytor pokolenia zgubionego* (Poznań: Wydawnictwo Poznańskiego Towarzystwa Przyjaciół Nauk, 2008).

108. Markiewicz, *Michał Spisak.*

109. Elżbieta Szczurko, *Antoni Szałowski. Person and Work* (Frankfurt am Main: Peter Lang Edition, 2013).

110. Ewa Wójtowicz, *Ludomir Michał Rogowski: sylwetka życia i twórczości* (Kraków: Akademia Muzyczna, 2009).

111. Roman Berger, *Zasada twórczości: wybór pism z lat 1984–2005*, ed. Krzysztof Droba, Stanisław Kosz (Katowice: Akademia Muzyczna, 2005).

112. Quoted in Jacek Marczyński, "Trauma zamieniona w muzykę," *Przekrój* 2013, no. 20, 21.

113. "'Lubię sytuacje, kiedy coś nie gra'. Z Mikołajem Laskowskim rozmawiają Agnieszka Grzybowska i Beniamin Głuszek," *Glissando* 2016, no. 29, 156.

114. Jan Topolski, "MUZYKA 2.1: Wojtek Blecharz," *Dwutygodnik* 2013, no. 98, http://www.dwutygodnik.com/artykul/4198-muzyka-21-wojtek-blecharz.html [accessed 18 December 2017].

115. Sebastian Smoliński, "Smrodek dydaktyczny," *Glissando* 2015, http://glissando.pl/aktualnosci/smrodek-dydaktyczny-soundwork-wojtka-blecharza/ [accessed 18 December 2017].

116. Ewa Szczecińska, "Ciało uwolnione z uwięzi," *Ruch Muzyczny* 2017, no. 9, 74–75.

117. Smoliński, "Smrodek dydaktyczny."

118. Szczecińska, "Ciało uwolnione z uwięzi," 7.

119. Barbara Bogunia, "Wizytówka Jagody Szmytki," *MEAKULTURA* 2013, http://meakultura.pl/publikacje/wizytowka-jagody-szmytki-798 [accessed 17 December 2017].

120. Tomasz Biernacki, "Warszawska Jesień 2015: LUCIER, NIBLOCK, ABRAHAMSEN, FERNEYHOUGH, CENDO, SZMYTKA, STEEN-ANDERSEN," *Glissando* 2015, http://glissando.pl/aktualnosci/wj2015_1/ [accessed 17 December 2017].

121. Jan Topolski, "Odgrzebując Zagrzeb," *Dwutygodnik* 2017, no. 211, http://www.dwutygodnik.com/artykul/7188-odgrzebujac-zagrzeb.html [accessed 17 December 2017].

122. This essay received an award in a competition celebrating the centennial of the ZAiKS Authors' Association: "Citizens of the World: Migrations of Polish Composers in the 21st Century."

123. From a 26 December 1830 letter from Chopin to Jaś Matuszyński, "I curse the moment of my departure and I admit, knowing my condition, that when Tytus left, everything fell onto my head at once. All the dinners, evenings, concerts, and dances, which I'm fed up with, bore me: I feel sad, deaf, and gloomy here. I like it, but not in such a cruel manner. I cannot do as I please, I have to dress up, wear fancy hair; in the salon, I pretend to be calm, but once I return, I thunder away on the piano." Quoted in Mariusz Wrona, *Fryderyk Chopin. Poeta fortepianu* (Warsaw: Świat Książki, 2010), 132–133.

124. "No, no. If I went back to Warsaw they might cancel my visa, I might be imprisoned there, I might not be able to get out again. No, I don't trust any countries east of the Iron Curtain." André Tchaikowsky, *A Musician Divided. André Tchaikowsky in his Own Words*, eds. David Pountney, Anastazja Belina-Johnson (London: Toccata Press, 2013), 37.

125. Jacek Marczyński, "Trauma zamieniona w muzykę," *Przekrój* 2013, no. 20.

126. Based on a phone conversation with Jagoda Szmytka, 8 October 2018.

127. Filip Lech, "Wojtek Blecharz," *Culture.pl* 2013, https://culture.pl/pl/tworca/wojtek-blecharz [accessed 1 October 2018].

128. Ewa Szczecińska, "Wojtek Blecharz" *Glissando* 2013, wiad [accessed 1 October 2018].

129. Ewa Chorościan, "Na co dzień zajmuję się tym, żeby uwrażliwiać odbiorcę – wywiad z Wojtkiem Blecharzem," *MEAKULTURA* 2017, http://meakultura.pl/wywiady/na-co-dzien-zajmuje-sie-tym-zeby-uwrazliwiac-odbiorce-wywiad-z-wojtkiem-blecharzem-1857 [accessed 05 October 2018].

130. I have spoken to Jagoda Szmytka, Prasqual, Szymon Brzóska, and Marcin Banasik.

131. Information from a conversation with Jagoda Szmytka, 7 October 2018.

132. Ewa Chorościan, "Na co dzień zajmuję się tym, żeby uwrażliwiać odbiorcę."

133. It is worth quoting a statement by Marta Ptaszyńska, who for years has divided her time between Poland and the United

States: "My American colleagues can only dream of an orchestral piece being performed by some orchestra that may not even be known. Here, it is unthinkable to have festivals such as the wonderful Festival of Premieres in Katowice, the Warsaw Autumn or the Warsaw Music Meetings, or various festivals in Kraków and Wrocław. This does not happen in America! Almost all composers are involved in teaching, and from time to time they have some local performance of a chamber piece, usually at the university where they teach. That's all. Of course, there are a few who are played more often, such as John Adams, Philip Glass, or Steve Reich, but for a nation of 250 million, that's probably not enough!" Aleksandra Masłowska, "Polska muzyka, a zwłaszcza kompozycja ma się doskonale. Wywiad z Martą Ptaszyńską," *MEAKULTURA* 2013, http://meakultura.pl/wywiady/polska-muzyka-a-zwlaszcza-kompozycja-ma-sie-doskonale-wywiad-z-marta-ptaszynska-598 [accessed 21 October 2018].

134. Jan Topolski, "Poematy egocentryczne," *Dwutygodnik* 2015, https://www.dwutygodnik.com/artykul/5877-poematy-egocentryczne.html [accessed 30 September 2018]; Krzysztof Stefański, "Barykady rosną," *Dwutygodnik* 2015, https://www.dwutygodnik.com/artykul/5877-poematy-egocentryczne.html [accessed 5 October 2018].
135. Elżbieta Burza, "Prasqual - ambasador muzyki współczesnej," *DW.com* 2015, https://www.dw.com/pl/prasqual-ambasador-muzyki-wsp%C3%B3%C5%82czesnej/a-18941742 [accessed 2 October 2018].
136. Quote based on a description provided by Prasqual in his email on 7 October 2018.
137. Marta Wryk, "Walka, taniec i muzyka," *Przegląd Polski* (weekly supplement to *Nowy Dziennik. Polish Daily News*), 19 November 2011, 6.
138. Based on a phone call with Szymon Brzóska, 3 October 2018.
139. Based on a phone call with Szymon Brzóska, 3 October 2018.
140. Marta Wryk, "Muzyka musi być po prostu dobra," *Przegląd Polski*, 29 February 2008, 5.
141. Based on email exchange with Jakub Ciupiński, 9 October 2018.
142. Based on a phone conversation with Marcin Banasik, 4 October 2018.
143. Based on a phone conversation with Jagoda Szmytka, 8 October 2018.
144. An earlier version of this article appeared in *MEAKULTURA* 2017, http://meakultura.pl/publikacje/muzyka--filmowa-tworcy-emigracyjni-1897 [accessed 20 August 2018].
145. Wojciech Kilar (1932–2013) contributed immensely to Hollywood film music, but he never emigrated from Poland.
146. In Polish culture, especially in the music community and among fans, jazz is perceived in opposition to pop music. The latter is thought to involve a large element of ambition, while jazz is considered to be a sophisticated, non-commercial art.
147. Andy Bennett, Barry Shank, Jason Toynbee, eds., *The Popular Music Studies Reader* (London: Routledge, 2006), 3.
148. For more about the influence of neoliberalism on music migrations, see Jason Toynbee and Byron Dueck, eds., *Migrating Music* (London: Routledge, 2011), 4.
149. When using the term jazz in reference to interwar Polish music, we have to remember that European concepts of this style for a long time didn't match the true nature of American, especially African-American jazz.
150. Krystian Brodacki, *Historia jazzu w Polsce* (Kraków: Polskie Wydawnictwo Muzyczne, 2010), 537f. Brodacki mentions Polish émigré jazz musicians and extensively describes the lives of the more prominent ones.
151. A band named Tea-Jazz, which had been started by Wars and Eugeniusz Bodo, was brought into Anders' Army in 1942 (without Bodo, who was arrested by the NKVD and died in a gulag in the Soviet Union). It was later renamed to Polish Parade.
152. Wars's career in Hollywood and the reasons for his misfortune are discussed in Iwona Sowińska, "Muzyka bez granic? Działalność Henryka Warsa po wybuchu wojny," *Kwartalnik Filmowy* 2016, no. 95, 14–16.
153. Ryszard Wolański, *Już nie zapomnisz mnie. Opowieść o Henryku Warsie* (Warsaw: Warszawskie Wydawnictwo Literackie Muza, 2010), 218–220.
154. Iwona Sowińska, "Muzyka bez granic?," 15.
155. Daniłowski's American life and his conflict with the Polish community and the omnipotent impresario Jan Wojewódka were described in Dariusz Michalski, *Powróćmy jak za dawnych lat…Czyli historia polskiej muzyki rozrywkowej (lata 1900–1939)* (Warsaw: Iskry, 2007), 550–553.
156. The pros and cons of these commercial travels, which lasted several years, were described in Urszula Dudziak, *Wyśpiewam wam wszystko* (Warsaw: Kayax, 2011), 36f.
157. Dariusz Michalski, *Trzysta tysięcy gitar nam gra. Czyli historia polskiej muzyki rozrywkowej (lata 1958–1973)* (Warsaw: Iskry, 2014), 428f.
158. Michalski, *Trzysta tysięcy gitar nam gra*, 648.

159. Aneta Norek-Skrycka, *Życie i twórczość Zbigniewa Seiferta: Man of the Light*, second ed. (Warsaw: Fundacja im. Zbigniewa Seiferta, 2016), 101.

160. Tomasz Stańko, *Desperado. Autobiografia* (Kraków: Wydawnictwo Literackie, 2010), 88.

161. Still, Stańko claims that: "In that arrangement [in the 1970s], Pagart functioned very well. You paid them 10 percent and they fixed everything. Before I went to Pagart, I had some cognac at the European Hotel, smoked a joint on the way, and, completely relaxed, I would go to the office where some of my friends worked….Passport offices were less pleasant, there were military officials there, but friends as well….Jazz existed on the side and they didn't care much about it." Stańko, *Desperado*, 249–250.

162. Brodacki, *Historia jazzu w Polsce*, 398.

163. Andrzej Makowiecki, *Ja, Urbanator: Awantury muzyka jazzowego* (Warsaw: Agora, 2011), 99.

164. Makowiecki, *Ja, Urbanator*, 132.

165. Quoted in Norek-Skrycka, *Życie i twórczość Zbigniewa Seiferta*, 130.

166. Stańko, *Desperado*, 249.

167. Norek-Skrycka, *Życie i twórczość Zbigniewa Seiferta*, 73.

168. Dudziak, *Wyśpiewam wam wszystko*, 242–244.

169. Grzegorz Piotrowski, K. Szymański, "Transnarodowa, czyli wszędzie Obca? Syndrom aktorstwa filmowego Anny Prucnal," *Kwartalnik Filmowy* 2016, no. 95, 108–110.

170. I offer an interpretation of this style in Grzegorz Piotrowski, "Ma dissidence. Sztuka piosenki Anny Prucnal," *Kwartalnik Filmowy* 2015, no. 91, 170–180.

171. Quoted in Brodacki, *Historia jazzu w Polsce*, 394.

172. On anomalies in the functioning of the Polish Jazz Association Concert Agency in Warsaw, Brodacki, *Historia jazzu w Polsce*, 394.

173. The example of Prucnal, whose return to Polish cinema and concert stages ultimately turned out to be impossible, despite a successful comeback in 1989, seems extremely interesting. It seems that this was predetermined by the peculiar resentment of Polish decision-makers and the public, analogous to what also affected, for example, Elżbieta Czyżewska.

174. Stańko, *Desperado*, 164.

175. Jan Błaszczak, "Kopenhaga nową stolicą polskich jazzmanów," *Polityka*, 5 September 2017, https://www.polityka.pl/tygodnikpolityka/kultura/1718362,1,kopenhaga-nowa-stolica-polskich-jazzmanow.read [accessed 18 December 2020]

176. Based on the author's phone conversation with Artur Tuźnik, February 2019.

177. From the author's phone conversation with Kuba Gudz, February 2019.

178. Romuald Czystaw, known for his involvement with Budka Suflera, had to leave the band due to problems with his voice. He performed with Romek's Band in exclusive hotels in the United Arab Emirates. He died in Poland.

179. Another Turbo member, percussionist Wojciech Anioła, moved to Great Britain.

180. The album was initially called *Izabela Trojanowska*. In 1992, it was re-released by Tripinicular Records under a new title, *Independence*.

181. Andrzej Icha, *Skaldowie. Historia i muzyka zespołu* (Gdynia: Professional Music Press, 2004), 221.

182. For more on this subject, see Dudziak's second book, *Wyśpiewam wam więcej* (Warsaw: Agora, 2018).

183. Igor Pietraszewski, *Jazz w Polsce. Wolność improwizowana* (Kraków: Nomos, 2012), 15.

184. This name is confusing; the band did not play rhythm and blues, but this name sounded safer than rock 'n' roll. As mentioned earlier, such music was also described as "big beat."

185. Franciszek Walicki, *Epitafium na śmierć rock'n'rolla* (Sopot: Fundacja Sopockie Korzenie, 2012), 69; Jacek Kurek "Chcemy być sobą…, czyli rock a sprawa polska," in *Rock i tożsamość. Notatki o muzyce i wartościach*. (Sosnowiec: GAD Records, 2014), 179–182.

186. Tomasz Jaśkiewicz, Witold Górka, *Byłem gitarzystą Niemena* (Warsaw: Grupa Wydawnicza Foksal, 2014), 127.

187. Jaśkiewicz, Górka, *Byłem gitarzystą Niemena*, 128–129.

188. Jacek Kurek: "Wichary Zygmunt," *Chorzowski słownik biograficzny* (Chorzów: Muzeum Chorzowskie, 2011), new series, vol. 3, 255–256; Jacek Kurek, [discussing the album *Zygmunt Wichary i jego soliści*], *Zeszyty Chorzowskie* vol. 12 (2008), 253–255. Wichary died due to injuries suffered during a private performance in Opole. The circumstances were never shared with the public. The artist was buried in Chorzów, where he lived.

189. Alicja Klenczon-Corona, "30 rocznica śmierci Krzysztofa Klenczona," *Dziennik bałtycki* 2011, https://dziennikbaltycki.

pl/30-rocznica-smierci-krzysztofa-klenczona/ar/389306 (accessed 10 July 2020).

190. The literature on this subject is rich, as musicians share knowledge in interviews and memoirs. See Leszek Winder, *Śląski Blues* (Skoczów: Śląskie Stowarzyszenie Artystów i Twórców, 2019); Bartosz Żurawiecki, *Festiwale wyklęte* (Warsaw: Wydawnictwo Krytyki Politycznej, 2019); Jacek Kurek, "Buntownicy i kolaboranci. Na rozdrożach polskiego rocka," in *Unisono w wielogłosie 6. Rock na pograniczach,* ed. Radosław Marcinkiewicz (Opole: GAD Records, 2019), 178–186; Jacek Kurek, "Marionetki," 47–58.
191. Mikołaj Lizut, *Punk. Rock. Later* (Warsaw: Wydawnictwo Sic, 2003), 47.
192. Dariusz Michalski, *Czesław Niemen. Czy go jeszcze pamiętasz?* (Warsaw: Wydawnictwo MG, 2009), 118.
193. Jaśkiewicz, Górka, *Byłem gitarzystą Niemena*, 126.
194. Tadeusz Prokop, who was associated with Blue Shadows [Błękitne Cienie], Drumlersi, and, mostly, PAKT, had lived in England since the late 1970s. He returned to Poland in 2001 and played in clubs in Wrocław. He died on 11 June 2015.
195. Born in Rzeszów in 1941 and the co-founder of Breakout, Józef Hajdasz emigrated to the United States in the 1980s, but returned to Poland just before his death. He played with a band comprised of members of Tadeusz Nalepa's band, Old Breakout. He died in Białystok on 4 May 2015.
196. The first, *My Life* [*Moje życie*], was published in Poland in 2013.
197. The artist released her first album, *Hashgachah*, in 2004. Music for the *Dracula* play staged by the Brunton Theatre Company received positive reviews for its display of "the spirit of a broken Eastern Europe."
198. Kurek, "Marionetki?," 51; Jacek Kurek, "Z tarczą słońca u boku, czyli Niemen w cieniu," in *Czesław Niemen i jego płytowe dzieła: 2*, eds. Piotr and Edyta Chlebowscy (Lublin: Wydawnictwo KUL, 2017), 157; Roman Radoszewski, *Czesław Niemen. Kiedy się dziwić przestanę: Monografia artystyczna* (Warsaw: Iskry, 2004), 399.
199. For more information, see Małgorzata Czermińska, *Autobiograficzny trójkąt. Świadectwo, wyznanie, wyzwanie* (Kraków: Universitas, 2000); Małgorzata Czermińska, "O autobiografii i autobiograficzności," in *Autobiografia*, (Gdańsk: Wydawnictwo Słowo, 2009).
200. Andrzej Chłopecki, "Muzyka 2.1: Aleksander Nowak," *Dwutygodnik* 2010, no. 30, https://www.dwutygodnik.com/artykul/1116-muzyka-21-aleksander-nowak.html [accessed 20 September 2020].
201. [Marian Buchowski], "Stachura stworzył życiopisanie. Jego pisarstwo było tożsame z jego życiem (fragment książki)," *Polska Times* 2017, https://polskatimes.pl/stachura-stworzyl-zyciopisanie-jego-pisarstwo-bylo-tozsame-z-jego-zyciem/ar/12510960, [accessed 12 June 2020].
202. "Wydobywanie dobra. Z Paulem Ricoeurem rozmawia Brat Emil z Taize," trans. M. Prussak, *Więź* 2001, no. 12, 22–23.
203. Domique de Roux, Witold Gombrowicz, *A Kind of Testament*, trans. A. Hamilton (London: Dalkey Archive Press, 2007).
204. A recorder of reality who still constantly indicates a kind of mask worn for the purpose of their own story can be observed in Hrabal's trilogy *Svatby v domě, Vita nuova, Proluky* (Prague, 1986).
205. Roland Barthes, *Roland Barthes par Roland Barthes* (Paris: Seuil, 1975); Roland Barthes, *L'Empire des signes* (Paris: Skira / Flammarion, 1970).
206. Wiesław Myśliwski, an excerpt from a speech given on 10 March 2009 at the University of Opole on the occasion of his honorary doctorate.
207. Frédéric Chopin, "Do Wojciecha Grzymały w Paryżu, Edynburg," letter from 30 October 1848, accessed 15 September 2020, https://pl.chopin.nifc.pl/chopin/letters/detail/text/r%C3%B3%C5%BC/page/6/id/355.
208. Edward Stachura, *Dzienniki: Zeszyty podróżne, 2* (Warsaw: Iskry, 2011), 122.
209. Edward Stachura, *Wszystko jest poezja: Opowieść – rzeka* (Warsaw: Państwowy Instytut Wydawniczy, 1987), 57.
210. Marcin Barski, "Ikona cudzych słów. Zbigniew Karkowski – wywiad," *Glissando* 2013, no. 22, http://glissando.pl/tekst/ikona-cudzych-stylow-zbigniew-karkowski-wywiad-2/ [accessed 26 September 2020].
211. Andrzej Chłopecki, Warsaw Autumn Festival program book, 1998, 78.
212. Zbigniew Granat, "*Marty Ptaszyńskiej portret w muzyce*," *Nowy Dziennik* (New York), 13 February 1997, quoted in Ewa Cichoń, Leszek Polony, *Muzyka to język najdoskonalszy. Rozmowy z Martą Ptaszyńską* (Kraków: 2001), 112.
213. M. Nogaj, J. Łukoszem, "Autobiografią jest każde pisanie," *Gazeta Wyborcza* 2005, no. 182, "Wrocław" supplement.
214. Benedict Anderson, *Imagined Communities: Reflections on the Origin and Spread of Nationalism* (New York: Verso Books, 1983).
215. If one were to imagine a pictorial example of compressing human history into 24 hours, the idea of seeing oneself as a member of a national community would appear about 45 seconds before midnight. Anderson, *Imagined Communities*; Krzysztof Jaskułowski, *Wspólnota symboliczna. W stronę antropologii nacjonalizmu* (Gdańsk: Wydawnictwo Naukowe

Katedra, 2012); Michael Billig, *Banal Nationalism* (London: Sage, 2009). A different vision, focusing on pre-national aspects of various communal forms, is presented by Antonina Kłoskowska in her famous *Kultury narodowe u korzeni* (Warsaw: Polskie Wydawnictwo Naukowe, 2015).

216. Akhil Gupta, James Ferguson, "Beyond Culture: Space, Identity, and the Politics of Difference," *Cultural Anthropology* 1992, vol. 7, no. 1.
217. Seyla Benhabib, *The Rights of Others: Aliens, Residents and Citizens* (Cambridge: Cambridge University Press, 2011).
218. Wolfgang Bauer, *Crossing the Sea: With Syrians on the Exodus to Europe* (Los Angeles: And Other Stories, 2016).
219. Patrick Kingsley, *The New Odyssey: The Story of the Twenty-First Century Refugee Crisis* (New York: Liveright, 2017).
220. Artur Domosławski, *Wykluczeni* (Warsaw: Wielka Litera, 2016).
221. As evidenced by the conjunction in the title of *Declaration of Human and Citizen Rights.* See Giorgio Agamben, *Homo sacer: Il potere sovrano e la nuda vita* (Turin: Einaudi, 1995).
222. Zygmunt Bauman, *Wasted Lives: Modernity and Its Outcasts* (Cambridge: Polity, 2004).
223. "Migracja," in *Słownik języka polskiego*, https://sjp.pl/migracja [accessed 18 December 2020].
224. The 28 July 1951 Geneva Convention relating to the status of refugees, https://www.unhcr.org/1951-refugee-convention.html [accessed 18 December 2020].
225. Pope Francis's speech to the European Parliament, Strasbourg 25 November 2014, http://www.vatican.va/content/francesco/pl/speeches/2014/november/documents/papa-francesco_20141125_strasburgo-parlamento-europeo.html [accessed 18 December 2020].
226. Yet another question: what is a "well-founded fear?" Are there strict criteria that can distinguish a well-founded fear from an unjustified, imaginary, or exaggerated fear, and if so, who should be the judge?
227. This is also the case for Poland. For several years in public discourse, we have been able to observe various attempts to create and instrumentalize, for the sake of power games, a division between "actual refugees" and "so called refugees," i.e., only "simple" or "ordinary" economic migrants. Piotr Jakubowski, "Brzydkie słowo na literę 'u'. Język jako narzędzie hegemonii i źródło oporu," *Czas Kultury* 2018, no. 3, 118–125.
228. A. Domosławski, *Wykluczeni*, 371. Other examples: Paweł Mościcki, justifying his own choices of language, writes: "In this book, I use many terms denoting people who experience migration. I make no difference between an emigrant, refugee, exile, displaced person, etc. The only clear network of such differences known to me is based on legal definitions," Pawel Mościcki, *Migawki z tradycji uciśnionych* (Bydgoszcz-Warszawa: Instytut Wydawniczy Książka i Prasa, Teatr Polski Bydgoszcz, 2017), 9. Patrick Kingsley says, in the context of the migrant/refugee crisis, which has lasted for over a decade now, that "when describing a large group of unfamiliar people, it is worth describing them by what they do (which you can be relatively sure of), not why they do that (which we cannot know)...[Many people claim that] refugees deserve special rights, while migrants do not. Refugees have justifiable reasons to leave their homes and migrants do not. This distinction is problematic. In fact… Various issues coexist, and the experiences of many people may fit into both categories," quoted in Kingsley, *The New Odyssey*.
229. J. Fudge,"Borders," in Anna Konik, *W tym samym mieście, pod tym samym niebem* (Warsaw: Centrum Sztuki Współczesnej Zamek Ujazdowski, 2016), 12–13; English version, *In the Same City Under This Same Sky* (Warsaw: CSW Ujazdowski, 2016). (Let's add that international legal regulations do not include such phenomena as migrations caused by climate crisis.)
230. Based on the International Organization for Migration (IOM), The UN Migration Agency, *World Migration Report: 2018*, https://publications.iom.int/system/files/pdf/wmr_2018_en.pdf [accessed 18 December 2020].
231. Konik, *W tym samym mieście*, 85–87.
232. See Olga Tokarczuk, *Bieguni* (Kraków: Wydawnictwo Literackie, 2008).
233. I. Kant, *Perpetual Peace. A Philosophical Sketch*, https://www.mtholyoke.edu/acad/intrel/kant/kant1.htm [accessed 18 December 2020].
234. Zbigniew Bargielski, "Czas teraźniejszy," in *Ekspresja formy – ekspresja treści: Marianowi Borkowskiemu w siedemdziesięciolecie urodzin*, ed. Alicja Gronau-Osińska (Warsaw: Chopin Academy of Music, 2004), 313.
235. Roman Berger, "…najpierw jest życie, a potem sztuka…Roman Berger (Bratysława)," in *Między Polską a światem: Kultura emigracyjna po 1939 roku*, ed. Marta Fik (Warsaw: Krąg, 1992), 129–130.
236. "'Skladateľ Roman Berger: Umenie spochybňuje údajnú všemohúcnosť svetskej moci," https://www.sme.sk/c/3567448/skladatel-roman-berger-umenie-spochybnuje-udajnu-vsemohucnost-svetskej-moci.html [accessed 12 October 2018].
237. Ewa Szczecińska, "Wojtek Blecharz: wywiad," *Glissando* 2013, http://glissando.pl/wywiady/wojtek-blecharz-wywiad/ [accessed 10 December 2020].

238. Bruce Duffie, "Joanna Bruzdowicz: A Conversation with Bruce Duffie," Chicago, 7 May 1991, http://www.bruceduffie.com/bruzdowicz.html [accessed 15 April 2015].

239. A. Bilińska, interview with the composer after the staging of *Penal Colony*, Musica Polonica Nova festival, Wrocław, February 2008.

240. Dorota Szwarcman, "Mistrz konstruktywizmu," https://szwarcman.blog.polityka.pl/2015/12/06/mistrz-konstruktywizmu [accessed 18 October 2018].

241. Simon Wynberg, "The Rediscovery of a Great Jewish Composer," *Mosaic Magazine*, 3 December 2005, https://mosaicmagazine.com/observation/arts-culture/2015/12/the-rediscovery-of-a-great-jewish-composer/?print [accessed 31 December 2020].

242. Beata Bolesławska-Lewandowska, *Górecki: Portret w pamięci* (Kraków: Polskie Wydawnictwo Muzyczne, 2013), 29.

243. Email from Maja Trochimczyk to editors of this book, 21 August 2018.

244. Beata Bolesławska-Lewandowska, *Górecki: Portret*, 33.

245. Roman Haubenstock-Ramati, "Zwischen Traum und Computer," *Wort und Wahrheit* 1971, no. 26.

246. Interview with Dobromiła Jaskot, *Glissando* 2004.

247. Jan A. P. Kaczmarek, interview for Culture.pl before the premiere of *Emigra – Symfonia bez końca*, https://vimeo.com/203999421, [accessed February 2017].

248. Jacek Kaczmarski, *Przejście Polaków przez Morze Czerwone* (Warsaw: NOWA, 1987).

249. Krzysztof Gajda, *To moja droga: Biografia Jacka Kaczmarskiego* (Wrocław: Wydawnictwo Dolonośląskie, 2009), 162.

250. Tony Thomas, cover for the album *The Film Music of Bronislaw Kaper*.

251. Jarosław Kapuściński, "Writing," www.jaroslawkapuscinski.com [accessed 10 December 2020].

252. *Zbigniew Karkowski we Wrocławiu*, https://www.muzyka.gildia.pl/news/2008/12/karkowski_piotrowicz [accessed 18 October 2018].

253. Interview with Dominik Karski, *Glissando* 2014, no. 23.

254. Letter from Kassern to Irena Sroczyńska, 27 March 1952, Warsaw University Library, Archiwum Kompozytorów Polskich, K-LXXXI.

255. Dorota Szwarcman, "Klecki, kompozytor, łodzianin," *Gazeta Wyborcza*, 11 November 2012.

256. Zofia Komeda speaking in the documentary *The Time of Komeda* [Czas Komedy], directed by Robert Kaczmarek and Mariusz Kalinowski (1994), about the success of the lullaby from *Rosemary's Baby*.

257. Witold Gombrowicz, *Ferdydurke*, quote used by the composer in the program to *Stelfer*, 2014.

258. Michał Kondracki [about himself], "O kierunkach współczesnej muzyki polskiej," *Muzyka Polska* 1937, no. 6, 273.

259. Adam Mrygoń, "Michał Kondracki," in *Muzyka źle obecna*, ed. Krystyna Tarnawska-Kaczorowska, vol. 1, 304.

260. Adam Mrygoń, "Michał Kondracki," in *Muzyka źle obecna*, vol. 1, 302.

261. Adam Mrygoń, "Michał Kondracki," in *Muzyka źle obecna*, vol. 1, 300.

262. Aleksandra Nowak, interview with Abel Korzeniowski, 2017, http://www.entertheroom.pl/life/22- wywiady/7058-wywiad-abel-korzeniowski [accessed 2 February 2018].

263. Emilia Stefańska, "W stroju perskim. Rozmowa z Martyną Kosecką." Unpublished interview, Emilia Stefańska's personal collection.

264. Hanna Kulenty, Tomasz Cyz, "Ja tworzę, nie komponuję. Rozmowa z Hanną Kulenty," *Ruch Muzyczny* 2014, no. 7, 40.

265. Ewa Szczecińska, Jan Topolski, "Andrzej Kwieciński: wywiad," *Glissando* 2012, no. 20, http://glissando.pl/tekst/andrzej-kwiecinski-wywiad/ [accessed 18 October 2018].

266. Szymon Laks, "Rozmowa z Tadeuszem Kaczyńskim," *Ruch Muzyczny* 1964, no. 21, 15–16.

267. Szymon Laks, *Gry oświęcimskie* (London: OPIM, 1979).

268. For the English version, see Szymon Laks, *Music of Another World* (Evanston: Northwestern University Press; London: Turnaround, 2000).

269. Laks, *Music of Another World*, 98–99.

270. André Laks, "O moim ojcu Szymonie Laksie i jego książce *Gry oświęcimskie*," *Muzykalia VI/Judaica I* 2008, 1.

271. Laks, *Music of Another World*, 7.

272. Bernard Gavoty, *Wanda Landowska* (Geneva: Kister-Limpert, 1956).

273. Tadeusz Kaczyński, "Rozmowa z twórcą *Requiem*," *Tygodnik Powszechny*, 8 January 1961, 6.

274. Lucyna Winnicka, *W poczekalni nieba: Rozmowy o życiu i śmierci* (Warsaw: Iskry, 1999), 139.

275. Winnicka, *W poczekalni nieba*, 138.

276. Marlena Wieczorek, *Roman Maciejewski. Kompozytor pokolenia zgubionego* (Poznań: Poznańskiego Towarzystwa

Przyjaciół Nauk, 2008).

277. Interview with Miłosz Magin, Paris 1993, https://www.youtube.com/watch?v=JCfdaKtOljU [accessed 18 October 2018].
278. Interview with Miłosz Magin, Paris 1993.
279. Interview with Miłosz Magin, Paris 1993.
280. Marek Strasz, *Grać pierwszy fortepian: Rozmowy z Adamem Makowiczem* (Kraków: Polskie Wydawnictwo Muzyczne, 2011), 95.
281. Z. Bargielski, B. Behr, L. Ciuciura, B. Matuszczak, K. Meyer, "Pytania i odpowiedzi," *Res Facta* 1971, no. 5.
282. Stefan Kisielewski, "Eugeniusz Morawski," in *Pisma i felietony muzyczne*, ed. Marek Włodarski (Warsaw: Prószyński Media, 2012), vol. 1, 494–497.
283. Krzysztof Stefański, "Piotr Moss," www.zamowieniakompozytorskie,pl/kompozytor/piotr-moss [accessed 4 September 2018].
284. "Rapsodia," www.culture.pl/pl/dzielo/rapsodia [accessed 4 September 2018].
285. Rafał Szczepański, *Fryderykowi Chopinowi – Ignacy Jan Paderewski* (Warsaw: Wydawnictwa Akcydensowe, 1991), 5.
286. Leszek Polony, "Spotkanie z Romanem Palestrem," *Tygodnik Powszechny* 1983, no. 42. (The meeting mentioned in the title took place in 1983, during the composer's visit to Poland.)
287. Artistic credo from 1952, preserved in the composer's archive and quoted in Beata Bolesławska, *The Life and Works of Andrzej Panufnik*, 264.
288. Quoted in Bolesławska, *The Life and Works of Andrzej Panufnik*, 245.
289. Jerzy Petersburski's words on Polish Radio, "Spotkanie z Jerzym Petersburskim w audycji z cyklu *Nestorzy polskiej piosenki* Andrzeja Jaroszewskiego," 16 June 1973.
290. Krzysztof Kwiatkowski, "Opery rosną we mnie jak drzewa. Prasqual odpowiada na pytania," *Ruch Muzyczny* 2012, no. 1.
291. Prasqual, Monika Pasiecznik, "Architektura muzyczna," *Odra* 2014, no. 12.
292. Kwiatkkowski, "Opery rosną we mnie jak drzewa", 13.
293. Prasqual, Pasiecznik, "Architektura muzyczna."
294. Marta Ptaszyńska in conversation with Ewa Uszpolewicz-Figurski, Chicago, September 2008, in E. Uszpolewicz-Figurski, "Baronowa perkusji i kompozycji," *Dziennik Związkowy Polish Daily News*, 30 April 2017, https://dziennikzwiazkowy.com/kultura/baronowa-%20perkusji-i-kompozycji/ [accessed 18 October 2018].
295. Ewa Cichoń, "Dźwięki w czterowymiarowej przestrzeni (wywiad z Marta Ptaszyńską)," *Kwarta* 2000, no. 5, 4.
296. From a letter sent by Karol Rathaus to conductor Jascha Horenstein.
297. Janusz Cegiełła, *Szkice do autoportretu polskiej muzyki współczesnej*, 151.
298. His life and career were described by Jerzy Stankiewicz in the entry "Regamey Konstanty Kazimierz Rudolfowicz," in *Encyklopedia Muzyczna PWM* (Kraków: Polskie Wydawnictwo Muzyczne, 2004), vol. 8, 331. He corrected a number of biographical inaccuracies found in previous literature and estimated, for the first time, the time and circumstances of his death. His family was told that he was sentenced to ten years of labor camp, where he died in 1941 (his son probably knew only this version). In reality, he was arrested by the NKVD on 15 July 1937, and shot on 20 January 1938. See also Jerzy Stankiewicz, "Między Kijowem a Warszawą – pieśni młodzieńcze Konstantego Regameya," in Konstanty Regamey, *Pieśni młodzieńcze na głos i fortepian* (Kraków: Musica Iagellonica, 2014), 43.
299. See Marek Mejor, "Konstanty Regamey (1907–1982), orientalista awangardowy," in Konstanty Regamey, "Zagadnienie nirwany według therawadinów cejlońskich," *Studia Buddhica* 2012, Supplement 1, 9–16.
300. In addition to publications in Indian studies (such as the book *Der Buddhismus Indiens*, 1964), Regamey is also the author of *Witold Małcużyński* (Kraków: Polskie Wydawnictwo Muzyczne, 1960); *Próba analizy ewolucji w sztuce* (Kraków: Polskie Wydawnictwo Muzyczne, 1973); a collection of analyses of 80 works of twentieth-century music (*Musiques du Vingtième Siècle. Présentation de quatre-vingts œuvres pour orchestre de chambre* (Lausanne: Éditions du Cervin, 1966); as well as articles on music published in Switzerland and in Poland.
301. Jean-Claude Poulin, "Constantin Regamey: L'éclectisme en musique n'est pas un défaut dans la mesure où il est cohérent," *Gazette de Lausanne. Samedi Littéraire*, 11 December 1976.
302. Witold Lutosławski, "Fascynująca prapremiera (wspomnienie z 1944 r.)," *Ruch Muzyczny* 1983, no. 10, 7–8. Reprinted in K. Tarnawska-Kaczorowska, ed., *Konstanty Regamey. Oblicza polistylizmu. Materiały sympozjum poświęconego twórczości Konstantego Regameya, Warsaw 29–30 May 1987* (Warsaw: Polish Composers' Union, 1988), 28–29.
303. Nicole Loutan-Charbon, *Constantin Regamey: Compositeur* (Yverdon: Éditions de la Thièle, 1978), 23–24.

304. Ludomir Michał Rogowski, "Ludomir Michał Rogowski," typescript, State Archive in Dubrovnik, sign. RO-180 4.VI.23.

305. Quote taken from "Roman Ryterband – Biography," https://polishmusic.usc.edu/files/2018/07/ryterband2016_web.pdf [accessed 6 December 2020]. See also *Roman Ryterband: Life and Work*, ed. Robert Eisele, author's private collection.

306. "Tomasz Stańko o Zbigniewie Seifercie," Seifert Competition 2014, https://seifertcompetition.com/seifert/news/87 [accessed 18 October 2018].

307. Wojciech Sitarz, "Gdyby nie trema zostałaby pianistką," http://wojciechsitarz.wordpress.com/2011/05/08/gdyby-nie-trema-zostalaby-pianistka-%E2%80%93-rozmowa-z-elzbieta-sikora/, quoted in W. Nowak, "Między emocją a abstrakcją. Wokół twórczości Elżbiety Sikory," http://meakultura.pl/artykul/miedzy-emocja-a-abstrakcja-wokol-tworczosci-elzbiety-sikory-728 [accessed 18 October 2018].

308. Elżbieta Sikora, "Zawód kompozytora nie ma płci. Sylwetka autorki opery 'Madame Curie'," *Wysokie obcasy*, 20 May 2017, http://www.wysokieobcasy.pl/wysokie-obcasy/7,127763,21825971,elzbieta-sikora-zawod-kompozytora-nie-ma-plci-sylwetka.html [accessed 30 November 2017].

309. Krzysztof Stefański, "Z archiwum KS: Festiwal to dobro konieczne," http://nibytygodnik.pl/2017/05/28/z-archiwum-ks-festiwal-to-dobro-konieczne/ [accessed 30 November 2017].

310. *Byłem w niebie. Mówi Stanisław Skrowaczewski w rozmowie z Agnieszką Malatyńską-Stankiewicz* (Kraków: Polskie Wydawnictwo Muzyczne, 2000), 44.

311. *Byłem w niebie*, 44, 56.

312. Bettina Skrzypczak, "Autoreferat," https://www.amuz.xn--krakw-3ta.pl/habilitacje/postepowania-habilitacyjne/bettina-skrzypczak, 35.

313. Skrzypczak, "Autoreferat," 31–32.

314. Skrzypczak, "Autoreferat," 14.

315. "Muzyka w kadrze," Grzegorz Dąbrowski and Mariusz Gradowski's music broadcast on Polish Radio, Program 2, 20 September 2015.

316. Letter from Michał Spisak to Seweryn Różycki, Paris, 8 December 1961.

317. Paweł Piotrowicz, "Tomasz Stańko: zło bywa konieczne," *Magazyn O!Kultura* June 2017, https://kultura.onet.pl/wywiady-i-artykuly/tomasz-stanko-zlo-bywa-konieczne-wywiad/j3er2fc [accessed 18 October 2018].

318. Tomasz Stańko, http://viva.pl/kultura/muzyka/tomasz-stanko-w-nowym-jorku-sesja-z-vivy-23782-r3/ [accessed 30 October 2018].

319. Paweł Piotrowicz, "To brzmienie, ten styl… Tomasz Stańko nie żyje," 29 July 2018, https://kultura.onet.pl/muzyka/wywiady-i-artykuly/to-brzmienie-ten-styl-tomasz-stanko-nie-zyje/ceenf8t [accessed 10 December 2020].

320. Tomasz Stańko, http://viva.pl/kultura/muzyka/tomasz-stanko-w-nowym-jorku-sesja-z-vivy-23782-r3/.

321. Tomasz Stańko, http://viva.pl/kultura/muzyka/tomasz-stanko-w-nowym-jorku-sesja-z-vivy-23782-r3/.

322. Zygmunt Stojowski, "Sztuka Chopinowska," in Sigismund Stojowski, Marek Szlezer, *Pisma wybrane*, trans. Marek Szlezer (Kraków: Akademia Muzyczna, 2015), 37.

323. Adam Krysiński, "Stanisław Syrewicz – wywiad rzeka z kompozytorem," http://www.soundtracks.pl/index.php?rssID=1375 [accessed 16 September 2018].

324. Krysiński, "Stanisław Syrewicz – wywiad."

325. Krysiński, "Stanisław Syrewicz – wywiad."

326. Krysiński, "Stanisław Syrewicz – wywiad."

327. Jacek Toczkowski, *Niezwykła rozmowa muzyczno-filmowa, czyli spotkanie ze Stanisławem Syrewiczem*, http://www.netkultura.pl/16240/niezwykla-rozmowa-muzyczno-filmowa-czyli-spotkanie-ze-stanislawem-syrewiczem/ [accessed 28 September 2018].

328. Iwona Szafrańska, "Wokół sonoryzmu. Z Witoldem Szalonkiem rozmawia Iwona Szafrańska," *Opcje* 1994, no. 2.

329. Zygmunt Mycielski, "Antoni Szałowski 21 IV 1907–21 III 1973," *Ruch Muzyczny* 1973, no. 10, 3.

330. Mycielski, "Antoni Szałowski."

331. Jagoda Szmytka in conversation with Marlena Wieczorek on Facebook, 9 October 2018.

332. Ewa Szczecińska, Jan Topolski, "Michał Talma-Sutt – wywiad," *Glissando* 2007, no. 12, http://glissando.pl/tekst/michal-talma-sutt-wywiad-2/.

333. Interview with Marek Zwyrzykowski, in the commentary to the album *Muzyka Polska Dzisiaj – Portrety Współczesnych Kompozytorów Polskich – Michał Talma-Sutt*, Polmic 096/PRCD/1748.

334. Irving Schwerke, *Alexandre Tansman: compositeur polonais* (Paris: Eschig, 1931).

335. Composer's diary entry dated 12 January 1980, in Anastasia Belina, *A Musician Divided: André Tchaikowsky in His*

Own Words (London: Toccata Press, 2013), 271.

336. Anna Niedźwiedź, interview with Ewa Trębacz published in a booklet to the album *Muzyka Polska Dzisiaj - Portrety Współczesnych Kompozytorów Polskich - Ewa Trębacz*, Polmic 097/PRCD/1749.
337. Ewa Trębacz, "Aletheia," https://polmic.pl/index.php?option=com_mwzbiory&view=publikacja&id=1356&Itemid=0&lang=pl [accessed 18 October 2018].
338. A. Chłopecki, "Raport z Paryża. Międzynarodowa Trybuna Kompozytorska 2009," *Ruch Muzyczny* 2009, nos. 16–17, 6.
339. Chłopecki, "Raport z Paryża."
340. Conversation conducted by Tomasz Furmanek with Michał Urbaniak, *Jazz Forum* 2014.
341. Ryszard Wolański, *Już nie zapomnisz mnie: Opowieść o Henryku Warsie* (Warsaw: Wydawnictwo Literackie Muza, 2010), 200.
342. Wolański, *Już nie zapomnisz mnie*, 200.
343. Michał Klubiński, "Pasażerka - opera o Pamięci. Z profesorem Michałem Bristigerem rozmawia Michał Klubiński," http://www.dziennikteatralny.pl/drukuj/pasazerka-8211-opera-o-pamieci.html, [accessed 13 October 2017].
344. Krzysztof Wołek composer, http://krzysztofwolek.com/w_about.htm [accessed 18 October 2018].
345. Andrzej Zieliński, transcription of an interview with Radio PiK, http://www.radiopik.pl/39,181,skaldo [accessed 19 August 2018].
346. M. Sienkiewicz, "Skaldowie," https://culture.pl/pl/tworca/skaldowie [accessed 19 August 2018].
347. "Andrzej Zieliński - polski Lenon," *Dziennik Polonijny*, http://www.poland.us/strona,9,591,0,andrzej-zielinski-polski-lenon.html [accessed: 19 August 2018].
348. "Zieliński - polski Lenon."
349. Wacław Krupiński, "'Pióra' i duma rockmana," *Dziennik Polski*, 3 October 2014, https://dziennikpolski24.pl/piora-i-duma-rockmana/ar/3596409 [accessed 19 August 2018].
350. Bartosz Chmielewski, *Skaldowie*, https://www.polskieradio.pl/6/11/Artykul/177462,Skaldowie [accessed 19 August 2018].

FRYDERYK FRANCISZEK CHOPIN 1810–1849

About the Publisher

Dear Readers,
We are glad that you are holding a book published by the MEAKULTURA Foundation in your hands!

The MEAKULTURA Foundation was established in 2012 on the initiative of Dr. Marlena Wieczorek, who is also its president. As such, she has designed and managed all of its projects. From the very beginning, the organization's vice president, Dr. Ewa Schreiber, has also been closely involved with its activities.

The priorities of the MEAKULTURA Foundation are music, education, and artists. Its goals are to promote valuable music regardless of genre, assist publishing efforts, organize concerts, develop educational projects, and support professional music journalism and cultural initiatives of high artistic quality.

The most important projects of the Foundation include publishing the MEAKULTURA online magazine (www.meakultura.pl), organizing the annual KROPKA Polish Music Critics Competition (www.konkurskropka.pl), launching the Save the Music social campaign (www.savethemusic.eu) and, together with Collegium Civitas in Warsaw, establishing a postgraduate Music in Media program (www.muzykawmediach.pl).

The tremendous number of people who have been engaged in the Foundation's activities—scholars, students, journalists, musicians, and teachers—prove its worth and potential.

In order to continue our work independently, to publish books like this one, and to cultivate and support Polish artists and culture, we always appreciate your help. Please donate to: account 70 1140 2004 0000 3502 7593 1654, Swift: BREXPLPWMUL, Subject: statutory activities.

Anyone who pays their taxes in Poland can also donate 1% tax to support us.
Your 1 % = 100% culture!

More about us: www.fundacjameakultura.pl

All of the illustrations in the book can be purchased on MEAKULTURA's website or by writing to kontakt@meakultura.pl.

Save
The Music